Tai-hoon Kim Stephen S. Yau
Osvaldo Gervasi Byeong-Ho Kang
Adrian Stoica Dominik

Grid and Dis[illegible] Computing, Control and Automation

International Conferences, GDC and CA 2010
Held as Part of the Future Generation
Information Technology Conference, FGIT 2010
Jeju Island, Korea, December 13-15, 2010
Proceedings

Volume Editors

Tai-hoon Kim
Hannam University, Daejeon, South Korea
E-mail: taihoonn@hnu.kr

Stephen S. Yau
Arizona State University, Tempe, AZ, USA
E-mail: yau@asu.edu

Osvaldo Gervasi
University of Perugia, Italy
E-mail: osvaldo@unipg.it

Byeong-Ho Kang
University of Tasmania, Hobart, Australia
E-mail: byeong.kang@utas.edu.au

Adrian Stoica
NASA Jet Propulsion Laboratory, Pasadena, CA, USA
E-mail: adrian.stoica@jpl.nasa.gov

Dominik Ślęzak
University of Warsaw & Infobright, Poland
E-mail: dominik.slezak@infobright.com

Library of Congress Control Number: 2010940173

CR Subject Classification (1998): C.2, I.2, H.4, H.3, D.2, F.1

ISSN 1865-0929
ISBN-10 3-642-17624-0 Springer Berlin Heidelberg New York
ISBN-13 978-3-642-17624-1 Springer Berlin Heidelberg New York

springer.com

Printed in Germany

Typesetting: Camera-ready by author, data conversion by Scientific Publishing Services, Chennai, India
Printed on acid-free paper 06/3180

Preface

Welcome to the proceedings of the 2010 International Conferences on Grid and Distributed Computing (GDC 2010), and Control and Automation (CA 2010) – two of the partnering events of the Second International Mega-Conference on Future Generation Information Technology (FGIT 2010).

GDC and CA bring together researchers from academia and industry as well as practitioners to share ideas, problems and solutions relating to the multifaceted aspects of high-performance and compound control systems, including their links to computational sciences, mathematics and information technology.

In total, 1,630 papers were submitted to FGIT 2010 from 30 countries, which includes 198 papers submitted to GDC/CA 2010. The submitted papers went through a rigorous reviewing process: 395 of the 1,630 papers were accepted for FGIT 2010, while 40 papers were accepted for GDC/CA 2010. Of the 40 papers, 8 were selected for the special FGIT 2010 volume published by Springer in LNCS the series. 28 papers are published in this volume, and 4 papers were withdrawn due to technical reasons.

We would like to acknowledge the great effort of the GDC/CA 2010 International Advisory Boards and members of the International Program Committees, as well as all the organizations and individuals who supported the idea of publishing this volume of proceedings, including SERSC and Springer. Also, the success of these two conferences would not have been possible without the huge support from our sponsors and the work of the Chairs and Organizing Committee.

We are grateful to the following keynote speakers who kindly accepted our invitation: Hojjat Adeli (Ohio State University), Ruay-Shiung Chang (National Dong Hwa University), and Andrzej Skowron (University of Warsaw). We would also like to thank all plenary and tutorial speakers for their valuable contributions.

We would like to express our greatest gratitude to the authors and reviewers of all paper submissions, as well as to all attendees, for their input and participation.

Last but not least, we give special thanks to Rosslin John Robles and Maricel Balitanas. These graduate school students of Hannam University contributed to the editing process of this volume with great passion.

December 2010

Tai-hoon Kim
Stephen S. Yau
Osvaldo Gervasi
Byeong-Ho Kang
Adrian Stoica
Dominik Ślęzak

GDC 2010 Organization

Organizing Committee

General Co-chairs	Stephen S. Yau, Chair (Arizona State University, USA) Osvaldo Gervasi (University of Perugia, Italy)
Program Co-chairs	Byeong-Ho Kang (University of Tasmania, Australia) Tai-hoon Kim (Hannam University, Korea)
Publication Co-chairs	Rosslin John Robles (Hannam University, Korea) Maricel Balitanas (Hannam University, Korea)

Program Committee

Albert Zomaya
Bilha Mendelson
BongHee Hong
Chao-Tung Yang
Cho-Li Wang
Chun-Hsi (Vincent) Huang
Damon Shing-Min Liu
Dan Grigoras
Dan Meng
Daniel S. Katz
Danilo Gonzalez
Dimitrios Serpanos
Domenico Laforenza
Domenico Talia
Eung Nam Ko
Farrukh Nadeem
Gail-Joon Ahn
Geoffrey Fox
George Bosilca
Hai Jin
Hung-Chang Hsiao
Hyeong-Ok Lee
Jan-Jan Wu
Jean-Louis Pazat
Jiannong Cao
Keecheon Kim
Kenichi Takahashi
Kuan-Ching Li
Liria Matsumoto Sato
Marcin Paprzycki
Marian Bubak AGH Krakow
Mark Baker
Minglu Li
Mohamed Jemni
Mohand-Said Hacid
Nabil Abdennadher
Omer F. Rana
Ramin Yahyapour
Ronald Perrott
Ruay-Shiung Chang
Susumu Date
Tomàs Margalef
Yangwoo Kim
Yeh-Ching Chung National
Yong Man Ro
Yongik Yoon
Yong-Kee Jun

CA 2010 Organization

Organizing Committee

General Chair	Adrian Stoica (NASA Jet Propulsion Laboratory, USA)
Program Co-chairs	Byeong-Ho Kang (University of Tasmania, Australia) Tai-hoon Kim (Hannam University, Korea)
Publicity Chair	Aboul Ella Hassanien (Cairo University, Egypt)
Publication Co-chairs	Rosslin John Robles (Hannam University, Korea) Maricel Balitanas (Hannam University, Korea)

Program Committee

Albert Cheng
Alessandro Casavola
Barry Lennox
Bernard Grabot
Choonsuk Oh
Christian Schmid
Chun-Yi Su
DaeEun Kim
DongWon Kim
Feng-Li Lian
Guang-Ren Duan
Guoping Liu
Gwi-Tae Park
Hideyuki Sawada
Hojjat Adeli
Hong Wang
Jong H. Park
Jong-Wook Kim
Jurek Sasiadek
Jus Kocijan
Kwan-Ho You
Kwon Soon Lee
Makoto Itoh
Manuel Haro Casado
Mitsuji Sampei
Myotaeg Lim
Peter Simon Sapaty
Pierre Borne
Pieter J. Mosterman
Pradeep Misra
S.C. Kim
Thomas Parisini
Zhong-Ping Jiang
Zuwairie Ibrahim

Table of Contents

Agent-Based Service Composition in Cloud Computing

J. Octavio Gutierrez-Garcia and Kwang-Mong Sim

Gwangju Institute of Science and Technology,
Gwangju 500-712 Republic of Korea
joseogg@gmail.com, kmsim@gist.ac.kr

Abstract. In a Cloud-computing environment, consumers, brokers, and service providers interact to achieve their individual purposes. In this regard, service providers offer a pool of resources wrapped as web services, which should be composed by broker agents to provide a single virtualized service to Cloud consumers. In this study, an agent-based test bed for simulating Cloud-computing environments is developed. Each Cloud participant is represented by an agent, whose behavior is defined by means of colored Petri nets. The relationship between web services and service providers is modeled using object Petri nets. Both Petri net formalisms are combined to support a design methodology for defining concurrent and parallel service choreographies. This results in the creation of a dynamic agent-based service composition algorithm. The simulation results indicate that service composition is achieved with a linear time complexity despite dealing with interleaving choreographies and synchronization of heterogeneous services.

Keywords: web service composition; Cloud computing; multi-agent systems.

1 Introduction

Cloud computing service composition must support dynamic reconfiguration and automatic reaction to new requirements as well as dealing with distributed, self-interested, and autonomous parties such as service providers, brokers, and Cloud consumers; these parties should interact and coordinate among themselves to achieve a proper service composition. This accentuates the need for an agent-based solution. Agents are autonomous problem solvers that can act flexibly (e.g., interacting with other agents through negotiation and cooperation) in a dynamic environment (e.g., a Cloud-computing environment).

Service composition can scale Cloud computing in two dimensions [3]: horizontal and vertical. Horizontal service composition refers to the composition of usually heterogeneous services that may be located in several Clouds. Vertical service composition deals with the composition of homogenous services to increase the capacity of a given Cloud node.

This work proposes an agent-based algorithm that supports both horizontal and vertical service compositions with linear time complexity (as demonstrated in section 4). In addition, each agent is only aware of the requirement it fulfills and possible requirements it may need from external agents. Furthermore, the algorithm handles

T.-h. Kim et al. (Eds.): GDC/CA 2010, CCIS 121, pp. 1–10, 2010.

the composition of atomic and complex web services. Moreover, a formal methodology for defining web services' workflows that handles synchronization and coordination aspects is defined through the use of colored Petri nets [2] and object Petri nets [5], which are endowed with a strong mathematical background.

The significance of this paper is that, to the best of the authors' knowledge, this work is the earliest research that adopts a multi-agent approach for supporting Cloud service composition.

This paper is structured as follows: Section 2 presents the agent-based architecture used to compose services. Section 3 presents Petri net models defined for the involved agents. Section 4 presents experimental results in both horizontal and vertical scenarios. Section 5 presents a comparison with related work and the conclusions.

2 An Agent-Based Cloud Service Composition Architecture

The multi-agent system architecture that supports Cloud computing service composition is presented in Fig. 1. The elements of the architecture are as follows:

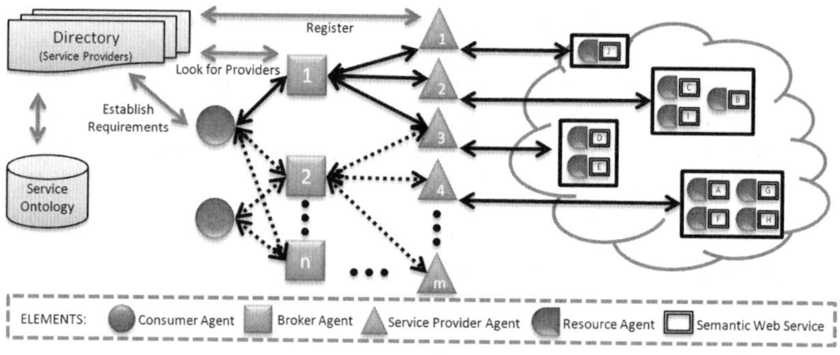

Fig. 1. Multi-agent system architecture

A *service ontology* is a formal representation of services and of the atomic requirements that these services can fulfill.

A *directory* is a listing of available service provider agents. Each entry associated to a service provider contains its name, location (e.g., URI address), and capabilities.

A *semantic web service* (SWS) is a web service whose definition is mapped to an ontology, which characterizes the service and its application domain.

A *consumer agent* (CA) submits a consumer's interests to broker agents.

A *resource agent* (RA) orchestrates a semantic web service. Furthermore, a RA contains a reference to an atomic requirement, which can be fulfilled by its SWS.

A *service provider agent* (SPA) handles a set of RAs. Its main function is to coordinate and synchronize RAs.

A *broker agent* (BA) accepts requests from consumer agents and creates a single virtualized service by means of composing services deployed on one or more Clouds. A BA utilizes consumer requirements to search for SPAs; it then starts the composition process by adopting the well-known contract net protocol [4] for selecting services and allocating tasks. However, an ad-hoc mechanism to collect results overrides the one provided by the contract net protocol. This ad-hoc mechanism synchronizes and coordinates interleaving service choreographies. In addition, as a result of the process for satisfying requirements, SPAs may need additional requirements, e.g., a computing provider may need a storage address to store its results. These requirements are handed to the BA. Further details of the composition algorithm are presented in section 3.

3 Petri Net Agent Models

In the context of agent interaction, transitions in colored Petri net models represent either the reception or transmission of messages, and internal actions performed by the agent. In contrast, places represent the interaction states.

3.1 Consumer Agents

The model of a consumer agent (Fig. 2) represents a Cloud consumer, whose actions and events are described as follows: (i) transition t_1 decomposes consumer requirements into a set of atomic requirements. *Input*: An initial mark from p_1. *Output*: A set of requirements (*Req*) in p_2; (ii) transition t_2 requests requirements to a BA. *Input*: A set of requirements (*Req*) from p_2; (iii) transition t_3 receives results from the BA. *Output*: A set of resolved requirements (*Req*, *Output*) in p_3; (iv) transition t_4 composes the atomic outputs into a single virtualized service. *Input*: A set of resolved requirements (*Req*, *Output*) from p_3. *Output*: A single virtualized service represented by an uncolored dot in p_4; (v) transition t_5 restarts the consumer agent's behavior. *Input*: An uncolored dot from p_4. *Output*: An uncolored dot (initial mark) in p_1.

The firing sequence $\sigma = \{t_1, t_2, t_3, t_4, t_5\}$ represents a complete cycle of the model, from providing consumer requirements to the reception of a single virtualized service.

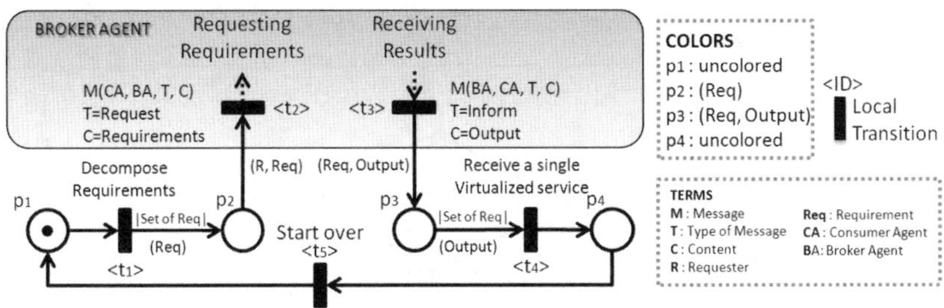

Fig. 2. Consumer agent model

3.2 Resource Agents

Resource agents are token objects, i.e., inner Petri nets contained in a system net. This follows the approach of Petri nets within Petri nets [5]. The system net is represented by the service provider agent model. The definition of resource agent models is limited to a set of design patterns that makes use of synchronized transitions to maintain a consistent behavior with respect to the system net that contains them.

The main structure of the resource agent model has two places and two synchronized transitions st_1 and st_2 (see Fig. 3). Transition st_1 synchronizes the beginning of the workflow with the reception of a request message from a SPA. This transition has a condition denoted by *if [Req = X_1]* in order to be triggered. The condition consists of accepting requirements that can be handled by the SWS in question. Transition st_2 reports the output to the outer level Petri net (a SPA).

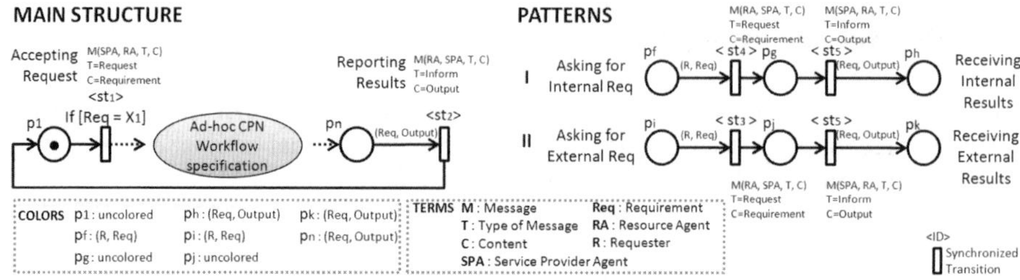

Fig. 3. Resource agent model

In addition to the main structure, a resource agent model has two design patterns (Fig. 3). Design pattern *I* allows a RA to ask for an internal requirement (st_4) and wait until this requirement is resolved by another RA (st_5) belonging to the same SPA. Pattern *II* is used to ask for external requirements (st_3); i.e., these requirements cannot be resolved by any existing token object of the current service provider system net. In this case, the SPA requests the requirement to a BA, which searches for another SPA who can fulfill the requirement. Both patterns *I* and *II* share the synchronized transition st_5 for receiving results and proceeding with the internal workflow.

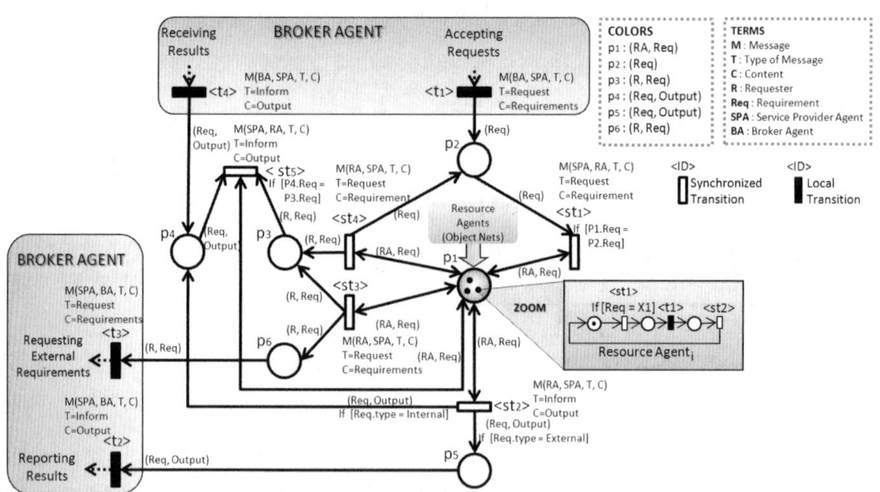

Fig. 4. Service provider agent model

3.3 Service Provider Agents

The model of a service provider agent (Fig. 4) represents the system net that contains RAs. The SPA coordinates independent and evolving resource agent tokens by means of five synchronized transitions.

Transition st_1 synchronizes the assignment of unfulfilled requirements to available RAs. *Input*: It needs two tokens, one unfulfilled requirement (*Req*) from p_2, and one available resource agent (*RA*) from p_1. The selection of an appropriate *RA* is determined by the condition *if* $[p_1.Req = p_2.Req]$. In addition, a *RA* is available if its transition $RA.st_1$ is enabled. *Output*: An evolved resource agent token in p_1.

Transition st_2 releases a resource agent by receiving its resolved requirement. This sends the *RA* back to its initial state, ready to accept another requirement. *Input*: A *RA* whose synchronized transition $RA.st_2$ is enabled in p_1. *Output*: An available *RA* in p_1 and a resolved requirement (*Req*, *Output*), which is placed in either place p_4 or p_5. This is according to the conditions attached to the output arcs regarding the type of requirement *if [Req.type = Internal/External]*.

Transition st_3 receives request messages from RAs asking for external requirements. *Input*: A resource agent token *RA* whose synchronized transition $RA.st_3$ is enabled in p_1. *Output*: An evolved resource agent token in p_1, and a requirement and its requester (*R*, *Req*) in both place p_3 and p_6; the token in p_3 is used to keep a record, and the token in p_6 is used to send an external request.

Transition st_4 receives request messages from RAs asking for internal requirements. *Input*: A resource agent token *RA* whose synchronized transition $RA.st_4$ is enabled in p_1. *Output*: An evolved resource agent token in p_1; a requirement (*Req*) to be internally solicited in p_2; and a record of the request (*R*, *Req*) in p_3.

Transition st_5 coordinates the delivery of recently arrived and fulfilled requirements to the corresponding resource agents. *Input*: It needs three tokens, one fulfilled requirement (*Req*, *Output*) from p_4; one previous solicited requirement (*R*, *Req*) from p_3; and one *RA* from p_1. The preconditions are $[p_4.Req = p_3.Req]$ and that $RA.st_5$ is enabled in p_1. *Output*: An evolved resource agent token in p_1.

In addition, local transitions are used to interact with the BA:

Transition t_1 accepts requests from BAs. *Output*: A requirement (*Req*) in p_2.

Transition t_2 reports resolved requirements to BAs. *Input*: A resolved requirement (*Req*, *Output*) from p_5.

Transition t_3 requests requirements to BAs. *Input*: A request (*R*, *Req*) from p_6.

Transition t_4 receives outputs from previous requests. *Output*: A resolved requirement (*Req*, *Output*) in p_4.

A firing sequence $\sigma_a = \{t_1, st_1, st_2, t_2\}$ represents the simplest coordination process for a SPA that contains one resource agent. Transition t_1 accepts a request from a BA to fulfill a requirement. Then, transition st_1 assigns the new requirement to an available *RA*. Transition st_2 receives the resultant output from the *RA*, and finally, transition t_2 delivers the output to the *BA*. This firing sequence is assumed to be accompanied by a resource agent's firing sequence $\sigma_b = \{st_1, t_1, st_2\}$, which corresponds to the model of the resource agent contained in Fig. 4. The resultant interleaving firing sequence is $\sigma = \{\sigma_a.t_1, \sigma_a.st_1, \sigma_b.st_1, \sigma_b.t_1, \sigma_b.st_2, \sigma_a.st_2, \sigma_a.t_2\}$.

3.4 Broker Agents

The model of a broker agent (Fig. 5) functions as a mediator among service provider and consumer agents. Its main functionality is contained in the following transitions:

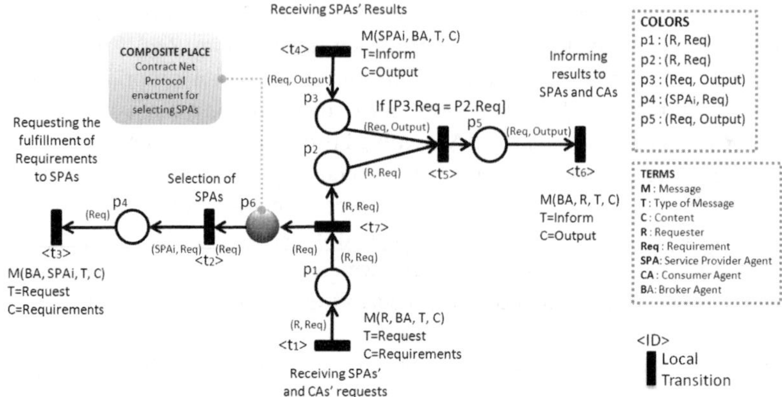

Fig. 5. Broker agent model

Transition t_1 receives requests from Cloud consumers. *Output*: An unresolved requirement (*R*, *Req*) in p_1.

Transition t_2 denotes the selection of SPAs based on the contract net protocol. The participants are all available SPAs who may fulfill the requirement(s) in question. *Input*: A requirement (*Req*) from p_6. *Output*: The selected SPA and the assigned requirement (SPA_i, *Req*) in p_4.

Transition t_3 represents the transmission of a request message to a SPA; the BA solicits the achievement of atomic requirements. *Input*: A requirement (*Req*) from p_4.

Transition t_4 receives outputs from previous requests. *Output*: A resolved requirement (*Req*, *Output*) in p_3.

Transition t_5 matches previous unfulfilled requests with incoming resolved requirements. *Input*: It needs two tokens, one unfulfilled requirement (*R*, *Req*) from p_2, and one resolved requirement (*Req*, *Output*) from p_3. Accompanied by the precondition *if* $[p_3.Req = p_2.Req]$. *Output*: A resolved requirement (*Req*, *Output*) in p_5.

Transition t_6 informs the results to either SPAs or CAs. *Input*: A resolved requirement (*Req*, *Output*) from p_5.

A firing sequence $\sigma = \{t_1, t_7, t_2, t_3, t_4, t_5, t_6\}$ represents a service composition solution to a consumer requirement as accepted by a BA (t_1). Subsequently, the requirement is assigned to an appropriate SPA (t_7, t_2, and t_3). Finally, the BA receives some provider's results (t_4), which are handed to the CA (t_5 and t_6).

4 Evaluation

A CA needs to apply several image filters to a huge amount of raw images; it then contacts a BA, which should contract several heterogeneous SPAs to satisfy that requirement. In this scenario, two different kinds of service providers are involved: computing service providers (CSP) and massive storage service providers (MSP).

A CSP has two types of resource agents: (i) an allocator service (AS) (Fig. 6(a)) and (ii) *n* processing services (PS) (Fig. 6(b)). The AS decomposes a computational task into several atomic tasks, which are handled by the PSs. Afterwards, the AS requests its service provider (a CSP) to assign the atomic tasks to the PSs and waits until all tasks are completed to join the outputs. At the same time, the AS divides the task, it computes the storage needed for saving the results, and asks the CSP for a storage address. In turn, the CSP passes the request to its BA, which again initiates the contract net protocol for contracting another SPA, which in this case is a MSP. The MSP only has one resource agent, a storage service (SS) (Fig. 6(c)) that provides a storage address; at the end, this is passed to the AS through the BA and corresponding service provider. Finally, the BA arranges the outputs of service providers and delivers a single virtualized service to the CA.

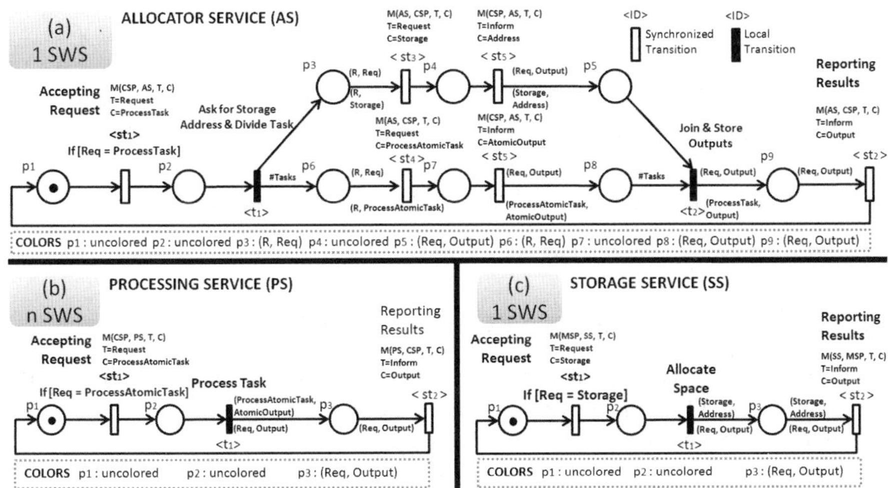

Fig. 6. Resource agents involved in the example scenario

Three experiments were conducted using the agent-based test bed described in sections 2 and 3. The test bed was implemented using the JADE agent framework [1].

4.1 Vertical Service Composition Experiment (Part A)

Objective. The first experiment was designed to explore the scalability and synchronization capabilities of the composition algorithm in vertical scenarios.

Scenario and experimental settings. A consumer agent was assumed to submit a task that has as an attribute the number of processing resources required to complete it (consumption level). The composition of services is carried out with different consumption levels of the consumer's task starting from 5 to 15, 5 being the exact number of available services per CSP. Thus, when this number is exceeded, the synchronization process of the service provider takes place in order to wait for available services and then assign them to the remaining requirements. In this experiment, the following were involved: one consumer agent, one broker agent, two MSPs, each containing one storage service, and two CSPs, each containing one allocator service and five processing services.

Results and observations. The number of exchanged messages increased at a constant rate of 4 messages per processing resource needed (see Fig. 7(a)). This shows that vertical service composition was achieved with a linear time complexity. In addition, all services were synchronized properly even with an insufficient number of resources. The number of exchanged messages is the result of adding up the required messages for (i) registering service provider agents; (ii) accessing the directory of services; (iii) selecting services by means of adopting the contract net protocol among possible service providers; and (iv) composing the involved services.

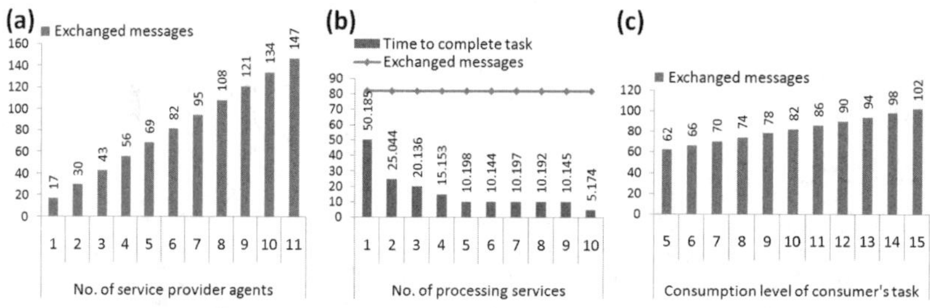

Fig. 7. Experimental results

4.2 Vertical Service Composition Experiment (Part B)

Objective. The second experiment was designed to explore the efficiency of the algorithm for parallelizing activities while dealing with heterogeneous services that may have different capacities (e.g., different processing rates).

Scenario and experimental settings. A consumer agent was assumed to submit a task that has the consumption level fixed to 10; however, in this case, the number of processing services contained in the CSPs was changed, starting from 1 to 10 processing services per CSP. In addition, the processing services were designed to spend 5 s processing each atomic task, while storage and allocator services did not take a considerable amount of time to execute their workflows. In this experiment, the following were involved: one consumer agent, one broker agent, two MSPs, each containing one storage service, and two CSPs, each containing one allocator service and n processing services, where $1 \leq n \leq 10$.

Results and observations. As Fig. 7(b) shows, (i) the number of necessary messages to compose services was constant even in the presence of scarce resources; and (ii) the allocator service efficiently exploited the available processing services by assigning the tasks in parallel. For instance, processing the consumer's task with four processing services, consumed 15 s; in the first 10 seconds, eight atomic tasks were processed by the four processing services, and in the remaining 5 s, just two processing services were used. This left 153 ms for composing and synchronizing. When the number of processing services was from 5 to 9, the consumed time was similar, and the milliseconds of difference were caused by message latencies. With ten resources, the ten atomic tasks were assigned in parallel, leaving 174 ms for the composition and synchronization processes. These results show that the proposed agent-based Cloud service composition algorithm handles the parallelization of tasks in a effective manner without involving additional messages. This parallelization was achieved even with heterogeneous resource agents having dissimilar times/capacities to fulfill the assigned requirements. In this regard, the execution of heterogeneous agents may evolve independently according to their capabilities and constraints.

4.3 Horizontal Service Composition Experiment

Objective. The third experiment was designed to explore the scalability and synchronization capabilities of the composition algorithm in horizontal scenarios.

Scenario and experimental settings. A consumer agent was assumed to require storing a huge amount of data, which must be stored by different service providers. It was first supposed that the data can be stored by one MSP, and then by two MSPs and so on until reaching eleven MSPs. In this experiment, the following were involved: one consumer agent, one broker agent, and n MSPs, each containing one storage service, where $1 \leq n \leq 11$.

Results and observations. The obtained results show that the number of exchanged messages increased at a constant rate of 13 messages per service provider added to the composition (see Fig. 7(c)). With this result, the agent-based service composition algorithm was shown to have a linear time complexity in both vertical and horizontal scenarios. Thus, it is suitable for handling the scalability necessary in Cloud-computing environments.

The specifications of the computer on which the experiments were carried out are as follows: Intel Core 2 Duo E8500 3.16 & 3.17 GHz, 4 GB RAM, with a Windows Vista Enterprise (32 bits) operating system, service pack 1.

5 Conclusions

5.1 Related Work

A previous research effort to achieve service composition in Cloud-computing environments was carried out in [7], which addressed service composition as a combinatorial optimization problem considering multi-Cloud environments, where each Cloud has a directory of available providers and their corresponding services. A search tree is created from these directories that maps the services deployed on the Cloud; artificial intelligence planning techniques are then applied to the tree in order to achieve the composition of atomic services. Another closely related work is [6], which presents a semantic matching algorithm that uses web services' descriptions to match the inputs and outputs of correlated web services.

Both approaches assume complete knowledge of all services deployed in different Clouds. Moreover, the composition process is centralized, and only atomic web services are considered. In contrast to [6] and [7], this work provides decentralized composition for both atomic and complex web services, which may require enacting an interaction protocol in order to fulfill their requirements.

5.2 Concluding Remarks

Throughout this research effort, the advantages of the agent paradigm as an underlying framework for supporting service composition in Cloud-computing environments were demonstrated. In addition, a Petri net–based methodology for defining web services' workflows capable of synchronizing concurrent and parallel execution of atomic and complex web services was developed. This design methodology provides a small set of requirements for assuring proper coordination and synchronization of web services in both horizontal and vertical scenarios.

Moreover, Cloud service composition is supported in a decentralized manner; no agent has dominant control over the others, and each agent knows only what it needs but not how to obtain it. Furthermore, RAs can be added dynamically even when a service composition is taking place due to the independent interfaces, which synchronize the acceptance and request of requirements. This fits well with the constantly changing Cloud infrastructure.

Finally, in the immediate future, work will be focus on deploying the agent-based architecture in a semantic web service framework using RESTful web services.

Acknowledgments. This work was supported by the Korea Research Foundation Grant funded by the Korean Government (MEST) (KRF-2009-220-D00092) and the DASAN International Faculty Fund (project code: 140316).

References

1. Bellifemine, F., Poggi, A., Rimassa, G.: JADE - A FIPA-Compliant Agent Framework. In: 4th International Conference and Exhibition on the Practical Application of Intelligent Agents and Multi-Agents, pp. 97–108 (1999)
2. Jensen, K., Kristensen, L.M., Wells, L.: Coloured Petri Nets and CPN Tools for Modelling and Validation of Concurrent Systems. J. Softw. Tools Technol. Transf. 9(3), 213–254 (2007)
3. Mei, L., Chan, W.K., Tse, T.H.: A Tale of Clouds: Paradigm Comparisons and Some Thoughts on Research Issues. In: Proc. of the 2008 IEEE Asia-Pacific Services Computing Conference, pp. 464–469. IEEE Computer Society, Washington (2008)
4. Smith, R.G.: The Contract Net Protocol: High-Level Communication and Control in a Distributed Problem Solver. IEEE Trans. Comput. 29(12), 1104–1113 (1980)
5. Valk, R.: Petri Nets as Token Objects: An Introduction to Elementary Object Nets. In: Desel, J., Silva, M. (eds.) ICATPN 1998. LNCS, vol. 1420, pp. 1–25. Springer, Heidelberg (1998)
6. Zeng, C., Guo, X., Ou, W., Han, D.: Cloud Computing Service Composition and Search Based on Semantic. In: Jaatun, M.G., Zhao, G., Rong, C. (eds.) CloudCom 2009. LNCS, vol. 5931, pp. 290–300. Springer, Heidelberg (2009)
7. Zou, G., Chen, Y., Yang, Y., Huang, R., Xu, Y.: AI Planning and Combinatorial Optimization for Web Service Composition in Cloud Computing. In: Proc. International Conference on Cloud Computing and Virtualization (2010)

Video Adaptation Model Based on Cognitive Lattice in Ubiquitous Computing*

Svetlana Kim and Yong-ik Yoon

Department of Multimedia Science, Sookmyung Women's University
Chungpa-Dong 2-Ga, Yongsan-Gu 140-742, Seoul, Korea
songsm0328@naver.com, yiyoon@sm.ac.kr

Abstract. The multimedia service delivery chain poses today many challenges. There are an increasing terminal diversity, network heterogeneity and a pressure to satisfy the user preferences. The situation encourages the need for the personalized contents to provide the user in the best possible experience in ubiquitous computing. This paper introduces a personalized content preparation and delivery framework for multimedia service. The personalized video adaptation is expected to satisfy individual users' need in video content. Cognitive lattice plays a significant role of video annotation to meet users' preference on video content. In this paper, a comprehensive solution for the PVA (Personalized Video Adaptation) is proposed based on Cognitive lattice concept. The PVA is implemented based on MPEG-21 Digital Item Adaptation framework. One of the challenges is how to quantify users' preference on video content.

Keywords: Content Adaptation, MPEG-21, Cognitive content, Personalized.

1 Introduction

In recently, personalization is on tailoring a multimedia service to the personal details or characteristics of a user. Due to the difference of users' device, network conditions, and especially their personal preference on multimedia content, multimedia systems need to personalized multimedia access aiming at enhancing the multimedia retrieval process by complementing explicit user requests with various user's environments [1,2,3]. Although these methods provide feasible ways for video adaptation, there is still a distance to satisfy user's preference on video content. Techniques for delivery have to be developed for content analysis and video adaptation to accommodate users' demands with little available time and their preference on video content. The other aspect is how to develop an adaptation system considering the characteristics of the media to be presented, the network constrains and the capabilities of the device used to access the media. Due to different video formats and various user environments, a generic solution for video adaptation is necessary.

In PVA scenarios, it is essential to personalize more easily and efficiently for the desired content. The major objective of this paper designs a video personalization system in heterogeneous usage environments and provides a new notion on their

* This Research was supported by the Sookmyung Women's University Research Grants 2010.

T.-h. Kim et al. (Eds.): GDC/CA 2010, CCIS 121, pp. 11–21, 2010.

associated issues in MPEG-7 and MPEG-21. The server maintains the content sources, the MPEG-7 metadata descriptions, the MPEG-21 rights expressions, and the content adaptability declarations. The client communicates the MPEG-7 user preference, MPEG-21 usage environments, and user query to retrieve and display the personalized content. The personalization engine and the adaptation engine affect the service adaptation middleware for video delivery.

Cognitive lattice concept refers to those semantic events in specific video domains, such as interesting events in sport videos. To bridge the gap between low-level features and user's perception, mid-level features, such as semantic video shots, specific audio sounds are detected to be further used for content detection. For affective content, we detect affective levels instead of detailed emotional categories. Within a certain genre of movie, affective levels can represent emotions more or less. For example, in horror movies, the content with high affective level most probably is the horror segment. Moreover, the adaptation is implemented based on MPEG-21 DIA (Digital Item Adaptation) framework[3].

2 Related Work

Video adaptation Video adaptation has been highly important research direction for many years. In order to reduce the bandwidth utilization, the early work was mostly concerned the capabilities of terminal devices [5,6], network conditions, [7,8], transcoding between video formats[9,10], or generating adapted video by dropping video frames[11,12], pixels and coefficients [13]. However, objectives of the adaptation process to reduce the bandwidth utilization cannot satisfy users' personal requests.

Nowadays, personalized video accesses become a crowded research area [14,15]. User access patterns are characterized to benefit the design of personalized multimedia system [3]. In W.H.Adams[4] introduces the important parts to construct the architectures for personalized multimedia. In digital TV field, a user-centered control system is proposed to provide personalized and automated channel selection service [8]. Some researches pay attention to certain user devices. In [9] describes a set of cooperative agents distributed over different sites that work together to provide personalized services for mobile users over the internet.

Most of user-specified adaptation focus on adapting low level features such as, color depth whereas users might pay more attention to high-level semantics than low-level features. Research works on semantic analysis provides a feasible way for user to access video according to their preference on video content. Applications of video-content analysis and retrieval are introduced in [4]. In Special Issue on Universal Multimedia Access[1], a systematic study of automatic classification of consumer videos into a large set of diverse semantic concept classes was presented. Multiple modalities have been considered to achieve good performance on semantic analysis in [2]. Some research focus on specific video domains. An event-based video indexing method taking account of semantically dependency between multi-modal information streams is introduced for sports videos.

Semantic analysis provides a feasible entry for users to access video based on their understanding on video content. However, users may prefer "emotional decisions" to find affective content because emotional factors directly reflect an audience's attention and evaluation. Multimedia affective computing attracts more and more research efforts. Affective content have also been detected for videos. In [5], Hanjalic and Xu utilized the features of motion, color, and audio to represent arousal and valence.

This paper presents a comprehensive video adaptation method according to users' preference on both cognitive and affective content.

3 PVA Framework Overview

Personalized Video Adaptation (PVA) refers to the ability to access by any user to any video contents over any type of network with any device from anywhere and anytime in ubiquitous computing. To support the adaptation, the application is required to directly execute an adaptation mechanism when the lower level informs about an occurred change. Even if an application is able to catch the change of the running environment, it is more efficient if the middleware manages such adaptation mechanisms. The middleware for ubiquitous computing has to be recognizable, and the applications executed on middleware have to be adapted to the changed context by using diverse logics [4][5]. PVA allows application developers to build a large and complex distributed system that can transform physical spaces into computationally active and intelligent environments. PVA applications need a middleware that can detect and act upon any context changes created by the result of any interactions between users, applications, and surrounding computing environment for applications without users' interventions.

User query response may be delivered through a network, eventually using a real-time connection. In this case, the streaming module will deliver the scalable or non-scalable content to the user; in the case, real-time transcoding is been performed. It may happen that real time adjustments to the transcoding process are implemented using measures which characterize, for example, the network fluctuations

This figure shows the framework of video content based personalized video adaptation. There are two main parts for personalized video adaptation which are Cognitive Lattice Analysis using Mining and FocusOfChoice algorithm for content delivery. The aim for video content analysis is to create tables of content for video sequence by detecting cognitive content or affective content. Table of content make it possible for us to easily access the corresponding part in video according to our interests. By considering users' request on video content and network conditions, the adaptation decision engine make adaptation decision according to QoS. Later on, FocusOfChoice algorithm in adaptation operation engine generates adapted video from the original video stream, generic Bitstream Syntax Description with the content annotation (Table of Content) according to the adaptation decision.

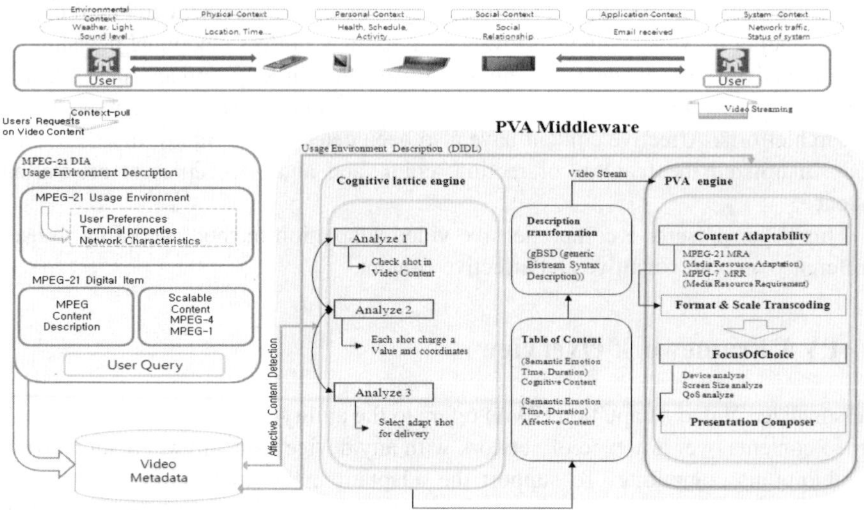

Fig. 1. Framework of Video Content based Personalized Video Adaptation

4 Video Content Analysis

4.1 Cognitive Lattice Engine

Cognitive lattice analysis bases on detecting those regular events which take place in some specific video contents. Sport videos possess an inherent structure due to the cameraman's technique and the constraints placed on the game through its rules.

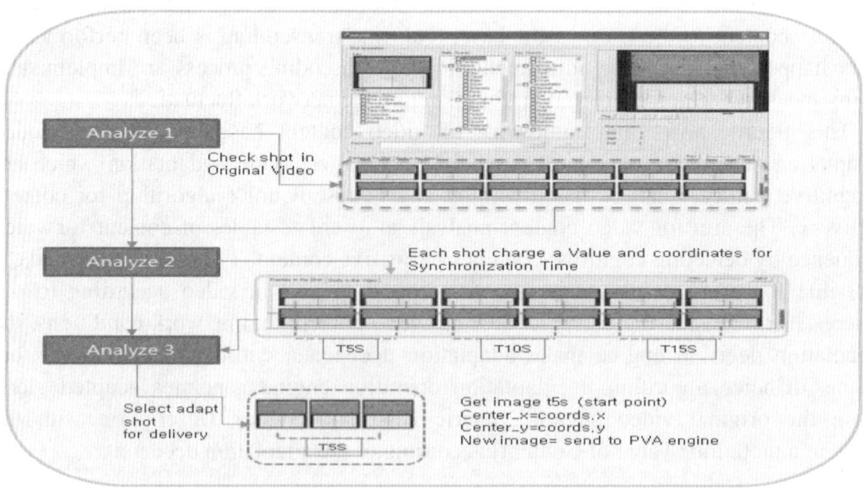

Fig. 2. PVA Cognitive lattice engine

Sports video has a rich events structure. The detection can be facilitated with the help of domain specific knowledge. Since an event is a typical semantic content, we choose sports video as a good test bed for studying semantic video indexing methods.

The objective of our system is to show a shortened video summary that maintains as much semantic content within the desired time constraint. The Cognitive lattice algorithm performs this process by three different matching analyzes and is described next in Fig. 2.

4.2 Cognitive Content Detection

4.2.1 Analyze 1 Check Shot in Original Video

Some video shot which contain interesting events, audio sounds have some correlation, and the occurrence of these audio sounds follows some potential rules. For example, during the stadium-view shot of soccer videos, silence and the sound of the ball being hit take place interlaced. After repeated sound of the ball being hit and silence, applause and commentator speech might be detected. In this paper, we use the frame number to represent shot-length, which indicated how many frames in the shot. The shot detector output the starting frame for each shot. Shot-length *SL* is calculated by $SL=N_i - N_{i+1}$, where N_i is the starting frame of shot *i*.

Using shot segments as the basic video unit, there are multiple methods of video summarization based on spatial and temporal compression of the original video sequence [13][14]. In our work, we focus on the insertion or deletion of each video shot depending on user preference. Each video shot is either included or excluded from the final video summary. In each shot, MPEG-7 metadata describes the semantic content and corresponding scores. Assume there are a total of *N* attribute categories.

Let $\vec{P} = [P_1, P_2, \ldots\ldots, P_n]^1$ be the user preference vector, where p_i denotes the preference weighting for attribute *i*, $1 \leq i \leq N$. Assume there are a total of *M* shots.

Let $\vec{S} = [S_1, S_2, \ldots\ldots, S_M]^T$ be the shot segments that comprise the original video sequence, where s_i denotes shot number *i*, $1 \leq i \leq M$. Subsequently, the attribute score $cor_{i,j}$ is defined as the relevance of attribute *i* in shot *j*, $1 \leq j \leq M$ and $1 \leq i \leq N$. It then follows that the weighted attribute w_i for shot *i* given the user preference $\vec{P}$ is calculated as the dot product of the attribute matrix **A** and the user preference vector $\vec{P}$.

Video summaries are composed of a set of independent shots or frame a unit that optimally matches the user preferences while limited by the total time constraint. The resulting video summaries do not take value and coordination for PVA. In this section, we examine a cognitive lattice analyze 2, where using cognitive lattice each shot charge a value and coordinates and duration relationship talks about the relationship between or among image.

First, we consider representing duration relationship by average motion intensity within one shot because of the following two considerations: 1) from durational relationships' point of view; 2) motion is estimated from the different between two frames. Next, we divide the shot into lattices $v\_num[k] = \sum (x_1)\, V_i[k]$, and divide the shot vertically and horizontally $h\_num[k] = \sum (x_2)\, H_i[k]$. Last, we have to number each lattice. Vertical lattice is assign the value *i*, horizontal lattice the value *j*. Finally, in analyze 3 select adapt shot for personalization delivery.

5 VA Adaptation Engine

The objective of the adaptation engine is to perform the optimal set of transformations on the selected content in accordance with the adaptability declarations and the inherent usage environment. The adaptation engine must be equipped to perform transcoding, filtering, and scaling such that the user can play the final adapted personalized content Fig 3.

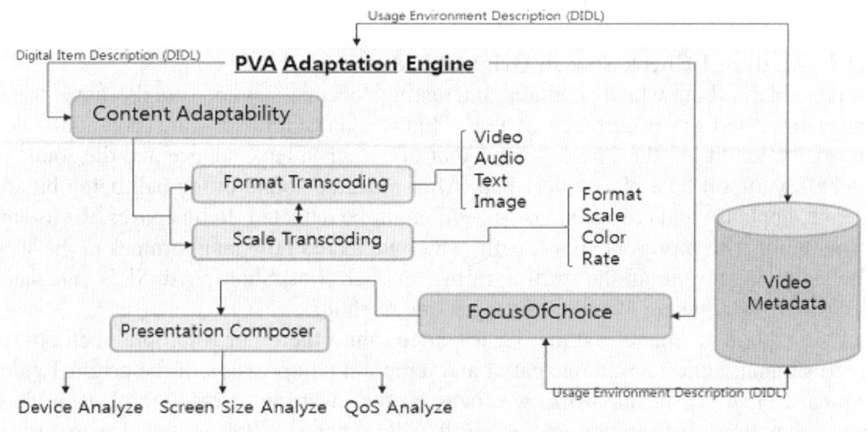

Fig. 3. PVA engine architecture

5.1 Content Adaptability

Content adaptability refers to the multiple variations that a media can be transformed into, either through changes in format, scale, rate, and/or quality. Format transcoding may be required to accommodate the user's terminal devices. Scale conversion can represent image size resizing, video frame rate extrapolation, or audio channel enhancement. Rate control corresponds to the data rate for transferring the media content, and may allow variable or constant rates. Quality of service can be guaranteed to the user based on any criteria including SNR or distortion quality measures. These adaptation operations transform the original content to efficiently fit the usage environment.

The *MPEG-7 media resource requirement* and the *MPEG-21 media resource adaptability* both provide descriptions for allowing certain types of adaptations. These adaptation descriptions contain information for a single adaptation or a set of adaptations. The descriptions may possibly include required conditions for the adaptation, the permissions, and the configurations.

5.2 Presentation Composer

The PVA adaptation engine performs the optimal set of transformation on the selected content in according with the adaptability declarations and the inherent usage environment [21]. The adaptation engine must be equipped to perform transcoding, filtering and scaling. Today, it does not provide the quantified measure of perceptibility indicating the degree of allowable transcoding. To overcome this problem, PVA adaptation engine uses a content value function V for any transcoding configuration C: C={I, r}, where $I \subset \{1,2\ldots,n\}$ represent a class of video and r is the resolution reduction factor of the transcoding video. The content value function V can be defined as:

$$V = C(I,r) = \sum_{i \in I} V_i(r) = \sum_{i \in I} (s_i \cdot u(r - r_i))$$

$$\text{where,} \quad u(x) = \begin{cases} 1, & \text{if} \quad x \geq 0 \\ 0, & \text{elsewhere} \end{cases}$$

Denoting the width and height of the client display size by W and H, respectively, the content adaptation is modeled as the following resource allocation problem:

$$\text{Maximize} \quad C(I,r),$$

$$\text{such that} \begin{cases} r|x_u - x_l| \leq W \\ r|y_u - y_l| \leq H \end{cases} and,$$

where the transcoding $C(I, r)$ is represented by a rectangle bounding box whose lower and upper bound point are (x_l, y_l) and (x_u, y_u) respectively.

6 Implementation on Analyzes

The soccer game include *LongShot(LS)* and *ShortShot(SS)* see in Fig4. *LongShot*, so there was the problem that the quality was low, serious random and low user preference because the displays are so small, many users have trouble viewing the content. For example, viewing soccer matches recorded with a *LongShot* camera it is very hard to see the ball and players because they are extremely small. Therefore it is necessary to develop a way of sending the part that interests the user to his device in a fitting way.

(a) (b)

Fig. 4. (a)*LS* and (b)*SS* in Soccer game

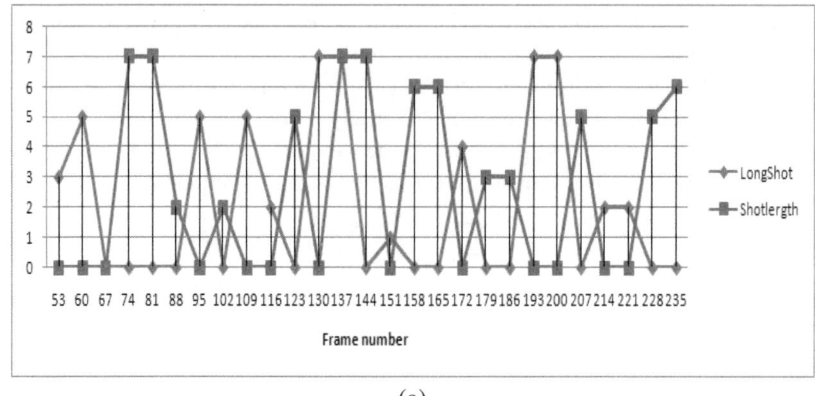

(a)

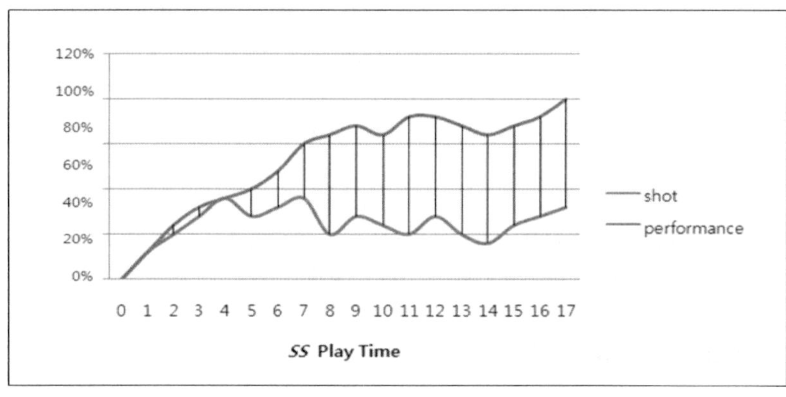

(b)

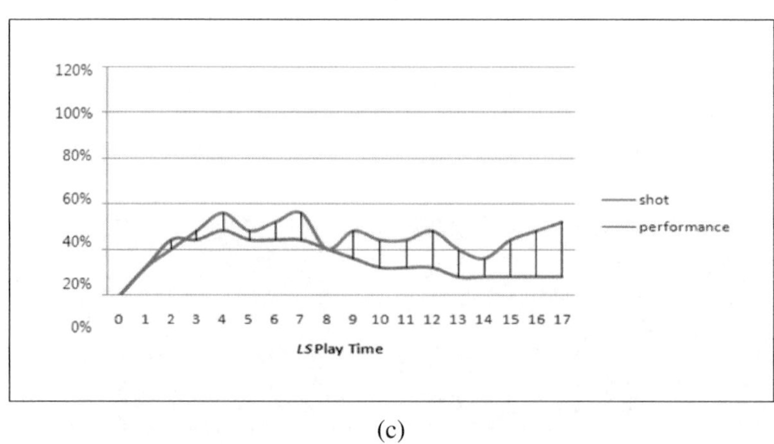

(c)

Fig. 5. Number of *LS* and *SS* (a),User performance Quality for *SS(*b) and User performance Quality for *LS*(c)

For Cognitive lattice algorithm, we divide the shot into lattice and divide the shot vertically and horizontally for indicated how many frames in the shot. Find value and coordinate we have classification shot. *LongShot LS), ShortShot (SS)* and *Shot-Length* are seen in Fig.5(a).This figure, shows how many *LongShot* and *ShortShot* including soccer video. The detailed explanation is in Fig.5 (b), (c). First, *ShortShot* valence recording performance which will be small gets better shows a result from the Fig.5(b), but Fig.5 (c), shows when delivered *LongShot* for user device, is performance very low. Therefore all *LongShot* in soccer video must change in the *ShortShot* for good performance Quality.

Next, we consider representing duration relationship by average motion intensity within one shot because of the following two considerations: 1) from durational relationships' point of view; 2) motion is estimated from the different between two frames. Motion intensity roughly estimates the gross motion in the whole frame, including object and camera motion. Motion intensity *MV* is computed as the average magnitude of motion vectors in a frame:

$$MV = \frac{1}{\Phi} \sum_{\Phi} \sqrt{v_x^2 + v_y^2}$$

where $\Phi = \{inter - coded\ macro\text{-}block\}$, and $v = [v_x, v_y]$ is the motion vector for each macro-block. Then the average motion intensity is calculated for the whole shot.

For this, we detect event in soccer game. Soccer event has the most dispersed structures. To detect each event exactly, shot transition becomes more important in soccer videos than in tennis and basketball as shown inf Fig. 6.

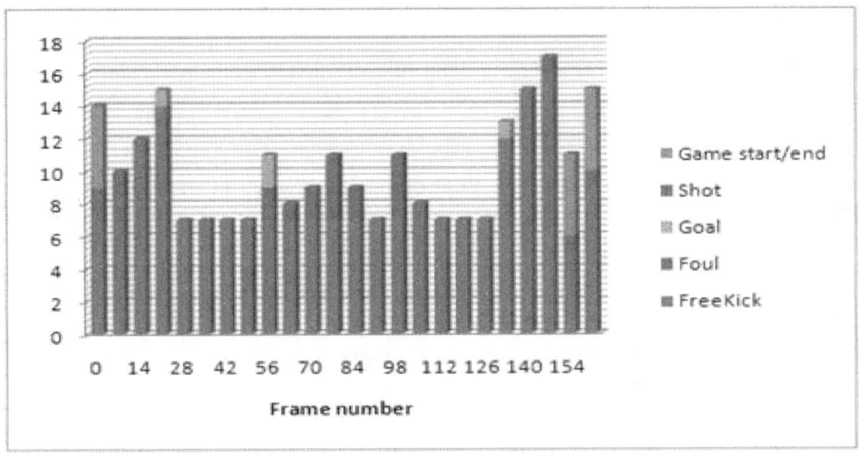

Fig. 6. Event detection in soccer video

When each event occurring, in the frame between happens the interval. Most like this interval the camera catches with *LongShot*. Uses an Cognitive lattice algorithm we, change from the *LongShot* with *ShortShot*. Therefore, object change goes out to user a same size, user performance gets better.

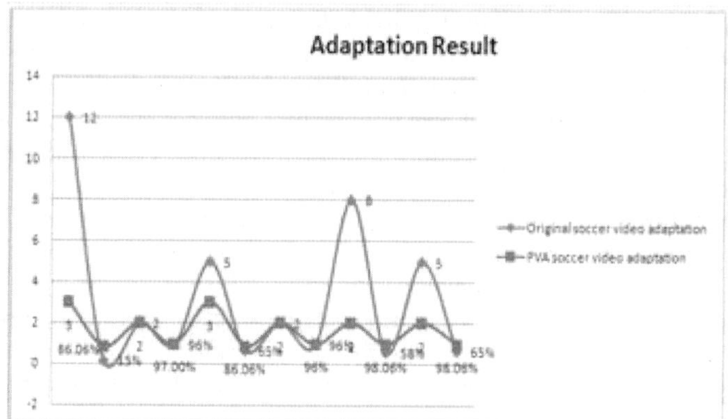

Fig. 7. Adaptation result using PVA framework

In the Fig.7 shows the difference of PVA soccer adaptation method and original soccer adaptation method. In the original adaptation performance result is low because original video adaptation sends *LongShot* it stands to the user. But using PVA adaptation, we get high performance results because before PVA had description process of *LongShot*.

7 Conclusion and Future Work

This paper we have proposed a comprehensive solution for personalized video adaptation including content analysis and MPEG-21 Digital Item Adaptation. Both cognitive content and affective content are considered for adaptation. Although the proposed adaptation solution has only been initially tested on sports video and some movies, it is not difficult to extend to other video domains, because of the following two reasons:

a. Cognitive content and affective content complement each other and almost cover all the highlights in different video domains. Users can access most of their interested video content by searching for either cognitive content or affective content.

b. MPEG-21 Digital Item Adaptation provides a generic adaptation solution, which is independent to video formats, user environments. Adaptation implementations based on MPEG-21 DIA framework are easily extended to other video adaptation environments.

Currently, the initial affective content analysis is based on affective level detection. In future, more detailed emotional categories can be further detected.

References

1. Issue on Universal Multimedia Access, IEEE Signal Processing Magazine 20(2) (March 2003)
2. Special Issue on Multimedia Adaptation. Signal Processing: Image Communication 18(8) (September 2003)

3. MPEG Requirement Group, MPEG-21 Multimedia framework, Part 1: Vision, technologies and strategy, Proposed Draft Technocal Report, 2nd edn., Doc. ISO/MPEG N6269, MPEG Waikaloa Meeting, USA (December 2003)
4. Adams, W.H., Iyengart, G., Lin, C.Y., Naphade, M.R., Neti, C., Nock, H.J., Smith, J.R.: Semantic indexing of multimedia content using visual, audio and text cues. EURASIP J. Appl. Signal Process. 2003(2) (February 2003)
5. Joyce, D.W., Lewis, P.H., Tansley, R.H., Dobie, M.R.: Semiotics and agents for integrating and navigating through multimedia representations. In: Proc. Storage Retrieval Media Databases, vol. 3972 (2000)
6. Belle, L.: Tseng, Ching-Yung Lim, John R.Smith, Video personalization system for usage environment. Multimedia Database Management System 15 (September 2004)
7. Tseng, B.L., Lin, C.-Y., Smith, J.R.: Video summarization and personalization for pervasive mobile devices. In: SPIE Electronic Imaging 2002—Storage and Retrieval for Media Databases, San Jose (January 2002)
8. ISO/IEC JTC 1/SC 29/WG 11/N 4242, Text of 15938-5 FDIS, Information Technology—Multimedia Content Description Interface—Part 5 Multimedia Description Schemes, Final Document International Standard (FDIS) edition (October 2001)
9. Butler, M.H.: Implementing content negotiation using CC/PP and WAP UAProf. Technical Report HPL-2001-190 (2001)
10. Tseng, B.L., Lin, C.-Y.: Personalized video summary using visual semantic annotations and automatic speech transcriptions. In: IEEE Multimedia Signal Processing MMSP, St. Thomas (December 2002)
11. ISO/IEC JTC1/SC29/WG11/M8321, MPEG-7 Tools for MPEG-21 Digital Item Adaptation, Fairfax, VA (May 2002)
12. National ISO/IEC JTC1/SC29/WG11/N5354, MPEG-21 Digital Item Adaptation, Awaji Island, Japan (December 2002)
13. Lin, C.-Y., Tseng, B.L., Smith, J.R.: VideoAnnEx: IBM MPEG-7 annotation tool. In: IEEE International Conference on Multimedia and Expo, Baltimore (2003)
14. Lin, C.-Y., Tseng, B.L., Naphade, M., Natsev, A., Smith, J.R.: VideoAL: a novel end-to-end MPEG-7 video automatic labeling system. In: IEEE International Conference on Image Processing, Barcelona, (September 2003)
15. Manjunath, B.S., Salembier, P., Sikora, T.: Introduction to MPEG-7: Multimedia Content Description Language. Wiley, New York (2002)

A Genetic-Based Scheduling Algorithm to Minimize the Makespan of the Grid Applications

Reza Entezari-Maleki and Ali Movaghar

Department of Computer Engineering, Sharif University of Technology, Tehran, Iran
entezari@ce.sharif.edu, movaghar@sharif.edu

Abstract. Task scheduling algorithms in grid environments strive to maximize the overall throughput of the grid. In order to maximize the throughput of the grid environments, the makespan of the grid tasks should be minimized. In this paper, a new task scheduling algorithm is proposed to assign tasks to the grid resources with goal of minimizing the total makespan of the tasks. The algorithm uses the genetic approach to find the suitable assignment within grid resources. The experimental results obtained from applying the proposed algorithm to schedule independent tasks within grid environments demonstrate the applicability of the algorithm in achieving schedules with comparatively lower makespan in comparison with other well-known scheduling algorithms such as, Min-min, Max-min, RASA and Sufferage algorithms.

Keywords: Task scheduling, grid environment, makespan, genetic algorithm.

1 Introduction

There are various computation- and data-intensive problems in science and industry those require weeks or months of computation to solve. Scientists involved in these types of problems need a computing environment that deliver large amounts of computational power over a long period of time. Such an environment is called a high throughput computing (HTC) environment [1], [2], [3]. The HTC field is more interested in how many independent tasks can be completed over a long period of time instead of how fast an individual task can complete which is interested in high performance computing (HPC) [4], [5]. HPC systems are mostly used to execute parallel dependent tasks and therefore they must execute within a particular site with low latency interconnections. Conversely, in HTC systems there are mostly numbers of independent and sequential tasks which can be individually scheduled on many different computing resources across multiple administrative domains. HTC systems can achieve this using various grid computing [6] technologies and techniques.

In order to achieve the HTC through grid environments, the overall response time to all the tasks, in a relatively long period of time, should be minimized. Thereby, the grid manager could schedule the submitted tasks on appropriate grid resources, considering the makespan of the environment. The makespan of a resource is the time slot between the start and completion of a sequence of tasks assigned to the resource [7], [8], [9]. The total makespan of a grid environment is defined as the largest makespan of the grid

T.-h. Kim et al. (Eds.): GDC/CA 2010, CCIS 121, pp. 22–31, 2010.

resources. Minimizing the total makespan of a grid environment, the throughput of the environment is increased, accordingly [4], [7].

To make effective use of the tremendous capabilities of the computational resources in grid environments and minimize the makespan of the grids, efficient task scheduling algorithms are required. Task scheduling algorithms are commonly applied by grid manager to optimally dispatch tasks to the grid resources [4], [7], [10]. Typically, grid users submit their own tasks to the grid manager to take full advantage of the grid facilities. The grid manager in a computational grid tries to distribute the submitted tasks among the grid resources in such a way that the total response time is minimized. There are relatively a large number of task scheduling algorithms to minimize the total makespan of the distributed systems [4], [7], [10], [11], [12]. Actually, these algorithms try to minimize the overall completion time of the tasks by finding the most suitable resources to be allocated to the tasks. It should be noticed that minimizing the overall completion time or total makespan of the tasks does not necessarily result in the minimization of execution time of each individual task [10].

Decision about the assigning of tasks to the resources and finding the best match between tasks and resources is NP-complete problem [4], [8], [9], [10]. In this reason, some heuristic methods are proposed to find the suitable and near optimal solutions for scheduling problem [7], [11], [13], [14]. This paper proposes a new task scheduling algorithm to minimize the makespan of the grid environments. The algorithm uses genetic heuristic and searches the possible assignments among tasks and resources to find the best matching between them. The algorithm proposed in this paper is simulated and compared with other well-known scheduling algorithms. The results obtained from comparing proposed algorithm and Min-min, Max-min, Sufferage and RASA algorithms show that the proposed algorithm overcomes the weakness of the other ones by finding task/resource pairs with lower makespan.

The remainder of this paper is organized as follows. Section 2 presents the related works based on previous literatures. In section 3, task scheduling algorithms are considered and four benchmarks used for evaluating the proposed algorithm are introduced. Section 4 proposes the genetic based scheduling algorithm and section 5 presents the experimental results obtained from comparing the scheduling algorithms. Finally, section 6 concludes the paper and presents the future works.

2 Related Works

Due to some specific attributes of the grid environments such as relatively high communication costs within resources, most of the previously introduced scheduling algorithms are not applicable in these systems [4], [10]. Therefore, there have been ongoing attempts to propose new scheduling algorithms specifically within heterogeneous distributed systems and grid environments [4], [7], [9], [10], [11], [12], [13], [14]. Some of these works are discussed below briefly.

He et al. [4] have presented a new algorithm based on the conventional Min-min algorithm. The proposed algorithm called QoS guided Min-min schedules tasks requiring high bandwidth before the others. Therefore, if the bandwidth required by different tasks varies highly, the QoS guided Min-min algorithm provides better results than the Min-min algorithm. Whenever the bandwidth requirement of all of the tasks is almost the same, the QoS guided Min-min algorithm acts similar to the Min-min algorithm.

Parsa et al. [10] have proposed a new task scheduling algorithm called RASA. RASA uses the advantages of both Min-min and Max-min algorithms and covers their disadvantages simultaneously. To achieve this, RASA firstly estimates the completion time of the tasks on each of the available resources, and then applies the Max-min and Min-min algorithms, alternatively. Applying Max-min and Min-min methods alternatively, the Min-min strategy is used to execute small tasks before the large ones, and the Max-min strategy is used to avoid delays in the execution of large tasks and to support concurrency in the execution of large and small tasks. Experimental results reported in [10] show that RASA demonstrates relatively lower makespan in comparison with both Min-min and Max-min algorithms within grid environments.

Munir et al. [12] have presented a new task scheduling algorithm for grid environments called QoS Sufferage. This algorithm considers network bandwidth and schedules tasks based on their bandwidth requirement as the QoS guided Min-min algorithm does. Compared with the Max-min, Min-min, QoS guided Min-min and QoS priority grouping algorithms, QoS Sufferage obtains smaller makespan.

Wang et al. [11] have presented a genetic-algorithm-based approach to dispatch and schedule subtasks within grid environments. Subtasks are produced from decomposition of tasks in grid manager and they should be scheduled appropriately to reach minimum completion time for the related entire task. The genetic-algorithm-based approach separates the matching and scheduling representations, provides independence between the chromosome structure and the details of the communication subsystem, and considers the overlap existing among all computations and communications that obey subtask precedence constraints. The simulation tests presented in [11] for small-sized problems (e.g., a small number of subtasks and a small number of machines), shows that the genetic-algorithm-based approach can found the optimal solution for these types of problems. The results obtained from simulation of the large size problems showed that this approach outperformed two non-evolutionary heuristics and a random search.

Levitin et al. [14] have proposed a genetic algorithm to distribute execution blocks within grid resources. The aim of the algorithm is to find the best match between execution blocks and grid resources in which the reliability and/or expected performance of the task execution in the grid environment maximizes. The illustrative and numerical examples presented in [14] shows that proposed algorithm can find the suitable solution for the problem.

3 Scheduling Algorithms

Suppose that m resources R_j ($j = 1, ..., m$) have to process n tasks T_i ($i = 1, ..., n$). A schedule for each task is an allocation of one or more time intervals to one or more resources. The expected execution time E_{ij} of task T_i on resource R_j is defined as the amount of time taken by R_j to execute T_i where R_j has no load when T_i is assigned. The expected completion time C_{ij} of task T_i on resource R_j is defined as the wall-clock time on which R_j completes T_i (after having finished any previously assigned tasks). Let b_i denote to the beginning of the execution of task T_i. From the above definitions, the expected completion time C_{ij} can be written as Eq. 1.

$$C_{ij} = b_i + E_{ij}. \tag{1}$$

Let C_i be the completion time for task T_i, and it is equal to C_{ij} where resource R_j is assigned to execute task T_i. The makespan for the complete schedule is then defined as Eq. 2.

$$Max_{T_i \in K}(C_i) \tag{2}$$

Where K is the set of tasks which has been assigned to the resources to be executed. Makespan is a measure of the throughput of the heterogeneous computing systems (e.g. computational grids) [7], [8], [10].

There are several scheduling algorithms attempting to minimize the makespan of the distributed systems. These algorithms are used as benchmarks to evaluate the new proposed algorithms. Min-min heuristic is one of the batch mode scheduling schemes used as a benchmark for many batch mode mappings [7], [8]. The Min-min algorithm can be applied to wide range of systems such as multiprocessors and homogenous and heterogeneous distributed systems by applying trivial modifications. This algorithm shows relatively low makespan in comparison with other similar algorithms. The Max-min heuristic is similar to the Min-min heuristic and has the same complexity as the Min-min heuristic but it is likely to do better than the Min-min heuristic in the cases where there are many shorter tasks than longer ones. Both Min-min and Max-min heuristics are implemented in SmartNet [7], [8].

RASA is a new proposed algorithm which combines two conventional algorithms, Min-min and Max-min, and achieves lower makespan in comparison with the basic algorithms [10]. RASA uses the number of the available resources when it determines the resource which should be allocated to a specific task. Whereas the number of the available resources is odd, the Max-min method is applied to the unscheduled tasks and when the number of the resources is even, the Min-min strategy is used. With this mechanism, RASA gives low makespan and consequently high throughput. Sufferage algorithm is a deterministic algorithm to schedule tasks within resources to achieve low makespan [7], [13]. The Sufferage heuristic is based on the idea that better mappings can be generated by assigning a resource to a task that would "suffer" most in terms of expected completion time if that particular resource is not assigned to it. In some of the simulated situations, Sufferage shows lower makespan compared to Min-min, Max-min and RASA algorithms. In this paper, four above mentioned algorithms are implemented and compared to the proposed genetic based algorithm.

4 The Proposed Algorithm

The task scheduling algorithm proposed in this paper is based on Genetic Algorithm (GA). GA is a promising heuristic and effective optimization approach to find near optimal solutions in large search spaces [11], [14]. To propose a new GA some steps should be specified. Fig. 1 shows these steps.

In the first step, it is necessary to encode any possible solution of the problem as a set of strings named as chromosome. Each chromosome represents one solution to the problem, and a set of chromosomes is referred to as a population. To represent the scheduling problem, the strings of integer numbers are used. Assume there are n independent tasks and m available resources to execute these tasks. Let first n integers (1, 2, ..., n) in a string representing the scheduling problem denote the tasks whereas the numbers from $n + 1$ to $n + m$ represent available resources (any number $n + i$ corresponds to resource i). The greatest number ($n + m$) always takes the last position in a code string.

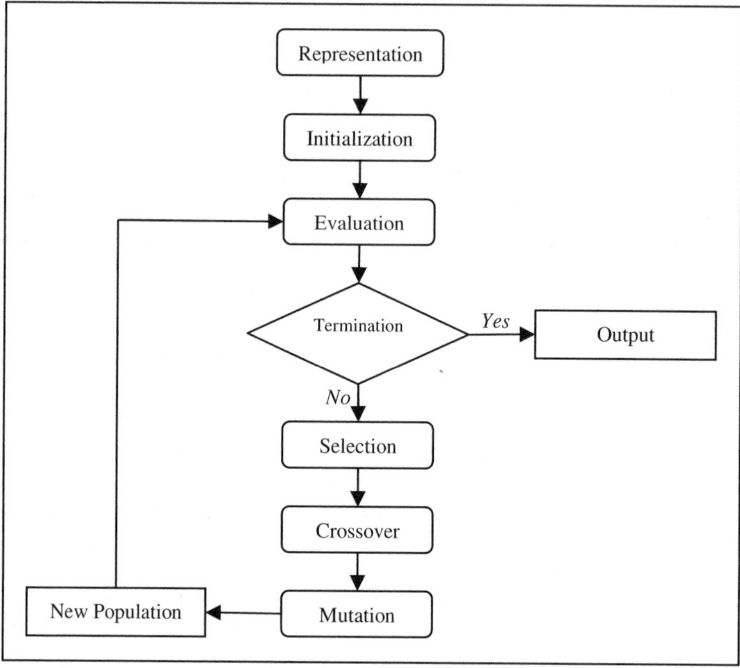

Fig. 1. Steps of Genetic Algorithms

The rule of representation decoding is as follows: any sequence of adjacent task numbers executed by the nearest resource placed in the right hand of the tasks. Consider several examples for $n = 5$ and $m = 3$, that are decoded and interpreted in Table 1. The numbers corresponding to the resources are marked in bold.

Table 1. Examples of task/resource encoding

String code	Interpretation
12**6**3**7**45**8**	Tasks 1 and 2 are assigned to resource 1, task 3 is assigned to resource 2 and tasks 4 and 5 are assigned to resource 3.
123**78**45**6**	Tasks 1, 2 and 3 are assigned to resource 2, tasks 4 and 5 are assigned to resource 1 and no task is assigned to resource 3.
7231**8**54**6**	Tasks 2, 3 and 1 are assigned to resource 3, tasks 5 and 4 are assigned to resource 1 and no task is assigned to resource 2.
1**6**2**7**34**8**4	An invalid string code.

The next step is to generate an initial population from valid chromosomes. A random set of chromosomes is often used as the initial population. This initial population is the first generation from which the evolution starts. In the proposed algorithm, 30 initial individuals from valid chromosomes are randomly generated.

The third step is to evaluate each of the chromosomes generated in the previous step. Each chromosome is associated with a fitness value, which is, in our algorithm, the completion time of the tasks represented by this chromosome. In other words, a fitness value is assigned to each of the chromosomes and the objective of the GA is to find a chromosome with optimal fitness value. In the algorithm proposed in this paper, each chromosome with a smaller fitness value represents a better solution. During each successive generation, a proportion of the existing population is selected to breed a new generation. In this step, certain selection methods such as roulette wheel selection, rank selection, tournament selection and so forth can be used to generate new population. There are two key concepts during the selection of the parents, elitism and diversity. Selection algorithm should be reserve these two concepts to reach a near optimal (not local optimal) solution for the problem in acceptable time. To do this, we use two well-known selection methods, tournament and rank selections, to select parents for offspring.

In the crossover step, all of the chromosomes selected in selection phase are paired up, and with a crossover probability they are crossed over. To use crossover probability, first a random number r in range [0, 1] is generated and then if the number is less than crossover probability, two pairs are crossed over else they are copied as two new chromosomes to the new population. The crossover procedure used in the proposed algorithm acts as follows: for each couple of chromosomes, two cross over points are randomly selected between 1 to $n + m$. Code string from beginning of chromosome to the first crossover point is copied from one parent (assume parent 1), the order of the genes existing in the part from the first to the second crossover point are inherited from second parent (assume parent 2) and the rest is copied from the first parent (parent 1). The following is an example of the crossover procedure on code strings described in Table 1. In this example, two random numbers are 2 and 7.

Parent 1: 12**6**3**7**45**8**
Parent 2: **7**231**8**54**6**
Children: 12**7**34**6**5**8**

After the crossover, for each of the genes of the chromosomes, the gene will be mutated to any one of the codes with a mutation probability. The mutation process transforms a valid chromosome into another valid one that may or may not already be in the current population. To perform mutation process on the chromosomes obtained from previous phase, a random number r in range [0, 1] is generated. If number r is less than the mutation probability, the selected chromosome is mutated else it is copied as a new chromosomes to the new population. The mutation method used in our algorithm just swaps genes initially located in two randomly chosen positions of a chromosome selected for mutation. After crossover and mutation, the new population is generated and fitness function can be applied to the new chromosomes. Crossover and mutation procedures should preserve validity of the newly obtained strings given where parent strings are valid. Both crossover and mutation methods introduced above are acceptable in our case and can be used to generate a new population.

The loop of chromosome generations is terminated when certain conditions are met. When the termination criteria are met, the elite chromosome as the best solution and its corresponding completion time as the makespan of the environment are returned. In our algorithm, the number of generations is used to specify the termination condition, but in general, other criteria such as allocation constraints (e.g. time), manual inspection, combination of the conditions and so forth can be used, too.

5 Experimental Results

To measure the performance of the proposed algorithm and compare the makespan of the algorithm to the others, randomly generated scenarios are considered. For the sake of brevity, only three figures showing the makespan of the five algorithms, Min-min, Max-min, RASA, Sufferage and the proposed algorithm (GA), are depicted in this paper. Fig. 2 shows the makespan of the above mentioned algorithms where the number of the resources is equal to 2 and the numbers of the tasks are varied from 5 to 50. As shown in Fig. 2, in almost all of the scenarios, the makespan of the GA is lower than other algorithms' makespans. It should be noticed that the makespan of the Min-min and Max-min algorithms is very depend on the number of small and large tasks, and therefore; in the random generated scenarios in which the size of the tasks is randomly varied, the makespan of these algorithms did not follow a specific pattern. RASA and Sufferage algorithms show low makespan in comparison with Min-min and Max-min algorithms, but the makespan of the GA is lower than them. Fig. 3 shows the makespan of the five mentioned algorithms in eight different case studies. In the first four case studies, the proportion of the tasks to the resources is relatively low number and in the four remaining cases, this proportion is relatively large number. These two cases are considered to simulate light and heavy load in grid environments, respectively.

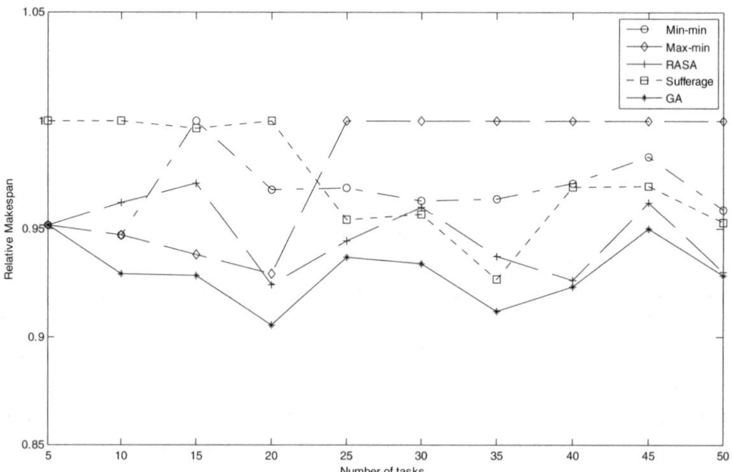

Fig. 2. The relative makespan of the five scheduling algorithms, Min-min, Max-min, RASA, Sufferage and GA. The number of the resources is assumed to be 2 and the numbers of the tasks are varied from 5 to 50 tasks.

As shown in Fig. 3, in almost all of the case studies (light and heavy loads), the proposed algorithm shows lower makespan. Specially, when the number of the tasks is low (light load), the makespan of the GA overcomes other algorithms' makespans.

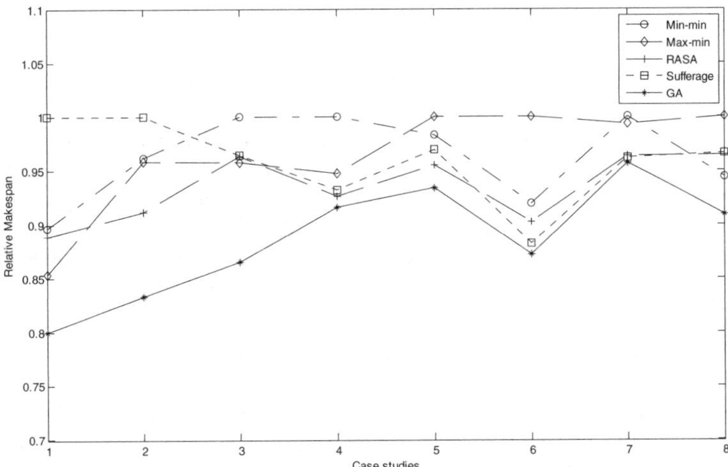

Fig. 3. The relative makespan of the five scheduling algorithms, Min-min, Max-min, RASA, Sufferage and GA where cases 1-4 and 5-8 show the grid environments with light and heavy loads, respectively

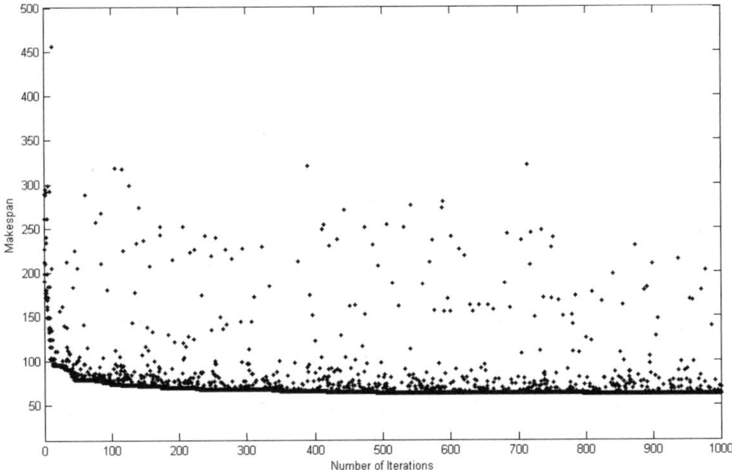

Fig. 4. The convergence of the proposed GA through 1000 iterations

In all of the above mentioned scenarios, the number of the iterations is used to determine the termination condition of the algorithm. This number is set to 1000 and lowers in above experiments. Based on the scenarios studied in this paper, the iteration number equal to 1000 is an acceptable value in almost all of the cases. In this point of view, it can be mentioned that the GA proposed in this paper is early convergence. Fig. 4 demonstrates the convergence of the GA in case study 2 given in Fig. 3. As Shown in Fig. 4, the variations in the makespans of the new populations after 500 iterations are very trivial and the best solution can be found after 500-1000 iterations.

6 Conclusion and Future Works

A new task scheduling algorithm based on genetic approach is presented. This algorithm can be applied to schedule tasks within grid environments to reduce the makespan of the tasks and thereby increase the throughput of the environment. The GA proposed in this paper not only uses very simple method to represent the resource allocation but also exposes lower makespan values in comparison with benchmark scheduling algorithms. Furthermore, the proposed GA converges to the suitable solution for a low number of iterations.

There are numbers of research issues remaining open for future works. One can use other QoS measures (instead of makespan) to evaluate the chromosomes of the population. Taking into account other criteria (e.g. cost of scheduling, grid resources idle times, number of the waiting tasks to be processed within grid resources, fault tolerant issues, performance and reliability of the grid environment and so forth) may result new scheduling algorithms in grid environment. In addition, combining two or more measures to propose a general objective function is an interesting issue in this field of research.

References

1. Montero, R.S., Huedo, E., Llorente, I.M.: Benchmarking of High Throughput Computing Applications on Grids. Journal of Parallel Computing 32, 267–279 (2006)
2. Xue, Y., Wang, Y., Wang, J., Luo, Y., Hu, Y., Zhong, S., Tang, J., Cai, G., Guan, Y.: High Throughput Computing for Spatial Information Processing (HIT-SIP) System on Grid Platform. In: Sloot, P.M.A., Hoekstra, A.G., Priol, T., Reinefeld, A., Bubak, M. (eds.) EGC 2005. LNCS, vol. 3470, pp. 40–49. Springer, Heidelberg (2005)
3. Condor Project, http://www.cs.wisc.edu/condor/overview/
4. He, X., Sun, X.-H., Laszewski, G.V.: QoS Guided Min-min Heuristic for Grid Task Scheduling. Journal of Computer Science and Technology 18, 442–451 (2003)
5. Hsu, C.-H., Chen, T.-L., Li, K.-C.: Performance Effective Pre-scheduled Strategy for Heterogeneous Grid Systems in the Master Slave Paradigm. Journal of Future Generation Computer Systems 23, 569–579 (2007)
6. Foster, I., Kesselman, C.: The Grid 2: Blueprint for a New Computing Infrastructure, 2nd edn. Elsevier and Morgan Kaufmann, San Francisco (2004)
7. Maheswaran, M., Ali, S., Siegel, H.J., Hensgen, D., Freund, R.F.: Dynamic Mapping of a Class of Independent Tasks onto Heterogeneous Computing Systems. Journal of Parallel and Distributed Computing 59, 107–131 (1999)
8. Braun, T.D., Siegel, H.J., Beck, N., Boloni, L.L., Maheswaran, M., Reuther, A.I., Robertson, J.P., Theys, M.D., Yao, B.: A Comparison of Eleven Static Heuristics for Mapping a Class of Independent Tasks onto Heterogeneous Distributed Computing Systems. Journal of Parallel and Distributed Computing 61, 810–837 (2001)

9. Tseng, L.-Y., Chin, Y.-H., Wang, S.-C.: A Minimized Makespan Scheduler with Multiple Factors for Grid Computing Systems. Journal of Expert Systems with Applications 35, 11118–11130 (2009)
10. Parsa, S., Entezari-Maleki, R.: RASA: A New Grid Task Scheduling Algorithm. International Journal of Digital Content Technology and its Applications 3, 91–99 (2009)
11. Wang, L., Siegel, H.J., Roychowdhury, V.P., Maciejewski, A.A.: Task Matching and Scheduling in Heterogeneous Computing Environments Using a Genetic-Algorithm-Based Approach. Journal of Parallel and Distributed Computing 47, 1–15 (1997)
12. Munir, E.U., Li, J., Shi, S.: QoS Sufferage Heuristic for Independent Task Scheduling in Grid. Information Technology Journal 6, 1166–1170 (2007)
13. Briceno, L.D., Oltikar, M., Siegel, H.J., Maciejewski, A.A.: Study of an Iterative Technique to Minimize Completion Times of Non-Makespan Machines. In: The 21st International Parallel and Distributed Processing Symposium, California, pp. 1–14 (2007)
14. Levitin, G., Dai, Y.-S.: Optimal Service Task Partition and Distribution in Grid System with Star Topology. Reliability Engineering and System Safety 93, 152–159 (2008)

An Adaptive Tradeoff Algorithm for Multi-issue SLA Negotiation

Seokho Son and Kwang Mong Sim*

Multiagent and Cloud Computing Systems Lab.,
Department of Information and Communication,
Gwangju Institute of Science and Technology (GIST), Gwangju, Korea
{shson,kmsim}@gist.ac.kr
http://mas.gist.ac.kr/

Abstract. Since participants in a Cloud may be independent bodies, mechanisms are necessary for resolving different preferences in leasing Cloud services. Whereas there are currently mechanisms that support service-level agreement negotiation, there is little or no negotiation support for concurrent price and timeslot for Cloud service reservations. For the concurrent price and timeslot negotiation, a tradeoff algorithm to generate and evaluate a proposal which consists of price and timeslot proposal is necessary. The contribution of this work is thus to design an adaptive tradeoff algorithm for multi-issue negotiation mechanism. The tradeoff algorithm referred to as "adaptive burst mode" is especially designed to increase negotiation speed and total utility and to reduce computational load by adaptively generating concurrent set of proposals. The empirical results obtained from simulations carried out using a testbed suggest that due to the concurrent price and timeslot negotiation mechanism with adaptive tradeoff algorithm: 1) both agents achieve the best performance in terms of negotiation speed and utility; 2) the number of evaluations of each proposal is comparatively lower than previous scheme (burst-N).

Keywords: Agent-based Cloud Computing and Cloud Economy, Cloud Business Models, Service Level Agreement, Negotiation Agents, Multi-issue Negotiation, Cloud Service Reservation, Timeslot Negotiation.

1 Introduction

In terms of Cloud service reservations, important questions for cloud participants include when to use a service (i.e., timeslot) and the price of the service. Before a consumer and a provider make a reservation, these two issues have to be settled. Whereas previous works have reported on advance reservations considering bandwidth or time constraints [1-3] and adopting a negotiation mechanism for SLA [4], as yet there is no definitive service reservation system that concurrently considers both the price and timeslot negotiation together except [5]. [5] designed a Cloud service reservation system that provides a negotiation for price and timeslot.

* Corresponding author.

T.-h. Kim et al. (Eds.): GDC/CA 2010, CCIS 121, pp. 32–41, 2010.

Since price and timeslot negotiation are in a tradeoff relationship—a consumer who pays a great deal of money for a service can demand to use the service at a more desirable timeslot—price and timeslot have to be negotiated concurrently. Accordingly, a multi-issue (i.e., multi-attribute) negotiation mechanism also has to be considered in this work. Even though there are several negotiation mechanisms for Grid resource negotiation (see [6] for a survey), these negotiation mechanisms are designed for Grid resource management and thus may not be appropriate for Cloud service reservation. Whereas [7] designed multi-issue SLA negotiations for Web service, these mechanisms are not specifically designed for timeslot and price negotiation in Cloud service reservation. There has been little work to date on Cloud service negotiation except for [8]; [8] proposes a complex Cloud negotiation mechanism for supporting concurrent negotiation activities in interrelated markets in which the negotiation outcomes between Cloud brokers and Cloud resource providers in one market can potentially affect and influence the negotiation outcomes of Cloud brokers and Cloud consumers in another market. The difference between this work and [8], however, is that whereas [8] focuses on a complex concurrent negotiations in multiple interrelated Cloud markets, in which the outcomes in one market can potentially influence another, this work is the earliest work to consider a multi-issue negotiation mechanism including a new adaptive tradeoff algorithm for Cloud service negotiation.

Finally, it should be noted that the earlier work of this paper were presented in [5]. In [5], the concurrent price and timeslot negotiation mechanism (CPTN) was designed. The design of CPTN includes a novel tradeoff algorithm, referred to as the "general burst mode" proposal, designed to enhance both the negotiation speed and aggregated utility of the price and timeslot in a multi-issue negotiation. With burst mode, agents are allowed to make a concurrent set of proposals, in which each proposal consists of a different pair of price and timeslot that generate the same aggregated utility. Increasing the number of proposals in concurrent set lets agents have an enhanced negotiation speed and aggregated utility. However, in [5], agents can specify only a definite number as the number of proposals in concurrent set, and burst mode does not consider adaptively selecting the number of proposals in concurrent set. Accordingly, this paper proposes a new tradeoff algorithm referred to as "adaptive burst mode" especially designed to increase negotiation speed and total utility and to reduce computational load by adaptively selecting the number of proposals in concurrent set.

As such, the purpose of this work is to: 1) introduce an overview of the concurrent price and timeslot negotiation mechanism (Section 2); 2) design new adaptive tradeoff algorithm for a negotiation strategy (Section 3); 3) evaluate performances of the proposed tradeoff algorithm in terms of the negotiation speed, the aggregated utility, and the number of proposals evaluated in each negotiation by conducting experiments using the testbed (Section 4). Finally, Section 5 concludes this paper by summarizing a list of future works.

2 Overview of Concurrent Price and Timeslot Negotiation

This section introduces the concurrent price and timeslot negotiation mechanism (CPTN) [5]. The design of CPTN includes: 1) design of a negotiation protocol; and 2) a decision making model that includes utility functions, in addition to a tradeoff algorithm for multi-issue negotiation.

2.1 Negotiation Protocol

The negotiation protocol of CPTN follows the Rubinstein's Alternating Offers protocol [10], in which agents make counter offers to their opponent in alternate rounds. Both agents generate counter offers and evaluate their opponent's offers until either an agreement is made or one of the agents' deadlines is reached. Counter proposals are generated according to the negotiation strategy in Section 2.3, and proposals are evaluated by the utility function in Section 2.2. If a counter-proposal is accepted, both agents can eventually reach a mutually acceptable price and timeslot. Conversely, if one of the agents' deadlines expires before they reach an agreement, their negotiation fails.

2.2 Utility Functions

The utility function $U(x)$ represents an agent's level of satisfaction of a negotiation outcome x. Since each user has different preferences for the price and position of the timeslot, a price utility function $U_P(P)$, timeslot utility function $U_T(T)$, and an aggregated utility function were defined in [5] to model the preference ordering of each proposal and each negotiation outcome. Let w_P and w_T be the weights for the price utility and the timeslot utility respectively; w_P and w_T satisfy $w_P + w_T = 1$. The aggregated price-timeslot utility $U_{total}(P,T)$ at each price P and timeslot T is given as

$$U_{total}(P,T) = \begin{cases} 0, & \text{if either } U_P(P)=0 \text{ or } U_T(T)=0 \\ w_P \cdot U_P(P) + w_T \cdot U_T(T), & \text{otherwise.} \end{cases} \quad (1)$$

By varying w_P and w_T, users can place different combinations of emphases on the price and position of timeslot for negotiation. If either $U_P(P)=0$ or $U_T(T)=0$, the aggregated total utility for P and T is 0 because both P and T should be within the acceptable range of each utility. Since there are numerous possible combinations of price and timeslot that can generate the same aggregated total utility, $U_{total}(P,T)$ can be expressed as a straight line, as shown in Fig. 1. Also, this line is represented as a dotted line since the timeslot utility used in the aggregated utility function is a discrete function.

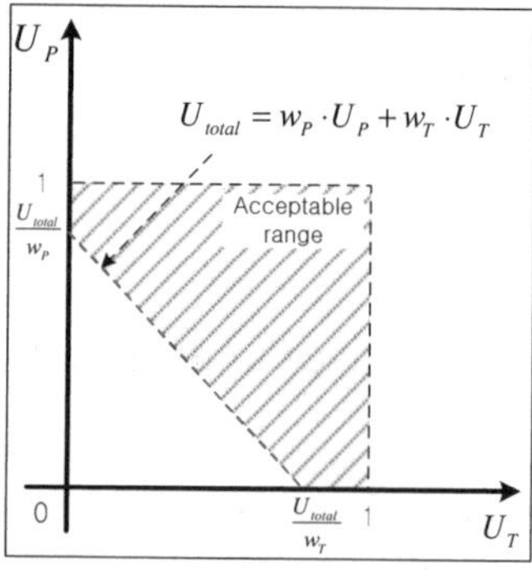

Fig. 1. Utility plane of the aggregated total utility function

2.3 Negotiation Strategy

This work considers bilateral negotiations between the consumer and provider, where both agents are sensitive to time and adopt time-dependent concession-making strategy for concurrent price and timeslot negotiations. Since both agents negotiate both price and timeslot, generating a counter proposal can either be making a concession or making a tradeoff between the price and timeslot. Hence, an agent's strategy for multi-issue negotiation can be implemented using both: 1) a tradeoff algorithm, and 2) a concession-making algorithm.

2.3.1 Concession-Making Algorithm

The concession-making algorithm determines the amount of concession ΔU_{total} for each negotiation round, and corresponds to the reduction in an agent's expectation based on its total utility. Agents in this work adopt the time-dependent strategies in [9] to determine the amount of concession required for the next proposal and the corresponding expectation. Let t, τ, and λ be the negotiation round, the negotiation deadline, and negotiation strategy respectively. Based on (2), the negotiation agent determines the amount of concession ΔU_{total} and then (3) determines its expectation of the total utility in the next round.

$$\Delta U_{total} = U^{t}_{total} \cdot \left(\frac{t}{\tau}\right)^{\lambda} . \tag{2}$$

$$U^{t+1}_{total} = U^{t}_{total} - \Delta U_{total} . \tag{3}$$

2.3.2 Tradeoff Algorithm

This section introduces a general idea of "burst mode", which is designed to enhance both the negotiation speed and the aggregated utility. In general, a multi-attribute proposal P from agent A to agent B during negotiation round t can be represented as $P^{A\to B,t} = (x^t_1, x^t_2, ..., x^t_n)$ where x_n is an element (i.e., $n-th$ attribute) of the proposal. Hence, a negotiation agent can make only one multi-attribute proposal in a negotiation round.

With burst mode, agents are allowed to make a concurrent set of proposals, in which each proposal consists of a different pair of price and timeslot that generate the same aggregated utility, but differ in terms of individual price and timeslot utility. A burst multi-attribute proposal x from agent A to B during negotiation round t can be represented as $BP^{A\to B,t} = \left[\left(x^t_1, x^t_2, ..., x^t_n\right), \left(y^t_1, y^t_2, ..., y^t_n\right), ..., \left(k^t_1, k^t_2, ..., k^t_n\right)\right]$ where $x, y, ..., k$ are a concurrent set of proposals; these concurrent proposals are uniformly selected from the utility line to generate a burst proposal. Therefore, with burst mode, a negotiating agent can provide more options for its opponent agent without having to make concession. [5] considered negotiation speed and total utility with burst modes increase as the number of proposals in the burst proposal increases. However, with the tradeoff algorithm in [5], agents can select a definite number for every negotiation rounds as the number of proposals in a burst proposal; there was no consideration of the appropriate number of proposals in a burst proposal to reduce computational load.

3 Adaptive Tradeoff Algorithm

The novelty of this work is in the adoption of a new tradeoff algorithm, referred to as "adaptive burst mode", which is designed to enhance both the negotiation speed and the aggregated utility and to select the efficient number of proposals encoded in a concurrent set of proposals (i.e., selecting value N for burst-N). An agent using adaptive burst mode adaptively selects N_P^t (the number of proposals encoded in a burst proposal for each negotiation round) according to two factors: a) the available range of the current utility space and b) the utility difference between the current utility expectation and the utility of the best-offer proposed by the opponent.

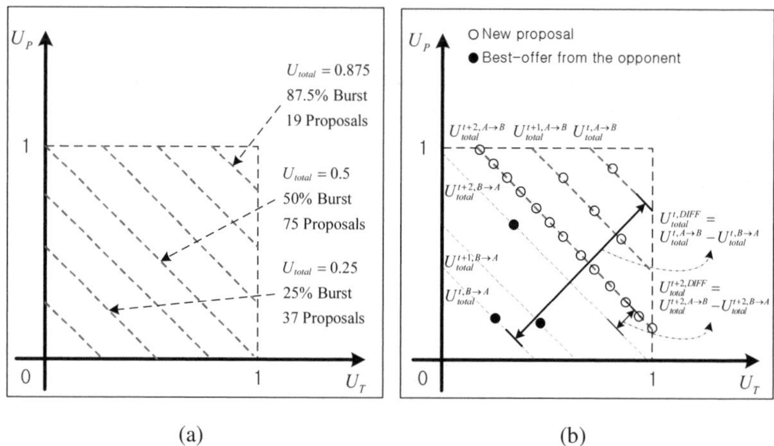

(a) (b)

Fig. 2. Adaptive selection of the number of proposals

3.1 The Available Range of the Current Utility Space

The utility line presents all combinations of price and timeslot which give the same aggregated utility, and it is bounded by the available utility plane (i.e., U_T axis and U_P axis of the available utility plane is bounded by 0 and 1). Aggregated utility changes for each negotiation round according to the concession making algorithm, and the length of the utility line changes. Consequently, the number of combinations of price and timeslot changes according to the aggregated utility value for each negotiation round.

Fig. 2(a) shows an example adaptively assigning the number of proposals for each negotiation round according to the available range of current utility space. When $w_P=0.5$, $w_T=0.5$, and $U_{total}^t=0.5$, the utility line has the longest length (i.e., the length of the utility line is $\sqrt{2}$); as U_{total}^t approaches 0 or 1, the length of the utility line decreases. Therefore, agents can relatively reduce the number of proposals encoded in a burst proposal when U_{total}^t approaches 0 or 1 from 0.5. Let $N_P^{t`}$ is the number of proposals in a burst proposal (intermediate assignment according to the factor (a)); $U^t_{total}$ is the aggregated utility at negotiation round $t$. Since the number of combinations of price and timeslot is relative to available timeslot range, $N^{t`}_P$ is adaptively selected to available timeslot range ($LT-FT$; FT is the first timeslot and LT is the last timeslot) and U^t_{total}. The $N^{t`}_P$ at negotiation round t is then given as

$$N^{t`}_P = \begin{cases} 1, & (U^t_{total}=0, U^t_{total}=1) \\ (LT-FT)\cdot(1-U^t_{total}), & (U^t_{total}>0.5) \\ (LT-FT)\cdot U^t_{total}, & (U^t_{total}\le 0.5) \end{cases} \quad (4)$$

3.2 The Utility Difference between the Current Utility Expectation and the Utility of the Best-Offer Proposed by the Opponent

$U^{t,DIFF}_{total}$ is the utility difference between the current utility expectation and the utility of the best-offer proposed by the opponent. As $U^{t,DIFF}_{total}$ decreases, the chance that the opponent accepts the proposal increases. A high $U^{t,DIFF}_{total}$ means that the current utility expectations between negotiating agents are too different to reach an agreement. In this case, a counter proposal using the tradeoff relationship is also hard to overcome $U^{t,DIFF}_{total}$. Therefore, with a high $U^{t,DIFF}_{total}$, N^t_P is not necessary to increase.

Fig. 2(b) shows an example adaptively assigning the number of proposals for each negotiation round according to $U^{t,DIFF}_{total}$. As negotiation round elapses, $U^{t,DIFF}_{total}$ decreases by the concession making algorithm, and the negotiation agent relatively increases the number of proposals in a burst proposal (N^t_P is determined by decreasing $N^{t`}_P$ relatively to $U^{t,DIFF}_{total}$). Finally, by the factor (a) and (b), the number of proposal encoded in a burst proposal N^t_P at negotiation round t is then given as

$$N^t_P = \begin{cases} 1, & (U^t_{total}=0, U^t_{total}=1, U^{t,DIFF}_{total}=1) \\ (LT-FT)\cdot(1-U^t_{total})\cdot(1-U^{t,DIFF}_{total}), & (U^t_{total}>0.5) \\ (LT-FT)\cdot U^t_{total}\cdot(1-U^{t,DIFF}_{total}), & (U^t_{total}\le 0.5) \end{cases} \quad (5)$$

4 Simulations and Empirical Results

These experiments were designed to observe the negotiation outcomes of the CPTN and to study the performance of "adaptive burst mode" of the CPTN and empirically compare with "general burst mode" proposed in [5].

4.1 Performance Measure

To evaluate the performance of the proposed burst mode in CPTN, we used 1) negotiation speed, 2) average total utility of the negotiation pair as the performance measures, and 3) The number of proposals evaluated. The negotiation speed S is a function of the negotiation round R spent in the negotiation. $S\to 0$ means the negotiation has a lower speed and $S \rightarrow 1$ means the negotiation has a higher speed. The average total utility of the negotiation pair shows the level of satisfaction in terms of price and timeslot with the agreed upon service. In addition, large N_P^{total} means the scheme requires a high computational load. A more detailed expression of the performance measures is given in Table 1.

Table 1. Performance measure

Negotiation speed (0–1)	$S = 1 - R / Min(\tau_C, \tau_P)$
Average total utility of negotiating pair (0–1)	$U_{total}^{aver.} = \left(U_{total}^{P}(P,T) + U_{total}^{C}(P,T)\right)/2$
Total number of proposals evaluated	$N_P^{total} = \sum_{t=1}^{\tau_C} N_P^{t,P\rightarrow C} + \sum_{t=1}^{\tau_P} N_P^{t,C\rightarrow P}$
R	Number of rounds spent until the end of negotiation
$Min(\tau_C, \tau_P)$	Shortest deadline among negotiation deadlines between consumer and provider
$U_{total}^{P}(P,T)$	$U_{total}^{P}(P,T) = w_P^P \cdot U_P^P(P) + w_T^P \cdot U_T^P(T)$
$U_{total}^{C}(P,T)$	$U_{total}^{C}(P,T) = w_P^C \cdot U_P^C(P) + w_T^C \cdot U_T^C(T)$
$N_P^{t,P\rightarrow C}$	The number of proposals evaluated by the consumer at round t
$N_P^{t,C\rightarrow P}$	The number of proposals evaluated by the provider at round t

4.2 Experimental Setting

Tables 2 and 3 show the input data sources for this experiment, and include the experimental settings for a Cloud market (Table 2) and user preference (Table 3) for a Cloud service. The input data sources of the Cloud market are parameters for the Cloud simulation controller. In the experiments, a Cloud market consists of 200 provider agents and 200 consumer agents to examine the performance of CPTN in a balanced Cloud market. They are automatically generated by the controller, and the controller randomly invokes a consumer 300 times for each simulation to start a service reservation. We note that market dynamics are not considered in this experiment.

Table 2. Input data source: Cloud market

Input Data	Possible Values	Settings
Cloud Load(CL)	$\mathrm{CL} = N_{res}/N_{tot}$	$0 \le \mathrm{CL} \le 1$
No. of provider agents	Integer	100 service provider agents
No. of consumer agents	Integer	200 consumer agents
Cloud services a provider lends	Strings	200 services/provider (randomly selected)
No. of negotiation sessions per each simulation	Integer	300 negotiation sessions

The Cloud load ($0 \le \mathrm{CL} \le 1$) in Table 2 represents and simulates different levels of utilization of the Cloud service in the Cloud environment. CL is defined here as the ratio of: 1) N_{res} —the total number of timeslots in the reservation queues of all service providers, and 2) N_{tot} —the number of timeslots already reserved. To simulate the uniformly distributed load to all service providers, each provider agent automatically fills their reservation queue with uniformly distributed virtual reservations from the simulation settings, up to a given CL.

For user preference values, settings are given in Table 3 for each consumer agent and provider agent. In this experiment, some variables (e.g., IP, RP, FT, LT, and job size) were controlled as extraneous variables to clearly observe the effects of independent variables such as CL, negotiation strategy, and negotiation deadline, because it is hard to simulate all possible combinations of input negotiation parameters due to space limitations.

Table 3. Input data source: user inputs for service reservation

Input Data	Possible Values	Settings	
		Consumer	Provider
Initial price (IP)	Integer(Cloud $)	10–60	200–250
Reserve price (RP)	Integer(Cloud $)	200–250	10–60
First timeslot (FT)	Integer, FT<LT	10–60	10–60
Last timeslot (LT)	Integer, FT<LT	300–350	300–350
Job size	Integer (Cloud time unit)	2–8	2–8
Negotiation Strategy(λ)	Conciliatory(< 1) Linear($= 1$) Conservative(> 1)	1.0	1.0
Negotiation deadline (τ)	Integer (Round unit)	50 rounds	50 rounds

4.3 Simulations

Empirical results were obtained for all representative combinations of the input data (i.e., { $\tau_C : \tau_P$ } = {50:50}, CL = {0.1, 0.3, 0.5, 0.7, 0.9}, and negotiation agents adopting λ_C= {1.0} and λ_P= {1.0}). The performance measures (i.e., negotiation speed, average total utility of the negotiating pair, and computational load) were then simulated for all burst modes while changing the number of proposals in each burst proposal (i.e., B1, B5, B50, and B100) and adaptive burst mode. To interpret the simulations, several graphs for each performance measure were plotted. Fig. 3 shows the performance results of the negotiation speed, Fig. 4 shows the performance results of the total utility, and Fig. 5 shows the performance results of the number of proposals evaluated in each negotiation.

4.4 Observations and Results

The following observations were made from the experiment results.

1) Among all types of the burst modes (B1, B5, B50, and B100) and the adaptive burst mode (AB), B100 and AB achieved the fastest negotiation speed.
2) Among all types of the burst modes (B1, B5, B50, and B100) and the adaptive burst mode (AB), B100 and AB achieved the highest average total utility except for conditions under a high Cloud loading (CL = 90%). However, the total utility for all types of tradeoff schemes decreased under the high Cloud loading.
3) Both performance measures with burst modes increase as the number of proposals encoded in the burst proposal increases, but the ratio of increments decreases

as the number of proposals increases. Although AB required comparatively fewer proposals in concurrent set than B100, the AB and B100 show the best performance in terms of average total utility and negotiation speed.

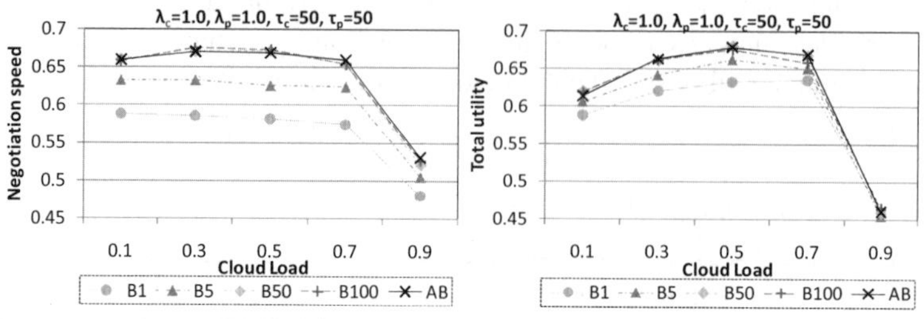

Fig. 3. Negotiation speed

Fig. 4. Total utility

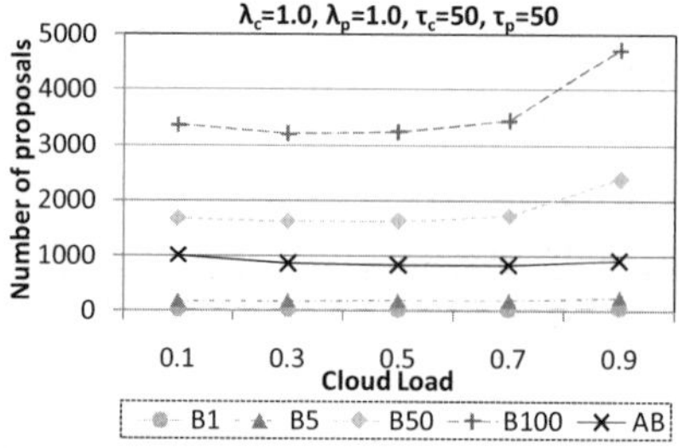

Fig. 5. The number of proposals evaluated

5 Conclusion and Future Work

The novelty and the significance of this work are the design of adaptive burst mode for multi-issue SLA negotiation. The contributions of this paper are detailed as follows:

1) Whereas [5] introduced "burst mode" to increase the negotiation speed and aggregated utility of the price and timeslot in a multi-issue negotiation, a novel tradeoff algorithm, referred to as the "adaptive burst mode", was designed to enhance the negotiation speed and aggregated utility with reduced computational load by adaptively assigning the number of proposals of a burst proposal.
2) Empirical results obtained from simulations carried out using the testbed show that the use of the proposed adaptive tradeoff algorithm enables Cloud participants to quickly reach agreements and successfully acquire/lease desired Cloud services in a higher utility than related approaches. In addition, adaptive burst mode requires comparatively fewer proposals in concurrent set than burst-100 which gives similar negotiation speed and total utility.

Finally, this paper can be extended by considering and specifying other negotiation issues. Since there have been many unconsidered and unspecified QoS attributes in multi-issue negotiations, it can be expected that extending this work by considering and specifying other negotiation issues will contribute to facilitating not only multi-issue negotiations but also Cloud service reservations.

Acknowledgments. This work was supported by a Korea Science and Engineering Foundation (KOSEF) grant funded by the Korea Government (MEST 2009-0065329) and the DASAN International Faculty Fund (project code: 140316).

References

1. Foster, I., Kesselman, C., Lee, C., Lindell, B., Nahrstedt, K., Roy, A.: A distributed resource management architecture that supports advance reservations and co-allocation. In: 7th International Workshop on Quality of Service (IWQoS 1999), London, UK. IEEE Computer Society Press, LA (March 1999)
2. Foster, I., Roy, A., Sander, V.: A Quality of Service architecture that combines resource reservation and application adaptation. In: 8th International Workshop on Quality of Service (2000)
3. Netto, M.A., Bubendorfer, K., Buyya, R.: SLA-Based Advance Reservations with Flexible and Adaptive Time QoS Parameters. In: Krämer, B.J., Lin, K.-J., Narasimhan, P. (eds.) ICSOC 2007. LNCS, vol. 4749, pp. 119–131. Springer, Heidelberg (2007)
4. Venugopal, S., Chu, X., Buyya, R.: A negotiation mechanism for advance resource reservation using the alternate offers protocol. In: 16th Int. Workshop on Quality of Service (IWQoS 2008), Twente, The Netherlands (June 2008)
5. Son, S., Sim, K.M.: A Multi-issue Negotiation Mechanism for Cloud Service Reservation. In: Annual International Conference on Cloud Computing and Virtualization, CCV (May 2010)
6. Sim, K.M.: Grid Resource Negotiation: Survey and New Directions. IEEE Trans. Syst., Man, Cybern. C, Applications and Reviews 40(3), 245–257 (2010)
7. Yan, J., Kowalczyk, R., Lin, J., Chhetri, M.B., Goh, S.K., Zhang, J.: Autonomous service level agreement negotiation for service composition provision. Future Generation Computer Systems 23(6), 748–759 (2007)
8. Sim, K.M.: Towards Complex Negotiation for Cloud Economy. In: Bellavista, P., Chang, R.-S., Chao, H.-C., Lin, S.-F., Sloot, P.M.A. (eds.) GPC 2010. LNCS, vol. 6104, pp. 395–406. Springer, Heidelberg (2010)
9. Sim, K.M.: Equilibria, Prudent Compromises, and the "Waiting" Game. IEEE Trans. on Systems, Man and Cybernetics, Part B: Cybernetics 35(4), 712–724 (2005)
10. Rubinstein, A.: Perfect equilibrium in a bargaining model. Econometrica 50(1), 97–109 (1982)

Framework for Behavior Adaptation of Distributed Applications

Narkoy Batouma and Jean-Louis Sourrouille

University of Lyon
INSA Lyon, LIESP, 69621, Villeurbanne, France
{Narkoy.batouma,Jean-Louis.sourrouille}@insa-lyon.fr

Abstract. In open environments, resource availability varies over time unpredictably. To tune resource use, adaptive systems provide the indispensable mechanisms to modify their behavior dynamically. This paper describes a decentralized framework aiming to increase the Quality of Service (QoS) of distributed applications by adapting their behavior. Based on information about applications and their execution context, the framework coordinates adaptation and finely controls applications. A model of applications exhibits the alternative behaviors that the framework selects according to the available resources. Finally, simulations show to what extent our approach improves the QoS, uses efficiently the CPU, and increases the number of completed applications.

Keywords: Behavior Adaptation; Adaptation Coordination; Application Model; QoS Management; Multi-Agent System.

1 Introduction

In an open environment, distributed applications with time-dependent resource requirements face to context fluctuations such as resource availability, network connectivity. These unforeseen contexts can affect the Quality of Service (QoS) provided by applications. The need to take into account context fluctuations, and QoS requirements to provide end-to-end QoS support, becomes more and more insistent. This is especially challenging in open environments with no underlying operating and networking system support for QoS [1][2]. The difficulty lies in unpredictability in resource availability when many distributed applications share resources such as processor, network bandwidth or memory, and in the inherent heterogeneity of distributed environments.

To address these issues, designers use either a reservation approach that controls admission and reserves resources to execute the applications, or an adaptation approach that proposes mechanisms to tune application requirements according to the execution context. The adaptation approach has the advantage of better controlling the execution of applications according to the available resources. Adaptation mechanisms aim to make the most effective use of resources in order to provide an acceptable level of QoS and to adapt to changing conditions of systems and networks [3][4][5][6][7][8].

T.-h. Kim et al. (Eds.): GDC/CA 2010, CCIS 121, pp. 42–53, 2010.

Numerous works have been proposed for QoS management. They tackle the problem at different levels: at low level, by introducing guarantees in communication protocols; at intermediary level, by modifying the operating system resource management policy; at high level, by introducing a middleware to manage the QoS. Our works stand at the high level: applications hold the required knowledge to set their alternative behaviors. They provide a description of their behavior and resource requirements to achieve adaptation under the control of a middleware.

We built and evaluated centralized approaches for QoS management in earlier works [7][8]. The former uses scheduling mechanisms to manage QoS while the latter is based on a reinforcement learning technique. Besides, we experimented with a decentralized approach [9] based on borrowing mechanisms for resource management that aims to guarantee application execution. In this paper, we investigate a decentralized middleware to adapt applications' behavior. The middleware addresses the problem of how to change application behavior at runtime in order to adapt to variations in the execution environment, such as resource availability. We designed a framework that is based on a general application model as the basis to support the construction of adaptive distributed applications and propose several strategies for adaptation.

The paper is organized as follows: first, we present the overview of previous works (section 2). Then, we describe our approach to adapt applications (section 3) and show how the system is implemented in practice (section 4). Finally, we give some results (section 5), we compare our approach to related works (section 6) before concluding (section 7).

2 Previous Work

In this paper we use some words or expressions which have the following meaning. A node (*Node*$_i$) is a separate piece of hardware that has at least one processor as in UML [10]. A resource is anything an application uses to execute. There are two types of resources: local resources (e.g., CPU, Memory) and shared resource (e.g., network bandwidth). A Local Manager (*LM*) is an entity that manages resources on a node. Our environment consists of a set of nodes connected via network. A local application has one part on a node whereas a distributed application has parts on several nodes.

In the sequel we describe briefly our previous works that are detailed in [9]. The previous approach presents a distributed middleware to manage resources in a decentralized manner. It is based on the use of approximate scheduling and a resource-borrowing schema to manage QoS. It aims to guarantee that as many applications as possible meet their deadline, to decrease the message exchange costs while increasing the use of resources. According to this approach, the time is subdivided into periods of length *T* and at the beginning of a period, each *LM* keeps a part of its resources and loans the remainder to other nodes. Shared resources such as bandwidth are managed in the same way. By this way, a *LM* constructs a comprehensive view of resource availability in the whole system. A *LM* uses this view to admit applications and control their execution on its node. A *LM* may exchange messages to request additional resources to other *LMs* when the available resources on its node do not meet application requirements. When a *LM* does not use its resource borrowings during some periods, it releases automatically a percentage of these resources. To avoid that several distributed applications attempt to use a shared resource at the same time, a protocol based on token is proposed ([9] for more detail). According to this protocol, shared resources are managed by the *LMs* collectively. Only two parts of a distributed application synchronize their two steps at a given time, e.g., send and receive data, and this application is triggered by the *LM* that holds the token. Moreover, the node that holds the token manages the queue of token requests according to a FIFO (First In First Out) principle.

The previous work describes how to coordinate *LMs* in a decentralized system in order to better use resources and to execute applications before their deadline while reducing the number of exchanged messages. However, the approach had no support for automatically adapting application's behavior. This paper deals with adaptation issues. We build adaptation strategies upon our previous work and we show how to use our application model to coordinate adaptation in a decentralized system.

3 The Proposed Middleware

The proposed middleware is a layer that copes with adaptation issues and controls application's behavior on each node. It cooperates with applications and schedules them based on run-time context. Any execution is decided by the middleware: the applications wait middleware orders before any step execution. Besides, applications run in a distributed context according to the following constraints: (i) any resource use should be declared, which means that applications all are registered; (ii) we assume that the underlying layers, including operating system and communication layers, supply all the required services to manage resources; (iii) we adopt an *intrusive* approach, i.e., the applications are specifically designed to collaborate with their environment (middleware, operating system, etc.), and to adapt their behavior; (iv) In this paper we adopt a resource reservation planning and an approximate dynamic scheduling solution to deal with unpredictable events that arise during execution.

3.1 Application Model

In order to provide QoS support a general model for managed applications is needed. An application is designed as a graph (Fig. 1). In the graph edges represent the execution of activities. An activity is a sequence of steps. Each activity (A_i) is associated with a mode (m_i) and a utility (U_i). Within applications, modes are alternative behaviors that provide the same service with different QoS properties (execution level in [1]) and utilities are a one-dimension index that specifies the benefit related to the mode choice. A step is associated with resource requirements (e.g., CPU use, memory consumption). Vertexes are *decision points*, from which several behaviors provide the same service with different QoS levels. A local application is designed as one graph while a distributed application is designed as a set of sub graphs. The number of sub graphs is equal to the number of distributed application parts. The whole application is a sequence of *Scheduling Units*. Each *Scheduling Unit* (SU_i) has a deadline d_i and is made up of a set of activities. A *SU* of the whole distributed application may concern one or more nodes, e.g., on Fig. 1, SU_1 on $Node_1$ and SU_1 on $Node_2$ belong to the same SU on several nodes while SU_j is a *SU* of the application on $Node_2$. When a *SU* is distributed on several nodes there is at least an *activity* that is distributed on these nodes.

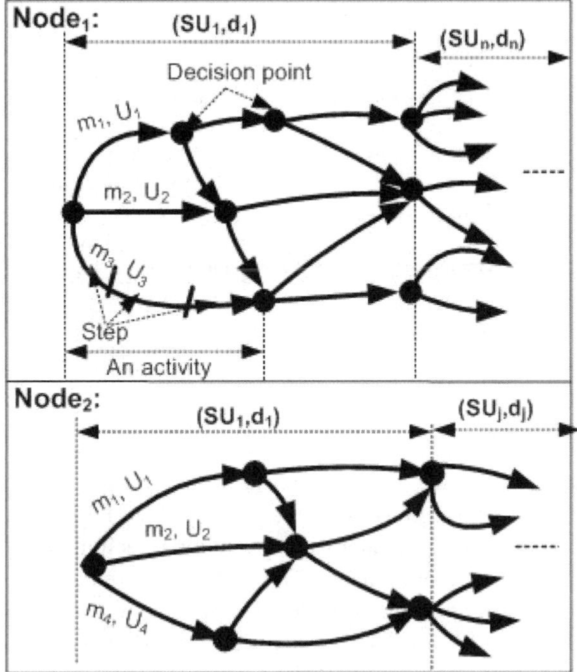

Fig. 1. General Application Model

A distributed *activity* is designed as sub-activities on nodes with the same *mode* and *utility*, e.g., on Fig. 1, (A_1, m_1, U_1) on $Node_1$ and (A_1, m_1, U_1) on $Node_2$ are parts of the same activity. It is important to know that the model of any application is provided by its designer and the information concerning the model is saved on each node (e.g., in a xml file) to be accessible to the middleware.

3.2 Application Example

Table I gives an example of a distributed application between two nodes: part A on $Node_1$ and part B on $Node_2$. This application supplies three data transmission modes. After application loading (*Load*) on node $Node_1$ and $Node_2$ and data acquisition (*Acquisition*) on node $Node_1$, data is either directly sent (*Transmission1*) or compressed (*compression1* or *compression2*) before being sent (*Transmission2 or Transmission3*). Node $Node_2$ receives data directly (*Reception1*) or receives data and decompresses it (*Reception2* and *Decompression1 or Reception3 and Decompression2*). Finally, data is displayed either in mode 1 (*Display1*) or in mode 2 (*Display2*) or in mode 3 (*Display3*).

Table 1. Application Example

Scheduling Unit	Activity	Mode	Step	Node
Start	A_Start	1	Load	$Node_1$
	A_Start		Load	$Node_2$
Sample	A_Acquisition	1	Acquisition	$Node_1$
	A_Transmission	1	Transmission1	$Node_1$
			Reception1	$Node_2$
	A_Transmission	2	Compression1, Transmission2	$Node_1$
			Reception2, Decompression1	$Node_2$
	A_Transmission	3	Compression2, Transmission3	$Node_1$
			Reception3, Decompression2	$Node_2$
	A_Display	1	Display1	$Node_2$
	A_Display	2	Display2	$Node_2$
	A_Display	3	Display3	$Node_2$
Analyze		…	…	…

3.3 Modes

Our middleware manages the available resources online to continuously keep the "satisfaction" level of applications as high as possible. On Fig. 1, the utility assesses this satisfaction while modes are alternative behaviors. Each mode is associated with both utility and resources requirements. The middleware tunes resources use by selecting the mode of each application while attempting to maximize the overall utility of the system. According to Table 1, when data compression is executed on node $Node_1$, for instance in mode 3, on $Node_2$ the decompression should be executed using the same policy: related local applications should run in the same mode on all the nodes. This is a major interest of the notion of mode as processed in our middleware: running modes are synchronized for all the local applications.

3.4 Adaptation Strategy and Scheduling Outlines

The basic idea behind QoS Adaptation is to change application behavior when possible according to the execution context. Activities have different resource requirements. A utility assesses the level of satisfaction of the provided QoS. According to our model, the lowest utility corresponds to a degraded service. In our work, a basic principle is "any degraded service is better than no service at all". Therefore, we have adopted the following strategy: at admission step, the *LM* chooses a schedulable path in a *SU* with the lowest *utility* and increases this utility when possible at execution step. This strategy aims to increase immediate availability of resources and executes as many applications as possible.

Our adaptation policy is based on the following rules:

- Resource reservation occurs at admission step to ensure resource availability. The SUs of applications are admitted in the mode with the lowest schedulable utility;

- Scheduling occurs at execution step; a *LM* chooses a step to execute according to EDF based on WCETs;
- A step can be preempted by a *LM* in order to execute steps that use a shared resource when it receives a synchronization event;
- Time saved by duration less than WCETs as well as free resources are used to increase application utility.
- Applications are rejected when available resources are not enough to run in the mode with the lowest utility.

3.5 Application Description

The easiest way to describe applications is to draw execution graphs adorned with QoS properties. The description lies on UML activity diagrams enriched with tagged values. At the higher level, an activity diagram describes the execution graph of the SUs: the Fig. 2 represents the higher level of the application given Table 1. The deadline comments define tagged values, i.e., attributes of SUs. Events and paths are simply described using UML notions.

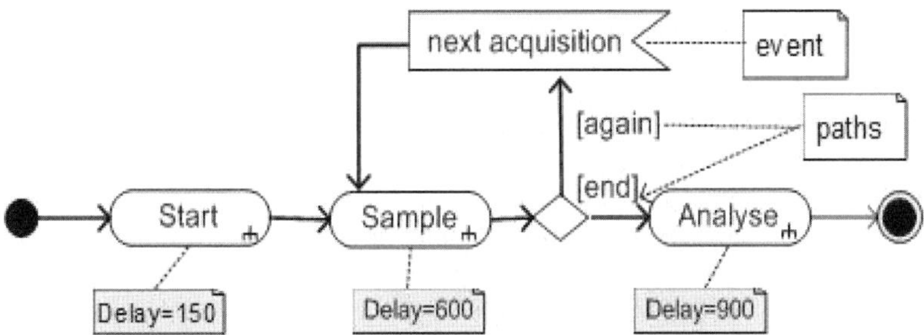

Fig. 2. Global Execution graph for the application Table 1

Again, each SU is described using a hierarchy of activity diagrams. The Fig. 3 describes the SU Sample. In this diagram, UML activities are steps while activities are not represented explicitly. However, any path between a mode-choice and any mode-choice, initial/final node represents an Activity. The mode-choice is a stereotype that extends the metaclass *DecisionNode* of UML, and it owns a specific icon. Guards on the outgoing edges are mode names. Parallel and sequential synchronization are described using join nodes and fork nodes. The swimlanes *APart1* and *APart2* represent the execution graphs for the two parts of the distributed application. For the sake of space, only two paths are drawn in this diagram and resources requirements are shown for Acquisition step only.

The two parts of the application run in parallel on their nodes. When LM_1 selects mode 2 with utility 100, after the execution of the step *compression1*, parallel synchronization ensures that the two nodes are ready to execute the activity in the next step.

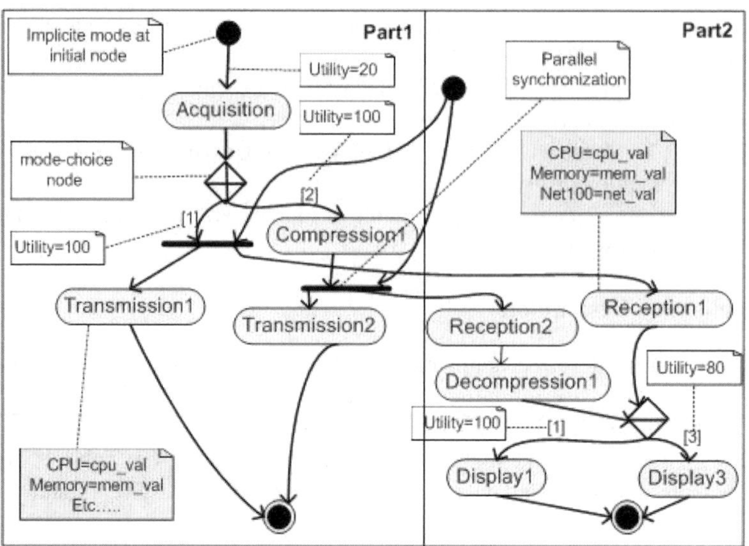

Fig. 3. Execution graph for the SU Sample

4 Experimentation and Evaluation

This section summarizes the practical environment of our simulations. It describes the adopted technology and the platform in which our framework is implemented. As we experiment with a decentralized architecture, the use of autonomous entities such as agents seems suitable. There are several definitions of software agent [13]. The term agent will be used to refer to a computer program that has the ability to take independent action, to react and to communicate. The agents communicate in the same host or over the network in order to coordinate their action. They can exchange information. A multi-agent system is a set of agents [14]. A multi-agent application consists of an environment and agents. The environment contains information that the agents use and manipulate to execute tasks. To implement agent-based software, a multi-agent platform is required since it provides both a model for developing multi-agent systems and an environment for running distributed agent-based applications. Within the area of multi-agent systems, efficiency is a key issue. The efficiency of an agent system relies on both its design and the underlying agent platform. The choice of JADE platform is based on investigation made by numerous works on several existing multi-agent platforms performance (e.g., [15], [16]). Besides, JADE is widely known, easy to use, and well documented.

5 Results

To validate our approach, several simulations have been done. We consider several models of applications such as Table I. A *LM* (Fig. 4) consists of three agents. A *Scheduler agent* implements adaptation strategy and performs admission and scheduling tasks. The Scheduler makes decision based on execution context and information about applications (application models). It communicates (1) with other schedulers on remote nodes for synchronization issues or adaptation coordination. Before any execution of a step that uses a shared resource, it communicates (2) with the *Global Resource Manager* agent that implements mechanisms to manage shared resources; Shared resources are managed by the *Global Resource Managers* collectively (3). On a node a *Generator* agent generates (5) applications according to arrival law as explained in the following subsection. On a node, agents use a common interface (4) to communicate with remote agents. The applications are integrated into the agent architecture as follows: one single agent simulates local applications while several agents simulate distributed applications.

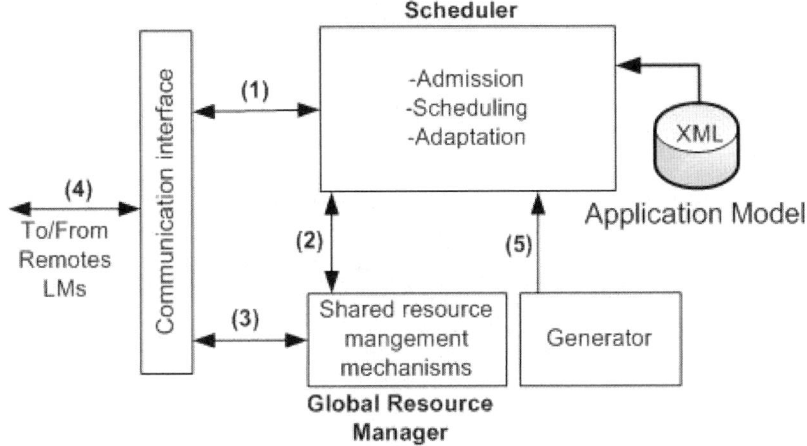

Fig. 4. LM Functionalities on a node

5.1 Experimental Conditions

Each *LM* holds a description of all the applications in the system. The results below were measured under the following conditions: (i) The deadline of each generated application is set to 2**SW* + *random [1*SW..2*SW]*, with *SW* = *Sum* of *WCET* (Worse Case Execution Time) of the application steps (path in the graph); (ii) The execution time of each step, is set to 2**WCET*/3 + *random* [0..*WCET*/3]; (iii) The arrival law of applications is simulated by the random time random [0..*C*], where *C* is a positive number: the smaller is *C*, the more applications arrive frequently and the more the system load increases; (iv) *WCETs* of applications' steps are defined in such a way that the sum of *WCETs* of all distributed applications is three time longer than the sum of *WCETs* of all local applications.

5.2 Measures

Fig. 5 shows the CPU useful time. It defines the effective time used by applications that completed their execution before their deadline. The CPU used reaches some maximum in our approach.

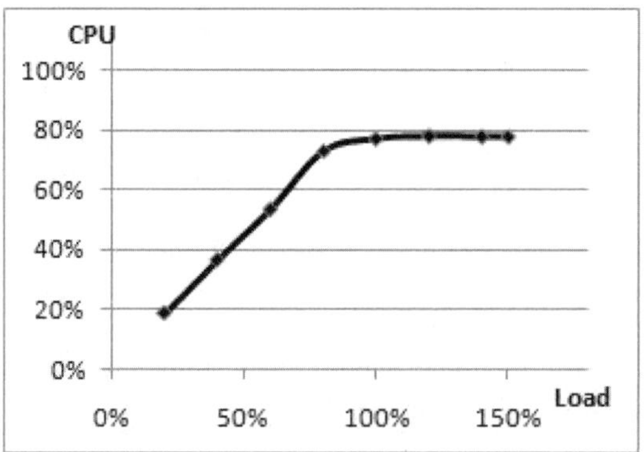

Fig. 5. Useful Time

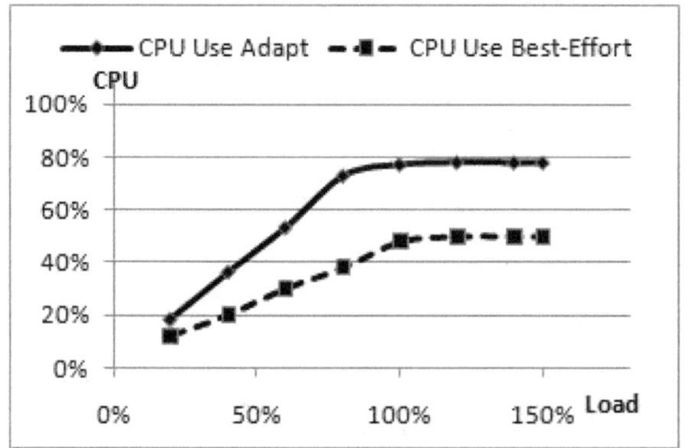

Fig. 6. Best-effort vs. Our Approach

Fig. 6 compares our adaptation policy (Adapt) and the best effort policy (Best-effort) based on CPU useful time as defined previously. The Best effort policy admits all applications and set their behavior to the highest utility *U*. Fig. 6 shows that the CPU use in Adapt policy is greater than the CPU use in best effort policy. This is due to the fact that the best-effort does not check admission; many applications abort because they are not completed before their deadline. Consequently Adapt is more efficient than best-effort.

Fig. 7 compares two approaches. The first is our approach without adaptation (*Max*). It admits the applications with the highest *U*. The second is our approach that performs adaptation. It admits applications with the lowest *U* and increases the utility when resources become available (*Adapt*). The comparisons are based on useful time.

From about 50% the *Adapt* policy performs adaptation when the system increasingly becomes loaded while with the *Max* policy the applications are always executed with the highest utility. Therefore considering only the utility, we could conclude that *Max* policy is efficient. However, Fig. 7 shows that the useful time in the approach with adaptation is greater than in the approach without adaptation. Besides, not represented here for the sake of space, the number of completed applications before their deadline in *Adapt* policy is greater than in *Max* policy when le system becomes loaded. In this context, at admission phase, *Max* rejects applications that could be executed when *Adapt* had been adopted. Hence, adaptation approach is more efficient.

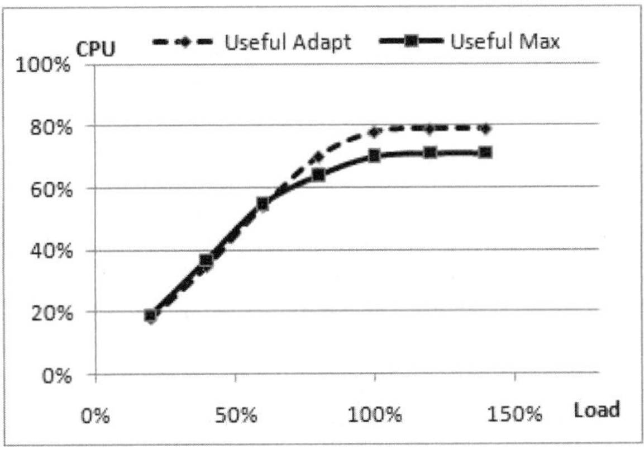

Fig. 7. Comparison of two Approaches

6 Related Works

[4] proposes a hierarchical, recursive, resource management architecture. It supports provision of integrated services for real-time distributed applications and offers management services for end-to-end QoS Management. This work changes the application behavior as a whole while in our approach adaptation is performed at activity level. Besides, it deals with multimedia applications that belong to periodic systems while our approach deals with aperiodic systems in which events arrival law is unpredictable. A periodic system is a particular case of aperiodic system.

Others approaches propose an intrusive policy and are based on application models [7][8]. The former proposes an efficient centralized approach aiming at adapting application behaviors. A unique scheduler tunes and schedules the use of the whole resources for all the concurrent applications in order to maximize the overall QoS of the supplied services. The latter integrates scheduling algorithms into reinforcement learning strategies in order to control resource use. It implements a centralized architecture. Our approach implements a decentralized approach and is based on an approximate scheduling.

In [18], two policies are distinguished: reservation-based system using reservation and admission control, and adaptation-based system attempting to adapt the system behavior to available resources. Our approach mixes these policies. The reservation-based policy ensures that an application is admitted when resources are available and the adaptation policy aims to increase the utility of applications according to context. In [19], authors propose a model for dynamic adaptation that can be customized by application designers in order to satisfy adaptation needs. The model is based on a set of mandatory functionalities and an optional functionality. Adaptation mechanisms are associated to entities such as the whole application, processes, services, components or data and each entity is considered as composed of a set of components, leading to a hierarchical organization of adaptation mechanisms. In our approach, adaptation is associated to decision points only and is performed at activity level, which is more flexible. [21] proposes a reflexive framework to modify application behavior in the underlying runtime environment or in the adaptation framework itself. In our approach common adaptation mechanisms are in the middleware while specific mechanisms such as step execution at a decision point are included in the code.

7 Conclusion

We have presented a framework for QoS management to cope with variations of resources in distributed environment. In order to provide QoS support, a general model of applications is described. This model exhibits several alternative behaviors of applications to provide the same service with different resource requirements. From this model, application designers may deal with application requirements according to their own policy. To ensure QoS properties when event arrivals are unpredictable, resource reservation is required. We used resource reservation and a heuristic algorithm to schedule the resource use for all distributed applications. Our framework manages the QoS of distributed applications by adapting dynamically their behavior to fit the current context. Adaptation relies on operating modes and is performed at predefined decision points where an activity with the higher utility is selected. Coordination between nodes ensures a consistent global adaptation.

Future works will focus on the refinement of the middleware functions. Besides, we plan to add a tool to help the designers to capture and evaluate QoS requirements and provide the required QoS specification. Finally, we also plan to attempt to take into account others application models and to include load balancing concepts.

References

[1] Brandt, S., Nutt, G., Berk, T., Mankovich, J.: A dynamic quality of service middleware agent for mediating application resource usage. In: RTSS, pp. 307–317 (1998)

[2] QoS-Basic Framework (ISO/IEC JTC1/SC21 N9309) (1995)

[3] Abdelzaher, T.F., Shin, K.G., Bhatti, N.: Performance Guarantees for Web Server End-Systems: A Control-Theoretical Approach. IEEE Trans. Parallel and Distributed Systems 13(1), 80–96 (2002)

[4] Cardei, I., Jha, R., Cardei, M., Pavan, A.: Hierarchical Architecture for Real-Time Adaptive Resource Management. In: Coulson, G., Sventek, J. (eds.) Middleware 2000. LNCS, vol. 1795, pp. 415–434. Springer, Heidelberg (2000)

[5] Ensink, B., Adve, V.: Coordinating Adaptations in Distributed Systems. In: Proceedings of the 24th International Conference on Distributed Computing Systems, USA, pp. 446–455 (2004)

[6] Abeni, L., Buttazzo, G.: Hierarchical QoS management for time sensitive applications. In: Proceedings of the 7th IEEE Real-Time Technology and Applications Symposium, pp. 63–72 (2001)

[7] Vienne, P., Sourrouille, J.-L., Maranzana, M.: Modeling Distributed Applications for QoS Management. In: 4th Int. Workshop On Soft. Eng. and Middleware, pp. 170–184 (2005)

[8] Vienne, P., Sourrouille, J.L.: A Middleware for Autonomic QoS Management based on Learning Software. In: Proceedings on Engineering and Middleware (SEM 2005). ACM, New York (2006)

[9] Batouma, N., Sourrouille, J.-L.: A Decentralized Resource Management Using a Borrowing Schema. In: Proceedings of the 8th ACS/IEEE International Conference on Computer Systems and Applications, AICCSA 2010, Hammamet, Tunisia (to appear, 2010)

[10] UML: Unified Modeling Language, http://www.uml.org

[11] Alhalabi, F., Narkoy, B., Aubry, R., Maranzana, M., Morel, L., Sourrouille, J.-L.: Centralized vs. Decentralized QoS Management Policy. In: 3rd IEEE Inter. Conf. on Information and Communication Technologies: From Theory to Applications, ICCTTA 2008, pp. 1–6 (2008)

[12] Lee, C., Lehoczky, J., Rajkumar, R(R.), Siewiorek, D.: On Quality of Service Optimization with Discrete QoS Options. In: RTAS, pp. 276–286 (1999)

[13] Hyacinth, S.N.: software agents: An overview, Intelligent Systems Research Advanced Application and Technology Department. Knowledge Engineering Review 11, 1–40 (1996)

[14] Avouris, N.A., Gasser, L.: Object Oriented Concurrent Programming and Distributed Artificial intelligence. In: Distributed Artificial Intelligence: Theory and praxis, pp. 81–108. Kluwer Academic Publishers, Dordrecht (1992)

[15] Kresimir, J., Gordon, J., Mario, K.: A performance Analysis of Multi-agent Systems. Published in the Journal: Inter. Transaction on Systems Sciences and Applications 1(4) (2006)

[16] Luis, M., Jose, M.S., Juan, M.A.: Performance Evaluation of Open-Source Multi-agent Platforms. In: AAMAS 2006. ACM, Japan (2006)

[17] Schantz, R.E., Loyall, J.P., Rodrigues, C., Shimidt, D.C., Krishnamurthy, Y., Pyarali, I.: Flexible and Adaptive QoS Control For Distributed Real-time and Embedded Middleware. In: Endler, M., Schmidt, D.C. (eds.) Middleware 2003. LNCS, vol. 2672. Springer, Heidelberg (2003)

[18] Li, B., Nashrstedt, K.: QualProbes: Middleware QoS Profiling Services for Configuring Adaptaive Applications. In: Coulson, G., Sventek, J. (eds.) Middleware 2000. LNCS, vol. 1795, pp. 256–272. Springer, Heidelberg (2000)

[19] Segarra, M.T., André, F.: A Distributed Dynamic Adaptation Model for Component-Based Applications. In: Proceedings of the International Conference on Advanced Information Networking and Applications, pp. 525–529. IEEE, USA (2009)

[20] Vadhiyar, S., Dongarra, J.: Self Adaptability in grid Computing, Concurrency and Computation: Practice and Experience, Special issue: Grid performance, pp. 235–257 (2005)

[21] Keeney, J., Cahil, V.: Chisel: a policy-driven, context-aware, dynamic adaptation framework. In: 4th International Workshop on Policies for Distributed Systems and Networks (2003)

A Multilateral Negotiation Model for Cloud Service Market

Dongjin Yoo and Kwang Mong Sim*

Multi-Agent and Cloud Computing Systems Laboratory,
Department of information and Communication,
Gwangju Institute of Science and Technology (GIST), Gwangju, Republic of Korea
{dongjinyoo,kmsim}@gist.ac.kr
http://mas.gist.ac.kr/

Abstract. Trading cloud services between consumers and providers is a complicated issue of cloud computing. Since a consumer can negotiate with multiple providers to acquire the same service and each provider can receive many requests from multiple consumers, to facilitate the trading of cloud services among multiple consumers and providers, a multilateral negotiation model for cloud market is necessary. The contribution of this work is the proposal of a business model supporting a multilateral price negotiation for trading cloud services. The design of proposed systems for cloud service market includes considering a many-to-many negotiation protocol, and price determining factor from service level feature. Two negotiation strategies are implemented: 1) MDA (Market Driven Agent); and 2) adaptive concession making responding to changes of bargaining position are proposed for cloud service market. Empirical results shows that MDA achieved better performance in some cases that the adaptive concession making strategy, it is noted that unlike the MDA, the adaptive concession making strategy does not assume that an agent has information of the number of competitors (e.g., a consumer agent adopting the adaptive concession making strategy need not know the number of consumer agents competing for the same service).

Keywords: Agent-based Cloud Computing, Cloud Business Models, Cloud Economy, Negotiation Agents, Service Level Agreement. Price Negotiation.

1 Introduction

To support the trading of cloud services, a business model is needed. This work proposes a many-to-many negotiation model to facilitate the trading of cloud services among providers and consumers. The idea of cloud negotiation model was first proposed in [2]. Whereas [1] devised a one-to-one negotiation model for price and time slot negotiation between a consumer and a cloud provider, this work address some of the issue in [2] by implementing a many-to-many negotiation mechanism to facilitate the trading of cloud services among multiple consumers and providers.

* Corresponding author.

T.-h. Kim et al. (Eds.): GDC/CA 2010, CCIS 121, pp. 54–63, 2010.

This work focused on agent-based multilateral price negotiation model for cloud service market. First, an overview of agent-based negotiation model in cloud market is introduced at Section 2. The details of the agent-based negotiation model consist of the framework of multilateral negotiation, price determinant factor considering service level, utility functions for consumers and providers. Second, two negotiation strategies: 1) Market Driven Agent model, and 2) adaptive concession making mechanism reacting change of bargaining position are explained at Section 3. The evaluation for proposed negotiation strategy is described at Section 4.

2 Overview of Agent-Based Negotiation in Cloud Market

This section introduces an agent-based negotiation model for cloud resource market. The techniques and designs of agent-based negotiation in cloud service market include: 1) multilateral negotiation framework, 2) price determining factor to determine price considering the aspect of service level feature, and 3) utility function.

2.1 Framework of Multilateral Negotiation in Cloud Market

The framework of a cloud service market is described in Figure 1. Cloud service providers register service registry in cloud market place. A consumer can access the service registry and get service information to communicate with service providers. The service registry provides information of services and providers to consumers.

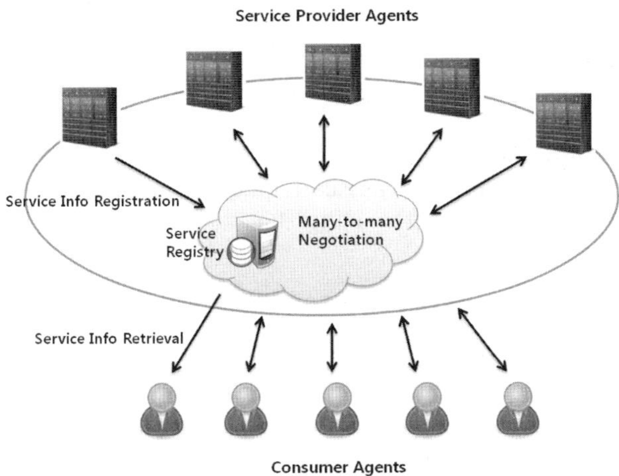

Fig. 1. Test bed for Agent based Cloud Service Market

A multilateral negotiation has a collection of multiple one-to-many negotiations. A consumer may send a same request for a service to multiple providers and negotiate with them, and a provider may receive multiple concurrent service requests. The structure of negotiation between providers and consumers is basically adopting Rubinstein's alternating protocol [3]. The distinction of the proposed negotiation protocol from traditional bilateral negotiation is that consumers take greedy actions, which means that consumers consider the most preferred option from providers to make decision how much to concede at the next round.

2.2 Price Determinant Factor

For both consumers and providers in the cloud service market, service level is the key factor to determine the price to negotiate. The initial price (IP) is the most preferred price, and the reserve price (RP) is the least acceptable price for both consumers and providers. Various details of service level for cloud service can affect the price unit to negotiate. Taking into consideration of service level, IP and RP is determined as follows:

$$IP = \sum (IPF_{s_i} \bullet L_{s_i}) \quad (1)$$

$$RP = \sum (RPF_{s_i} \bullet L_{s_i}) \quad (2)$$

s_i is a kind of services described in a SLA(Service Level Agreement) contract, which can affect the price. IPF_{s_i} is the factor from the service s_i to determine IP. RP is determined in the same way as IP. RPF_{s_i} is the determinant factor affecting RP. L_{s_i} is the level of service s_i. Level of service can be storage capacity, computational speed, network bandwidth, supported software, or any factors affecting degree of services in SLA. IPF and RPF is varied preference for each agent. As a provider receives service requests with different level of services, provider has different IP and RP for each request.

2.3 Utility Function

By using the utility function showing degree of satisfaction, each agent evaluates counter proposals. The negotiating issue is price, so the utility function represents price preference of an agent. The utility functions for consumer and provider is defined as

$$U(x_c) = U_{min} + (1 - U_{min})\{(RP - x_c) / (RP - IP)\} \quad \text{(for consumer)} \quad (3)$$

$$U(x_p) = U_{min} + (1 - U_{min})\{(x_p - RP) / (IP - RP)\} \quad \text{(for provider)} \quad (4)$$

$U(x)$ is in the range between [0,1]. x_c, x_p are the price to evaluate proposals for consumer, and provider repectively. U_{min} is the minimum utility when concession is made at RP. For experimental purpose, U_{min} is set to 0.1. If negotiation fails, $U(x) = 0$.

3 Negotiation Strategy

Agents in this work mainly follows time-dependent concession making strategy with principles of time discounting and deadline [4]. An agent may have different attitude toward time. In addition to time dependent strategy, agents also need to consider market factors in many-to-many negotiation situation. In this section, two conceding strategies for many-to-many negotiations are adopted: 1) Market Driven Agent (MDA) model [5], and 2) Adaptive concession making strategy considering change of bargaining position [6].

3.1 MDA with Complete Information

MDA [5] is designed for making adjustable amounts of concessions in multilateral negotiation. A market driven agent determines adjustable amount of concession using three functions: 1) Time, 2) Competition, and 3) Opportunity.

3.1.1 Time

The time function determines the amount of concession by considering an agent's deadline and its attitude toward time. (e.g., an agent that is more (respectively, less) sensitive to time will concede more (respectively, less) rapidly to its reserve price) Taking into account current time position t, deadline τ, strategy reacting time λ, time function is defined as

$$T(t, \tau, \lambda) = 1 - (t / \tau)^{\lambda} \tag{5}$$

Three classes of time-dependent concession making strategies responding time are used: 1) linear ($\lambda = 1$), 2) Conciliatory ($1 < \lambda < \infty$), and 3) Conservative ($0 < \lambda < 1$). A linear strategy makes concession at constant rate. A conciliatory (respectively, conservative) strategy makes larger (respectively, smaller) concession at early rounds and makes smaller (respectively, larger) concession at later rounds.

3.1.2 Competition

The competition function determine the amount of compromise by the probability which the agent is not considered as the most preferred partner, and this function is defined as

$$C(m, n) = 1 - [(m-1)/m]^{n} \tag{6}$$

m is the number of competitors in the market and n is the number of trading partners to negotiate. However, to apply competition function to make concession, an agent must have information about the number of competitors. For instance, to apply the competition function, a cloud consumer needs to know how many other consumers are competing for the same cloud service. This information may be difficult to obtain since consumers do not transmit their service requests to other consumers.

3.1.3 Opportunity

The opportunity function determines the amount of concession by 1) alternative options, 2) difference in proposal (utility), given as follows:

$$O(n_t^{B}, v_t^{B \to Sj}, < w_t^{Sj \to B} >) = 1 - \prod_{j=1}^{n_t^B} \frac{v_t^{B \to Sj} - w_t^{Sj \to B}}{v_t^{B \to Sj} - c^{B}} \tag{7}$$

where n_t^{B} is the number of trading partner, $v_t^{B \to Sj}$ is the proposal proposed by MDA, and $< w_t^{Sj \to B} >$ is the set of altanative trading options.

3.2 Adaptive Concession Making Strategy with Incomplete Information

Due to lack of information about competitors in cloud market, MDA may not be applicable if market doesn't support it. Thus in this section, adaptive concession making strategy considering change of bargaining position with incomplete information is proposed.

3.2.1 Bargaining Position

The concept of bargaining position (BP) is initially devised and formulated in a previous work of [6]. $P_j(t)$ is denoted as the counter proposal from trading partner j where $0 \leq j \leq n$ and n is the number of trading partners. Each agent has set of counter proposals $P_j(t)$ over negotiation. BP can be derived from patterns of the counter proposals $P_j(t)$, as defined in

$$BP(t) = Avg_j\left(\frac{\Delta P_j(t-1,t)}{\Delta P_j(0,t)/t}\right)$$
$$(\text{ where } \Delta Pj(t', t) = P_j(t') - P_j(t)) \tag{8}$$

$\Delta P_j(t', t)$ means the difference between counter proposals at round t´ and t. Thus $\Delta P_j(t - 1, t)$ is the difference between the counter proposal at previous round and current round t from trading partner j. Bargaining position BP(t) is the ratio of diference with previous counter proposal to average differences of counter proposal from trading partner j at round t. If BP(t) is 1, the recent amount of concesion is same as prior average amount of concession, which means neutral. If BP(t) is larger(smaller) than 1, agent is in the advantageous(disadvantageous) position.

3.2.2 Reacting Change of Bargaining Position

From change of bargaining position, strategy toward time over negotiation of each agent can be derived as

$$\lambda_{t+1} = \begin{cases} Max(\lambda_{min}, \lambda_t + \Delta BP(t)(\lambda_t - \lambda_{min})), & \lambda_t \leq 1.0 \\ \lambda_t + \Delta BP(t), & \lambda_t > 1.0 \end{cases} \tag{9}$$

The proposed conceding strategy adapts to time dependent strategy by responding to variation of bargaining position from the previous round. For example, if bargaining position is becoming more advantageous ($\Delta BP(t) > 0$), and an agent should adopt a more conservative strategy to enhance its utility. If the bargaining position is becoming more disadvantageous ($\Delta BP(t) < 0$), an agent should adopt a more conciliatory strategy to enhance its success rate. The amount to change time strategy is determined by changes of BP ($\Delta BP(t)$) and current strategy. Due to the asymmetry of intervals between conciliatory strategy including linear strategy ($\lambda \in [0, 1]$) and conservative strategy ($\lambda \in (1, \infty]$), different amount of changing strategy should be applied as above. λ_{min} is the minimal utility which is manulally set to 0.1. Since MDA has the limitation on cloud market, adaptive concession making using characteristic of BP can be the complementaty strategy. The proposed reacting strategy is not the optimal strategy with incompete information, but the best effort strategy. The better applications of using BP and ΔBP can be also proposed.

4 Experiment and Empirical Results

4.1 Objectives and Motivation

Experiments are designed to evaluate and compare performances from three different categories of strategies: 1) time-dependent strategy, 2) market driven strategy (MDA), and 3) adaptive concession making strategy.

4.2 Performance Measure

Three criteria: 1) negotiation success rate, 2) expected consumer's utility, and 3) expected utility of negotiating pairs (see Table 1) are used to evaluate performances of each bargaining strategy. Negotiation success rate is the consumer's probability accomplishing negotiation to get resources from providers in deadline. Expected utility of negotiating pairs is expected utility from average of a consumer and a provider paring at each negotiation. Negotiation success rate and consumer's utility were measured in distinct conditions of time dependent strategies. U^C, U^P are extracted from the utility function denoting levels of satisfaction from negotiation. (The utility function is described in Section 2.3)

Table 1. Performance Measure

Negotiation success rate	$P_{suc} = N_{suc} / N_{tot}$
Expected consumer's utility	$\sum U^C / N_{tot}$
Expected utility of negotiating pairs	$\sum((U^C + U^P)/2) / N_{tot}$
N_{suc}	The number of success
N_{tot}	Total number of resources requested by consumers
U^C	Expected consumer's utility
U^P	Expected provider's utility

4.3 Experiment Setting

For this experiment, two classes of input data source are required: 1) properties of agents who participate cloud resource market (Table 2), and 2) characteristics of market environment (Table 3). Consumers and providers determine initial price (IP) and reserve price (RP) by using IP factor, RP factor, and resource capacity, as described in Section 2.2. In this experiment, a computational virtual machine is assumed to be the product for bargaining, so it is assumed that there are two kinds of quantity factors of resources: 1) CPU-capacity and 2) memory-capacity. Consumer's CPU and memory capacity factor is capacity of requesting resources to service providers. Provider's CPU and memory factor is the total amount of possessing resources.

Table 2. Input data source: Properties of Consumers and Providers

Input Data	Possible Values	Settings	
		Consumer	Provider
Initial Price Factor (IPF_c, IPF_p)	Positive Real number	1 – 15	66 – 80
Reserve Price Factor (RPF_c, RPF_p)	Positive Real number	66 – 80	1 – 15
CPU Capacity Factor (C^c_{cpu}, C^p_{cpu})	Integer (Cloud resource unit)	500 – 5000	5000 – 20000
Memory Capacity Factor (C^c_{mem}, C^p_{mem})	Integer (Cloud resource unit)	250 – 2500	2500 – 10000
Time Dependent Strategy (λ_c, λ_p)	Conciliatory (< 1) Linear (= 1) Conservative (> 1)	0.3 1.0 3.0	0.3 1.0 3.0
Negotiation Deadline (τ_c, τ_p)	Integer(Round-based)	20 - 40	20 – 40

For examining performances in dynamic market situation, experiments were carried out in different market type. Three kinds of market types are used for this experiment as shown in Table 3: 1) favorable, 2) balanced and 3) unfavorable market. Market type is determined by ratio of providers and consumers. The graphs in the experiments we're plotted from the perspective of consumers. When market type is (consumer) favorable, the number of provider is larger than consumer. Balanced market is when the number of consumer is same as providers. In unfavorable market, the number of consumer is less than providers. Each agent is generated in 0.1 second with probability 0.3. In this experiment given ratio of providers and consumer is maintained constantly following market composition. The total number of providers is manually set to 250 due to space limitation.

Table 3. Input data source: Cloud Resource Market

Market Type	Favorable	Balanced	Unfavorable
Consumer-Provider Ratio	1:10, 1:5, 1:3	1:1	3:1, 5:1, 10:1
No. of total provider agents	250	250	250
No. of total consumer agents	≅ 500, 600	≅ 900	≅ 1170, 1350
Probability of generating agent (per 0.1 seconds)	0.3	0.3	0.3

4.4 Simulation and Results

Empirical results were obtained for all representative combinations of the input data. (i.e., consumer-provider ratio = {1:10, 1:5, 1:3, 1:1, 3:1, 5:1, 10:1}, negotiating agent adopting strategy as λ_c = {0.3, 1.0, 3.0}, and λ_p = {0.3, 1.0, 3.0}) Agents' properties are randomly picked from ranges given in Table 2, and each agent's property is uniformly distributed. (IPF, RPF, $C_{cpu,}$ C_{mem} are uniformly distributed and randomly selected to each agent.)

Three negotiation strategies are experimented and compared. Results in terms of expected consumer's utility and success rate with particular time-strategy λ (= {0.3,

1.0, 3.0}) include all the cases corresponding provider's possible time-strategies. For example, when getting consumer's expected utility with time dependent strategy 1.0, results should be made considering all the cases that λ_p = {0.3, 1.0, 3.0}. To get expected utility of negotiating pair, results should be obtained in all the possible combinations of λ_c, λ_p. Comparison of expected utility with different λ among time function, MDA, and adaptive strategy is shown as below Figure 2, 3, and 4. Negotiation success rate is given in Figure 5, 6, and 7. Performances regarding expected utility of negotiating pair are also given in Figure 8.

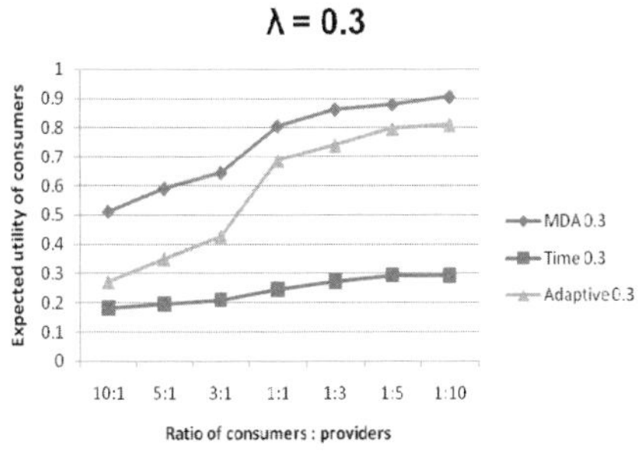

Fig. 2. Expected utility (λ = 0.3)

Fig. 3. Expected utility (λ = 1.0)

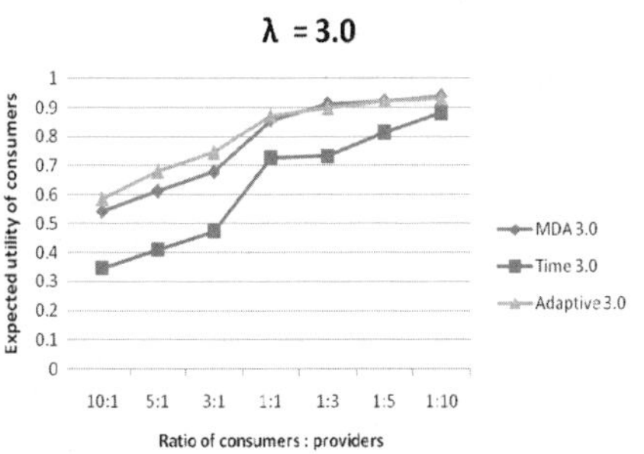

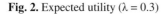

Fig. 4. Expected utility (λ = 3.0)

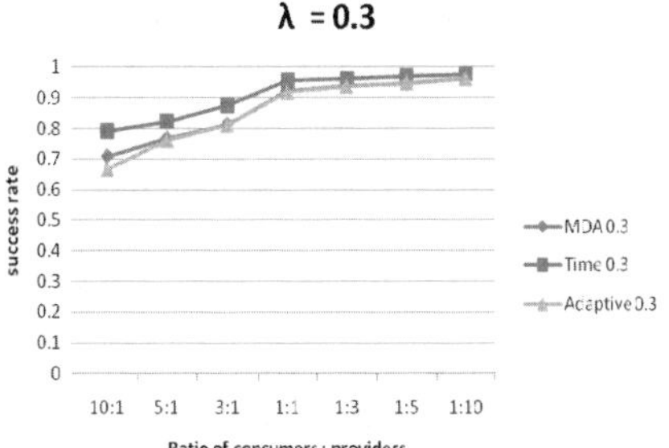

Fig. 5. Success rate (λ = 0.3)

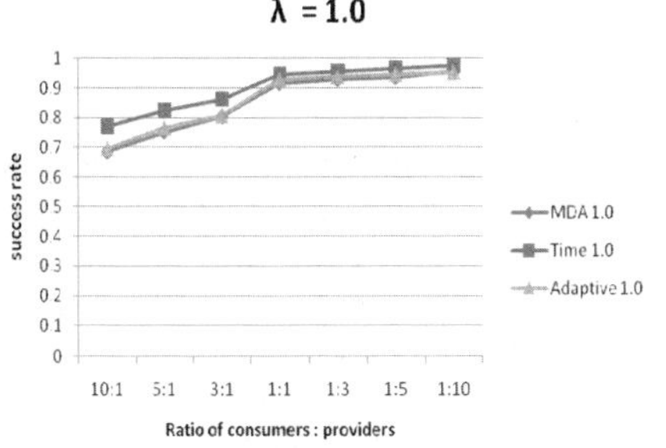

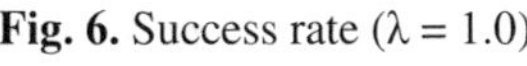

Fig. 6. Success rate (λ = 1.0)

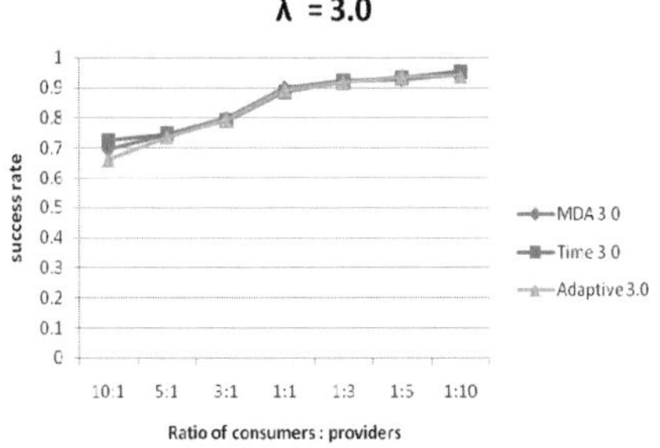

Fig. 7. Success rate (λ = 3.0)

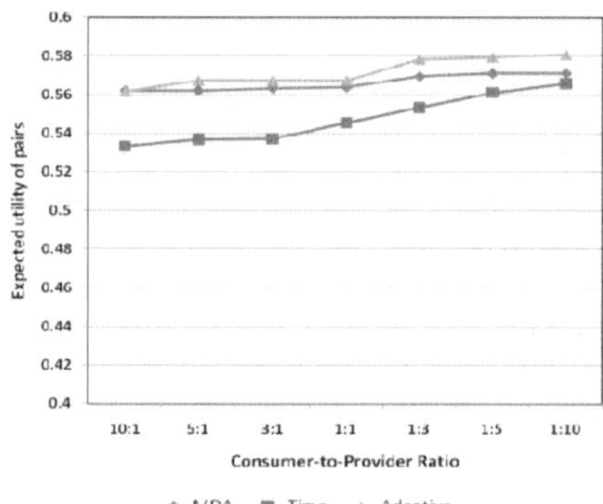

Fig. 8. Expected utility of negotiating pairs

5.5 Observation

The following observations are made.

1) Given complete information consumer agents adopting the MDA strategy generally achieved the highest expected utility of consumer.

2) For the expected utility of consumers, adaptive concession making strategy with incomplete information accomplished higher utility than time function and less than MDA strategy. When initial λ is 3.0, adaptive concession making strategy is slightly better than MDA.

3) Time function achieved higher success rate than MDA, and adaptive concession making strategy when λ is 0.3, and 1.0. Three strategies got similar success rate with λ = 3.0.

4) Both the MDA and adaptive concession making strategy achieved significantly higher expected utility of negotiating pair than the time-only strategy. Even though the adaptive strategy achieve only slightly expected utility of negotiating pair than the MDA strategy, unlike the MDA strategy, the adaptive strategy does not assume complete knowledge of the numbers of consumers and providers.

5 Conclusion and Future Work

The contributions of this work are: (i) designing of multilateral negotiation model promoting trading among multiple consumer and provider, (ii) proposing two negotiation strategies in cloud market: 1) MDA with complete information, and 2) the adaptive concession making strategy with incomplete information. From the empirical experiments, MDA achieves the highest excepted utility but MDA has the limitation to be used in cloud market. The adaptive concession making strategy reacting change of bargaining position can be complement strategy since the adaptive strategy with incomplete information still gets better expected utility of consumers than only-time function. Also, in some cases (favorable market, λ=3.0) market the adaptive strategy achieves similar expected utility of consumers as MDA. In case of expected utility of negotiating pair, the adaptive strategy accomplished slightly better than MDA, even though the adaptive strategy has no complete information about competitors. Future work would be making adaptive strategy using the concept of bargaining position more concrete (i.e., near optimal strategy) in the environment with incomplete information.

Acknowledgments

This work was supported by a Korea Science and Engineering Foundation (KOSEF) grant funded by the Korea Government (MEST 2009-0065329) and the DASAN International Faculty Fund (project code: 140316).

References

1. Son, S., Sim, K.M.: A Multi-issue Negotiation Mechanism for Cloud Service Reservation. In: Annual International Conference on Cloud Computing and Virtualization, CCV 2010 (May 2010)
2. Sim, K.M.: Towards Complex Negotiation for Cloud Economy. In: Bellavista, P., Chang, R.-S., Chao, H.-C., Lin, S.-F., Sloot, P.M.A. (eds.) GPC 2010. LNCS, vol. 6104, pp. 395–406. Springer, Heidelberg (2010)
3. Rubinstein, A.: Perfect equilibrium in a bargaining model. Econometrica 50(1), 97–109 (1982)
4. Fishburn, P.C., Rubinstein, A.: Time preference, Internat. Econom. Rev. 23, 677–694 (1982)
5. Sim, K.M.: Equilibria, Prudent Compromises, and the "Waiting" Game. IEEE Trans. on Systems, Man and Cybernetics, Part B: Cybernetics 35(4), 712–724 (2005)
6. Sim., K.M., Shi, B.: Adaptive Commitment Management Strategy Profiles for Concurrent Negotiations. In: Proceedings of the first International Workshop on Agent-based Complex Automated Negotiations (ACAN), held in Conjunction with 7th Int. Conf. on Autonomous Agents and Multi-Agent Systems (AAMAS), Estoril Portugal, pp. 16–23 (2008)

Intelligent Smart Cloud Computing for Smart Service

Su-mi Song and Yong-ik Yoon

Department of Multimedia Science, Sookmyung Women's University
Chungpa-Dong 2-Ga, Yongsan-Gu 140-742, Seoul, Korea
songsm0328@naver.com, yiyoon@sm.ac.kr

Abstract. The cloud computing technology causes much attention in IT field. The developments using this technology have done actively. The cloud computing is more evolved than the existing offer. So, the current cloud computing only has a process that responds user requirements when users demand their needs. For intelligently adapting the needs, this paper suggests a intelligent smart cloud model that is based on 4S/3R. This model can handle intelligently to meet users needs through collecting user's behaviors, prospecting, building, delivering, and rendering steps. It is because users have always mobile devices including smart phones so that is collecting user's behavior by sensors mounted on the devices. The proposed service model using intelligent smart cloud computing will show the personalized and customized services to be possible in various fields.

Keywords: Smart Cloud, Intelligent, Cloud Service, Smart Service.

1 Introduction

Cloud service is the main attention to the IT business and is currently a lot of service companies throughout the growing commercialization. Cloud service means that Internet space is featured as the huge new workspace or repository, a large number of content including the platform and infrastructure to provide. However, existing cloud computing technology have passive mode depending on user's needs. Users can access Internet anywhere, anytime because spreading mobile devices including Smart phones and expending Wireless Internet spaces. This situation shows that cloud service should be evolution passive mode to proactive mode. As so, users always carry mobile devices on body, information acquired and services received is expected to increase. So we propose an intelligent smart cloud computing (ISCC) model for providing personalized contents through intelligent processing based on the user behavior what are acquired by user's mobile devices. ISCC doesn't provide the same contents to each of the users. This will provide other contents depending on the user behavior to each of the users accurately, personally. ISCC can be possible that users are able to get contents or services they want without searching, requirements. This point means service quality improve than now. Furthermore, ISCC will be appropriate technology in new lifestyle service.

T.-h. Kim et al. (Eds.): GDC/CA 2010, CCIS 121, pp. 64–73, 2010.

On this paper, we will summary about existing cloud computing simply and introduce mobile cloud computing. Then, we will have explain an intelligent smart cloud service and define the ISCC (intelligent smart cloud computing) what it is in detail.

2 Related Work

In this section, the concept of cloud computing and mobile cloud computing will explore.

2.1 Cloud Computing

The cloud computing is defined as a technology to provide to users IT resources by using the Internet as a service. Users can be freed from the inconvenience required to install the software on their computers because users can select necessary resource and use in the cloud by internet access without purchasing. After using resources, they should pay cost as much as their usage. This point has any economic advantages benefits personally, in companies. The cloud computing was born in complex combination from Distributed computing, Grid computing, Utility computing and so on. Cloud computing has three type of services as follows; SaaS(Software as a Service), PaaS(Platform as a Service), and IaaS(Infrastructure as a Service). Cloud contains from small-scale contents to computing environments and users can use those resources optionally in the Cloud.

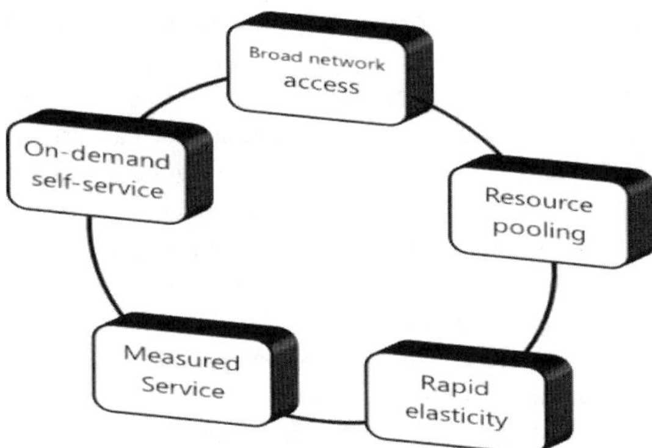

Fig. 1. Main features of cloud computing

Cloud computing has several key features as shown in [Fig. 1]. The most important feature of cloud computing is not directly required contents providers. When contents and services are needed, users can directly select the required services and contents, like on-demand self-service. This process will be carried through the Internet connection and users can be provided the desired service on the network freely using a mechanism for supporting different client's platforms (broad network access).

Services are pooling to each of users who need through Multi-Tenant model, such as Resource pooling. The requested resources are allocated dynamically depending on need and demand.

In short, users register their want service in cloud server and server provides the contents to each of users according to the registered details. So the cloud computing has the ability to quickly process, like Rapid elasticity. It is because the server must respond to the needs for users quickly to provide. Server requires fees of each user as usage and controls to optimize usage automatically via measured service. These features allow that users can be provided the service which they want in desired time away from the constraints of time and space. Also, users can use SW for service or other contents of ownership being hard in the cloud space. Because of this, cloud computing is the most notably technology in the IT market. Many services has been developed and been continue based cloud computing.

2.2 Mobile Cloud Computing

Simply, a target device of mobile cloud computing is mobile phones. In other words, mobile services are provided to mobile phones for mobility in cloud. The mobile phones can be avoided from hardware failures because of a continuous service through accessing the Cloud. Cloud allows mobile phones to have larger storage than own, use augmented reality service and find location by GPS. This is quite different from the past mobile service. In the past, mobile services work inside phone alone and are not interactive. Also, the small size of the storage requests to using large amounts of data for the cloud. But now it is solved in the mobile cloud.

Currently, a variety of mobile cloud service is going to such as Apple MobileMe, Microsoft Myphone and Soonr, representative of services. MobileMe provides a service which can synchronize e-mail, calendar, contacts between the server and devices automatically in real time. All registered devices including a mobile phone are applied to synchronize. The key point of the service is that user can use same data on device anywhere, anytime. Myphone is a service for smart phone applications based on Windows Mobile platform to provide through online access. Especially, locking is the best feature. The Lock function protects important information stored in smart phone. Because the server is connected to phone, maintenance and updating are easy through synchronizing. If users lose their smart-phone, they can lock phone through accessing server and will find easily more than past. Soonr is a service for mobile office application to target the iPhone through cloud. Users are able to open the file (DOC, PPT, XSL, and so on) on iPhone without installation. Soonr shows users only result using Remote UI technology.

3 Smart Cloud Service

'Smart' means 'be clever', 'be intelligence', 'be clear' and 'be correct'. The smart has many meanings in dictionary. We often listen this word in various fields. As spreading smart phone, smart becomes more familiar and service markets are changing to target smart devices rapidly. Limitation of time and space is slowly disappearing. People always have a smart phone all around and enjoy some internet services using smart phones. Further, a need for more smart service will be expected. So, service types are expected to change from simply providing service that responds to user needs to automatic service that delivery to user correct contents through analysis user's information. At this time, the cloud computing technology is appropriated to take advantages. Intelligently processing is done through the cloud server. Then the cloud server makes new contents which is befitting and provide to user using Internet. In other word, user can be given desired services automatically in cloud when they feel the needs. We will call this cloud 'smart cloud'.

The Cloud server collects user information for processing through the sensors in user's device. USN (Ubiquitous Sensor Network), RFID (Radio Frequency Identification) tag, Gyro Sensor and other sensing information are transmitted to server that collects data precisely. User is provided a personalized service that is made by server with analysis their status and needs in real time based information collected.

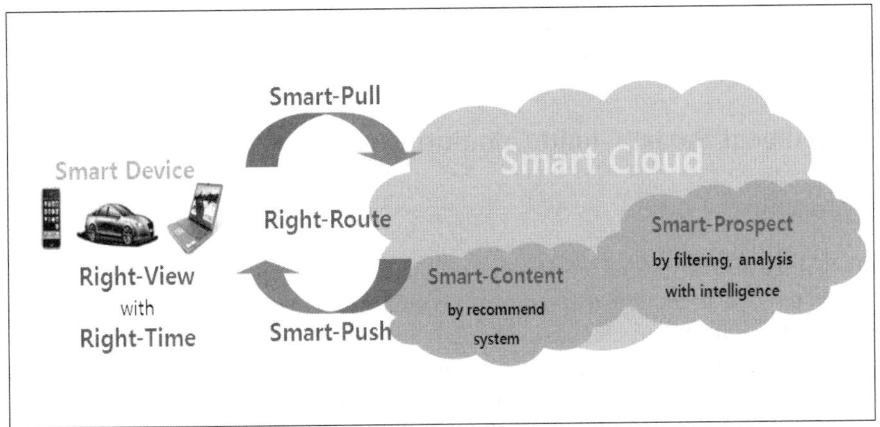

Fig. 2. Smart cloud service model

A overall model of the Smart Cloud services is shown by [Fig. 2]. This model suggests a new notion that defined 4S/3R that is essential needs in smart cloud service. The description of elements for 4S/3R is below.

- Smart-Pull/Smart-Push
  Server gathers good information to analyze user behavior patterns and to determine easily though filtering. Server determines the priority of contents which are made through all processing. In addition, the process of synchronizing occurs to the registered devices for user.
- Smart-Content
  This element is fusion-media offering user. Server creates fusion-media from various contents (image, text, video, animation, and so on). Content generated will be provided by the user recommend system.

- Smart-Prospect
  Server forecasts user's needs, contents by powerful analysis, filtering process using user's situational information.
- Right-Route
  Server considers band-width, data size, user place for delivering on best speed without delay. So decide the best route.
- Right-View
  Service offers Views moderately various devices(smart-phone, laptop, PDA, PC, etc) through rendering.
- Right-Time
  User can receive contents at desired time, space.

The Smart Cloud service is expected to improve the quality of service in life, culture, medical, business and all aspects. It is because the smart cloud will be applied variously depending on domains.

4 Intelligent Smart Cloud Computing (ISCC)

4.1 Concept

The intelligent smart cloud computing enables the server to provide user services actively through a additional intelligent process on existing cloud system. The demand condition for Smart cloud computing is shown in [Fig. 3]. Most importantly, the server always performs Elastic processes such as Elastic Computing for IaaS, Elastic Management for PaaS, and Elastic Deployment for SaaS. Simply, the Elastic Processing is collecting user information that is pulled by the sensing of context information from user's hold devices and being ready to the right service according to the changing information of user situation.

The intelligent smart cloud computing enables the server to provide user services actively through a additional intelligent process on existing cloud system. The demand condition for Smart cloud computing is shown in [Fig. 3]. Most importantly, the server always performs Elastic processes such as Elastic Computing for IaaS, Elastic Management for PaaS, and Elastic Deployment for SaaS. Simply, the Elastic Processing is collecting user information that is pulled by the sensing of context information from user's hold devices and being ready to the right service according to the changing information of user situation. For supporting the requirements of IaaS, like storages limitation and processing power, the server prepares the virtualization for mass storages and infrastructures in Cloud by considering of Elastic Computing. That is, the Elastic Computing supports a dynamic adaptation for the need of computing environment that is accomplished by a decision policy based on the change of user's situation. Also, Elastic Management performs a provisioning and scheduling for a decision of the smart activity. The provisioning and scheduling is performed through a inference engine that consists of some rules based on three attributes as follows; an object id for user context, a predicate relationship for user behavior, and a value for thinking. Through the result of Elastic Management, a smart activity, like a Platform as a service, is supported.

By considering the priority of service and the elastic result of provisioning, The Elastic Deployment makes a right service for user to keep stable condition and to avoid delays and collision. Also, a user interface configuration, like personalized view and content rendering, is generated by according of the right service for user-centric. Such as SaaS, support, in order to satisfy user requirements in SaaS, the Elastic Deployment supports a right view in right time based on the right delivery. These processing is accomplished with rendering and playing functions, such as attach, playing, and view of the right contents received in user device.

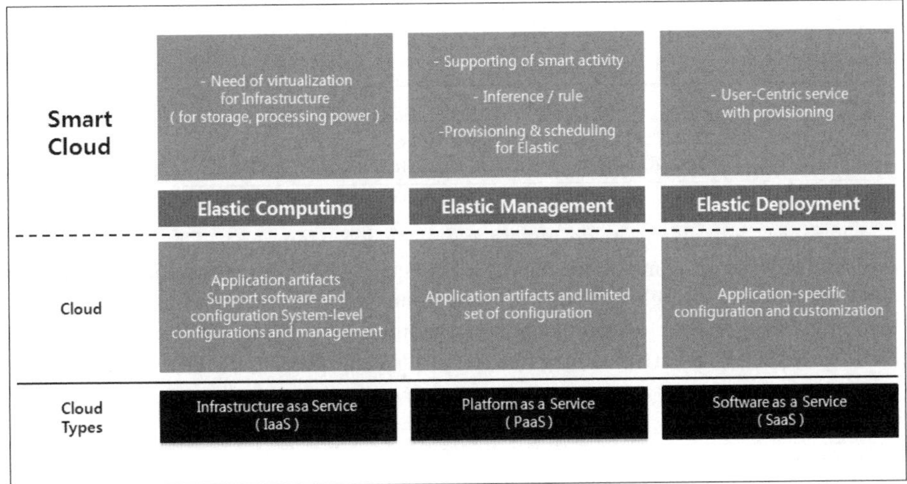

Fig. 3. Elastic service of smart cloud

4.2 Handling Process

4S/3R is introduced in the previous section. This section will demonstrate intelligent process of the smart cloud computing according to 4S/3R with simple example. The sensing contexts, like current location and activity, are caught by sensors inside user's device. Through Internet connection between smart devices and the Smart cloud, the sensing contexts for user behaviors are sent to server in the Smart cloud. This process is called to 'Smart-Pull'. Updating user behavior should be done at regular intervals so that user status is figured out exactly. Also the repetitive behaviors cycles of user are registered as patterns.

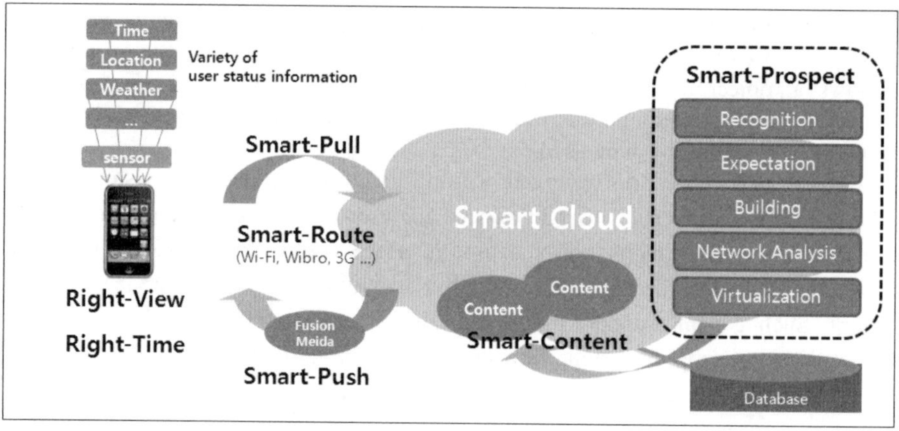

Fig. 4. Intelligent processing in smart cloud

The patterns are materials of prospection useful contents for user.

> example 1 :
>
> - Mr. Smart often go to watch the movies on Saturday night.

Mr. Smart behavior is made pattern based on the example 1. The smart cloud is ready to provide contents about movies. The smart cloud collects a current location and time for him, as well as favorite movie genre information about user. This information collection is performed by the smart cloud itself without user's awareness. The Smart-prospect in Smart cloud performs as following processes: recognition and expectation for user preference

> example 2 :
>
> - He enjoys the usual romantic movie. Over the last month, 3 of 4 films were romantic genre films.
> - L theater, and C theater are often used especially. Because he' been membership of two theater.

The smart cloud firstly starts to anticipate necessary data based on the example 2. Then gathering data and contents is started with anticipation. It finds nearest location of theaters with priority L and C from current user's location. And it prepares the list of movies in each theater as first preferred genre by reordering. Only necessary data and contents, like right contents, are edited and made as fusion-media by the Smart cloud. Fusion-media is processed considering with the condition of hardware, software of devices and the user interface. The whole processes are 'Smart-Prospect'.

The smart cloud produces contents for users convenience actively without requirements. At this point, a fusion-media is made through Smart-Prospect process is 'Smart-Content'. The Fusion-media has a complex shape (with text, image, video, sound, and so on). When the smart cloud is ready to deliver the right contents being provided, the smart cloud determines the 'Right-Route' to deliver it accurately and quickly. For the right-route, the smart cloud considers the data-capacity of content, user's routes to access the web from current location, and band-width to avoid interruption of delivery. Step to determine the Right-Route process is included in the 'Smart-Push'. If the user uses multiple devices, the smart cloud has to synchronize the all devices which are registered.

example 3 :

- He uses Smart phone in free Wi-Fi zone.

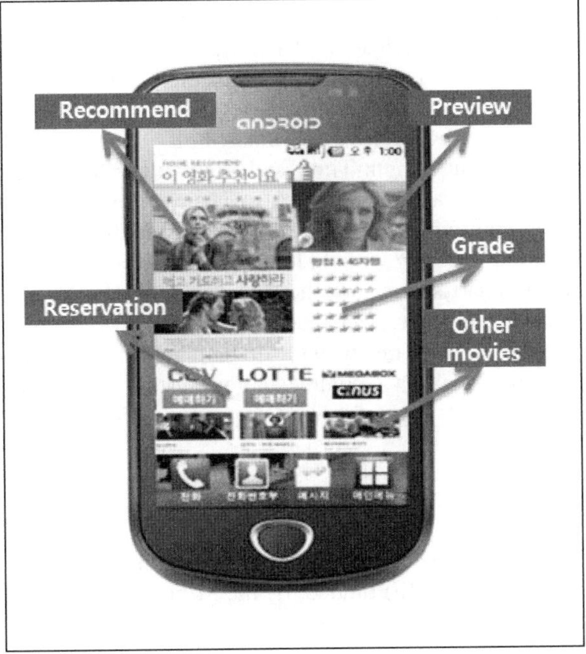

Fig. 5. Example of smart-content

Now, smart phones can use Internet by Wi-Fi and 3G. Wi-Fi is free and easy to transfer large data. But the rate is reduced if it has many number of network users. In contrast, 3G has ability to transfer data quickly regardless of connectors but capacity limit. When the size of content to delivery is not big, then the smart cloud determines 3G route. The smart cloud concerns a transmission delays because of the number of Wi-Fi network connectors. Then the content transmission is done with notification what is using 3G. 'Right-Time' is most essential element in transmission. If the movie information is delivered to out of time, the content becomes the garbage even though the content is very nice. In addition, the user may feel uncomfortable for such service. The Right-Time also has relationship with user's devices and is most important consideration element for the smart cloud. The smart cloud selects the best content type and route for the Right-Time. Finally, the content delivered in user's device will be shown with 'Right-View'. In Smart device, resolution, screen size, optimal placement are belong to Right-View. The Right-View also is performed with rendering and playing function for Smart contents. As shown in [Fig. 5], Mr. Smart will take a user-centric content, like a reservation for watching movie, on his smart phone.

5 Conclusion

In this paper, the intelligent smart cloud model through intelligent processing that can provide users necessary contents correctly has introduced. This cloud computing collects user's behavior information periodically. And It forecasts and prepares contents by analysis collecting information. Then it provides the contents at appropriate time and place actively. For the intelligent smart cloud, this paper has presented a model for intelligent processing for user-centric. The smart cloud service model has the requirements like 4S/3R as follows: Smart-Pull, Smart-Push, Smart-Prospect, Smart-Contents, Right-Route, Right-Time, and Right-View. These requirements need in aspects of user, networks and the cloud. Also The requirements must be considered for the best service environment. As a result, users will be able to receive a right content when they want correctly without looking.

For the intelligent smart service, we have a plan to study intelligent smart cloud computing more detail and more technically than now. The intelligent smart cloud model will apply to real environment with domain information based on ontology. For the results, we will make a recommendation system and a looking service by according to various domains (age, gender, occupation, region, etc).

Acknowledgment

“This was supported by Basic Science Research Program through the National Research Foundation of Korea(NRF) funded by the Ministry of Education, Science and Technology(2010-0008848)“.

References

1. Sheng, Q.Z., Yu, J., Dustdar, S.: Enabling Context-Aware Web Services: Methods, Architectures, and Technologies. CRC Press, Boca Raton (2010)
2. Yoon, Y.: Smart Cloud Model for Future Services. Sookmyung Women’s University
3. Cloud computing, next-generation computing technology/market trends and business strategies
4. Lee, B., et al.: Personal user-centric cloud computing technology. Korea Institute of Information Technology Review, 15–21 (December 2008)

5. Yoon, Y., et al.: Mobile Cloud Technical Trends. Sookmyung Women;s University
6. Sun MicroSystems, Inc.: Introduction to Cloud Computing Architecture, White Paper 1st Edition (June 2009)
7. Perez, S.: Why Cloud Computing is the Future of Mobile, http://www.readwriteweb.com/archives/why_cloud_computing_is_the_future_of_mobile.php/
8. Dargie, W.: Context-aware computing and Self-Managing Systems. CRC Press, Boca Raton (2009)

VMcol: A Collector of Garbage for Virtual Machine Image Files

Xiao Ling, Hai Jin, Song Wu, and Xuanhua Shi

Service Computing Technology and System Lab
Cluster and Grid Computing Lab
School of Computer Science and Technology
Huazhong University of Science and Technology, Wuhan, 430074, China
hjin@hust.edu.cn

Abstract. Virtual disk for a *virtual machine* (VM) is a virtual image file on a physical node. Inside a VM, the guest VM operates the virtual disk as the general OS, while outside the VM, the virtual image file grows larger and larger with the data operation of the VM, because of the semantic gap between the guest VM and the *virtual machine monitor* (VMM), the *delete* operation in guest VM cannot be received to the VMM. This leads to data space vanishing on physical node, even there are a large volume of data space released inside the VM. To target this, we present the design, implementation and evaluation of the VMcol, a system that collects the garbage space lively which has been deleted in the guest VM. When a file is deleted in the guest VM, VMcol will reclaim the deleted data for the corresponding virtual image files without interrupting the service of the VM and requiring additional physical space. The performance evaluation shows that VMcol improves the storage utilization with little performance penalty of VMs in terms of CPU utilization and I/O bandwidth.

Keywords: virtual machine image file, semantic gap, storage utilization, virtual disk.

1 Introduction

Nowadays, virtualization draws more attention since energy saving issues and resource utilization concerns. The primary merit of virtualization technology is to present the illusion of many small *virtual machines* (VMs), each of which runs a separate operating system instance. The virtual disks for VMs are VM image files on physical nodes, and the VM image file encapsulates the applications and environment of the *VM* and the private data of users. Virtual machine image files are the storage medium of virtual disks. The image file is convenient for the *virtual machine monitor* (VMM) that executes these images.

While the semantic gap between the VMM and guest VM causes that the driver domain, which manages virtual machine image files outside the guest VM, receives no deletion request from guest VM. So the virtual machine images preserve all the useless data, even it has been deleted in guest VM permanently. Unfortunately, the growing

T.-h. Kim et al. (Eds.): GDC/CA 2010, CCIS 121, pp. 74–83, 2010.

useless data of virtual machine image files leads to lowering storage utilization, so that no enough space meets the growing VMs' capacity requirement.

Besides, the growing useless data of image file cause the storage footprint of virtual machine larger than the size of virtual disk space. So users have to pay for the unused space in the virtual disk of VM. The worse thing is that, data centers, which serve a large-scale VM farm, cannot provide their storage capacity infinitely due to the related problems on space, maintenance, and cooling. So, how to collect garbage in virtual machine image has been one of the most important challenges in the virtualization environment.

Some methods have been provided to effectively reclaim unused space in virtual machine image storage. For example, VMware offers a disk shrinking function in Virtual Disk Manger to release the space taken by deleted data in virtual machine image [16]. Microsoft makes use of Hype-V to shrink *virtual hard disk* (VHD) [17, 18]. IBM also uses the shrink-vDisk technology [9]. These methods require users to mark the deleted data in guest VM and then reclaim the corresponding space manually after shutting down VMs. Therefore, these methods have the shortcomings of additional service interruption, low recovery rate, and high overheads. Besides, parallax [5], a storage system for Xen, reclaims the unused space in virtual machine image without interrupting the service of virtual machines. But it is not transparent to users because the system has a mechanism similar to a mark-and-sweep collector.

This paper describes VMcol, a system that collects the garbage lively in virtual machine image storage. Unlike existing work, VMcol does not halt the guest VM and scan virtual machine image file. VMcol can real-timely perceive data deletion in the guest VM and get the information of deleted data in virtual disks without the help of users. Based on the information of deleted data and with the format of disk image files, VMcol locates the area of useless data of disk image files directly instead of scanning the disk image file. In addition, VMcol can lively reclaim the useless data of disk image file with ongoing service of guest VM, which never produces a temporary disk image file. So user deletes file in a guest VM, meanwhile, physical free-space increases by the same space automatically. The prototype of VMcol is implemented based on Xen 3.3.0 to reclaim the unused space in locate *qcow* image storage. *qcow* is a kind of virtual machine image format supported by qemu in the full-virtualized environment.

The rest of this paper is organized as follows. We discuss the related work in section 2. Section 3 presents the design and implementation of VMcol. Section 4 provides a quantitative evaluation of our system. Finally, we conclude and present the future work in section 5.

2 Related Work

Much work has been done towards the garbage collection of virtual machine image files to improve the storage utilization.

VMware offers the shrinking virtual disk function of Virtual Disk Manger, named shrink [16], the third part tools, to release the worthless data of virtual machine image file for collecting the garbage blocks. Users start the function while shutting down the corresponding guest VM. It is notable fact that VMware shrinks the virtual disks after rescanning and defragmenting the virtual disks with interrupting the service of guest virtual machines. During shrinking, the system needs the other same space as the virtual disks, which are stored, for a while, the old virtual machine image file, the storage medium of virtual disk. Although defragmenting the virtual disk and using extra space transferring reduce disk fragment which collecting deleted data for the virtual machine image file produces, the process takes a long time and interrupts the service of guest VMs.

Moreover, Microsoft also uses the regularly manual way to compact *virtual hard disk* (VHD) [17, 18], a virtual machine image file, after shutting down the guest VM, the process, compacting VHD, takes a long time and brings high overheads. Lately Microsoft makes use of Hype-V to shrink VHD. Despite decreasing the overhead and cutting down the time of shrinking the virtual machine image file, the process requires the high configuration.

In view of reducing the size of the image file with processing the worthless data of the virtual machine image file, IBM also provides the shrink-vDisk technology [9]. These methods might alleviate this problem to some extent but service which the guest VMs offer is still interrupted and restarted which results in extra overheads, or the high configuration is required in environment.

Besides, Parallax [5], an effective cluster volume manager for virtual disks, provides an approach to reclaim deleted data for the virtual machine image files without interrupting the services. The approach is to have users mark the position of the deleted data, similar to do checkpoint, when deleting data in the guest virtual machine, and then run a garbage collector that tracks metadata references across the entire shared block store and frees any unallocated blocks. Unfortunately, a garbage collector must scan the metadata references to locate the position before reclaim the deleted data in the virtual machine image files.

Compared with above tools, VMcol brings some advantages. First, the system never shuts down guest VMs to collect garbage for the virtual machine image files, which avoids the overhead of restarting guest VMs. Besides, the system locates the garbage in the virtual machine image files without rescanning the image files. What's more, the system automatically runs without the high configuration.

3 Design and Implementation

In this section, we describe the design and implementation of VMcol to collect the garbage for virtual machine image file in Xen. The two objections behind VMcol are user-level transparent and live collection of garbage. So the idea of VMcol is that when guest OS deletes data in the virtual disks the corresponding useless data of virtual machine image file is also reclaimed automatically.

3.1 System Overview

We present an overview of VMcol's architecture in Fig. 1 and discuss components in more detail in the following subsections. VMcol consists of a *File Operation Control* (FOC) layer responsible for getting information of file deletion in the guest VMs in real-time and a *File Operation Execution* (FOE) layer responsible for deleting useless data of virtual machine image files.

Taking into accounts the semantic gap and the encapsulation of VM, FOC layer inserts a foreground monitor in a guest OS to perceive the file deletion. The foreground monitor is capable of recording the virtual addresses of deleted data for collecting garbage. The foreground monitor is to capture and get the virtual addresses of deleted file dynamically using a real-time analysis mechanism described later in section 3.2.

In FOE layer, a deletion module is inserted in user space of driver domain. The deletion module is capable of lively deleting the useless data of the virtual machine image file based on the virtual addresses of the data from the FOC layer. Before deleting data, the deletion module implements a content hash based on the format of *qcow* image [16] to map the virtual addresses of data into the beginning and end offset of useless data in virtual machine image file.

Given that the ownership of writing file is only one in OS, VMcol offers a mid-deletion system call to support the deletion module deleting the data of the image file directly. The mid-deletion system call detailed in section 3.3 ensures that while the tapdisk process [6] reads and writes a virtual machine image file the deletion module also deletes the data of the image file transparently.

In the full-virtualized Xen environment, transmitting information of file deletion between the FOC layer and the FOE layer needs to avoid damaging the inter-domain communication, reducing the complexity of system. The resolution is done with the help of XML-RPC between a transmitter in each guest VM and a receiver in the driver domain. The receiver offers a mapping table that stores the identity, as [Image Position, MAC] of pair, of each other guest VM in the same physical machine. This table is updated when a guest VM is configured.

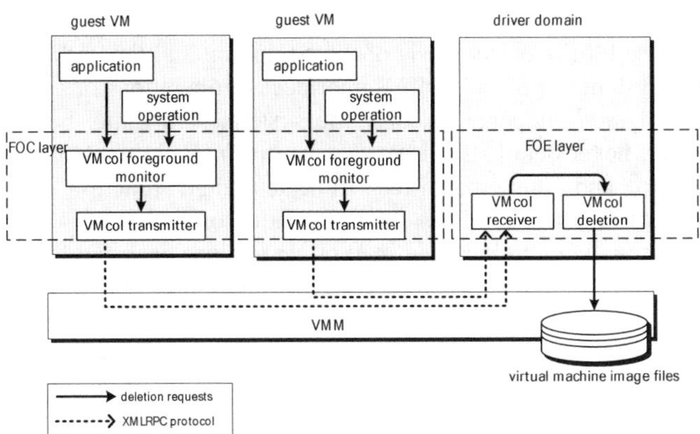

Fig. 1. System Structure

3.2 Deletion Monitor and Analyzer

In order to get the information of file deletion from the guest VMs transparently, the foreground monitor in the kernel of each guest OS monitors file deletion in real-time. To enable such real-time and low-overhead procedure of monitoring the virtual addresses of the deleted file, VMcol employs a real-time analysis mechanism. When a guest OS invokes the deletion function, the foreground monitor captures and analyzes environment information of the goal file to get the inode of the file. Before the OS's deletion function deletes file, the foreground monitor based on the *inode* takes advantage of layout of file system to get a set of offset addresses and start address of virtual disk in memory, which reduces extra virtual disk I/O. But the foreground monitor still brings in a little VCPU cost for analyzing the file deletion.

Given that the information of file deletion monitored in kernel space is read by transmission process in user space, the foreground monitor makes use of relay file system [28], which Linux offers to transmit data from kernel to user space efficient, to record the information of deletion in a log directly.

3.3 Lively Collect Data Block

The heart of VMcol is to reclaim the goal blocks of virtual machine image file with ongoing service of guest VM. Xen-Linux based on ext3 file system, however, never allows multi-process to modify a file at the same time or offers a function of reclaiming blocks of a file directly on the basis of beginning and end offsets in the file. Thus, we design a mid-deletion system call which meets the goal of VMcol on reclaiming the useless data of the image files directly. In Xen-Linux, the mid-deletion system call is to add an interface, which is provided to the VMcol's deletion module, and a mid-deletion function, which details reclaiming blocks of file. The interface of the mid-deletion system call includes three parameters, the handle of the file, the beginning and the end offsets in the file.

In order to ensure the compatibility of VMcol, the mid-deletion function invokes the interface of the truncate range function. The truncate range function is an operation of *inode* to release blocks on the basis of the beginning and the end offset in the file. The virtual file system (VFS) only offers interfaces of operations of *inode*, implementing operations of *inode* depends on disk file system. Xen-Linux based on ext3 file system, however, never details the truncate range of *inode* in ext3 file system. Therefore, we design and implement the truncate range function of ext3 *inode*, *ext3_truncate_range*, which modifies the information of ext3 *inode* to reclaim deleted blocks of file. The *i_block* field stored in ext3 *inode* maps each file block number into a logical block numbers in disk partition for accessing a file. The *ext3_truncate_range* function, therefore, modifies the *i_block* field and then informs the super block of file system to update the bitmap of disk. As shown in Fig. 2, the *i_block* field having 15 entries utilizes extra indirect blocks to form a four-layer tree structure. Each leaf node of the tree structure stores a logical block number of file data blocks in an order of file block numbers. So the function releases the leaf nodes in bottom-up according to the range of file block numbers.

As above discussed, the *ext3_truncate_range* function converts the beginning and the end offsets into the beginning and end file block numbers, so as to find and release the range of leaf nodes in the *i_block* field. Due to releasing range of leaf nodes across several layers, the function releases the leaf nodes of the same layers in batch to minimize memory and CPU cost. Deleting the leaf nodes is repeat and trivial, so we implement an iterative algorithm which deletes the leaves in bottom-up. So the time cost of the algorithm is $4N$ (N is the value at each level). In order to lower the additional overhead, the function never handles the data of which size is less than a block.

Although the procedure of deleting the leaf nodes of *i_block* field of original *inode* brings in *file hole*, the original *inode* corresponding to file never be replaced with a new *inode* so as to keep the guest VM running. The procedure never requires a lot of memory or extra disk space to store the temporary file.

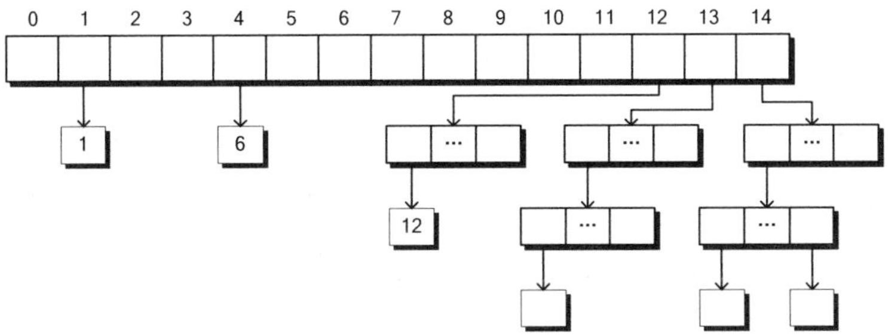

Fig. 2. Tree structure of *i_block* field in *ext3 inode*

Given that modifying the *inode* results in the data inconsistency between disk and memory, the mid-deletion function modifies page cache before invoking the interface of the truncate range operation of *inode*. Xen-Linux provides a system function, *vmtruncate_range*, to ensure the consistency of the range from the beginning to the end offset of the file between memory and disk. The mid-deletion function, with the help of *vmtruncate_range* function, grabs a truncate mutex on the *inode* and then unmaps the deleted data in pages. After clearing the trace of deleted data in page cache, the function invokes the interface of the truncate range operation. The mid-deletion function does not release the mutex on the *inode* until the truncate range operation returns.

4 Evaluation

We have implemented a functional prototype of VMcol based on *ext3* file system in the Xen 3.3.0 environment. In this section, we present an experimental evaluation of our VMcol with realistic workloads. There are two questions that this evaluation attempts to answer. First, how much space VMcol saves? Second, what are the overheads that VMcol imposes on the different sizes of larger files? To address these questions, we delete a set of files (with size of 100MB, 300MB, 500MB, 700MB, and 900MB files, respectively) as workloads in a guest VM with VMcol (called VMcol VM), which is compared with a guest VM without VMcol (called native VM).

In all experiments, the application server is server-class machine with one Pentium Dual-Core E5200 CPU (2.5GHz and two cores) running at 2GB of memory, and 500GB SATA disk (rotation speed is 7200rps). In addition, the server runs Xen 3.3.0 distribution along with full-virtualized Linux domains using linux-2.6.18, and both used x86_64-bit mode. The two guest VMs are allocated 512MB memory and 20GB virtual disk.

4.1 Improvement of Storage Utilization

Table 1 presents the real-time incremental free space in the virtual disk and the physical disk when the files are deleted in the VMcol VM. When the free space of virtual disk increases by a value, the free space of physical disk also increases by almost the same value. Therefore, the storage utilization is improved. The reason is that our system reclaims all the corresponding garbage space when files are deleted in the VMcol VM.

Table 1. The real-time incremental free space in the virtual disk and in the physical disk

Size of deleted file	Incremental free space of virtual disk	Incremental free space of physical disk	Accuracy
100MB	102604KB	102501KB	99.9%
300MB	307604KB	306681KB	99.7%
500MB	512604KB	511066KB	99.7%
700MB	717604KB	716168KB	99.8%
900MB	918508KB	917589KB	99.9%

4.2 Overall Performance

VMcol consists of FOC layer in a guest VM and FOE layer in the driver domain, so we evaluate performance of VMcol in the guest VM and in the driver domain, respectively.

In the Guest VM. In each guest OS, the VMcol's foreground monitor as a main part of VM-level layer is to capture and analyze the file deletion. Therefore, we concern the performance of the foreground monitor and overheads introduced by it when deleting files in a guest VM.

Fig. 3 shows the user and total VCPU utilization in the VMcol VM and in the native VM respectively when files are deleted in the two guest VMs. Comparing Fig. 3(a) and Fig. 3(b), the total VCPU utilization in the VMcol VM is almost the same in the native VM and the user VCPU utilization in the VMcol VM increases only a little. The reason is that VMcol costs some CPU to analyze the file deletion in the guest VM. Therefore, the low extra VCPU cost introduced by VMcol never impacts the performance of VCPU in the guest VM.

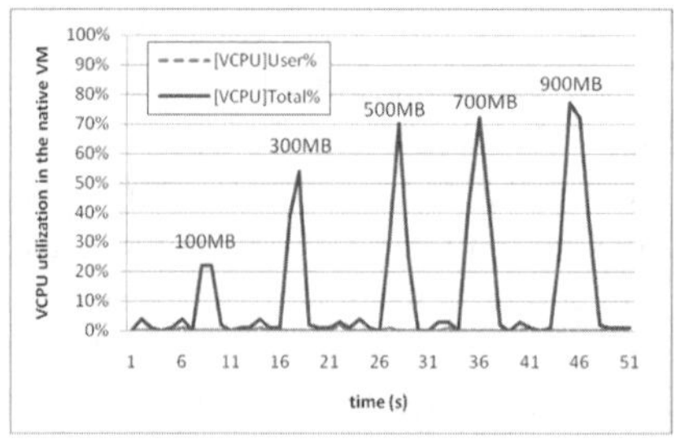

(a) VCPU utilization in the native VM

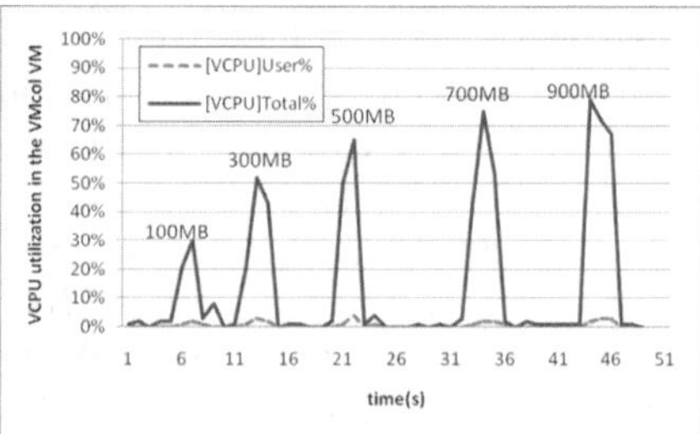

(b) VCPU utilization in the VMcol VM

Fig. 3. VCPU Utilization when files are deleted in the guest VM

As shown in Fig. 4, we compare the virtual disk I/O bandwidth of the two guest VMs when deleting the set of files. Fig. 4(a) shows the read bandwidth of two guest VMs is almost the same when deleting the files, same with the write bandwidth (shown in Fig. 4(b)), because VMcol uses relay file system to record the information of the deleted files in memory and transmits the information in real-time. The little difference is due to accessing the information of the deleted file.

As discussed above, the VMcol's foreground monitor impacts little the performance when deleting files in the guest VM.

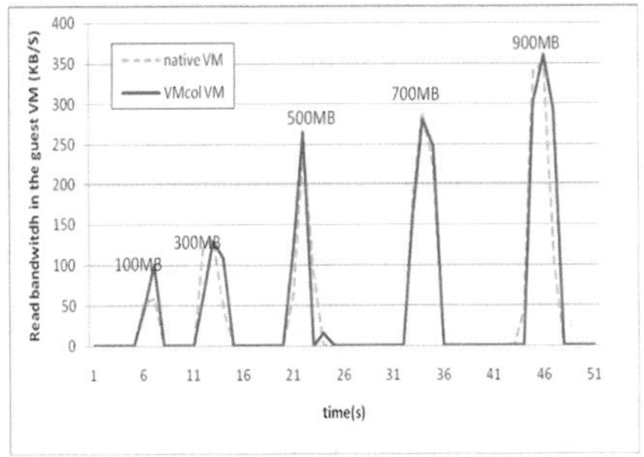

(a) Read bandwidth in two guest VMs

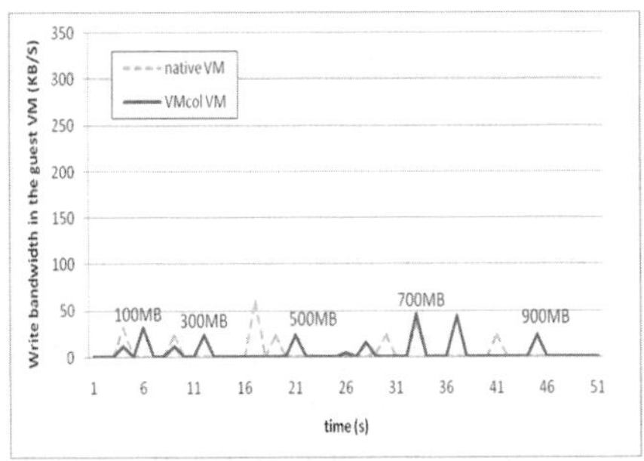

(b) Write bandwidth in two guest VMs

Fig. 4. Virtual disk I/O bandwidth when files are deleted in two guest VMs

In the Driver Domain. To evaluate the overheads introduced by VMcol in the driver domain, we evaluate the CPU utilization and bandwidth of disk I/O. Fig. 5 shows that the CPU utilization with VMcol is little higher than without VMcol. That means VMcol does not bring CPU overhead of server.

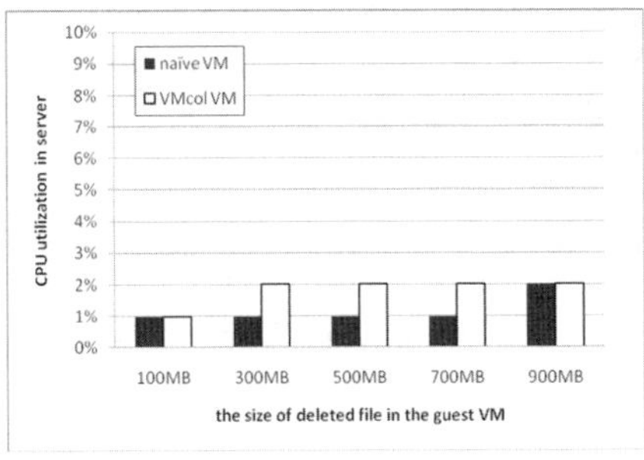

Fig. 5. The driver domain's CPU utilization when files are deleted in the guest VM

As shown in Fig. 6(a), the read bandwidths introduced by the VMcol VM and by the native VM are almost the same. However, the write bandwidth introduced by VMcol VM increases more than by the native VM in Fig. 6(b). The reason is that VMcol deletes the useless data of the *qcow* image file. We focus on the improvement of storage utilization, and the extra write bandwidth costs fewer than 25% of the whole write bandwidth, so the extra write overhead will not affect the privileged domain's performance.

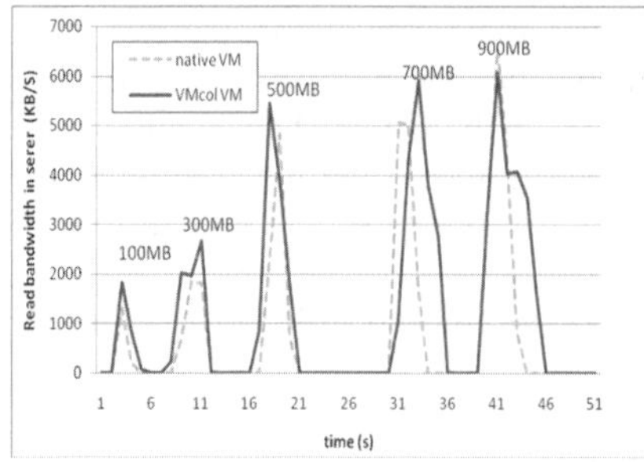

(a) Read overhead in the driver domain

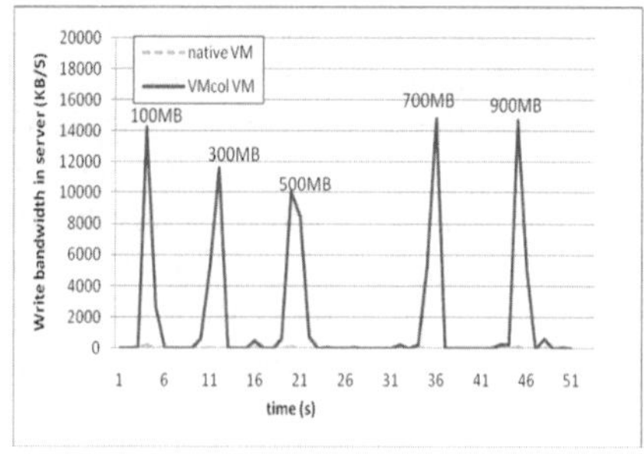

(b) Write overhead in the driver domain

Fig. 6. Disk overheads introduced by the VMcol VM and the native VM

5 Conclusion and Further Work

Due to the semantic gap between VMM and guest VM, there are lots of useless data deleted inside guest VM, as the VMM cannot notice the *delete* operation inside the VM, which leads to disk vanishing. To target this, we propose VMcol system, which provides a transparent and live disk space garbage collector for virtual machine images. The VMcol works as a transparent bridge between the VMM and guest VMs, part of VMcol is implemented inside the guest VM, and part of the VMcol is implemented in VMM. The VMcol perceives the data deletion in the guest VM, and reclaims the disk space which is released by guest VMs. Consequently, the available space inside the guest VMs are the same as the available space in the VMM. Our tests demonstrate that the VMcol can work transparently with low performance penalty in terms of CPU utilization and I/O bandwidth.

In the future, we will optimize the performance of VMcol with specific algorithms which can reduce the communication frequency between the VMM and guest VMs, and we will evaluate VMcol with intensive file deletion inside guest VM. We also will improve the universality of VMcol to make it applicable in other file system and even in cloud computing.

Acknowledgments. This work is supported by National 973 Key Basic Research Program under grant No.2007CB310900, NSFC under grant No.61073024 and 60973037, NCET under grant 07-0334, and Wuhan Chenguang Program under grant No.201050231075.

References

1. Barham, P., Dragovic, B., Fraser, K., Had, S., Harris, T., Ho, A.: Xen and the Art of Virtualization. In: Proceedings of the Nineteenth ACM Symposium on Operating Systems Principles, pp. 164–177
2. Clements, A.T., Ahmad, I., Vilayannur, M., Li, J.: Decentralized deduplication in SAN cluster file systems. In: Proceedings of USENIX 2009 (2009)

3. Fraser, K., Hand, S., Neugebauer, R., Pratt, I., Warfield, A., Williamson, M.: Safe Hardware Access with the Xen Virtual Machine Monitor. In: Proceedings of OASIS ASPLOS 2004 Workshop (October 2004)
4. Liguori, A., Linux, I.B.: Merging QEMU-DM upstream. Xen Summit (2007)
5. Meyer, D.T., Aggarwal, G., Cully, B., Lefebver, G., Feely, M.J., Hutchinson, N.C., Warfield, A.: Parallax: virtual disks for virtual machines. In: Proceedings of EuroSys 2008 (2008)
6. Matthews, J.N., Dow, E.M., Deshane, T., Hu, W., Bongio, J., Wilbur, P.F., Johnson, B.: Running Xen: a hands-on guide to the art of virtualization, April 10. Prentice-Hall, Englewood Cliffs (2008)
7. Reimer, D., Thomas, A., Ammons, G., Mummert, T., Alpern, B., Bala, V.: Opening black boxes: Using semantic information to combat virtual machine image sprawl. In: Proceedings of VEE 2008 (2008)
8. Shiyachk, D., Unterkircher, A., Habib, I.: Tools and Techniques for Managing Virtual Machine Images. In: César, E., et al. (eds.) Euro-Par 2008 Workshop. LNCS, vol. 5415. Springer, Heidelberg (2008)
9. Werner, E.: IBM system storage SAN Volume Controller (SVC 4.2), IBM Corporation (2008)
10. Zanussi, T., Yaghmour, K., Wisniewski, R., Moore, R., Dagenais, M.: relayfs: An efficient unified approach for transmitting data from kernel to user space. In: Linux Symposium (2003)
11. Bovet, D., Cesati, M.: Understanding the Linux Kernel, 3rd edn., pp. 729–757. O'Reilly, Sebastopol (2005)
12. Gupta, A., Hutchinson, N.C.: Efficient Disk Space Management for Virtual Machines, http://www.usenix.org/events/fast05/wips/slides/gupta.pdf
13. Jiang, L.S.: Hot Resize Multipath Storage Volume on Linux with SVC, http://www03.ibm.com/support/techdocs/atsmastr.nsf/WebIndex/TD105262
14. Sethuramalingam, A., Iyer, M., Thirupugalsamy, R.: Implementation of Insert/Delete System call for the Ext3 File system, http://www.cs.sunysb.edu/~aponniah/report/ext3insdel-report.pdf
15. Laverick, M.: Using and automating the virtual disks shrink feature, http://www.scribd.com/doc/2682740/Using-and-Automating-the-Virtual-Disk-Shrink-Featurewhitepaper
16. Vmware shrinking virtual disks, http://www.vmware.com/support/ws5/doc/ws_disk_shrink.html
17. VHD file format, http://en.wikipedia.org/wiki/VHD_file_format
18. VHD resize, http://www.windowsreference.com/free-utilities/vhd-resizer-resize-microsofts-vhd-hyper-v-files/
19. The qcow image, http://people.gnome.org/~markmc/qcow-image-format-version-1.html
20. Xen 3.0 Users' Manual, http://tx.downloads.xensource.com/downloads/docs/user

Predictable Cloud Provisioning Using Analysis of User Resource Usage Patterns in Virtualized Environment*

Hyukho Kim, Woongsup Kim, and Yangwoo Kim**

Dept. of Information and Communication Engineering, Dongguk University
Seoul, 100-715, South Korea
{hulegea,woongsup,ywkim}@dongguk.edu

Abstract. Cloud computing is emerging paradigm based on the virtualization technology which supports easily accessing and integrating heterogeneous computing resources which are dispersed in the different locations. One of challenges which Cloud system has to solve is resource provisioning. In Cloud system, users can run diverse applications and require varying amount of resources. Therefore it is imperative of implementing the execution environment that can guarantee the performance of various applications balancing resource requests and the amount of resources provisioned. In this paper, we propose a prediction-based resource provisioning model with which Cloud system can analyze the resource usage history and predict the needed resource amount in advance before applications start requesting new/additional resources. In our model, we define several resource usage patterns and we employ resource usage history to find out the best-fit usage pattern at the given time window. The best-fit patterns determine whether Cloud system allocates additional resources to guarantee performance or release resources to prevent resource over-provisioning. As a result, our approach successfully predicts the amount of needed resources, and hence reduces the time to prepare the needed resources. In addition, our experiments show our model can utilize resources effectively while providing high level of services.

Keywords: Cloud computing, Virtualization, Provisioning model, Resource usage pattern.

1 Introduction

Cloud is a virtualized resource pool that is able to handle the diversity of different workload through the resource provisioning based on virtual machine (VM) or physical machines [1, 2]. Cloud has to be able to provide monitoring service *about resource usage* for allocation and scheduling of resources, and support advanced resource management for automated resource and workload management. In other word, Cloud computing is the ultimate virtualization system and/or the virtual data

* This work was supported by a Ministry of Education, Science and Technology (MEST) grant funded by the Korea government(S-2010-A0104-0001, S-2010-A0004-00012).
** Corresponding author.

T.-h. Kim et al. (Eds.): GDC/CA 2010, CCIS 121, pp. 84–94, 2010.

center or virtual computing center to which the automated system management, workload balancing, and virtualization technology have been applied [3, 4].

Server consolidation using virtualization technology [5] can reduce over the use of resource provisioning efficiently but management cost and complexity for resource provisioning increase at the same time, because a system and/or several systems run on Cloud system concurrently and all the virtual machines in physical servers are competing with each other for satisfying of QoS requirements [6, 7]. So, it is imperative to allocate virtualized resources dynamically at the appropriate time over monitoring all VM's workload [8, 9, 10, 11]. Recently, efficient and advanced mechanisms [12, 13, 14, 15, 16] for Cloud resource management are studied. However resource management mechanisms still needs improvement for handling many resource requests at a appropriate time while reducing resource over-provisioning over time-varying resource requests, because it is difficult to predict the amount of resources which all virtual machines in physical servers need.

In this paper, we present the prediction-based Cloud provisioning model that it can prepare the needed resource amount before users request to by analyzing the resource usage using the resource usage patterns of each user. The proposed model generates the usage patterns per each user with information which is from user application on virtual machines. The resource usage patterns consist of resource type, service type, time using the services, the resource type and amount in process of time. This model can do resource provisioning in advance because it predicts the service and resource amount through the generated resource patterns. As a result, this model can reduce the time to prepare the needed resource amount and it can use resources efficiently. It can also provide high-level service to users. And we evaluated the proposed model with the threshold-based provisioning model.

The rest of this paper is organized as follows. In Section2, we present the limitation of the existing provisioning mechanism. In Section 3, we explain our proposed model and section 4 present our experiments and their analysis. Finally, we conclude in Section 5.

2 Problem Statement

In this section, we present limitations of the existing provisioning mechanism (e.g. Threshold-based provisioning) through experiments. Threshold-based provisioning in the existing systems uses a resource allocation policy which allocates additional resource only when the resource usage of system exceeds the particular point (threshold) over a period of time.

In experiments, we used two virtual machines in a physical machine and carried out threshold-based provisioning. If the resource usage of virtual machine exceeds 60%, we allocated second virtual machine. On the contrary, if the resource usage of virtual machine uses below 30%, we released second virtual machine.

For experiments of threshold-based provisioning, we made a system with a server that provides virtual machines for applications, and several workload-generating clients. Xen server 3.0.1 is installed in the server node which has dual Intel Xeon 3.2GHz CPUs and 2GB memory. We used Indexer Service in Grid IR system for measuring of system performance. We also use TRAC [17] data (784MB of 49,026 HTML files).

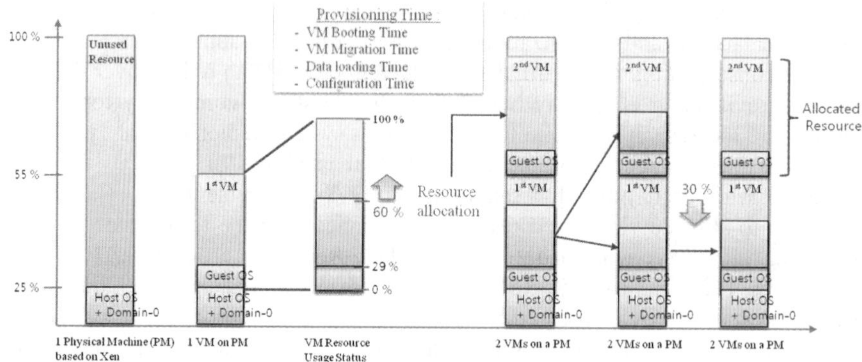

Fig. 1. The limitations of threshold-based resource provisioning

As you can see in Fig. 1, threshold-based provisioning took long time for allocation of the additional resource such as virtual machine migration time, booting time, data loading time, and configuration time. In resource allocation case, total provisioning time can slow down the system performance. Threshold-based provisioning holds the added resource until the particular conditions are satisfied because it doesn't have mechanisms for resource release. This leads to the system's resource waste in resource availability.

Fig. 2 shows the resource usage history of the threshold based system over a period of time. This system allocated or released the resource based on the particular threshold values (e.g. allocation threshold value is 60% and release threshold value is 30%). We marked the resource history with red circles and blue Xs that indicate the resource allocation time and the resource release time respectively.

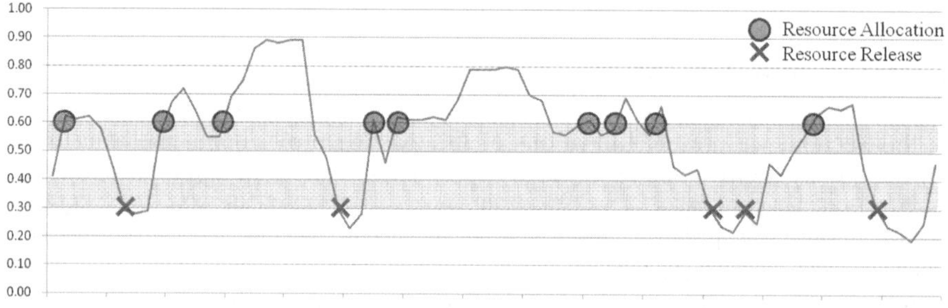

Fig. 2. The number of resource allocation and release in the threshold-based system

The total number of resource allocation and release in this system was 14 for the time period of this experiment. This system needs the advanced resource management mechanism for handling the lots of resource allocation and release requests if all requests are suitable. However, if not, we can regard 14 requests as an inappropriate request. We classified appropriate requests and inappropriate requests and marked them on the resource history graph again. As you can see Fig. 3, we marked with circles and triangles.

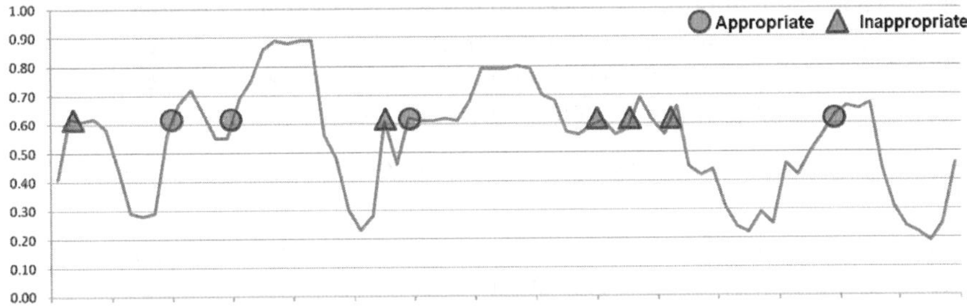

Fig. 3. The classification of resource allocation requests

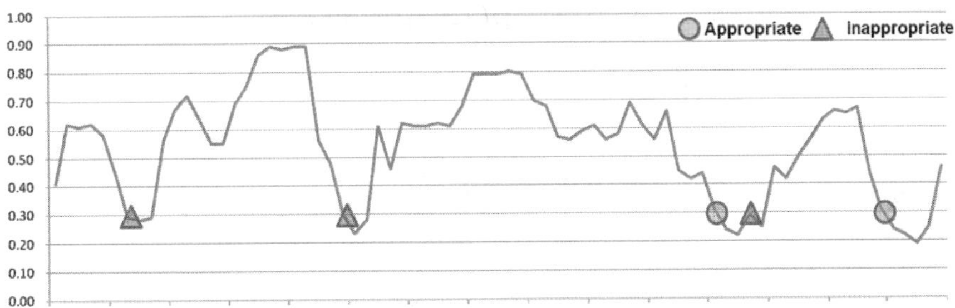

Fig. 4. The classification of resource release requests

In resource allocation case, three of nine requests are appropriate and six are inappropriate. And in resource release case, two of five requests are appropriate and three are inappropriate.

As a result, we figured out several limitations from the threshold based provisioning, which are as follows:

- Frequent provisioning request
- System performance degradation by inappropriate resource allocating and releasing
- Resource waste by the inappropriate request handling

3 Predictable Provisioning Model

3.1 Patterns Classification and Definition

Our proposed model employs the resource usage flow pattern to generate resource usage patterns with log data which is collected from virtual machines. Before generating usage patterns, we consider two cases: one is the case of resource utilization increase and the other is the case of resource utilization decrease (Fig. 5).

For the resource utilization increase case, we classify four types which are as follows:

1) The gradient of resource utilization increase is less than 15 degree
2) The gradient of resource utilization increase is less than 30 degree
3) The gradient of resource utilization increase is less than 45 degree
4) The gradient of resource utilization increase is above 45 degree

For the resource utilization decrease case, we also classify four types which are as follows:

1) The gradient of resource utilization decrease is less than 15 degree
2) The gradient of resource utilization decrease is less than 30 degree
3) The gradient of resource utilization decrease is less than 45 degree
4) The gradient of resource utilization decrease is above 45 degree

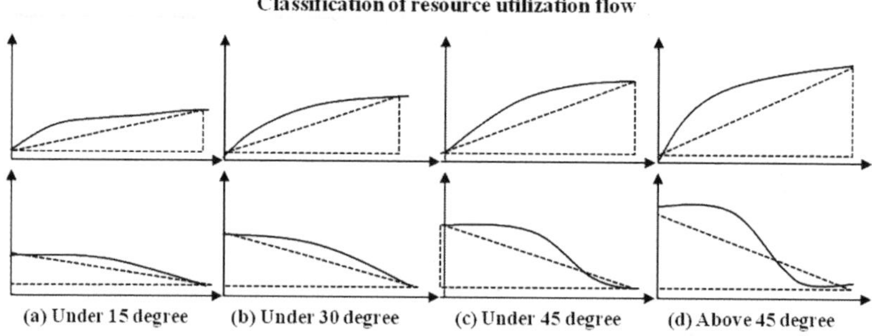

Fig. 5. Classification of resource utilization flow

We classified the resource utilization with the above method, and then we define pattern values based on classified types. Pattern values are shown as follow (see Table 1):

Table 1. The definition of pattern values

Value	Pattern	Conditions
0	000	Recorded increasing of less than 15 degree
1	001	Recorded increasing of less than 30 degree
2	010	Recorded increasing of less than 45 degree
3	011	Recorded increasing above 45 degree
-0	100	Recorded decreasing of less than 15 degree
-1	101	Recorded decreasing of less than 30 degree
-2	110	Recorded decreasing of less than 45 degree
-3	111	Recorded decreasing above 45 degree

3.2 Pattern-Based Resource Allocation and Release

The proposed provisioning calculates the inclination about the change of resource utilization after the pattern generation. For calculation, we used trigonometrical function and a table of trigonometrical function.

Fig. 6 shows pattern values which are generated by data it collected at five minutes intervals. In the proposed model, we used these pattern values to allocate or release the additional resource. And the proposed model makes a decision to allocate the additional resource if the total value is over 5 which is added pattern values for twenty minutes. In contrary, the proposed model makes a decision to release the added resource if the total value is under -5. The proposed model not only uses pattern values, but also uses the threshold value (e.g. resource utilization 60% and 30%). For example, we set the threshold value on 60% for resource allocation in Fig. 6.

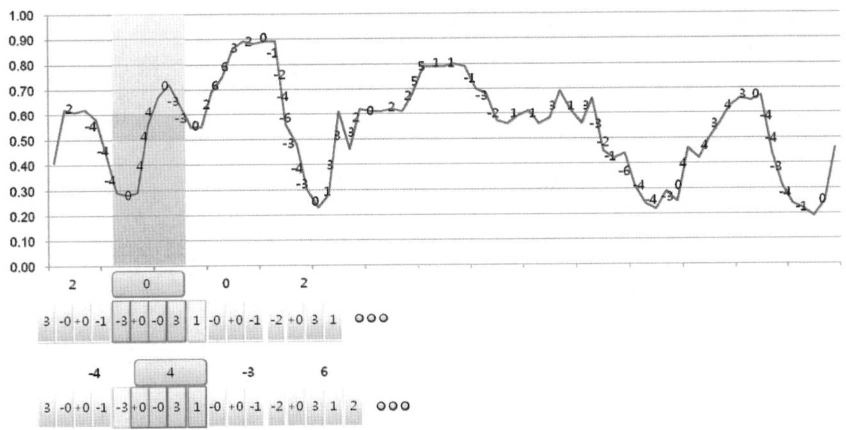

Fig. 6. Pattern values from resource utilization flow

Fig. 7 shows the points of resource allocation and release with pattern values. The number of allocation requests is 4 and the number of release requests is 4. In comparison with threshold-based provisioning model, the proposed model can reduce the total number of allocation and release requests significantly.

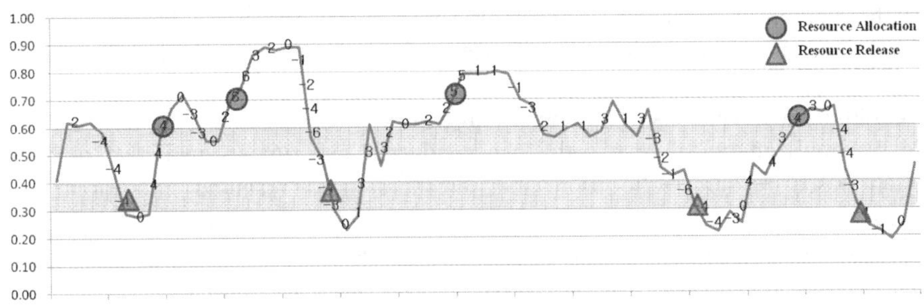

Fig. 7. Resource allocation and release based on pattern values

4 Experiments

4.1 Experimental Configuration

We used 6 nodes in our experiments. Each computing node has two 3.00 GHz CPUs, 1GB Memory, 120 GB local disk space, and connected to the others by Ethernet. We used only a 1Gbps Ethernet for the network communication. Every node uses Fedora Linux Core 8. The home directory is shared by NFS, and each node has own local disk. We also designed and implemented Indexer Service in Grid IR system for measuring of system performance. We also use TRAC data (784MB of 49,026 HTML files). And we used additional tools for experiments such as Apache Ant 1.6.5, J2SDK 1.5.0.19, Apache Lucene 2.4.1, and Apache Log4j-1.2.8.

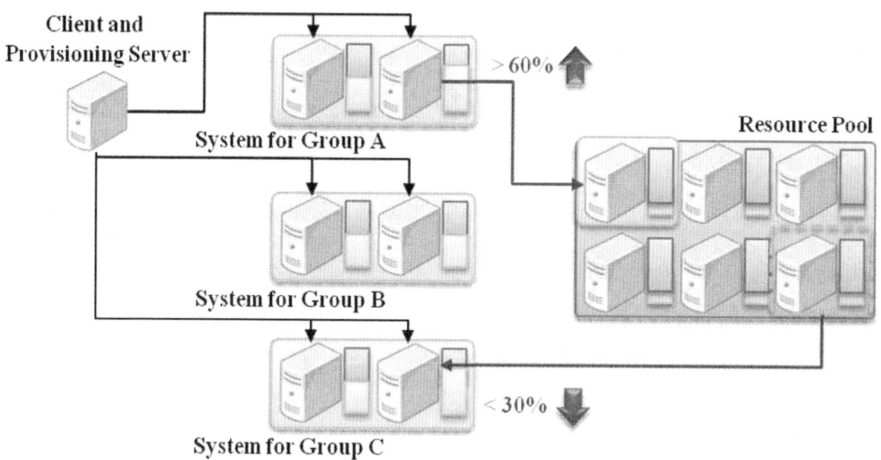

Fig. 8. The Experiment environment

4.2 Pattern-Based Analysis Experiments with the Existing Resource History

Firstly, we conducted experiments with the existing resource history which is made in advance. As we mentioned before, we conducted comparative experiments with threshold-based provisioning. In threshold-based model, the threshold value is 60% for resource allocation and the threshold value is 30% for resource release.

1) Comparative Analysis of Resource Allocation

Fig. 9 shows analytical results that we conducted experiments with two model - pattern-based resource allocation and threshold-based resource allocation. The number of resource allocation in threshold-based model is eight and only four of eight requests are appropriate. In contrary, the number of resource allocation in pattern-based model is five and four of five allocations are appropriate.

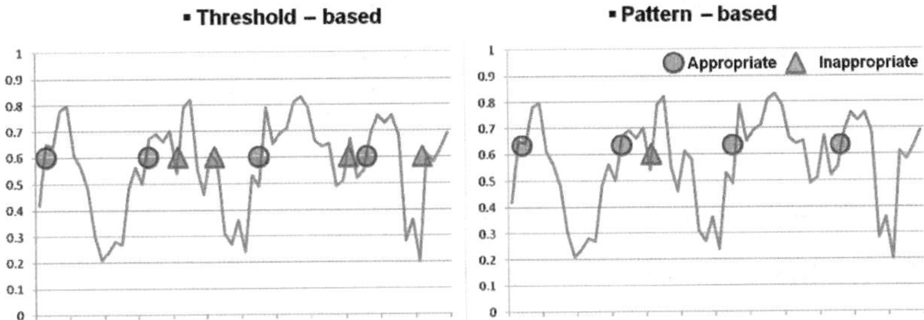

Fig. 9. Resource allocation with the existing resource history

Table 2 is the overall results. The success rate of threshold-based model is 50% and the success rate of pattern-based model is 80%. As a result, our proposed model is 60% better than threshold-based model.

Table 2. Comparative analysis of resource allocation

	Appropriate	Inappropriate	Total	Rate
Threshold	4	4	8	50%
Pattern	4	1	5	80%

2) Comparative Analysis of Resource Release

Fig. 10 shows analytical results from the experiments of pattern-based resource release and threshold-based resource release. The number of resource release in threshold-based model is 5 and three times of total requests are appropriate only. In contrary, the number of resource release in pattern-based model is 3 and all requests are appropriate.

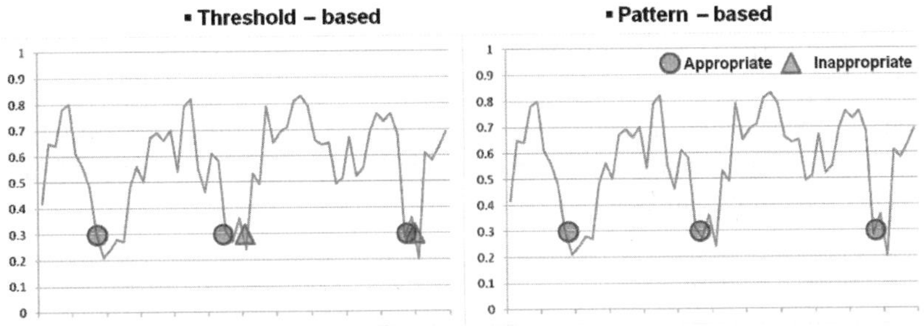

Fig. 10. Resource release with the existing resource history

Table 3 shows the overall results. The success rate of threshold-based model is 60% and the success rate of pattern-based model is 100%. As a result, the proposed model is 60% better than threshold-based model.

Table 3. Comparative analysis of resource release

	Appropriate	Inappropriate	Total	Rate
Threshold	3	2	5	60%
Pattern	3	0	3	100%

4.3 Pattern-Based Analysis Experiments in a Physical Server

Secondly, we conducted experiments with a server that the load generator was generating lots of workload in real time. We also conducted comparative experiments with threshold-based provisioning.

1) Comparative Analysis of Resource Allocation

We marked the resource history graph with red circles, red Xs, blue circles, and blue Xs. Red circle and blue circle present appropriate allocation time and red X and blue X present inappropriate allocation time. Fig. 11 shows analytical results that we conducted experiments with two models. The number of resource allocation in threshold-based model is seven and four times of total requests are appropriate only. In contrary, the number of resource allocation in pattern-based model is five and four times of total requests are appropriate.

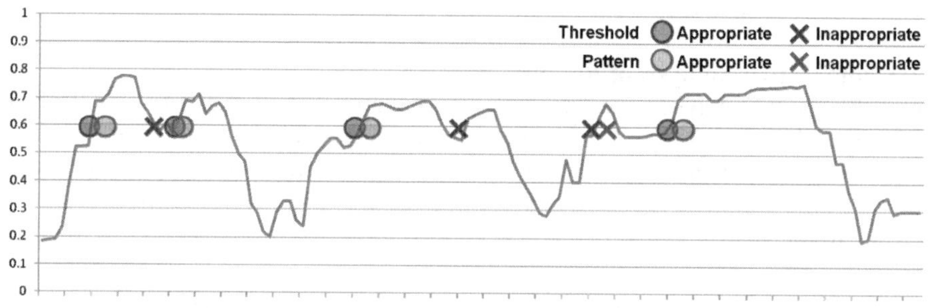

Fig. 11. Resource allocation in resource history in real time

Table 4 is the overall results. The success rate of threshold-based model is 57% and the success rate of pattern-based model is 80%. As a result, the proposed model is 23% better than threshold-based model.

Table 4. Comparative analysis of resource allocation in a server in real time

	Appropriate	Inappropriate	Total	Rate
Threshold	4	3	7	57%
Pattern	4	1	5	80%

2) Comparative Analysis of Resource Release

Fig. 12 shows analytical results that we conducted experiments with two models. The number of resource release in threshold-based model is five and two times of total requests are appropriate only. In contrary, the number of resource release in pattern-based model is two and all requests are appropriate.

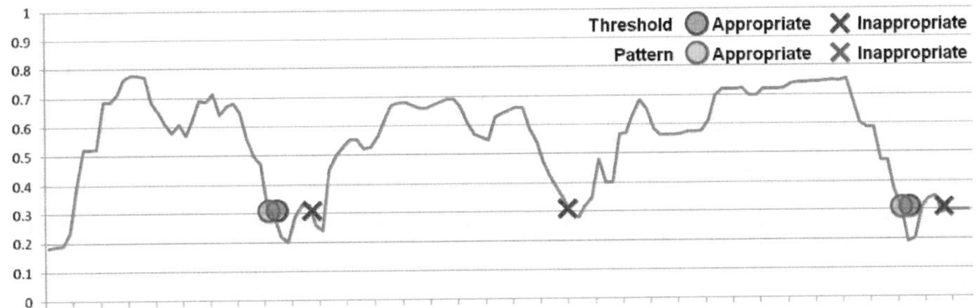

Fig. 12. Resource release in resource history in real time

Table 5 is the overall results. The success rate of threshold-based model is 40% and the success rate of pattern-based model is 100%. As a result, the proposed model is much better than threshold-based model.

Table 5. Comparative analysis of resource release in a server in real time

	Appropriate	Inappropriate	Total	Rate
Threshold	2	3	5	40%
Pattern	2	0	2	100%

5 Conclusions

In this paper, we proposed the prediction-based Cloud provisioning model that can prepare the needed resource amount before users begin to request by using the resource usage patterns based on analysis of resource usage history. We conducted various experiments for showing the advantages of the proposed model in comparison with the existing provisioning model. The proposed model, as experimental results have shown, can reduce the number of resource allocation requests and resource release requests. The success rate of resource allocation in the proposed model is better than the threshold-based model and the success rate of resource release also is better than the existing model. As a result, this model can reduce the time to prepare the needed resource amount and use resources efficiently.

Although the proposed model has several advantages on the resource allocation and release aspects, still there are more areas for further improvements. We plan to conduct additional experiments with various types of data to find accurate patterns and pattern values. Moreover it remains to simulate the applicability and the usefulness of the proposed model in real system.

References

1. Buyya, R., Yeo, C.S., Venugopal, S.: Market-Oriented Cloud Computing: Vision, Hype, and Reality for Delivering IT Services as Computing Utilities. In: Proc. Of the 10th IEEE International Conference on High Performance Computing and Communications (2008)
2. Vaquero, L.M., Rodero-Merino, L., Caceres, J., Lindner, M.: A Break in the Clouds: Towards a Cloud Definition. ACM SIGCOMM Computer Communication Review 39(1) (2009)
3. Li, H., Sedayao, J., Hahn-Steichen, J., Jimison, E., Spence, C., Chahal, S.: Developing an Enterprise Cloud Computing Strategy. Korea Information Processing Society Review (2009)
4. Vouk, M.A.: Cloud computing — Issues, research and implementations, Information Technology Interfaces. In: 30th International Conference (ITI 2008), pp. 31–40 (2008)
5. Barham, P., Dragovic, B., Fraser, K., Hand, S., Harris, T., Ho, A., Neugebauery, R., Pratt, I., Wareld, A.: Xen and the Art of Virtualization. In: Proc. of 19th ACM in Symposium on Operating Systems Principles (2003)
6. Sotomayor, B., Keahey, K., Foster, I.: Combining batch execution and leasing using virtual machines. In: Sotomayor, B., Keahey, K., Foster, I. (eds.) ACM 17th International Symposium on High Performance Distributed Computing, pp. 87–96 (2008)
7. Keahey, K., Foster, I., Freeman, T., Zhang, X.: Virtual workspaces: Achieving quality of service and quality of life in the Grids. Scientific Programming 13(4), 265–275 (2006)
8. Irwin, D., Chase, J., Grit, L., Yumerefendi, A., Becker, D., Yocum, K.G.: Sharing networked resources with brokered leases. In: USENIX Annual Technical Conference, pp. 199–212 (2006)
9. Emeneker, W., Jackson, D., Butikofer, J., Stanzione, D.: Dynamic Virtual Clustering with Xen and Moab. In: Min, G., Di Martino, B., Yang, L.T., Guo, M., Rünger, G. (eds.) ISPA Workshops 2006. LNCS, vol. 4331, pp. 440–451. Springer, Heidelberg (2006)
10. Ruth, P., McGachey, P., Xu, D.: VioCluster: Virtualization for dynamic computational domain. IEEE International on Cluster Computing, 1–10 (2005)
11. Montero, R.S., Huedo, E., Llorente, I.M.: Dynamic deployment of custom execution environments in Grids. In: 2nd International Conference on Advanced Engineering Computing and Applications in Sciences, pp. 33–38 (2008)
12. Ruth, P., Rhee, J., Xu, D., Kennell, R., Goasguen, S.: Autonomic Live Adaptation of Virtual Computational Environments in a Multi-Domain Infrastructure. In: Proceedings of the 3rd IEEE International Conference on Autonomic Computing (ICAC 2006), pp. 5–14 (2006)
13. Bennani, M.N., Menasce, D.A.: Resource Allocation for Autonomic Data Centers Using Analytic Performance Models. In: Proceedings of the 2nd IEEE International Conference on Autonomic Computing (ICAC 2005), pp. 229–240 (2005)
14. Zheng, T., Yang, J., Woodside, M., Litoiu, M., Iszlai, G.: Tracking time-varying parameters in software systems with extended Kalman filters. In: Proceedings of the 2005 conference of the Centre for Advanced Studies on Collaborative Research, CASCON (2005)
15. Jiang, G., Chen, H., Yoshihira, K.: Discovering likely invariants of distributed transaction systems for autonomic system management. In: Proceedings of the 3rd IEEE International Conference on Autonomic Computing (ICAC 2006), pp. 199–208 (2006)
16. Ghanbari, S., Soundararajan, G., Chen, J., Amza, C.: Adaptive Learning of Metric Correlations for Temparature-Aware Database Provisioning. In: Proceedings of the 4th International Conference on Automatic Computing, ICAC 2007 (2007)
17. Text REtrieval Conference (TREC), `http://trec.nist.gov/`

Deployment of Solving Permutation Flow Shop Scheduling Problem on the Grid

Samia Kouki[1], Mohamed Jemni[1], and Talel Ladhari[2]

[1] Ecole Supérieure des Sciences et Techniques de Tunis, Research Laboratory UTIC, Tunis, Tunisia
Samia.kouki@esstt.rnu.tn, mohamed.jemni@fst.rnu.tn
[2] Ecole Polytechnique de Tunisie, Laboratory of Mathematical Engineering, Tunis, Tunisia
talel_ladhari2004@yahoo.fr

Abstract. This paper describes a parallel algorithm solving the m-machines, n-jobs, permutation flow shop scheduling problem as well as its deployment on a Grid of computers (Grid'5000). Our algorithm is basically a parallelization of the well known Branch and Bound method, which is an exact method for solving combinatorial optimization problems. We present, in particular, a new strategy of parallelization which uses some directives of communication between all processors in order to update the value of the Upper Bound. The purpose is to obtain the optimal scheduling of all the jobs as quickly as possible by modifying and adapting the classical sequential Branch and Bound method. The deployment of our application on the Grid gives good results and permits the resolution of new instances not yet resolved.

Keywords: Grid computing, Scheduling; Permutation Flow Shop, B&B algorithm, parallel algorithms, Parallel computing.

1 Introduction

Because of the increasing competition caused by globalization, companies have been forced to reduce the costs and improve the quality in order to maintain competitive position in the fast changing markets. Cost and quality are considered as key success factors of modern manufacturing industry. New sophisticated scheduling techniques play a crucial role in achieving such factors and help production planners and production managers to better organize and master the production activities.

Many practical environments and modern production systems such as paper bag factory, printing, oil, pharmaceutical, and textile industry can be modeled as a permutation flow shop problem. The permutation flow shop problem is one of hard problems in combinatorial optimization and scheduling theory. The interest in this classical NP-hard problem is motivated by its practical relevance and its challenging hardness. However, there exist efficient exact and heuristic methods for solving this problem [1] and [2]. Exact methods, give the optimal solution of the problem however, heuristics give approximation. For exact methods, the most known method is the

T.-h. Kim et al. (Eds.): GDC/CA 2010, CCIS 121, pp. 95–104, 2010.

Branch and Bound algorithm (B&B). Nevertheless, with serial machine, this method is limited, as it can solve only small size instances. For large scale instances, an exact resolution is often impractical due to the limited amount of resources. Therefore, parallel computing and grid computing can be good alternatives to reduce the computation time of large size problems.

Crainic and al. presented in [3], an exhaustive review of the state of the art related to B&B method. At the same context, in our previous paper [4] we presented a parallel distributed algorithm to solve the PFSP based on B&B method and dedicated to a cluster of machines. Our application treated the simplest lower Bound (LB1), and has been tested with Taillard's Benchmarks and gave good parallelization results.

In this paper we present the gridification of our parallel version of the B&B algorithm to solve the permutation flow shop problem (PFSP) with makespan criterion, using the national French Grid (Grid'5000). In fact, thanks to the huge number of resources provided by the grid computing, our objective is to propose a new solution in order to solve the permutation flow shop problem and in particular some unsolved instances of Taillard [5], or to reduce the running times of instances requiring many hours and even years to be solved.

Another originality aspect of our work is the use of the so-called LB7 lower bound of [1] to solve the PFSP. This lower bound is composed of tree levels; in every level a different lower bound is computed. To our knowledge, this lower bound had never been implemented in parallel. Our algorithm presents the first parallel implementation of the B&B.

This paper is organized as follows, first, we describe the Branch and Bound algorithm based on the lower bound (LB7), and then we present the gridified version of this algorithm. Finally we present our computational results performed on well-known benchmarks (Taillard), using the Grid'5000 [6]. We conclude the paper by a conclusion and the presentation of our future perspectives.

2 The Sequential B&B Algorithm Solving the PFSP with Makespan Criterion

In this paper, we investigate the permutation flow shop problem. This problem can be described as follows. Each job from the job set J = {1, 2… n} has to be processed on m machines M_1, M_2… M_m, in this order. The processing time of job j on machine M_i is p_{ij}. All jobs are ready for processing at time zero. The machines are continuously available from time zero onwards (no breakdowns). At any time, each machine can process at most one job and each job can be processed on at most one machine. No pre-emption is allowed (that is, once the processing of a job on a machine has started, it must be completed without interruption). Only permutation schedules are allowed (i.e. all jobs have the same ordering sequence on all machines). The problem is to find a processing order of the n jobs, such that the time C_{max} (makespan) is minimized. Based on the notation presented in [7], this problem is denoted $F \mid prmu \mid C_{max}$.

It is well-known that the case of two machines ($F_2 \mid \mid C_{max}$), could be easily solved using Johnson's rule which generates an optimal schedule in O(n log n) time [18][20]. For $m \geq 3$, however, the problem is shown to be strongly NP-hard [8].

To solve such kind of problems (hard combinatorial optimization problem), there exist mainly two classes of methods: exact methods and approximate methods.

Indeed, the B&B algorithm is an exact method applied in order to obtain the optimal solution to a wide class of combinatorial optimization and scheduling problems. It was introduced by Ignall and Shrage [19]. The principle of the B&B method is to make an implicit search through the space of all possible feasible solutions of the problem. These enumerative optimization methods require a substantial computing time and can subsequently only solve relatively small sized instance problems. In this subsection, we try to briefly describe the basic components of a classical B&B algorithm. Suppose that we have a discrete set S, and an optimal solution $x^* \in S$, such that $F(x^*) = \min F(x)\ \forall x \in S$, where F is called the objective function, S is called feasible region or domain and x feasible solution.

B&B is characterized by the three following basic components:

- A branching strategy splits the region of feasible solutions into subregions or subproblems through the addition of constraints. Convergence of B&B is assured if the size of each new generated subproblem is smaller than the original problem, and the number of feasible solutions to the original problem is finite.
- The lower bounding is an algorithm which provides a lower bound (LB), on the value of each solution in a subproblem generated by the branching scheme. A stronger bound eliminates relatively more nodes of the search tree. But if its computational requirements turn excessively large, it may become advantageous to search through larger parts of the tree, using a weaker but more quickly computable bound.
- A search strategy or exploration strategy selects a node from which to branch. For instance, there is the depth first strategy, the large first strategy and the best first strategy.

The following algorithm describes the ideas presented above:

1. LIST={S};
2. UB: value of some heuristic solutions. CurrentBest: heuristic solution
3. While LIST≠ Ø Do
4. Choose a branching node k from LIST
5. Remove k from LIST
6. Generate children child(i) for i=1,…,n_k and compute the corresponding lower bounds LB_i.
7. For i=1 To n_k DO
8. IF LB_i<UB Then
9. IF child(i) consists of a single solution THEN
10. UB= LB_i
11. CurrentBest= solution corresponding with child(i)
12. ELSE add child(i) to LIST

The figure (Fig.1) shows an example for the resolution of the PFSP using the B&B algorithm, in a single processor.

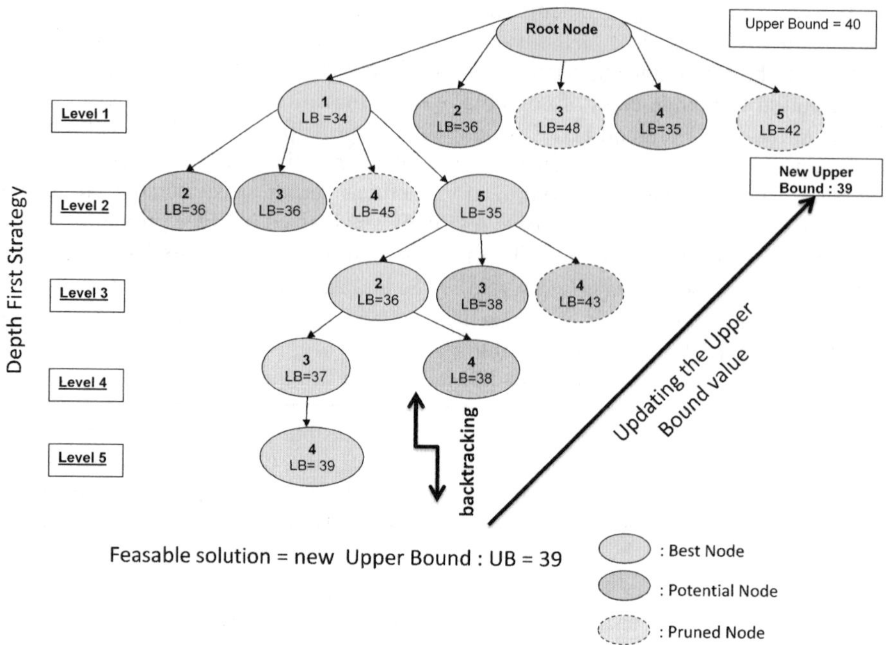

Fig. 1. Sequential resolution steps of the PFSP with B&B

3 The Use of Grid Computing

3.1 Introduction

In the past few years, new approaches of distributed and parallel architectures have emerged in order to coordinate the use of geographically dispersed underused resources and/or to solve hard and complex problems which require a large number of resources (processors).

The implementation of a parallel and distributed algorithm for solving a combinatorial optimization problem depends strictly on the hardware architecture on which the application will be deployed. In this context, in order to use the grid computing for solving the PFSP, we have to make some readjustment of our parallel algorithm that we presented in [4].

We have chosen the grid Grid5000 [6] for several reasons: Grid'5000 is suitable for complex scientific applications, large-scale simulations and data analysis, also it is a safe environment based on a high speed dedicated network.

3.2 Grid'5000 Architecture

Grid'5000 is a French research grid offering a large scale nationwide infrastructure for large scale parallel and distributed computing research. Seventeen laboratories are involved in France with the objective of providing the community a test bed allowing experiments in all the software layers between the network protocols up to the

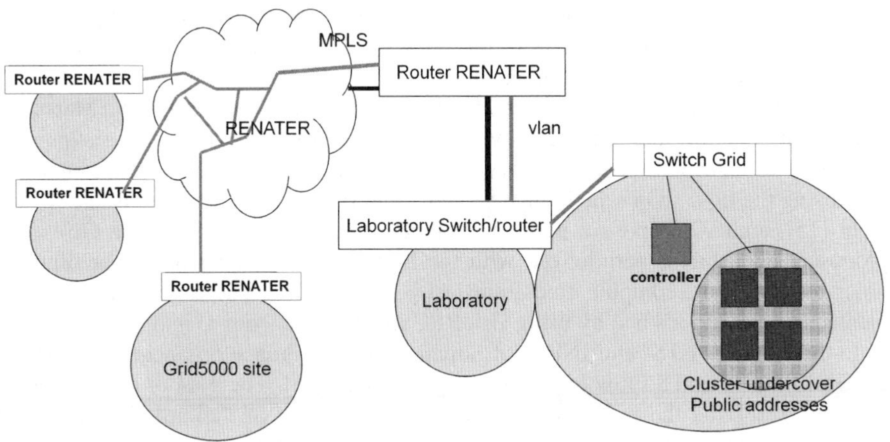

Fig. 2. The Grid'5000 architecture [10]

applications [6]. Fig. 2 shows clearly the hardware architecture of the Grid'5000, and its principal components.

3.3 Use of Grids to Solve Combinatorial Optimization Problems: State of the Art

The use of large scale architectures such as Grid computing in many scientific purposes is to satisfy the requirement of applications which are very time consuming and require a large number of processors to be solved. For example, in the combinatorial optimization field, and in particular for NP-hard problems, the use of grids is the best cure to decrease running times of some problems, and even to solve some problems not yet solved. In this context, several studies have been interested in Grid computing, which continues to attract more researchers.

In the following, we will present a review of state of the art related to the use of grids to solve combinatorial optimization problems.

In [11], authors were interested in the particular optimization problem; the quadratic assignment, in their paper they showed clearly that grid and cluster computing provide tremendous power to optimization methods, and especially for large instances of data.

Moreover, several researchers from the combinatorial optimization community have focused on the programming environment of large scale. In [12], M. Mezmaz, N. Melab and E.-G. Talbi present a parallel B&B algorithm using Grid'5000, they resolved the tail056 Taillard's benchmark in 25 days. In fact, although this may be considered as a promising result, more investments have to be investigated to reduce the running time which is still huge.

In [13], authors propose a dynamic load balancing approach for the parallel Branch and Bound algorithm on the computational grid. They perform their experimentations on the bi-objective permutation flow shop problem.

In [9], Bendjoudi, A., Melab, N., Talbi, E.-G propose a P2P design and implementation of a parallel B&B algorithm on the ProActive grid middleware. They applied their application to the flow shop scheduling problem and experimented it on a computational pool of 1500 CPUs from the GRID'5000. Remark that the authors used other benchmarks than we used in our study.

After that, in 2009, D. Caromel, A. di Costanzo, L. Baduel and S. Matsuoka propose in [14], a framework built over the master-workers approach that helps programmers to distribute problems over grids. They performed their experimental results using the flow shop scheduling problem, with randomly generated instances.

In [15], authors propose a parallel B&B algorithm which runs on the Grid. The proposed algorithm is parallelized with the hierarchical master-worker paradigm in order to efficiently compute fine-grain tasks on the Grid. The algorithm is implemented on the Grid testbed by using GridRPC middleware, Ninf-G and Ninf.

In this context, ETSI and INRIA at Sophia Antipolis France organized in 2005 the 2nd Grid PLUGTESTS Flow Shop Challenge Contest [16]. The goal of this contest is focused on solving the well known benchmarks problems of Taillard [5]. Indeed, in 2007, a challenge was launched in order to solve some of the instances of combinatorial optimization problem, for instance the PFSP, and a call for competition has been announced in the web [17].

4 Deployment of Our Parallel Distributed Application on Grid'5000

The high computing time of the PFSP solved by B&B algorithm is due to the computation of bounds which accomplished at each node of the search tree (as presented in Fig.1). The size of this tree is huge and can attempt several billions of nodes. Furthermore, not all combinatorial optimization problems can be parallelized, since this depends strictly on the nature and the characteristics of the problem to treat, and in particular on the quality of the upper and lower bounds.

Our implemented algorithm is based on updating the upper bound value in order to make the algorithm converging rapidly to the optimal solution. Also, the strategy of exploring the search tree is very important for the resolution of hard problems. In this paper we use the depth first strategy.

Our parallelization strategy is based on dividing the PFSP to many sub-problems to be performed independently and simultaneously by different processors. However, the parallel execution of the B&B solving the PFSP, can lead to the treatment of some needless sub problems. Especially, when sub problems are treated in parallel, although some of these problems may be pruned in sequential execution. For this reason, in our algorithm we used an intelligent technique to distribute and update the upper bound values in order to reduce the size of the search tree and therefore to obtain as quickly as possible the optimal solution.

In this parallel algorithm we have to distribute all the jobs to be scheduled among all processors while maintaining a load balancing between different processors. This task is ensured by the master. Each processor is responsible of its local sub problem (set of jobs). Each processor has to use the operating times of different jobs on different machines in order to build its complete local sub tree.

While developing the nodes of its sub tree, when the processor reach a feasible solution (which has a lower bound value less than the upper bound value), it updates the value of the Upper bound (if LB <UB) and sends this new value to all other processors in order to prune the maximum of local not promising branches. We need then communication between all processors in this step of the algorithm.

Remark that for the parallel execution of the algorithm, the structure of the search tree may be different from the tree developed in sequential since it may explore some branches of the tree which are not developed in sequential. However the time investigated in the development of unexplored branches may be awarded by a fast pruning of non promising branches.

Initially, the lower and the upper bound are assigned by the lower and upper bounds of Taillard and since we have a fairly high number of processors, we can decompose our problem into a number of smaller sub-problems at least equal to the number of processors. In this algorithm we use especially the update of the current best upper bound denoted by (NUB: New Upper Bound).

In our parallel algorithm we use the paradigm master/slave in order to distribute and compute the Upper and Lower Bounds for each portion of the tree.

The master has to distribute the input data (root node) among all the processors with respect to the load balancing between all of them. We consider the case where the number of processors is less or equal to the number of jobs. The different steps of our algorithm are described as follows:

- **A master/Slave paradigm:**

The *master* process has the responsibility of controlling all the system; however the *Worker* processors concurrently execute independent tasks. The Figure 3. shows our parallel algorithm performed in the grid.

In our algorithm a sub problem corresponds to a set of nodes to be examined and scheduled.

We present below the general parallel algorithm.

```
BEGIN
     Distribute the jobs among all processors
     If (nb of jobs < nb processors) Then
       Portion = nb of jobs / nb of processors
     Else if (nb of jobs = nb processors) Then
       Portion = one job for each processor
       End if
     End if
     For each processor:
  -    Step 1: Explore the node
  -    Step 2: Branch the child of the node
  -    Step 3: Construct a feasible solution : A New lower bound (feasible solution)
       = NLB = candidate to a NUB
  -    Step 4: Compare the LB with the NUB:
            If (NLB < NUB) then update the NUB and broadcast it to all the
          processors (all to all communication).
            Else return to the step 1
            End if
END
```

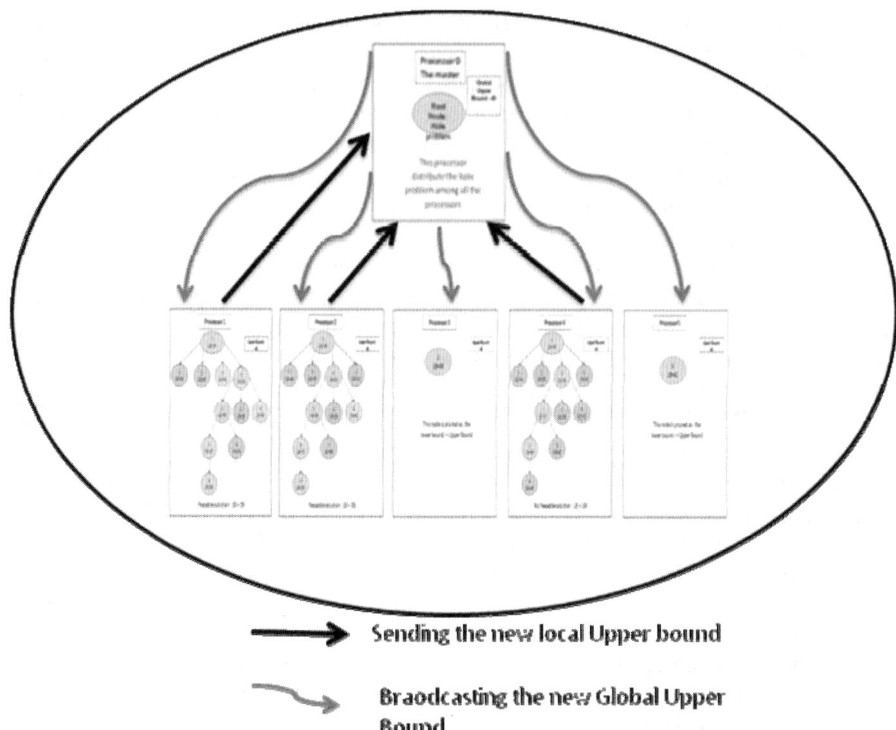

Fig. 3. Parallel resolution of the PFSP with B&B

5 Experimental Results

We implemented our algorithm with C, we used also the MPI library (Message Passing Interface) in order to ensure communication between processors. All the computational results were carried on the French national Grid (Grid'5000).

In order to validate practically the efficiency of our gridified algorithm we performed our experimental tests on a well-known set of benchmark instances from the literature [5]. These instances are known to be very hard and about a decade after their publication, many of them are still open (instances with 20 machines and some others with 10 machines).

In our experimentations we tested our application with the following instances of Taillard: 50X10, 100X10 and 200X10 instances.

We focused particularly in the 50X10 instances and we successfully solved two instances to optimality which have never been resolved before neither with sequential programs nor with parallel ones.

The table bellow (Table 1) shows the two instances of the 50X10 instances, Tail042 and Tail050 that could not be solved in sequential. The table gives also the optimal solution obtained by our algorithm.

Table 1. Resolution of the 50X10 instances in the Grid

50X10 instances				
Instance -Name	**Sequential running time**	**Parallel running time (50 processors)**	C_{max}	**Optimal Solution**
Tail042	Unsolved	1 hour and 55 minutes	2867	49-3-33-28-50-31-35-7-10-38-12- 6-37-20-9-39-47-34-23-1-19- 44-21-18-29-42-16-14-43-27-25- 40- 22-26-17-8-4-46-36- 24-41-32- 5-30-13-2-45-11-15-48
Tail050	Unsolved	33 minutes and 55 seconds	3065	49-38-10-27-17-28-42-15-39-6-1-8-16-47-20-44-26-24-29-11-22-18-48-7-25-35-34-46-9-43-31-21-3-30-40-5-32-4-50-36-45-33-19-13-37-41-23-2-12-14

Remark here, that the resolution of the PFSP depends also on the instance to solve. In fact, from the experiments we have done, we noticed that when several nodes are pruned from the first level of the search tree, the use of parallelism is not very significant. However, when the processors share the workload that is normally assigned to a single processor, we can achieve reasonable running times for some instances.

6 Conclusion and Perspectives

In this paper, we proposed a new parallel algorithm for resolution of the PFSP as well as its deployment on a Grid of computers (Grid'5000). Our algorithm is basically a parallelization of the well known B&B method, which is an exact method for solving combinatorial optimization problems. We presented, in particular, a new strategy of parallelization which uses some directives of communication between all processors in order to update the value of the Upper Bound value. The deployment of our application on Gird'5000 gives good results and permits in particular the resolution of two new instances not yet resolved which are the Tail043 and Tail050 from Taillard's benchmarks. In our future work, in order to improve our algorithm, we plan to use a bigger number of the processors and to solve other instances not yet solved and to use other paradigms, such us, the multithreading paradigm in order to more improve load balancing between all processors and then the possibility of resolution of new unsolved instances of data.

References

1. Ladhari, T., Haouari, M.: A computational study of the PFSP based on a tight lower bound. Computers & Operations Research 32, 1831–1847 (2005)
2. Reza Hejazi, S., Saghafian, S.: Flowshop-scheduling problems with makespan criterion: a review. International Journal of Production Research 43(14), 2895–2929 (2005)
3. Gendron, B., Crainic, T.G.: Parallel B&B Algorithms: Survey and synthesis. Operation Research 42(6), 1042–1066 (1994)

4. Kouki, S., Jemni, M., Ladhari, T.: A parallel Distributed Algorithm for the permutation flow shop scheduling problem. In: Hsu, C.-H., Yang, L.T., Park, J.H., Yeo, S.-S. (eds.) ICA3PP 2010. LNCS, vol. 6082, pp. 328–337. Springer, Heidelberg (2010)
5. Taillard, E.: Benchmarks for basic scheduling problems. European Journal of Operational Research 64, 278–285 (1993)
6. http://www.grid5000.fr/
7. Pinedo, M.: Scheduling: theory, algorithms, and systems. Prentice-Hall, Englewood CliKs (1995)
8. Garey, M.R., Johnson, D.S., Sethi, R.: The complexity of flow shop and job shop scheduling. Mathematics of Operations Research 29, 1:117 (1976)
9. Bendjoudi, A., Melab, N., Talbi, E.-G.: P2P design and implementation of a parallel B&B algorithm for grids. International Journal of Grid and Utility Computing 1, 159–168 (2009)
10. http://www.lri.fr/~fci/Grid5000/downloads/Compte-rendu.ppt
11. Fujisawa, K., Kojima, M., Takeda, A., Yamashita, M.: Solving large scale optimization problems via Grid and Cluster Computing, Research Report B400 (December 2003)
12. Mezmaz, M., Melab, N., Talbi, E.-G.: A Grid-enabled B&B Algorithm for Solving Challenging Combinatorial Optimization Problems. In: IEEE International Parallel and Distributed Processing Symposium, pp. 1–9 (March 2007)
13. Mezmaz, M., Melab, N., Talbi, E.-G.: An efficient load balancing strategy for grid-basedbranch and bound algorithm. Parallel Computing, Large Scale Grids 33(4-5), 302–313 (2007)
14. Caromel, D., Di Costanzo, A., Baduel, L., Matsuoka, S.: *grid'BnB*: A parallel branch and bound framework for grids. In: Aluru, S., Parashar, M., Badrinath, R., Prasanna, V.K. (eds.) HiPC 2007. LNCS, vol. 4873, pp. 566–579. Springer, Heidelberg (2007)
15. Aida, K., Yoshiaki Futakata, Y., Osumi, T.: Parallel Branch and Bound Algorithm with the Hierarchical Master-Worker Paradigm on the Grid Information and Media Technologies 2(1), 17–30 (2007)
16. http://www-sop.inria.fr/oasis/plugtest2005/2ndGridPlugtestsReport/
17. http://www2.lifl.fr/~talbi/challenge2007/
18. Johnson, S.M.: Optimal two- and three-stage production schedules with setup times included. Naval Research Logistics Quarterly 8, 1–61 (1954)
19. Ignall, E., Schrage, L.E.: Application of the branch-and-bound technique to some flow shop problems. Operations Research 12, 400–412 (1965)
20. Carlier, J., Rebai, I.: Two branch-and-bound algorithms for the permutation flowshop problem. European Journal of Operational Research 90(2), 238–251 (1996)

Result Verification Mechanism Based on Availability and Reputation of Resources in P2P Desktop Grid Systems*

Joon-Min Gil[1], Soo-Jin Koo[2], and SungJin Choi[3]**

[1] School of Computer and Information Communications Engineering, Catholic University of Daegu
jmgil@cu.ac.kr

[2] R&D Team, Visual Display, Samsung Electronics Co., LTD.
soojin.koo@samsung.com

[3] Cloud Business Unit, KT
lotieye@gmail.com

Abstract. The recent tendency of transfer from centralized desktop to P2P desktop grids requires redesigning the result verification mechanism that has been developed for the former. Since there is no central server to verify the correctness of task results in P2P desktop grids, it is difficult to intactly apply the existing mechanisms to P2P environments. In this paper, we propose a result verification mechanism based on a task tree that can efficiently provide the result correctness against malicious resources in P2P desktop grids. In the mechanism, a task tree is built based on the availability and reputation of resources, and different result verification methods are used according to level characteristics in the task tree. Numerical analysis results show that our mechanism performs better than the existing ones, in terms of the correctness of task results.

Keywords: P2P desktop grids, result verification, task tree, availability, reputation.

1 Introduction

Desktop grids are a computing paradigm that enables the parallel processing of large-scale applications using idle computing power obtained from a number of desktop computers connected over the Internet [1]. To date, they have attracted attention toward successful projects such as SETI@Home [2], Distributed.net [3], etc. and the development of underlying platforms such as BOINC [4], XtremWeb [5], Korea@Home [6], etc.

In general, each resource in desktop grids can freely join and leave for task execution, and thus task volatility inevitably occurs. Because of this, the task

* This research was supported by Basic Science Research Program through the National Research Foundation of Korea (NRF) funded by the Ministry of Education, Science and Technology (No. 2009-0077638).

** Corresponding author.

T.-h. Kim et al. (Eds.): GDC/CA 2010, CCIS 121, pp. 105–116, 2010.

completion cannot always be guaranteed. Moreover, as unspecific resources are basically used in desktop grids, their malicious and selfish behavior incurs the unexpected errors that may eventually lead to the invalidation of the whole task results. Therefore, result verification procedure is essential to obtain reliable and trusty task results in desktop grids [7].

According to whether there is a central server that globally manages resources, desktop grids can be classified into two types: one is centralized and the other is decentralized [1]. In the centralized desktop grids, a central server directly performs fundamental functions such as task scheduling, fault tolerance, result verification, etc. Whereas, in the decentralized desktop grids, such functions should be autonomically performed by each resource due to the absence of a central server. Thus, it is crucial to utilize P2P technology in the second type. In this paper, we will refer to this type as *P2P desktop grids*.

Typically, two methods have been used to guarantee the correctness of task results: one is the majority voting that utilizes task replication [4] and the other is the spot-checking that utilizes the small-size spots whose results are known previously [8]. However, both methods have been devised focusing on the centralized desktop grids, which can cause a scalability problem due to the bottleneck effect on the central server. To overcome this problem, recent studies have adopted P2P technology for the result verification of desktop grids [9,10,11,12]. However, the result verification in P2P desktop grids cannot help utilizing those resources which have much lower availability and reliability than that in centralized desktop grids. The following points should be taken into account:

- There is structurally no central server in a P2P environment. Result verification should be done by cooperations between resources.
- In the P2P environment, not only could malicious resources make unreliable task results, but also the resources executing the tasks received from the malicious resources could make unreliable task results.
- It is difficult to directly apply the result verification schemes devised for centralized desktop grids to P2P desktop grids without any changes. For example, the existing result verification mechanisms have mostly used the task stealing based on tree or graph structure [13]. If a task replication policy for majority voting is used in the upper level of this structure, redundant replications will occur in the lower level, degrading the system performance.

In this paper, we propose a result verification mechanism for P2P desktop grids, considering the points mentioned above. First of all, our mechanism constructs a task tree based on the availability and reputation of resources. It then uses different result verification methods according to the characteristics of each tree level. Therefore, as compared with the existing mechanisms used for centralized desktop grids, our mechanism can reduce result verification loads while guaranteeing the correctness of task results. Numerical analysis results show that our mechanism has a better performance than the existing mechanisms.

The rest of this paper is organized as follows. In Section 2, we describe a P2P desktop grid environment assumed in this paper. Section 3 presents the definition

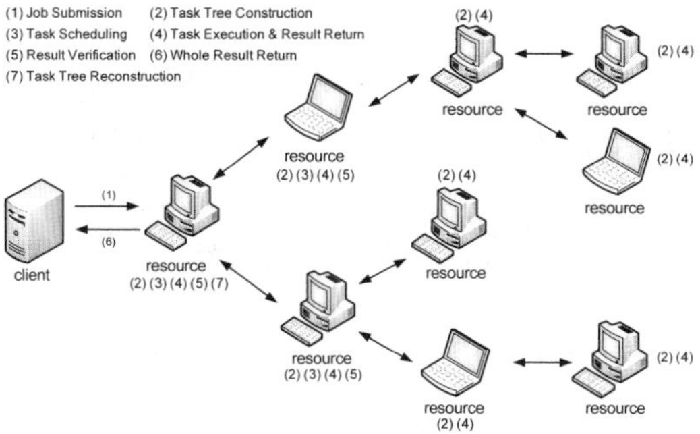

Fig. 1. Execution procedure

of resource availability and reputation. In Section 4, we describe a task tree constructed by resource availability and reputation. Section 5 proposes a result verification mechanism based on task tree that can verify the correctness of task results. In Section 6, we evaluate the performance of the proposed mechanism by mathematical analysis and compare it with the existing mechanisms in terms of the correctness of task results. Section 7 concludes the paper.

2 P2P Desktop Grid Environment

We describe a P2P desktop grid environment used in this paper. This environment largely consists of two entities: one is a client that takes the responsibility of submitting a large-scale application to a desktop grid system, and the other is a number of resources that take the responsibility of executing tasks while acting as a server at the same time. The resources receiving tasks from the client construct a task tree. Task scheduling and result verification are performed based on the task tree. Figure 1 shows a task execution procedure in the P2P desktop grid environment. This procedure has the following steps:

Step 1. A client submits the whole tasks to a resource.

Step 2. The resource (to which tasks are submitted) becomes a root node of task tree and constructs a task tree using the availability and reputation information of other resources.

Step 3. Based on the task tree, upper-level resources perform the task scheduling that allocates tasks to lower-level resources.

Step 4. These resources (to which tasks are assigned) execute the tasks, and return task results to upper-level resources.

Step 5. Upper-level resources verify the correctness of task results, and update the availability and reputation of lower-level resources.

Step 6. When the whole task results are verified, they are returned to the client.

Step 7. The task tree is reconstructed based on the updated availability and reputation.

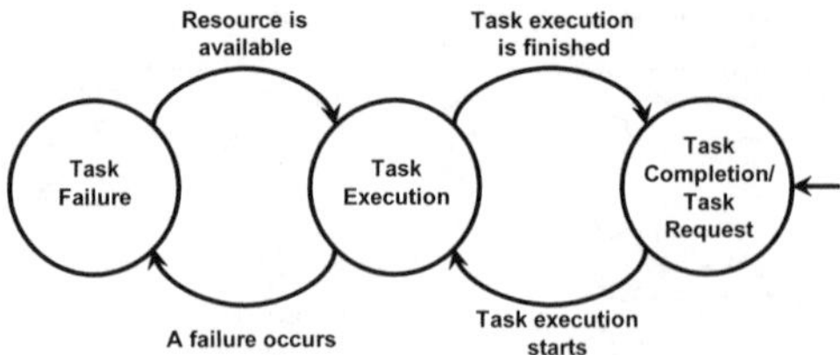

Fig. 2. State transition diagram

3 Definition of Availability and Reputation

3.1 Definition of Availability

In our P2P desktop grid environment, each resource has a state that can be updated by its execution behavior [14]. Figure 2 shows a diagram for the state transition. In the beginning, a resource has the "task completion/request" state for the request of a task, and then transits to the "task execution" state when it starts to execute the task. If it fails during the execution of the task, the resource falls into the "task failure" state. Upon recovering from the failure, the resource returns to the "task execution" state. If the task execution is finished, the resource transits to the "task completion/request" state, and again to the "task execution" state again, etc.

In Figure 2, the time during which a resource stays in the "task execution" state represents the amount of time the resource takes when participating in actual execution. During this time, the resource repeatedly joins and leaves the execution until the task is completed. When the resource often leaves the execution, the execution volatility will increase; when the join rate is higher than the leave one, the availability will increase.

In general, the availability in desktop grid environments can be classified into three types: host availability, task execution availability, and CPU availability [15]. The task execution availability is suitable for desktop grids, because unavailable time for task execution can arise from a keyboad/mouse hooking. Thus, the availability of a resource p_i, $A(p_i)$, is defined as follows:

$$A(p_i) = \frac{MTTF(p_i)}{MTTF(p_i) + MTTR(p_i)} \tag{1}$$

where MTTF (Mean Time To Failure) is the average time that p_i participates in task execution, and MTTR (Mean Time To Repair) is the average time from task stop to task restart.

3.2 Definition of Reputation

Since there is no central server that manages the trust of resources in P2P desktop grid environments, the trust of each resource must be evaluated based on the trust of other resources. Typically, this trust can be evaluated by using reputation among various evaluation methods [16]. Reputation is a measure that predicts the trust of a specific resource based on the previous experience between resources. In this paper, we define the reputation in terms of the number of execution performed and the correctness ratio of such executions. Due to the P2P desktop grid environments where there is no central server, we use two evaluation methods: one is a direction recommendation and the other is an indirect recommendation.

Direct recommendation. Let us assume that the two resources p_i and p_j are in friend relations contained in a friend list. Then, the reputation of p_j directly evaluated by p_i, $R_D(p_i \rightarrow p_j)$, is defined as follows:

$$R_D(p_i \rightarrow p_j) = \frac{O_S(p_i \rightarrow p_j)}{O_T(p_i \rightarrow p_j)} \tag{2}$$

where $O_T(p_i \rightarrow p_j)$ represents the total number of tasks that p_i has executed with p_j, and $O_S(p_i \rightarrow p_j)$ represents the number of correct results among these tasks.

Indirect Recommendation. When it is not possible to obtain the reputation of a certain resource only from direct recommendation, an alternative is to rely on the recommendation of other resources. This is called as an *indirect recommendation.* Let us assume that two resource pairs, p_i and p_k, and p_k and p_j, are respectively in friend relations contained in a friend list from the previous observations, but p_i and p_j are in neighbor relations that are not contained in the friend list. Then, the reputation of resource p_j that resource p_i can obtain from an indirect recommendation, $R_{ID}(p_i \rightarrow p_j)$, is defined as follows:

$$R_{ID}(p_i \rightarrow p_j) = R_D(p_i \rightarrow p_k) \cdot R_D(p_k \rightarrow p_j) \tag{3}$$

Using Eqs. (2) and (3), each resource can have the reputation obtained from the direct and indirect recommendations. The overall reputation of resource p_i, $R(p_i)$, is then defined as follows:

$$R(p_i) = \sum_{p_i \in F} (\omega \cdot R_D(p_j \rightarrow p_i) + (1 - \omega) \cdot R_{ID}(p_j \rightarrow p_i)) \cdot \frac{1}{|F|} \tag{4}$$

where F and $|F|$ represent p_i's friend list and the number of resources that belong to F, respectively. ω represents a weight parameter of direct and indirect recommendations.

4 Task Tree Using Availability and Reputation

In this section, we present a task tree using the availability and reputation of resources that are used to verify the correctness of task results in P2P desktop grid environments.

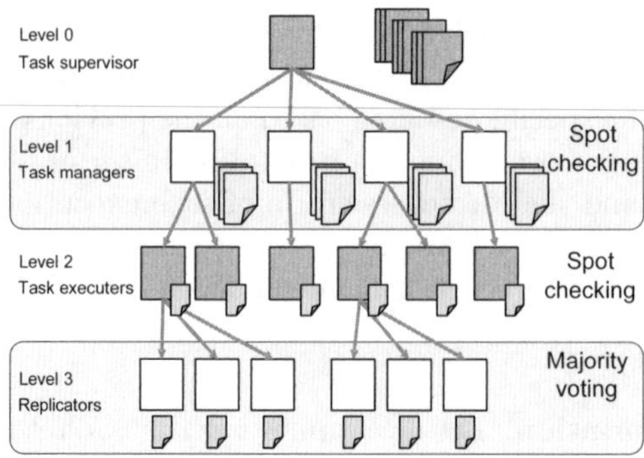

Fig. 3. Task tree and result verification in each level

4.1 Structure of Task Tree

A task tree is built by setting a threshold value for each level and by differently deploying resources in each level according to their availability and reputation. Also, to guarantee the continuous and reliable task execution despite volatility, the resources with high availability and reputation are deployed in the upper level of the task tree. Accordingly, the upper-level resources take responsibility for task scheduling and result verification for the lower-level resources.

As shown in Figure 3, a task tree has four levels. Each resource plays a role of one among task supervisors, task managers, task executers, and replicators according to its location in the task tree. First of all, the whole tasks are submitted to a task supervisor in level 0, which assigns task bundles to task managers in level 1 and verifies the correctness of the task results executed by these managers. The task managers in level 1 allocate tasks to resources in sub-levels (levels 2 and 3) and verifies the correctness of the task results executed by these resources. The task executors in level 2 execute the unit task and return a task result to upper-level resources. The replicators in level 3 performs task replication to cope with execution stops or failures due to the volatility of task executors in the upper levels. Therefore, the resources in levels 0 and 1 are deployed in the task tree in such a way that they have higher availability and reputation than those in levels 2 and 3, as they are responsible for the task scheduling and result verification of the lower-level resources.

4.2 Procedure of Constructing a Task Tree

A task tree is built by the following steps:

Step 1. The task supervisor (p_0) constructs a task tree as soon as it receives the whole tasks from a client. As shown in Figure 4(a), it calculates the level in which each resource can be deployed, based on the availability and reputation of resources in its own friend list. By this calculation, p_1 is deployed in level 1, p_2 in level 2, and p_3 and p_4 in level 3.

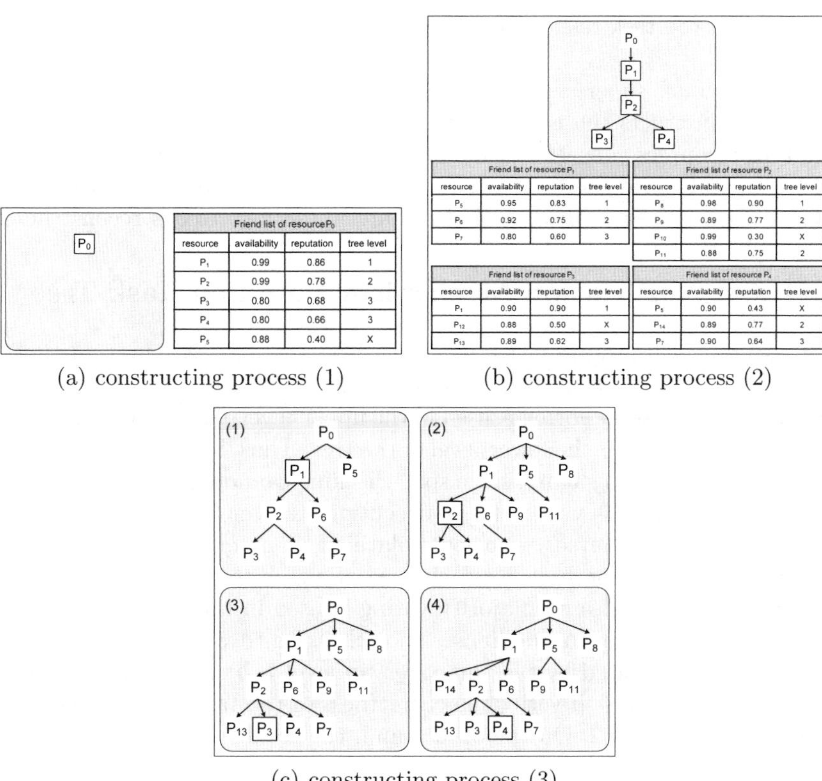

Friend list of resource P0			
resource	availability	reputation	tree level
P_1	0.99	0.86	1
P_2	0.99	0.78	2
P_3	0.80	0.68	3
P_4	0.80	0.66	3
P_5	0.88	0.40	X

(a) constructing process (1)

Friend list of resource P1			
resource	availability	reputation	tree level
P_5	0.95	0.83	1
P_6	0.92	0.75	2
P_7	0.80	0.60	3

Friend list of resource P2			
resource	availability	reputation	tree level
P_8	0.98	0.90	1
P_9	0.89	0.77	2
P_{10}	0.99	0.30	X
P_{11}	0.88	0.75	2

Friend list of resource P3			
resource	availability	reputation	tree level
P_1	0.90	0.90	1
P_{12}	0.88	0.50	X
P_{13}	0.89	0.62	3

Friend list of resource P4			
resource	availability	reputation	tree level
P_5	0.90	0.43	X
P_{14}	0.89	0.77	2
P_7	0.90	0.64	3

(b) constructing process (2)

(c) constructing process (3)

Fig. 4. Example of constructing a task tree

Step 2. After the process of Step 1, we can obtain the task tree presented in Figure 4(b). Then, each of the resources $p_1 \sim p_4$ expands the task tree with resources in its own friend list, as shown in Figure 4(c). When each parent node can have up to three child nodes, (1), (2), (3), and (4) of Figure 4(c) represent the task trees that have been built using the friend list of these resources ($p_1 \sim p_4$), respectively. If the maximum number of child nodes is exceeded, they are allocated to the sibling nodes of their parent.

Step 3. This process is repeated for a given TTL (Time to Live). The value of TTL is decreased by one whenever the task tree is extended with new resources.

4.3 Reconstruction of a Task Tree

Once the construction of a task tree is completed, a task supervisor in level 0 and task managers in level 1 allocate tasks to lower-level resources. These resources return task results to upper levels when their task execution is completed. The task supervisor and task managers receiving the task results then verify the correctness of the task results and update the availability and reputation of the resources.

When the task supervisor receives the submission of other tasks from the client, it reconstructs the task tree based on the updated availability and reputation of resources; *i.e.*, the task supervisor in level 0 and the task managers in level 1 recalculate the level where each of the lower-level resources can be deployed. Using the modified level of resources, the task tree is reconstructed.

5 Result Verification Mechanism Based on Task Tree

In this section, we propose a result verification mechanism based on the task tree that is constructed by the availability and reputation of resources.

Typically, if majority voting is used in the upper-level of a task tree, redundant replication will occur in the lower-level of the tree. Thus, it should be used in the lower-level. On the other hand, since spot-checking cannot aggressively deal with execution volatility, it is vulnerable to execution stops or failures; thus, it should be applied to the resources with low volatility. Consequently, our mechanism uses one of these two methods for each level of a task tree; *i.e.*, spot-checking is used in the upper-level, and majority voting is used in the lower-level. In more detail, a task supervisor in level 0 uses spot-checking to verify the correctness of the task results executed by task managers in level 1. The spot-checking is also used by task managers to verify the correctness of the task results executed by task executors in level 2. On the other hand, the result verification in level 3 is done by majority voting.

The number of replications and spots are the important parameters to determine the performance of result verification mechanisms when spot-checking and majority voting are used. In this paper, these two parameters are calculated based on resource reputation. First of all, let us consider the number of replications for majority voting. If a resource p_i absolutely trusts a resource p_j (*i.e.*, $R(p_i \rightarrow p_j) = 1$), the number of replications becomes $2m - 1$ (where m represents a majority factor). Thus, the number of replications for majority voting, $V(p_i \rightarrow p_j)$, can be calculated by

$$V(p_i \rightarrow p_j) = 2 \cdot \left(\frac{m}{R(p_i \rightarrow p_j)} \right) - 1 \quad (5)$$

Next, let us consider the number of spots needed when spot-checking is performed. If a resource p_i absolutely trusts a resource p_j, it is sufficiently to use only one spot per task. However, if the trust between two resources is low, more spots per task will be used. Thus, the number of spots needed when p_i performs spot-checking on p_j, $S(p_i \rightarrow p_j)$, can be calculated by

$$S(p_i \rightarrow p_j) = \lceil \frac{1}{R(p_i \rightarrow p_j)} \rceil \quad (6)$$

From Eqs. (5) and (6), it can be seen that the number of both replications and spots depends on the reputation of resources ($R(p_i \rightarrow p_j)$), and more specifically,

```
// Check the level of the resource that sent a task result.
if (Resource.level=1) or (Resource.level=2) then
    if spotter.result = false then
        excludeChild(childResource)
        replaceChild()
    else
        updateReputation(childResource)
    end if
end if
if Resource.level=3 then
    majorityVoting(childResource)
    updateReputation(childResource)
end if
```

Fig. 5. Result verification algorithm based on task tree

this number increases as the reputation decreases. Figure 5 shows a task tree-based result verification algorithm in which different result verification methods (majority voting and spot-checking) are used for each level of a task tree. This algorithm is performed when a resource in the upper level receives task results from resources in the lower level.

6 Performance Evaluation

We evaluate the performance of our result verification mechanism in terms of the correctness of task results and compare it with other mechanisms.

6.1 Performance Environments

The correctness of task results is calculated as how reliable task results are according to resource reputation. In this paper, we compare the correctness of task results for cases where (1) no result verification is applied, (2) only spot-checking is used, (3) only majority voting is used, and (4) our result verification mechanism is used. The correctness of task results for each mechanism can be defined by the following equations:

Not applied

$$\sum_{i=1}^{n}(1 - f_{p_i}) \cdot (1 - f_{par(p_i)}) \cdot \frac{1}{n}$$

Spot-checking

$$\left(\sum_{i=1}^{n}\left(1 - \frac{f_{p_i}}{1-f_{p_i}} \cdot \frac{1}{s \cdot e}\right) \cdot \left(1 - \frac{f_{par(p_i)}}{1-f_{par(p_i)}} \cdot \frac{1}{s \cdot e}\right)\right) \cdot \frac{1}{n}$$

Majority voting

$$\left(\sum_{i=1}^{n}\left(1 - \frac{(4 \cdot f_{p_i} \cdot (1-f_{p_i}))^m}{2 \cdot (1-2 \cdot f_{p_i}) \cdot \sqrt{\pi \cdot (m-1)}}\right) \cdot \left(1 - \frac{(4 \cdot f_{par(p_i)} \cdot (1-f_{par(p_i)}))^m}{2 \cdot (1-2 \cdot f_{par(p_i)}) \cdot \sqrt{\pi \cdot (m-1)}}\right)\right) \cdot \frac{1}{n}$$

Table 1. Parameters and values used for result verification

Parameters	Values
Total number of tasks (t)	269
Total number of nodes (n)	126
Number of spots (s)	2
Majority factor (m)	2
Level threshold of task tree (α)	0.7
False probability of resource p_i (f_{p_i})	0.1, 0.3, 0.5
False probability of the resource that verified the task results of resource p_i ($f_{par(p_i)}$)	0.0, 0.1, 0.2

Our result verification mechanism

$$\left(\sum_{i=1}^{n}\left(1-\frac{f_{p_i}}{1-f_{p_i}}\cdot\frac{1}{S(p_i \to p_j)\cdot e}\right)\cdot\left(1-\frac{f_{par(p_i)}}{1-f_{par(p_i)}}\cdot\frac{1}{S(par(p_i)\to p_j)\cdot e}\right)\right)\cdot\frac{1}{n} \quad \text{if } (\alpha < R(p_i) \le 1)$$

$$\left(\sum_{i=1}^{n}\left(1-\frac{(4\cdot f_{p_i}\cdot(1-f_{p_i}))^{V(p_i\to p_j)}}{2\cdot(1-2\cdot f_{p_i})\cdot\sqrt{\pi\cdot(V(p_i\to p_j)-1)}}\right)\cdot\left(1-\frac{f_{par(p_i)}}{1-f_{par(p_i)}}\cdot\frac{1}{S(par(p_i)\to p_j)\cdot e}\right)\right)\cdot\frac{1}{n} \quad \text{if } (0 \le R(p_i) \le \alpha)$$

In the above equations, f_{p_i} and $f_{par(p_i)}$ indicate the false probability of resource p_i and the false probability of the resource that verifies the task results of p_i, respectively. These two false probabilities are defined as the ratio of incorrect results to total tasks executed. The equations of spot-checking and majority voting are derived based on the equations presented in [17,18]. In these equations, s and m represent the number of spots and a majority factor, respectively. In the correctness equation of our mechanism, spot-checking and majority voting are applied differently according to the threshold value (α) determining the level of a task tree. Moreover, it can dynamically determine the number of spots and replications by Eqs. (5) and (6).

To evaluate the effect of resource reputation on the correctness of task results, we divided f_{p_i} and $f_{par(p_i)}$ into three cases, respectively: 0.1, 0.3, 0.5 for f_{p_i} and 0.0, 0.1, 0.2 for $f_{par(p_i)}$. The performance of four mechanisms for each of the total nine cases was evaluated. Table 1 shows the parameters and values used for the performance evaluation of four mechanisms.

6.2 Performance Results

Figure 6 compares the result correctness of each mechanism according to the change of f_{p_i} for three cases of $f_{par(p_i)}$. Figure 6(a) shows the result correctness obtained in the case that the resources verifying task results has no false probability. It can be seen that, as the false probability decreases, the correctness of each mechanism increases. We can observe from this figure that the lowest

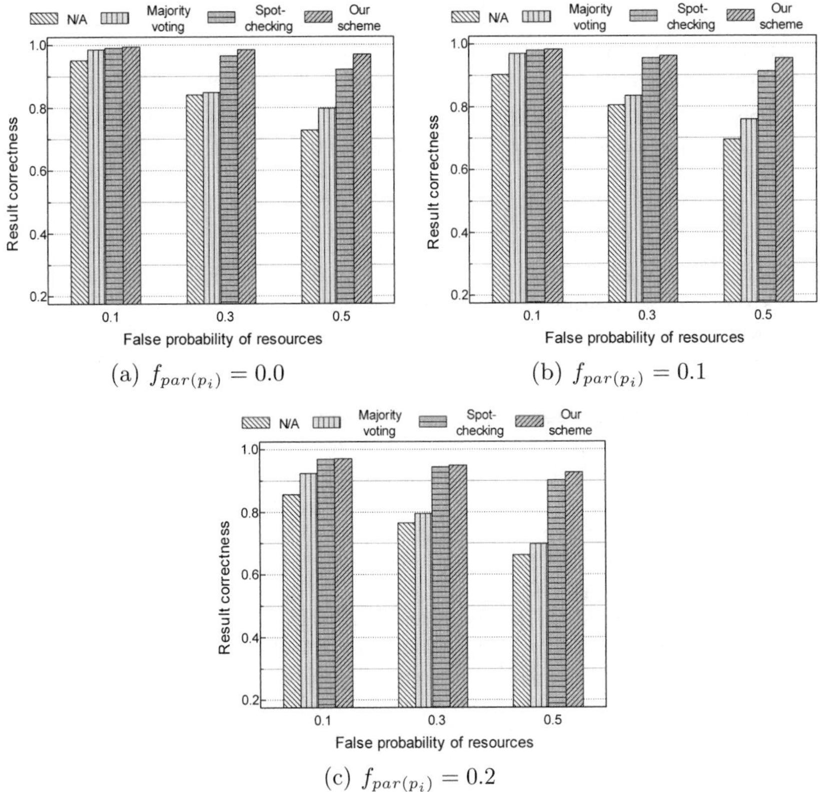

(a) $f_{par(p_i)} = 0.0$

(b) $f_{par(p_i)} = 0.1$

(c) $f_{par(p_i)} = 0.2$

Fig. 6. Comparison of result correctness

result correctness is when no result verification is applied. The result correctness of majority voting and spot-checking mechanisms appears to be $0.7 \sim 1.0$, which is lower than that of our result verification mechanism.

On the other hand, the result correctness of Figures 6(b) and (c) (cases that the resources verifying task results have a false probability) is lower than that of Figure 6(a), but our mechanism has higher result correctness than others. Generally, as f_{p_i} and $f_{par(p_i)}$ decrease, p_i' reputation increases. The high reputation of resources leads to the increment of reliable task results. Therefore, it is obvious that our mechanism steadily have good performances compared with others. This results from the fact that different result verification methods are used for each level of the task tree according to resource reputation.

7 Conclusion

In this paper, we proposed a task tree-based result verification mechanism to efficiently cope with incorrect task results from malicious resources in P2P desktop grid environments. The proposed mechanism constructs a task tree based on the availability and reputation of resources, and then differently applies spot-checking and majority voting to each level of the task tree in order to guarantee the result correctness. Numerical analysis results showed that the proposed mechanism can improve the performance of result verification compared with that of other mechanisms, even if resources have a false probability.

References

1. Kacsuk, P., Lovas, R., Németh, Z.: Distributed and Parallel Systems. In: focus: Desktop Grid Computing. Springer, Heidelberg (2008)
2. Korpela, E., Werthimer, D., Anderson, D., Cobb, J., Lebofsky, M.: SETI@home-massively distributed computing for SETI. Computing in Science & Eng. 3(1), 78–83 (2001)
3. Distributed.net, `http://www.distributed.net/`
4. Anderson, D.P.: BOINC: A system for public-resource computing and storage. In: 5th IEEE/ACM Int. Workshop on Grid Computing, pp. 4–10 (2004)
5. Cappello, F., Djilali, S., Fedak, G., Herault, T., Magniette, F., Neri, V., Lodygensky, O.: Computing on large scale distributed systems: XtremWeb architecture, programming models, security, tests and convergence with Grid. Future Generation Computer Systems 23(3), 417–437 (2005)
6. Korea@Home, `http://www.koreaathome.org/eng/`
7. Molnar, D.: On Patrol: The SETI@Home problem, E-Commerce (2000)
8. Germain-Renaud, C., Playez, N.: Result-checking in global computing systems. In: Proc. of the 17th Annual Int. Conf. on Supercomputing, pp. 226–233 (2003)
9. Charkravarti, A.J., Baumgatner, G., Lauria, M.: The organic grid: self-organizing computation on a peer-to-peer network. IEEE Trans. on Systems, Man, and Cybernetics 35(3), 373–384 (2005)
10. Dou, W., Jia, Y., Wang, H., Song, W., Zou, P.: A P2P approach for global computing, Int. Parallel and Distributed Processing Symp., p. 248b (2003)
11. Andrade, N., Brasileiro, F., Cirne, W.: Discouraging free riding in a peer-to-peer CPU-sharing grid. In: Proc. of the 13th IEEE Int. Symp. on High Performance Distributed Computing, pp. 129–137 (2004)
12. Lo, V., Zhou, D., Zappala, D., Liu, Y., Zhao, S.: Cluster computing on the fly: P2P scheduling of idle cycles in the Internet. In: Proc. of the IEEE 4th Int. Workshop on Peer-to-Peer Systems, pp. 227–236 (2004)
13. Blumofe, R.D., Joerg, C.F., Kuszmaul, B.C., Leiserson, C.E., Randall, K.H., Zhou, Y.: Cilk: an efficient multithreaded runtime system. SIGPLAN Not. 30(8), 207–216 (1995)
14. Kondo, D., Chien, A., Casanova, H.: Scheduling task parallel applications for rapid turnaround on desktop grids. J. of Grid Computing 5(4), 379–405 (2007)
15. Bhagwan, R., Savage, S., Voelker, G.: Understanding availability. In: Proc. of the 2nd Int. Workshop on Peer-to-Peer Systems II, pp. 256–267 (2003)
16. Suryanarayana, G., Taylor, R .: A survey of trust management and resource discovery technologies in peer-to-peer applications, ISR Technical Report #UCI-ISR-04-6 (2004)
17. Sarmenta, L.: Sabotage-tolerance mechanism for volunteer computing systems. In: Proc. of the 1st Int. Symp. on Cluster Computing and the Grid, pp. 337–346 (2001)
18. Zuev, Y.A.: The estimation of efficiency of voting procedures. Theory of Probability and Its Applications 42(1), 78–84 (1997)

Mobile Grid System Based on Mobile Agent

JongHyuk Lee[1], SungJin Choi[2], JongBeom Lim[1],
Taeweon Suh[1], JoonMin Gil[3], and HeonChang Yu[1,*]

[1] Dept. of Computer Science Education, Korea University
Anam-dong, Sungbuk-gu, Seoul 136-701, Korea
{spurt,jblim,suhtw,yuhc}@korea.ac.kr
[2] Cloud Service Business Unit, KT
17 Umyeon-dong, Seocho-gu, Seoul 137-792, Korea
lotieye@gmail.com
[3] School of Computer and Information Communications Engineering,
Catholic University of Daegu
330 Geumnak, Hayang-eup, Gyeongsan-si, Gyeongbuk 712-701, Korea
jmgil@cu.ac.kr

Abstract. Mobile Grid is a branch of Grid where the infrastructure includes mobile devices. The mobile Grid exhibits different challenges such as resource-constraints and users' movements, compared to the traditional Grid. Mobile agent is an attractive technology to overcome these challenges. In this paper, we present a new mobile Grid system based on the mobile agent. This paper describes the architecture of the new system: multi-proxy based mobile grid environment with location management and message delivery mechanism. Our system is lightweight enough to be installed on mobile devices. It also provides the physical and logical mobility of mobile agents. We implemented the mobile Grid system based on Globus Toolkit and ODDUGI mobile agent system.

Keywords: mobile Grid, mobile agent, mobility.

1 Introduction

Emerging Grids [1] are extending the scope of resources to mobile devices (e.g., laptop computers and smart phones) and sensors that are loosely connected through wireless networks (e.g., Wi-Fi, Wibro/WiMAX, HSPA, and Satellite), which is referred to as mobile Grid. Mobile Grid is a branch of Grid [2] in which the infrastructure includes mobile devices. Due to the characteristics of mobile devices, the mobile Grid exhibits different challenges such as resource-constraints and users' movements, compared to the traditional Grid.

A mobile agent is a software program that migrates from one node to another while performing given tasks on behalf of users and provides the following benefits: 1) A mobile agent can reduce network load and latency. 2) It can be used in an environment where the network disruption occurs frequently or intermittently. 3) It enables the dynamic service customization and software deployment.

* Corresponding author.

T.-h. Kim et al. (Eds.): GDC/CA 2010, CCIS 121, pp. 117–126, 2010.

4) It enables the dynamic adaptation to the heterogeneous environment as well as the environmental changes. Due to these benefits, a convergence of Grid and the agent system has been discussed steadily [3-6]. However, these studies lack the discussion of the imperatives that enable mobile Grid such as location management and message delivery.

We implemented a mobile agent system, referred to as ODDUGI in our prior work [7], which aims to support high reliability, security, and efficient location management and message delivery mechanism between mobile agents. In this paper, based on our work, we present a new mobile Grid system that uses mobile devices as resource providers in the service-based Grid. Our mobile Grid system is lightweight enough to be installed on mobile devices, which are typically equipped with components of less performance. Our system also provides two key functionalities for the physical and logical mobility of a mobile agent: Location management and Asynchronous message delivery. The location management keeps track of the locations of mobile devices that can be moved physically across network domains or logically among mobile devices located in the same or other domain. The asynchronous message delivery guarantees the delivery of a message to a destination even when the network disruption occurs. To guarantee the delivery, we implement a queue that temporarily stores a message upon submission. These location management and asynchrony are essential in coping with the users' movement and realizing the mobile Grid.

The rest of the paper is organized as follows. Section 2 describes why mobile agent should be used in mobile Grid. Section 3 presents the system model. Section 4 details the implementation of the mobile Grid system. Finally, we conclude our paper in Section 5.

2 Mobile Agent in Mobile Grid

Mobile Grid has characteristics that distinguish from the traditional Grid [8, 9]. Notable characteristics are as follows.

- *Mobile devices are typically designed with components of less performance.* In other words, they have resource limitations. For example, they are equipped with low-performance CPUs, small amount of memory and storage space, and small display size, operating from batteries, as opposed to the static counterparts such as desktop computers.
- *Mobile network connectivity varies in performance and reliability.* Depending on locations, some mobile devices have high-bandwidth connectivity, whereas others have low-bandwidth connectivity. The users' movement makes the connection unreliable and unstable from one network domain to another or to no-network domain.

Table 1 summarizes the differences between traditional Grid and mobile Grid environments. These differences make it infeasible to use the traditional middleware such as Globus [13] in the mobile Grid since it is originally devised for non-mobile devices. New strategies should take the characteristics of the mobile

Table 1. Differences between traditional Grid and mobile Grid environments

Criteria		Traditional Grid	Mobile Grid
Resource	Availability	High	Low
	Capacity	High	Low
Network	Bandwidth	High	Low
	Communication	Sync & Async	Async
	Connectivity	Stable	Unstable
Etc.	Mobility	No	Yes
	Context	Static	Dynamic
	Power supply	Stable	Unstable

Grid environment into account. We propose a mobile agent-based technology for the mobile Grid middleware.

The mobile agent provides the following benefits:

– *The mobile agent reduces a network load and latency by dispatching mobile agents to remote nodes where data is located.* For example, u-HealthCare system requires a high-bandwidth network connection to send data collected by body sensors of a patient located in a remote area. The requirement is mitigated by dispatching mobile agents to the remote area [10, 11]. The mobile agent aggregates monitoring data of the patient from the sensors, processes data, and sends outcome typically with a small amount of data to the central office. That is, the mobile agent provides the data processing capability in the dispatched place.
– *The mobile agent addresses the network disconnection problem in job execution.* After a mobile agent is dispatched to a destination node, the task is executed autonomously by the mobile agent, and its outcome is returned asynchronously when the network connection is re-established. Thus, in the u-HealthCare example, the remote node does not have to be online all the time.
– *The mobile agent dynamically provides customized services based on information of mobile devices.* In other words, the mobile agent provides adaptability to the mobile Grid environment. For example, in mobile Grid, diverse mobile devices freely join and leave the Grid. They have various static and dynamic properties such as resource capacity (e.g., CPU, storage, network bandwidth, etc.), location, availability, and reliability. For this environment, a scheduling mechanism is implemented in mobile agents assigned for scheduling after mobile devices are classified into groups [12].

3 Mobile Agent-Based Mobile Grid System

Mobile Grid is a convergence of wired and wireless computing environment to efficiently utilize both static and mobile resources. It typically consists of physically static devices, mobile devices, and proxies. Consequently, it requires a

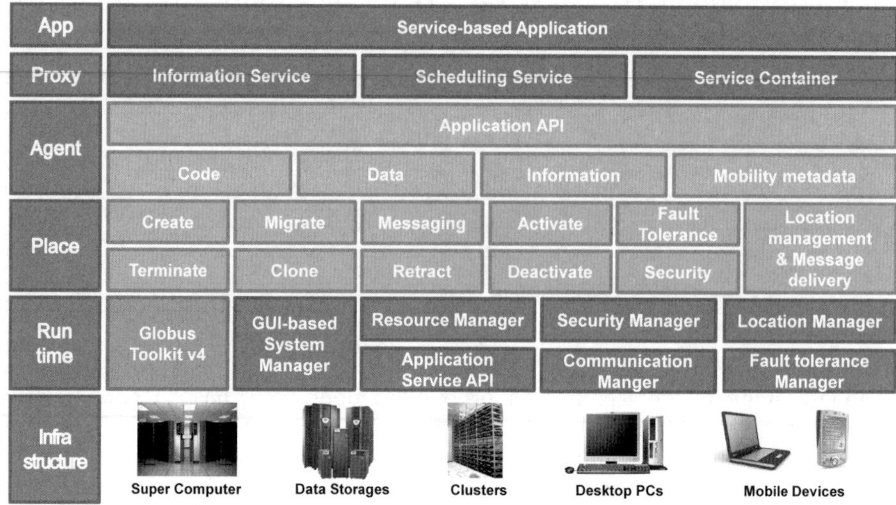

Fig. 1. Mobile Grid system architecture

new system model incorporating various homogeneous and/or heterogeneous resources. The new system should be lightweight to be ported to mobile devices with limited resources. It also should guarantee the delivery of messages in an unreliable communication environment. In this section, we first present a Mobile Grid System (MGS) architecture based on mobile agents. Then, we describe a multi-proxy environment where MGS is deployed to. Finally, we discuss location management and message delivery protocol to control mobile agents and guarantee communication between mobile agents. A detailed design concept of fault tolerance and security is described in [7].

3.1 Mobile Grid System Architecture

In [7], we proposed ODDUGI, a mobile agent system, that enables the creation, execution, transfer, and termination of mobile agents. ODDUGI provides primitives necessary for the development and management of mobile agents. Basic primitives support the creation, execution, clone, migration, activation, deactivation, and termination of a mobile agent. Extended primitives provide communication, fault tolerance, security, location management and message delivery, and monitoring tools. Mobile devices typically do not provide enough capacity to accommodate service-based Grid middleware such as Globus. One of the distinct features in ODDUGI is that it is lightweight enough to be installed on mobile devices such as PDA. Based on ODDUGI, we propose MGS architecture to utilize mobile devices as resource providers. MGS is composed of infrastructure, runtime, place, agent, proxy, and application layers as shown in Fig. 1.

- *Infrastructure layer*: The infrastructure layer includes physical devices such as supercomputer, data storage, cluster, desktop PC, laptop, smartphone, and PDA.
- *Runtime layer*: The runtime layer contains the Globus toolkit, GUI-based system manager, application service API, and various managers: resource manager, security manager, location manager, communication manager, and fault tolerance manager. The runtime layer for mobile agents is implemented as a GUI-based system manager, which helps manage mobile agents systems more conveniently. The resource manager manages the system properties and resources used in ODDUGI. The security manager is responsible for maintaining security in ODDUGI. It cooperates with the security unit in the place layer. The location manager has responsibility for location management of mobile agents. The communication manager is a daemon that listens to a certain port, waiting for mobile agents and messages from proxy and other nodes. The location and communication managers cooperate with the location management & message delivery and messaging units in the place layer. The fault tolerance manger is responsible for fault tolerance of ODDUGI mobile agent. It is related with fault tolerance unit in the place layer.
- *Place layer*: The place layer is an execution environment for mobile agents. It provides core functionality such as creation, execution, clone, migration, retraction, activation, deactivation, termination and messaging. It also provides enhanced functionality such as fault tolerance, security and location management and message delivery of mobile agents.
- *Agent layer*: The agent layer provides application developers with APIs for migration, clone, activation and communication to implement mobile agents. It allows application developers to create, execute, clone, retract, activate, deactivate and terminate mobile agents as well as interact with other agents. A mobile agent object that consists of code, data, various information (i.e., identifier, creator, time, codebase, etc.), and mobility metadata (i.e., itinerary, state, results, etc.) is manipulated in the agent layer.
- *Proxy layer*: The proxy layer provides service-based delegation functionality so that users and mobile devices do not have to be online all the time when requesting or executing jobs. It is composed of information service, scheduling service, and service container. The information service collects resource information via information providers such as Network Weather Service (NWS). The scheduling service chooses suitable resources to execute requested jobs according to the scheduling algorithm. Our scheduling algorithm takes into account user mobility, load-balancing, adaptability, and fault tolerance [12, 14].

3.2 Multi-proxy Based Mobile Grid Computing Environment

We use a multi-proxy environment where multiple proxies exist in a system and each proxy manages its own domain. The environment is composed of five components: mobile agent, node (i.e., static or mobile devices), domain, proxy

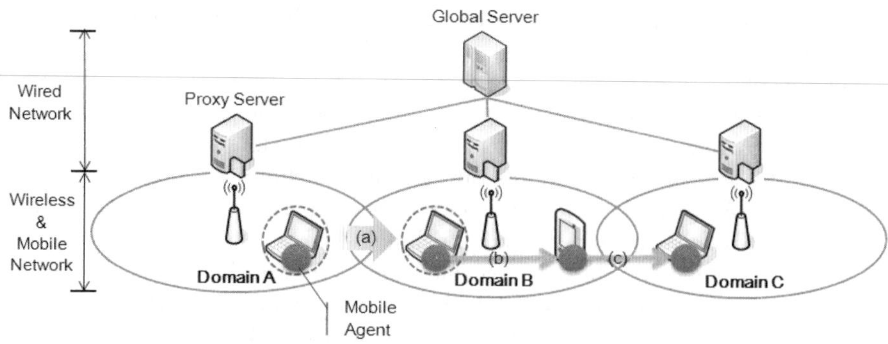

Fig. 2. Multi-proxy based mobile Grid computing environment: (a) a mobile node moves to other domain but a mobile agent remains in the same node, (b) and (c) only the mobile agent moves to a different mobile node located in the same or other domain

server, and global server. Fig. 2 shows a multi-proxy mobile Grid computing environment.

- *Mobile Agent*: A mobile agent is a mobile object that consists of code, data, state, and mobility metadata. The mobile agent is able to migrate from one node to another autonomously while performing a task. When a mobile agent migrates, it chooses the next destination according to its itinerary that is either a predefined travel plan or a dynamically determined path according to the execution result. A path from a source to the final destination is called a *migration path.*
- *Node*: A node is a place (i.e., a mobile device) where mobile agents can be executed on. Thus, the node should be installed with a mobile agent system. The node offers specific services such as computation and location awareness. A mobile agent executes tasks either on a single node or migrating through a sequence of nodes. The node that creates a mobile agent is called a *home node* (HN).
- *Domain*: A domain contains a set of nodes under one authority (such as proxy). One domain typically contains mobile devices around one access point (AP).
- *Proxy Server*: A proxy server (PS) is responsible for managing its domain. The PS provides the naming service for mobile agents created within its domain, cooperating with its global server. It performs the location management for the mobile agents within its domain with the naming table that associates the names of mobile agents with the addresses of the home nodes. In addition, the PS provides the information service, scheduling service, and service container. The information service collects information of mobile devices such as machine and network availabilities. Using this information, the scheduling service makes a decision on which mobile devices are available for the job execution. Jobs are delegated via a service-based interface to the

PS (i.e., service container), which creates and deploys mobile agents for the jobs.
– *Global Server*: A global server (GS) provides the lookup service for mobile agents and nodes. The GS maintains the location information as well as the list of service information for the mobile agents created and delivered in all domains.

In such an environment, a mobile agent executes tasks migrating through a sequence of nodes possibly located in different domains. Each action that a mobile agent performs on a node is called a *stage*. The execution of mobile agents on a node results in a new internal state of mobile agent as well as potentially a new state of the node. Therefore, the mobile agent status in the previous stage is different from one in the current stage.

As shown in Fig. 2, there are two types of mobility: physical mobility and logical mobility. The *physical mobility* means that a mobile node moves to other domain but a mobile agent remains in the same node, as depicted in (a) of Fig. 2. The *logical mobility* means that only the mobile agent moves to a different mobile node located in the same or other domain, as depicted in the migration paths (b) and (c) of Fig. 2. In all cases, the proxy server should be informed the new locations of mobile agents. Therefore, the mobile Grid system provides the location management to interact with mobile agents in a multi-proxy mobile Grid environment.

3.3 Location Management and Message Delivery

We propose a location management and message transfer protocol based on our prior works: Broadcast-based Message Transferring protocol [15] and Reliable Asynchronous Message Delivery (RAMD) protocol [16]. The Broadcast-based Message Transferring protocol broadcasts only the notification of changes instead of message content itself, so subscribers may request the details of changes if necessary. Therefore, it reduces the amount of network traffic. This protocol is useful for the event notification in mobile agent-based mobile Grid. In service-based Grid, WS-Notification specification allows the event-driven programming between Grid services. However, it would not be applied to the mobile agent system because it demands the web services, which typically require the modest computing power. The RAMD protocol consists of a location management procedure and a blackboard-based asynchronous message delivery procedure. In order to reliably and asynchronously deliver messages, RAMD exploits a blackboard (i.e., a shared information space for message exchange). In addition, the message delivery is tightly related with the agent migration. It guarantees the message delivery by placing a blackboard in each domain. That is, this protocol is useful for the reliable delivery of messages in mobile Grid where mobile agents can be frequently moved.

The RAMD protocol for mobile Grid consists of three phases: creation, migration, and message delivery phases.

- *Creation phase*: A mobile agent registers its location to the GS and the PS upon creation. In the migration phase, a mobile agent registers its location to the HN or its associated PSs when the agent migrates from one node to another.
- *Migration phase*: It is divided into intra-domain migration (i.e., when a mobile agent migrates to a node within the same domain) and inter-domain migration (i. e., when a mobile agent migrates to a node in other domain). According to the migration type, the location registration procedure is executed differently. In the intra-domain migration, a mobile agent sends a location update message only to the PS with which the mobile agent is associated. In the inter-domain migration, a mobile agent sends the location update message to the HN, previous PS and current PS.
- *Message delivery phase*: A message is delivered to a mobile agent after looking up the naming table and locating the agent. First, a sender finds the address of the HN by contacting the GS and sends a message to the PS. Then the PS puts the message on its blackboard. Finally, when the PS receives a location update message from a mobile agent, the PS checks its blackboard. If there is a message, the PS retrieves it from the blackboard and delivers it to the mobile agent.

In this way, the RAMD protocol for mobile Grid decreases the cost of the location management and the message delivery. Furthermore, the RAMD protocol for mobile Grid takes care of the location management and message delivery of cloned, parent and child mobile agents, so that it ensures the message delivery of these mobile agents.

4 Implementation

We implemented the Mobile Grid System (MGS) based on Globus Toolkit Version 4 and ODDUGI mobile agent system. In MGS, a proxy server plays key roles as follows: job reception from clients, creation and management of mobile agents, and outcome delivery from mobile agents to clients. Globus supports a stateful web service keeping stateful resource information. We assume that a resource corresponds to a mobile agent. A multiple-resource stateful web service is implemented by using separate classes for service and resource. The service class is implemented with a design pattern known as the factory/instance pattern, which is shown in Fig. 3. The client interacts with two services (factory service and instance service) to submit a job. The client requests a resource home to create a resource through the factory service (Fig. 3 (a)). Then the client receives EPR (endpoint reference, i.e., Agent ID) from the resource home through the factory service (Fig. 3 (b)). The client executes a resource operation through the instance service by using a given EPR (Fig. 3 (c)).

When the client executes the resource operation, it may have to wait for a response synchronously until timeout. Asynchrony in mobile agent system prevents the wasteful pauses since the client is notified when the mobile agent completes

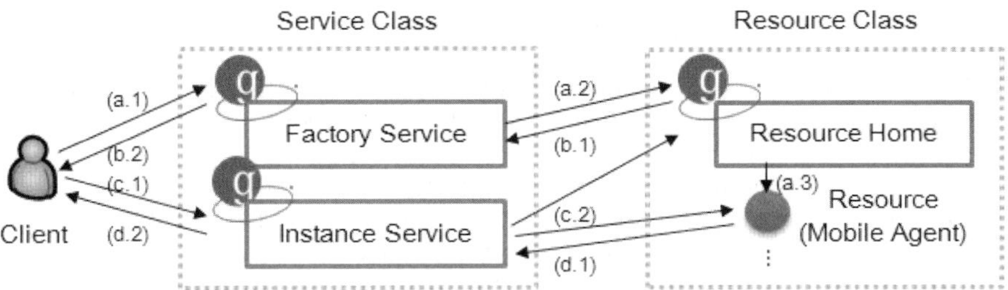

Fig. 3. Factory/instance pattern (a) resource creation (b) EPR reception (c) execution of a resource operation (d) notification of a result to a client

a job. However, in mobile Grid, the asynchrony is maintained between proxies and mobile agents. Thus, there should be a communication mechanism between proxies and clients. The simplest approach is that a client keeps track of outcome status in a proxy using polling. That is, the client periodically contacts a proxy server to check whether the requested job is finished. However, this approach incurs an overhead because the client repeatedly sends a polling message to a server and there is a scalability problem if many clients exist in a system. Therefore, we implemented the response message delivery using the WS-Notification family of the specification. This approach notifies the result to the client when the proxy server receives the result from the mobile agent (Fig. 3 (d)). We used different protocols among clients, proxies, and mobile devices. Between proxies and mobile devices (i.e., mobile agents), we implemented Broadcast-based Message Transferring and RAMD protocols for the asynchronous message delivery. Between proxies and clients, we used WS-Notification specification for the asynchronous message delivery.

5 Conclusions

This paper presents a mobile Grid system based on mobile agent that enables a convergence of wired and wireless computing environments. Our system architecture makes use of static and mobile resources. In the multi-proxy based mobile Grid, a mobile agent executes tasks migrating through a sequence of nodes located in multi-domains. Mobile devices can be moved physically across network or logically among mobile devices located in the same or other domain. The location management and asynchronous message delivery are two key enablers of mobile Grid to harness the mobile devices. The location management locates mobile agents by keeping track of the locations of mobile devices. The asynchronous message delivery guarantees the delivery of messages to a destination by implementing a queue that temporarily stores a message upon submission. Finally, we implemented our mobile Grid system based on Globus Toolkit and ODDUGI mobile agent system. We plan to develop and deploy the Ubi-Campus service application on our system.

References

1. Kurdi, H., Li, M., Al-Raweshidy, H.: A Classification of Emerging and Traditional Grid Systems. IEEE Distributed Systems Online 9 (2008)
2. Foster, I., Kesselman, C.: The Grid 2: Blueprint for a New Computing Infrastructure. Morgan Kaufmann, San Francisco (2004)
3. Foster, I., Jennings, N.R., Kesselman, C.: Brain Meets Brawn: Why Grid and Agents Need Each Other. In: Kudenko, D., Kazakov, D., Alonso, E. (eds.) AAMAS 2004. LNCS (LNAI), vol. 3394, pp. 8–15. Springer, Heidelberg (2005)
4. Zahreddine, W., Mahmoud, Q.H.: An Agent-based Approach to Composite Mobile Web Services. In: 19th International Conference on Advanced Information Networking and Applications (AINA 2005), pp. 189–192 (2005)
5. Bellavista, P., Corradi, A., Monti, S.: Integrating Web Services and Mobile Agent Systems. In: 25th IEEE International Conference on Distributed Computing Systems Workshops, pp. 283–290 (2005)
6. Athanaileas, T.E., Tselikas, N.D., Tsoulos, G.V., Kaklamani, D.I.: An Agent-Based Framework for Integrating Mobility into Grid Services. In: Proceedings of the 1st international Conference on MOBILe Wireless MiddleWARE, Operating Systems, and Applications. ICST (Institute for Computer Sciences, Social-Informatics and Telecommunications Engineering), Innsbruck, Austria (2007)
7. Choi, S., Choo, H., Baik, M., Kim, H., Byun, E.: ODDUGI: Ubiquitous Mobile Agent System. In: Gervasi, O., Taniar, D., Murgante, B., Laganà, A., Mun, Y., Gavrilova, M.L. (eds.) ICCSA 2009. LNCS, vol. 5593, pp. 393–407. Springer, Heidelberg (2009)
8. Satyanarayanan, M.: Fundamental Challenges in Mobile Computing. In: Proceedings of the Fifteenth Annual ACM Symposium on Principles of Distributed Computing. ACM, Philadelphia, pp. 1–7 (1996)
9. Satyanarayanan, M.: Mobile Information Access. IEEE Pers. Commun. 3, 26–33 (1996)
10. Kang, E., Im, Y., Kim, U.: Remote Control Multi-Agent System for u-Healthcare Service, pp. 636–644 (2007)
11. Kirn, S.: Ubiquitous Healthcare: The OnkoNet Mobile Agents Architecture, pp. 265–277 (2009)
12. Lee, J., Choi, S., Suh, T., Yu, H., Gil, J.: Group-based Scheduling Algorithm for Fault Tolerance in Mobile Grid. In: Kim, T.-h., Stoica, A., Chang, R.-S. (eds.) Security-Enriched Urban Computing and Smart Grid. Communications in Computer and Information Science, vol. 78, pp. 394–403. Springer, Heidelberg (2010)
13. Foster, I.: Globus Toolkit Version 4: Software for Service-Oriented Systems. Journal of Computer Science and Technology 21, 513–520 (2006)
14. Lee, J., Song, S., Gil, J., Chung, K., Suh, T., Yu, H.: Balanced Scheduling Algorithm Considering Availability in Mobile Grid. In: Proceedings of the 4th International Conference on Advances in Grid and Pervasive Computing, pp. 211–222. Springer, Heidelberg (2009)
15. Baik, M., Yang, K., Shon, J., Hwang, C.: Message Transferring Model between Mobile Agents in Multi-region Mobile Agent Computing Environment. In: Chung, C.-W., Kim, C.-k., Bilò, V., Ling, T.-W., Song, K.-H. (eds.) HSI 2003. LNCS, vol. 2713, pp. 166–166. Springer, Heidelberg (2003)
16. Choi, S., Kim, H., Byun, E., Hwang, C., Baik, M.: Reliable Asynchronous Message Delivery for Mobile Agents. IEEE Internet Computing 10, 16–25 (2006)

An Improvement on the Weighted Least-Connection Scheduling Algorithm for Load Balancing in Web Cluster Systems

DongJun Choi, Kwang Sik Chung, and JinGon Shon*

Dept. of Computer Science, Korea National Open University
169, Dongsung-dong, Jongro-ku, Seoul, Korea
hotfeel7@daum.net, {kchung0825,jgshon}@knou.ac.kr

Abstract. Web cluster systems consist of a load balancer for distributing web requests and loads to several servers, and real servers for processing web requests. Previous load distribution scheduling algorithms of web cluster systems to distribute web requests to real servers are Round-Robin, Weighted Round-Robin, Least-Connection and Weighted Least-Connection(WLC) algorithm. The WLC scheduling algorithm, in which a throughput weight is assigned to real servers and the least connected real server is selected for processing web requests, is generally used for web cluster systems. When a new real server is added to a web cluster system with many simultaneous users, previous WLC scheduling algorithm assigns web requests to only the new real server, and makes load imbalance among real servers. In this paper, we propose a improved WLC scheduling algorithm which maintains load balance among real servers by avoiding web requests being assigned to only a new real server. When web requests are continuously assigned to only a new real server more than the maximum continuous allocation number(L), the proposed algorithm excepts the new real server from activated real server scheduling list and deactivates the new real server. And after L-1 allocation round times, the new real server is included into real server scheduling list by activating it. When a new real server is added to web cluster systems, the proposed algorithm maintains load balance among real servers by avoiding overloads of the new real server.

Keywords: Weighted Least-Connection algorithm, Web Cluster System, Load Balancing.

1 Introduction

As web services and internet usage get popular, a web server has received thousands and thousands web requests per one millisecond. A web server which receives overflowed web requests is stuffed and shut down. Web service administrators try to device method which can improve the performance of a web service in spite of overflowed web requests in web cluster systems. Methods to improve the performance of web

* Corresponding author.

T.-h. Kim et al. (Eds.): GDC/CA 2010, CCIS 121, pp. 127–134, 2010.

service consist of hardware extension and software-based extension using clustering technology. Since software-based extension on a single server's upgrade technology is cheaper than hardware extension and guarantees scalability, it is more useful and effective [1][2][3]. Software-based extension on a single server is that servers is clustered and managed as like virtual one server and called cluster systems. Cluster systems connect several web servers with a high speed network and serve many requests as like a single server.

Since new servers can be added more and more, cluster systems guarantees scalability and is cheaper than a super computer and a parallel computer. Cluster system is divided into High Performance Computing cluster computing, High Availability cluster computing, and Load Distribution cluster computing according to the purpose of computing system. Web cluster systems are a load distribution cluster computing system which makes web requests distributed on several real servers[2][4]. Web cluster systems consist of real servers which process a web request and a load balancer which distributes web requests on several real servers. A load balancer invokes Weighted Least-Connection(WLC) scheduling algorithm in order to avoid load concentration on one real server[5][9][10]. WLC Scheduling algorithm assigns the performance weight(web request connection number) to each real server and selects least weighted real servers. But previous WLC Scheduling algorithm cannot effectively maintain load balance when a new real server is added to web cluster systems with many simultaneous users, since web requests are assigned to only the new real server among real servers.

We proposes the improved WLC scheduling algorithm, that excepts a newly added new real server from activated real server scheduling list by deactivating the added real server, which keeps maintaining load balance among real servers in spite of adding a new real server to web cluster system.

2 Related Works

Load distribution scheduling algorithms in web cluster systems are classified into round-robin scheduling algorithm, weighted round-robin scheduling algorithm, least-connection scheduling algorithm, and weight based least-connection scheduling algorithm. Round-Robin scheduling algorithm selects a real server and forwards a web request to the real servers by using a Round-Robin method. Round-Robin scheduling algorithm does not consider a connection number of real servers and response time, and uniformly assigns web requests to real servers. Weighted Round-Robin scheduling algorithm considers various performance of real servers. Performance weight is defined as a constant number which means capacity of each real server. In this scheduling algorithm, web connection state is not used for selecting a server. However, if web requests change suddenly, load imbalance will be brought about among real servers in this weighted Round-Robin scheduling algorithm. Least-Connection scheduling assigns a web request to a real server that has least web connection number. Since this algorithm does not unfairly assign web requests to only one real server with the same capacity, it is effective when web requests are overloaded to web cluster systems. However, among real servers with various performance capacity, load imbalance occurs as like other scheduling algorithms. In Weighted Least-Connection scheduling(WLC), various performance weight numbers can be assigned to each real server. The real server with a higher weight receives more web requests and more web connections than others.

If we assume that *n* is the number of real server, real server *i* has a weight W_i (i= 1, …, n) and the number of connection C_i(i=1,…,n), then a web request is assigned to real server *j* that satisfies with the below equation[6].

$$C_j/W_j = \min\{C_i/W_i\}\ (i=1,\ldots,n)$$

WLC scheduling algorithm has a problem that when a new real server is added to web cluster systems with many simultaneous users, WLC scheduling algorithm assigns web requests intensively to the new real server.

3 Improved Weighted Least-Connection Scheduling Algorithm

3.1 Real Server Selection Algorithm

Real server selection algorithm counts the number of activated real servers and selects a real server by a same way as WLC scheduling algorithm. Fig. 1. is a real server selection algorithm by that load balancer selects a real server processing a web request. This algorithm compares all real servers and selects a real server that has the least web connection per performance weight of a real server. At that time, if the selected real server is at deactivated state, then the real server is excepted and the other real server, that has the least web connection per performance weight of a real server, is selected. When there is no real server that is compared to select a real server, Reduce_Overload function (overload decrease algorithm) is invoked with the number of activated real server and selected real server.

```
 WLCI_Schedule(A[], n)
Input : A[0:n-1] : Arrangement of real server
n : Numbe of arrangement element
output : least : Selected real server
{
   var least : Save of selected real server
   var active : Number of server to be vitality state

   f or ( i = 0; i < n; i++ ) {
      if ( A[i].flag == DISABLE ) {
         A[i]; Real server in scheduling exception
      }
      if ( least.conns / least.weight > A[i].conns / A[i].weight ) {
         least = A[i];
      }
      active++;               /* New add part */
   }

   Reduce_Overload(least, active);      /* New add part */
   return least;
 }
```

Fig. 1. Real server selection algorithm

3.2 Overload Reduce Algorithm

Overload reduce algorithm uses maximum series assignment number (L) in order to avoid concentrated web request assign to new added real server. L is a maximum web request assignment number of times within that web requests can be continuously assigned to a real server. If web requests are assigned to a real server more than L, the real server's state is set to 'deactivated state' and excepted from activated real server list. And after L-1 times web requests, the real server is set to 'activated state' and included in activated real server list. Fig. 2. is overload reduce algorithm.

```
Reduce_Overload(s, n)
  s : Selected real server
  n : Number of activated real servers
  {
    var old_s : Previously Selected Real Server
    var count : Series assignment number
    var flag : Overload flag
    var L : Maximum series assignment number

        /* Overload mode */
    if ( flag == 1 ) {
      if ( --count < 1 ) {
        old_s.flag = ENABLE;
        flag = 0;
      }
      return;
    }

      /* Normal mode */
    if ( n < 2 ) {
      return;
    }
    if ( old_s != s ) {
      old_s = s;
      count = 1;
      return;
    }

    if ( ++count >= L ) {
      count = L - 1;
      old_s.flag = DISABLE;
      flag = 1;
    }
  }
```

Fig. 2. Overload reduce algorithm

Overload reduce algorithm receives a selected real server and the number of activated real servers as parameters. If there is only one real server in activated real server list, real server selection algorithm resumes since a web request cannot be continuously assigned to same real server. Overload reduce algorithm is executed in normal operation mode or overload mode. Normal operation mode is the state in which load distribution scheduling is executed normally and periodically checks web requests concentration on one real server. Overload mode is the state in which web requests are assigned to maximum web request assignment number overload state allocated as maximum series assignment number to real server that web request is equal, reduce overload. In normal operation mode(a flag value is 0), the count number increases by 1 if a newly selected real server is equal to a previously selected real server(old_s), otherwise a newly selected real server(s) is stored and count number is set to 1. If the count number is bigger than maximum web request assignment number(L), the selected real server is deactivated and excepted from web request assignment scheduling. Count value is set to L-1 and overload flag is set to 1 so that the real server is excepted from scheduling list for L-1 times round. During overload mode(flag value is 1), the count decreases by 1 whenever overload reduce algorithm is called. If the count is less than 1, then the real server is included in activated real server list and overload flag is set to 0.

4 Performance Assessment

4.1 Simulation Environment

In this chapter, we analyze the performance in an aspect of number of web request and web tasks. A web request arrives by average 250 times of uniform distribution. When a real server is connected, a web request follows Poisson distribution with average 3 times, a next web request time follows Poisson distribution with average 10 seconds. And average throughput time of a real server follows normal distribution with 2 seconds and standard deviation is 1 second. If there is no web re-request to the connected real server within 20 seconds, the web connection of the real server is disconnected. Maximum continuous allocation number is 10 in order to avoid concentration of web requests assignment to only one newly added real server. We simulated our proposed algorithm on web clustering systems with 9 real servers for 51 seconds.

We assume that a real server *i* has performance weight W_i $(i = 1, \cdots, n)$, web task number J_i $(i = 1, \cdots, n)$, and web connection number C_i $(i = 1, \cdots, n)$.

Table 1. Before input R10 server, state of virtual web cluster system

Real server (i)	weight(Wi)	Work number(Ji)	Connection number (Ci)
R1	1	126	761
R2	2	227	1522
R3	1	120	760
R4	3	329	2282
R5	1	120	761
R6	2	233	1521
R7	1	115	761
R8	1	120	761
R9	3	324	2282

Table 1. is state of web cluster systems at t = 51. While the number of a real server R1's web connection is 761, number of web task that is executed in server actually is 126. And real server R2 is 1522 that connection number is double more than real server R1's connection number because weight is 2. Weight inputs 1 is R10 server in addition and compared existing techniques and proposed connection number of techniques and work number in such state.

4.2 Simulation Results

The proposed algorithm is compared with WLC algorithm and a comparison factor is a web connection number of real server R1. A Fig. 3. is the result of simulation. A Fig. 4. is the result of a web connection number of real server R10 that is newly added to an activated real server list A proposed algorithm shows the similar result of real server R1 with previous WLC algorithm. In previous WLC algorithm, all of web requests are assigned to only a newly added real server R10 until a web connection number of the

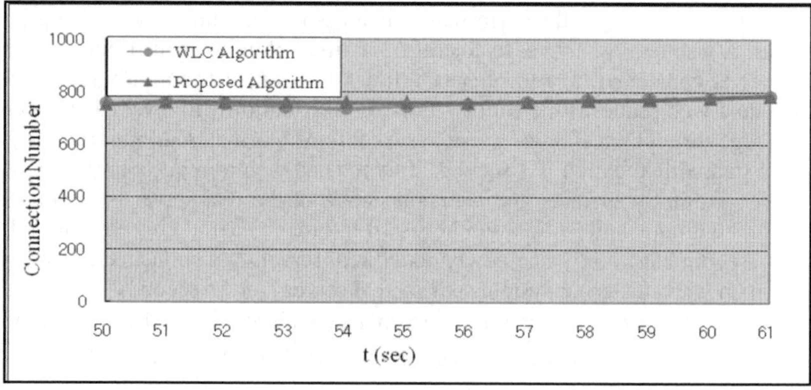

Fig. 3. Connection number comparison of existing R1 server

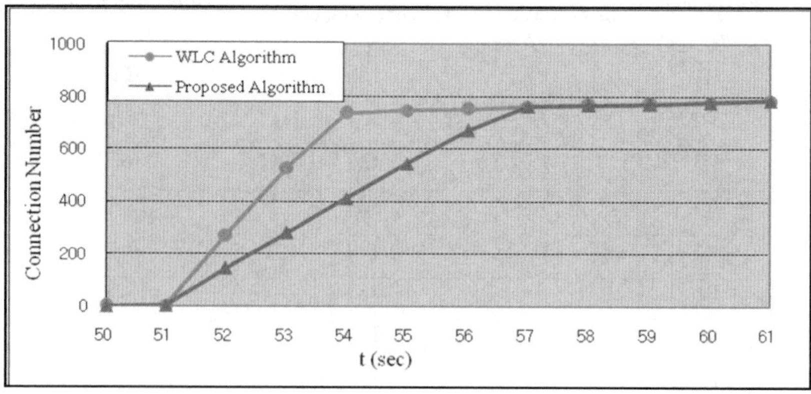

Fig. 4. New connection number comparison of added R10 server

real server R11 is same as an average web connection number of other real servers. And a web connection number of newly added real server rapidly increases. But in proposed algorithm, only one web request is assigned to the newly added real server and nine web requests are assigned to other real servers. Thus a web connection number of newly added real server moderately increases.

A Fig. 5. is a comparison result of task number of real server R1 in previous WLC algorithm and proposed algorithm. A Fig. 6. is a comparison result of task number of real server R10 in previous WLC algorithm and proposed algorithm. In a <Figure 4-3>, a proposed algorithm shows a similar result of task number of real server R1 with previous WLC algorithm. But in a <Figure 4-4>, around 250 web requests per second are assigned to the newly added real server R11. And the web task number of newly added real server rapidly increases. But in our proposed algorithm, around 140 web requests per second are assigned to the newly added real server. Thus a web task number of the newly added real server moderately increases. We can conclude that our proposed algorithm effectively maintains load balance among real servers than the previous WLC algorithm.

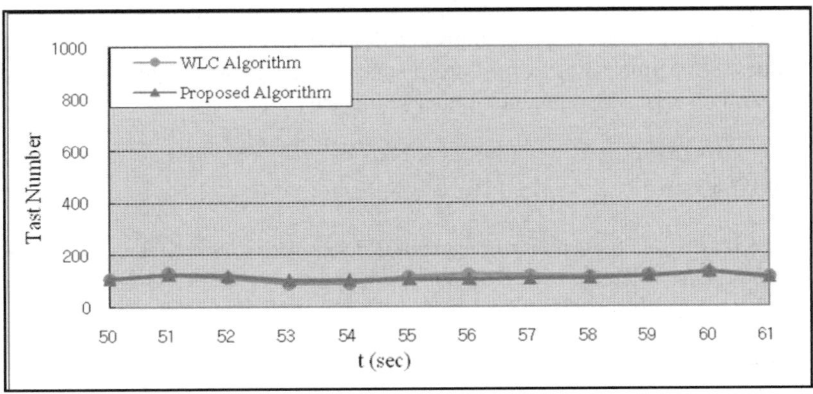

Fig. 5. Work number comparison of existing R1 server

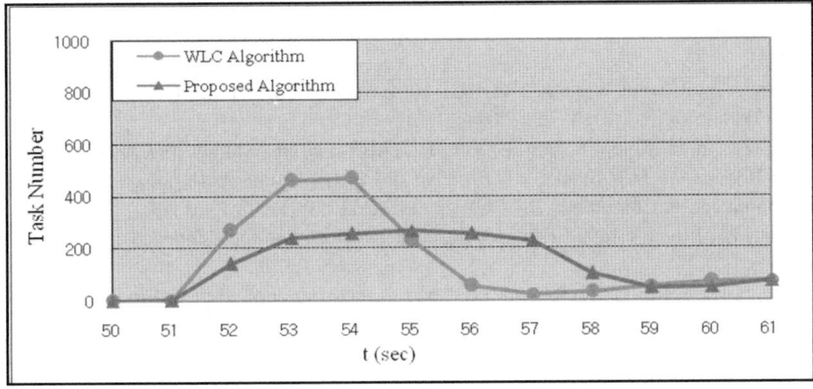

Fig. 6. New work number comparison of added R10 server

As a simulation result, maximally 508 web tasks are assigned to a newly added real server in previous WLC algorithm and maximally 260 web tasks are assigned to a newly added real server in our proposed algorithm.

5 Conclusion

In this paper, we proposed the improved WLC algorithm that maintains load balance among real servers by avoiding web requests being assigned to only a new real server when the real server is newly added to a activated real server list. Proposed algorithm consists of real server selection algorithm and overload reduce algorithm. In proposed algorithm, a real server is selected by real server selection algorithm and the selected real server is passed to overload reduce algorithm as a parameter. If web requests are assigned to a real server more than L times, the real server is set to be deactivated state and excepted from activated real server list in overload reduce algorithm. As a result, proposed algorithm maintains load balance among real servers by avoiding overloads on the new real server.

We have plan to study a new algorithm that can deal with the case in that two real servers are added to web cluster systems and dynamically adjust maximum continuous web request allocation value according to state of web cluster system without specifying maximum series assignment number voluntarily.

References

1. Kim, S.C., Lee, Y.: System Infrastructure of Efficient Web Cluster System to Decrease the Response Time using the Load Distribution Algorithm. Journal of Korea Information Science Society C(10), 507–513 (2004)
2. Nortel Networks, Alteon Web Switch, `http://www.nortel.com/` (2006.5.20 visit)
3. Zhang, W., et al.: Linux Virtual Server Project, `http://www.linuxvirtualserver.org/` (2006.5.20 visit)
4. Kwon, O.Y.: Cluster system abstract, Technical.Policy same native place, Korea Institute of Science and Technology Information news (2000)
5. Yun, C.G.: A Load Distribution Technique of Web Clustering System based on the Real Time Status of Real Server. Journal of Korea Information Science Society A(5), 427–432 (2005)
6. Kuzmin, A.: Cluster Approach to High Performance Computing. Computer Modeling & New Technologies 7(2), 7–15 (2003)
7. Shao, Z., Jin, H., Chen, B., Xu, J., Yue, J.: HARTs: High Availability Cluster Architecture with Redundant TCP Stacks. In: Proc. of the International Performance Computing and Communication Conference(IPCCC), pp. 255–262 (2003)
8. Zhang, W.: Linux Virtual Server for Scalable Network Services. Ottawa Linux Symposium (2000)
9. Santana, C., Leite, J.C.B., Mossé, D.: Load forecasting applied to soft real-time web clusters. In: Proceedings of the 2010 ACM Symposium on Applied Computing (2010)
10. Zhou, H., Hu, Y., Mu, D., Hu, W.: Proportional Delay Differentiation Service and Load Balancing in Web Cluster Systems. In: INFOCOM IEEE Conference on Computer Communications Workshops (2010)

Design and Implementation of User-Created Information Systems with Mobile RFID

Jae Kwoen Lee[1], SungHo Chin[2], Hee Cheon Kim[3], and Kwang Sik Chung[*]

[1] Hanmi IT Ltd.
[2] Dep. of Computer Science Education, Korea University
[3] Dept. of Computer Science, Korea National Open University
jaekwonyi@naver.com, wintop@korea.ac.kr,
{hckim,Kchung0825}@knou.ac.kr

Abstract. RFID (Radio Frequency Identification) has been usually applied at physical distribution field. The Mobile RFID can be the only technology that we can lead the market. In our country, ETRI standardizes MOBION (MOBile Identification ON), and the mobile-telecommunication companies provide the trial-mobile RFID service from 2006. In the trial-mobile RFID services, the Broker model is used to decode the mobile RFID code. However, the Broker model has some problems, such as communication overhead caused by the frequent ODS query, service performance, and various services for users. In this paper, we developed device application that is capable for filtering unrelated code from RFID service to improve the decoding performance. We also improve the performance through simplifying connection process between device application and the broker. Finally, we propose and develop the user-created information system to widely distribute the Mobile RFID service.

Keywords: mobile RFID, dongle RFID reader, user-created information system.

1 Introduction

RFID (Radio Frequency Identification) has been usually applied at physical distribution field. A mobile RFID service provides useful information to users with the cell-phone, in which RFID reader is attached or embedded. Although the developed countries dominate most of the RFID technologies, the Mobile RFID can be the only technology that we can lead the market. In our country, ETRI standardizes MOBION (MOBile Identification ON), and the mobile-telecommunication companies provide the trial-mobile RFID service with the reader embedded mobile devices[1][2][3].

A mobile service model can be classified based on the existence of the decoding broker. If the broker is included in a model, the model is called Broker model, and the contrary is Basic model. In the trial-mobile RFID services, the Broker model is used. The model easily reflects the revised standard through only modifying the broker, not the application, because the device does not query to the ODS (Object Directory

[*]Corresponding author.

T.-h. Kim et al. (Eds.): GDC/CA 2010, CCIS 121, pp. 135–144, 2010.

Service)[4][5]. The code converting and interaction with ODS are not implemented in the relatively low-capacity mobile device, but in the broker. Because of this implementation, the overhead in the mobile devices can degrade and traffic and transactions can be controllable[6][7][8][9]. Thereby, the trial service is selected to improve more stable services. However, to widely distribute the RFID service, some problems, such as communication overhead caused by the frequent ODS query, service performance, and various services for users, need to be addressed.

In this paper, we developed device application that is capable for filtering unrelated code from RFID service to improve the decoding performance. Through the definition of the packet format between device application and Broker, We also implement broker application to directly transfer service data. Finally, we propose and develop the user-created information system, in which users can create and update information by themselves, based on the convergence of the UCC (User Created Contents) paradigm to the Mobile RFID technology.

2 Paper Preparation

As mentioned above, the mobile RFID service model can be classified by whether the broker is included or not. The basic model can get the URLs through direct interaction between mobile device and ODS. The minor aspects of the model are to make device application more complex, and the model also requires the modification of application when the standard is renewed or revised because the communication traffic might occur in the low-performance device[10]. Therefore, the trial-mobile RFID service is based on the broker model in which the Broker is located between devices and ODS. A device can demand decoding only by communicating with the Broker. Once the socket connection between the Broker and devices is established, the broker is responsible for data transmission, traffic management and decoding through interaction with the ODS[11][12][13][15][16].

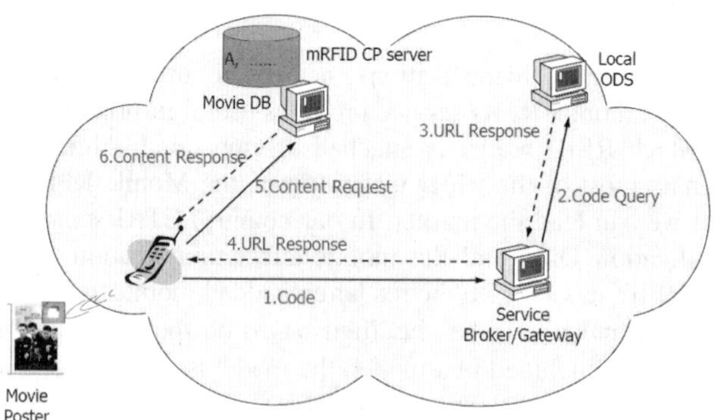

Fig. 1. Broker model

In the mobile RFID decoding process, a device application scans the tag code and delivers the RFID code based on the HTTP (HyperText Transfer Protocol). To decode the code, the Broker queries to the DOS after converting the code to the FQDN (Fully Qualified Domain Name) format. The local ODS queried by the Broker generates the URL about the query and sends back it based on the HTTP. If the ODS cannot generate URL by itself, the URL can be produces through the higher-level ODS server[14][16][17].

One problem of the existed mobile RFID service model is to request decoding caused by sending even the unrelated code. Another problem is that Web server and WAS (Web Application Server) are mandatory to implement the Broker as the HTTP is used for the interaction between devices and the Broker[13][14][16].

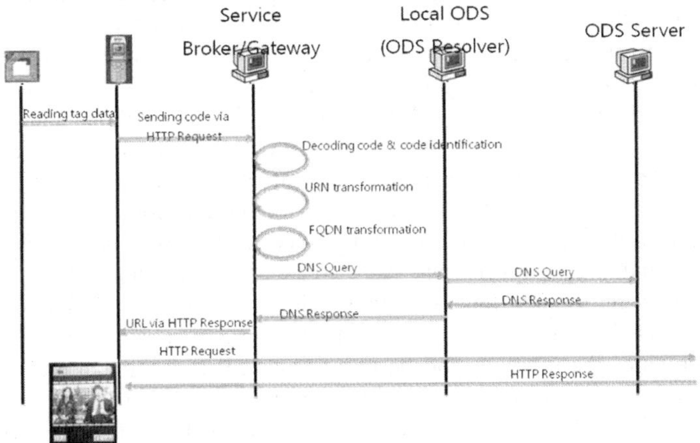

Fig. 2. Dataflow of the Broker model

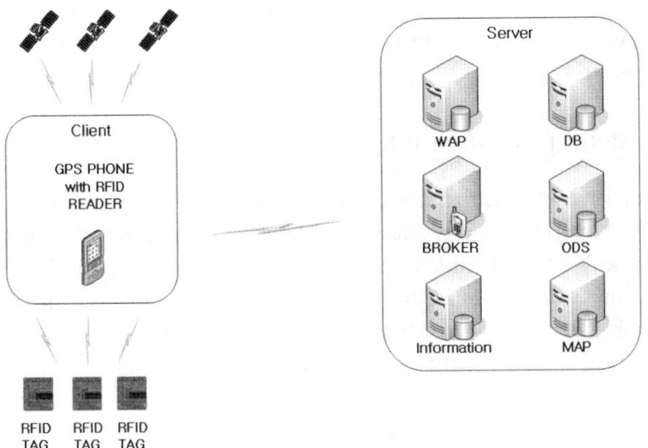

Fig. 3. The system composition of the user-created information system

3 The Composition of User-Created Information System

The user-created information system with the mobile RFID reads the POI (Point Of Interest) tags through the GPS location system or RFID code reader attached device, and then, it utilizes the information generated based on the location measured by the GPS system. To compose the system that generates and queries a user's POI information, the server includes ODS (Object Directory Service) server, MAP application, Broker application, information application, WAP server and DBMS. The client consists of GPS enabled device and dongle RFID reader.

3.1 Information Application

The information application is responsible for control of the user-created information system, user authentication, and log management, through the interactions among WAP server, Broker application, MAP application and DB systems. We divided the system into the six parts. The parts are Connection Manager, User Manager for user registration and authentication, Billing Manager for accounting service, Statistic Manager for management various statistics, POI manager for management POI information and categorization. The detail description of each part is as follows. The Connection Manager establishes and maintains the connections among WAP server, Broker application, Map application, and DB server. The User Manager is capable for management the user information, such as registration, modification, and access control of service information. The POI manager builds the DB about the POI information that is main context for the sharing among server users. The Location Manager provides the interface for the user-requested measurement and the latitude-longitude coordination can be changed to the administrative district name or vice-versa. The Billing Manager stores and retrieves the accounting information for the using contents. When the location measurement is performed, which usually charging is happened, the manager notifies the result of charging and stores the charging information. The transaction is used for the information transmission to ensure more accuracy delivery. The Statistic Manager provides various statistics with respect to user, menu, service, time, location and accounting based on the collected information by the collection processes.

3.2 User-Created Information Databases

To store and retrieve POI information created by a user through the scanning of RFID tags, we use the Sybase ASE (Adaptive Server Enterprise) version 12.5 and the relational DB model based tables are in it. The user table contains the information about users in our system. To log the access information for each table, the user ID as a FK (Foreign Key) belongs to other tables. The location information table has the data about location, name, evaluate-rate, etc. of the POI and the table can be stored and retrieved data based on the reply and address table. The accounting table maintains the accounting information, and the log table stores access history for each user. The RFID table includes the code list, and the system table holds the information about system status and environment, data for system monitoring.

3.3 Broker Application

The role of the Broker is the interface between WIPI (Wireless Internet Platform for Interoperability) an application and ODS server. Another role is returning the URI information of the RFID tag code to the WIPI application after receiving the RFID tag from the WIPI application. That is, (1) the broker decodes the RFID tag code read from the WIPI application, (2) convers the code to FQDN format and queries to the ODS as NAPTR type and (3) delivers the URI to the WIPI application. To implement basic operations of the Broker, the Broker application must has several functionalities such as, RFID code identification, FQDN formatting for the ODS query, inquiry for taking URI from DNS and delivery of the URI and its kind. To meet these requirements, we modulate the Broker application and define the packet formats between Broker application and WIPI application as in the table 6 and 7. We present each module more detail in the next part. The Connector module is responsible for connection and data transmission between WIPI application and Broker. Through this module, WIPI application sends RFID code to Broker application and Broker application delivers the URI to the device for accessing the RFID code. The Analyzer module analyzes the data transmitted from the WIPI application based on the packet transmission protocol. It also reads the format field of the data and delivers each code to each corresponding formatter, the formatter convert delivered code to the URN following the RFID code from the analyzer. The converter changes the URN to FQDN that feasible to the mobile RFID code type, and sends it to the Resolver. The Resolver extracts the URI information by referencing the DNS packet protocol document, which is returned from the DNS query with FQDN. The connect send the extracted URI information to mobile application. The Version field is located at the first byte of the packet to manage the data packet based on the various versions between WIPI and Broker application. The Message ID field records the request time of the packet and its format is 'YYYYMMDDHHMMSS'. In the response data, this field is same as in the request, and it also used to differentiate the response code for packet sending. The Message Type is code for classifying sender and receiver. The Format field is for distinguishing the type of the code when RFID code is scanned. Because the tags supporting ISO/IEC-18000-6C(EPC Class1 Gen 2) Air-Interface, which is the most popular tag in our country's RFID market, can record kCode, mobile RFID code (mCode, mini-mCode, micro-mCode), URL Code, EPC, etc., the Format field is used to give the information to Broker application about what type of the code is recorded. The reason why WIPI application examines the field about the kind of tag is that if the broker application inspects the kind of tag, unrelated decode requests are always delivered to the Broker application, and this can cause traffic and overhead of Broker application. To prevent the problem, WIPI application checks the kind of code when reader scans the tag code. The Code Length informs that the length of tag according to the type in the code-part. In the mobile RFID code, the length of mCode is various from 48 to 128 bits, but the lengths of mini-mCode and micro-mCode are static with 32 bits. The Code field stores the contents of each code. The Result field returns the result of the query about RFID code is success or not. If the query is failed, the description of the reason of the result is stored in the field. The field value is same as the Response code in the RFC 1035. The URL Length field is the length of the URL if the query is successfully performed and the length is transferred to the client.

3.4 MAP Application

Map application is responsible for converting location information measured by GPS and administrative district name each other in the device, and the latitude-longitude coordination is represented by the WGS84(World Geodetic System) coordination system type. Table 8 and 9 show the defined packet formats between MAP application and client. The Message ID field composed of the user's globally unique key from of 'YYYYMMDDHHMMSS'. The Message Type field decides the form of query. '0x00, 0x01' means address and latitude-longitude coordination request and '0x10, 0x11' means response about that. X, Y fields is a latitude, longitude coordination, respectively, and SIDO, SIGUNGU, GU, EMDONG fields represent the administrative district of our country.

3.5 WAP Server

WAP server consists of JEUS and WebtoB application that is developed by of Tmax cooperation. JEUS, WAS(web application server) provides transaction management, session management and load balancing management. WebtoB, that is WEB server and processes browser requests through HTTP protocol, provides high performance and stability. Proposed system answers to WML(Wireless Markup Language) requests of JEUS and WebtoB. WAP server provides services that are read function of RFID tag code, location awareness function, and interesting information finding function with RFID tag location. We propose a service example of user-created information system that can be used in various service types.

3.6 WIPI Applications

Clients application of proposed system consists of WIPI application and WAP browser. WAP browser is mobile phone embedded browser. WIPI application consists of RFID reader module, RFID analyzer module, Broker module, and GPS communication module. RFID reader module reads RFID code tag, Broker module requests RFID code encoding, and GPS communication module requests position coordination(latitude and longitude) for RFID location.

RFID Reader module controls Dongle RFID Reader and read RFID tag code. RFID Analyzer module analyzes RFID code for performance, decides whether RFID code is RFID mobile code or the code related with the RFID service, and filters codes. memory structures of ISO/IEC 18000-6C and EPC Class1 Gen2 specification consists of Bank00(Reserved), Bank01(UII/EPC), Bank10(TID), and Bank11(USER)and memory structure of Bank01 is only different name from others.

In Bank01, encoded code structure and related information for identifying object as like EPC code are inserted. Bank01 consists of CRC-16(Cyclic Redundancy Check), PC(Protocol Control) and UII(Uinque Item Identifier). CRC-16 detects data errors between tag and reader. PC(Protocol Control) records information for sending tag information to reader. UII(Uinque Item Identifier) is data area for encoded tag information.

In order for WIPI application to read and analyze RFID code, it is determined whether RFID code is for EPC or Non-EPC, by checking toggle bits of PC data area and whether fields value of AFI(Application Family Identifier) data area is '0000 00012' or not. And UII data area analysis of OID(Object ID) determines code structures.

<table 10> shows OID in code structure and mini-mCode structure is used in proposed system. Thus WIPI application decides whether Toggle bits is “12”, AFI가 '0000 00012', OID가 "0 2 450 4" or not, and whether TLC, Class, CC value of mini-mCode is assigned by KISA(Korea internet & Security Agency) or not. Mobile RFID code analysis is implemented only by bits comparisons, and Broker requests are decreased so that proposed system's performance is improved. After Broker module connects with Broker server, it deliver analyzed code by RFID Analyzer module to Broker application and receives response value, URI. GPS module initiate GPS device for position coordination(latitude and longitude) requests, requests position coordination(latitude and longitude) requests, and receives position coordination(latitude and longitude) value.

4 Implementation of User Created Information System

After user-created information system reads RFID tag code of interesting spot, receives response of Broker application, then it fetches URI of WAP pages and retrieves and presents information of user interesting spot.

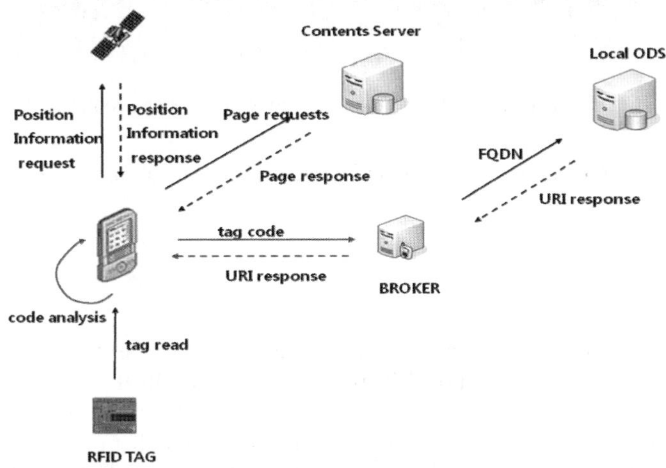

Fig. 4. User-created information Systems operation flow

A user reads RFID tag code of interesting spots with WIPI application. WIPI application analyzes RFID tag codes and determines whether RFID tag codes are related with user-created information system or not and send RFID tag codes to Broker application and delivers the results to user-created information system.

Broker application receives analyzed RFID tag codes from WIPI application and transforms them into FQDN types and requests URI information to local ODS. And local ODS analyzes FQDN and determines whether it can process FQDN by itself or not.

If local ODS can not process FQDN by itself, then local ODS requests FQDN process to upper ODS and send the result of FQDN process to Broker application. Broker application delivers the results from ODS.

If user's mobile phone needs position coordination(latitude and longitude), then it collects GPS' position coordination(latitude and longitude). Collected position coordination(latitude and longitude) and URI are sent to WAP server and WAP pages are requested. A user can retrieves interesting spot information from user-created information system.

Lastly Information application manages transaction control and records user authentication and logs. MAP application transforms position coordination(latitude and longitude) into an administrative district name. WIPI application confirms that mobile RFID tag codes matches with mobile RFID code types and, after filtering mobile RFID codes, then directly connects with Broker application.

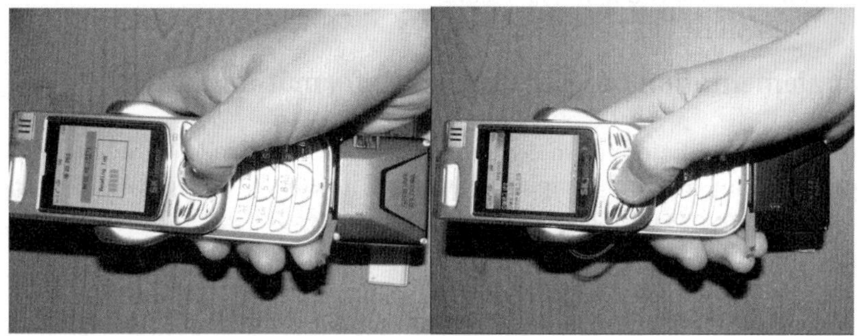

Fig. 5. RFID tag read **Fig. 6.** WAP page connection

Fig. 5 and Fig. 6 shows mobile phone presents WAP page through URL of Broker application.

5 Conclusion

This paper presents the design and implementation of the RFID-based Mobile Information System which can read RFID tag codes using RFID readers, get URIs as query responses, request some services to its WAP server and utilize them. This system consists of several basic components including a number of RFID tags, dongle type RFID readers operating at 900MHz band developed by ETRI, a Sybase ASE, a Tmax Webtob as a web server, and a Tmax JEUS middleware as a web application server. Our major results are as follows.

- Development of a WIPI application in C language installed on RFID terminals with dongle type RFID readers
- Construction of a WAP server in Java using a Tmax middleware and a Tmax JEUS
- Implementation of a Broker application in C to read a RFID tag code and transform it to a URI through ODS queries

- Construction of local ODS servers to answer ODS queries
- Implementation of a map application in C to convert between addresses and longitude/latitude values

We also implement a RFID code analyzer for the WIPI application to filter out unnecessary RFID codes before the mobile RFID Broker interprets the RFID tag codes. As both incorrect RFID codes and irrelevant ones are surely removed, the Broker don't have to make undesirable queries. Consequently, the WIPI application, capable of tag code filtering with direct socket connection to the Broker, can definitely make performance improvements that results from reduction in system load, process simplification, and decreasing time in code interpretation. If future RFID technology offers capability to make full use of user memory in RFID tags, we could get some benefits by storing user location information to that memory, such as reduction in location sensing time, better accuracy in user location, minimizing shadow areas, etc. The information can be applicable to various fields, such as personal navigation systems and car navigation systems, as well. Our system implemented in this paper can be upgraded to store and utilize location information in user memory and we leave it as a follow-up study.

References

1. Kim, Y.Y.: Network Architecture Models for Mobile RFID Services (2006)
2. Kim, W., Yim, H.D., Kim, H.J., Park, S.W.: RFID Code Structure Encoding Guidelines. Korea Mobile RFID Forum Technical Report (2006)
3. Qian, Y., Jin, B., Cao, D.: A Heuristic Algorithm for Broker Deployment in RFID Applications. In: 2009 IEEE International Conference on e-Business Engineering (2009)
4. Korea TTA, Format of URN and FQDN for RFID Service, TTAS.KO-06.0109/R1 (December 2007)
5. Korea TTA, Common Application Requirements for Mobile RFID Services, TTAS-KO-06.0108 (December 2005)
6. Preishuber-Pflüg, J.: RFID Application and System Design based in Simulations (2006)
7. Lee, Y.J.: Trends of RFID Middleware Technology and Its Applications, vol. 12(5), pp. 43–51 (2005)
8. Jung, S.H., Lee, B.K., Lim, J.H.: Implementation of Mobile Computing based RFID Reconition System. In: Proc. of KIMICS conference, vol. 6(2), pp. 119–122 (2005)
9. Cho, H.T., Choi, H., Lee, W.H., Baek, Y.J.: A Development of Active RFID System for Ubiquitous Logistics Environment. In: Proc. of the 32th KIISE Fall Conference, vol. 32(2), pp. 274–276 (2005)
10. Kong, M.K., Kim, H.J., Lee, J.S.: Analysis on Technical Regulation of RFID in the 860 MHz to 960 MHz band. In: Proc. of the 32th KIISE Fall Conference, vol. 32(2), pp. 487–489 (2005)
11. Korea TTA, Mobile RFID Code Structure and Tag Data Structure for Mobile RFID Services. TTAS.KO-06.0105/R1 (December 2006)
12. Korea TTA, Architecture of the mobile RFID services. TTAK.KO-06.0186 (December 2008)
13. Kim, W., Yim, H.D., Kim, H.J., Park, S.W.: RFID Code Structure Encoding Guidelines. Korea Mobile RFID Forum Technical Report (2006)

14. Korea TTA, RFID Object Directory Service Architecture, TTAK.KO-06.0103/R2 (December 2009)
15. Korea TTA, Mobile RFID Code Registration Protocol, TTAS.KO-06.0137 (December 2006)
16. Korea Internet & Security Agency, Guidelines for constructing and operating RFID Object Directory Service, NIDA Technical Report (2006)
17. Zheng, F., Huang, J., Zhang, Y.: RFID Information Acquisition: An Analysis and Comparison between ONS and LDAP. In: Proceedings of International Conference on Information Science and Engineering, ICISE (2009)

An Experimental Performance Measurement of Implemented Wireless Access Point for Interworking Wi-Fi and HSDPA Networks

Tae-Young Byun

School of Computer and Information Communications Engineering,
Catholic University of Daegu, Gyeonsan-si, Gyeongbuk, Rep. of Korea
tybyun@cu.ac.kr

Abstract. This paper presents a prototype of WAP(Wireless Access Point) that provides the wireless Internet access anywhere. Implemented WAP can be equipped with various wireless WAN interfaces such as WCDMA and HSDPA. WAP in the IP mechanism has to process connection setup procedure to one wireless WAN. Also, WAP can provide connection management procedures to reconnect interrupted connection automatically. By using WAP, several mobile devices such as netbook, UMPC and smart-phone in a moving vehicle can access to HSDPA network simultaneously. So, it has more convenient for using the WAP when there are needs to access wireless Internet more than two mobile devices in restricted spaces such as car, train and ship.

Keywords: Wireless Access Point, Wireless WAN, Ubiquitous Computing.

1 Introduction

Recently, the concept of ubiquitous computing has broadly been adopted to real world to provide more convenient computing environments and services to people. More creative applications and services have been emerged as convergence of wired and wireless communications are fastened. Especially, the convergences of technologies among a variety of industries lead more innovative services to come out in business, and fusions of services are promoted to make more revenue. For example, development of ubiquitous healthcare system requires the knowledge of both medical treatment and information technology to deliver proper medical service to patients in convenient ways. Also, intelligent car communication system needs advanced infrastructure of wireless communications, development of embedded software and a variety of sensors in vehicle. Thus, fusions of technologies make the novelty of service released in market.

Wireless Internet subscribers have been increased rapidly. With wired Internet access, subscribers can enjoy ubiquitous Internet access via wireless communications. The importance of wireless Internet increases in view of convenience of Internet access regardless space and time. Most countries of cellular communication system have tries to increase the capacity of data channel in air interface, thus, WCDMA(wideband code division multiple access), HSDPA(high speed downlink protocol access) and

T.-h. Kim et al. (Eds.): GDC/CA 2010, CCIS 121, pp. 145–154, 2010.

WiBro(wireless broadband) services prevails across the world. These high-speed wireless WANs are inevitable to deliver various services to subscribers.

There have been many studies to provide user mobility and service mobility in Internet. IETF (Internet Engineering Task Force) defined mobile IP facilities to provide roaming schemes in a wireless computing. The IETF NEMO (NEtwork MObility) working group improved roaming schemes such that subscribers could use a mobile router for data transmission and do not need to worry about service environments[1].

Wireless access point can be installed on any vehicle. Wireless access point is responsible for communicating with external mobile networks. When a vehicle moves, mobile nodes within the vehicle do not need to perform handoffs individually the whole car is a sub-network and performs handoff procedures using the installed wireless access point.

This study embeds a network mobility system on an SAMSUNG S3C2440A processor platform to deploy wireless access point. Embedded Linux is the operating system. The interworking scheme between HSDPA and Wi-Fi, which includes NAT(network address translation) and half-bridge modes, packet formatting, receiving, sending and processing, is implemented in wireless access point. This study also increases connectivity of mobile devices via Wi-Fi in a vehicle.

2 Related Works

2.1 Mobile Router

Mobile IP is designed to keep current IP settings and connections and resolve security faults while roaming to another network. Mobile IP uses an agent for network roaming and establishes an encapsulated tunnel to transmit packets to a new subnet to ensure security. The mobile IP concept indicates that when a Mobile Node (MN) moves to another network, it obtains a Care-of Address (CoA) and informs its Home Agent (HA) by a binding update. Subsequently, a Correspondent Node (CN) only needs to send packets to the HA when it wants to send messages to the MN, and the HA can forward packets to the MN by the mobile node's most recent recorded position. Once the MN wants to reply to messages, it can send packets directly to CN using the source address in packets without HA interception

2.2 Embedded System

Embedded systems, in which hardware and software are typically inseparable, differ from general computers (such as desktop computer, tablet PC) in more ways. An embedded micro-processor differs from a central processor unit in a traditional computer. Most micro-processors in embedded systems are developed with System on Chip (SoC), and software is usually developed into firmware.

The architecture of an embedded system includes a user interface, simulation environment, several modules and design programs between software and hardware. After designing the system, a ROMization is required to build an executable image file. This file can be burned into a ROM or Flash of the target platform and execute programs on the target platform.

2.3 Well-Known Network Mobility Systems

The Connexion system was developed by Boeing™ and Cisco Systems. In this system, a mobile platform is established to setup a Mobile Router. The Ethernet connects to the Mobile Router to form a Local Area Network in a cabin. The Mobile Router maintains a stable subnet and connects with a satellite to transmit network packets. Thus, the Mobile Router has two interfaces: an Ethernet interface and a satellite signal interface.

The NEMO basic support protocol published by Mobility, KEIO University, Japan, Nokia and Motorola became RFC3963 in January 2005. Related projects, such as Internet car (ICAR System), establish a Mobile Router and connect with sensors, GPS and cameras to achieve a mobile network in a car [2].

Almost all works related to Mobile IPv6 quotes the well-known MIPL (Mobile IPv6 for Linux) package for implementation [3]. The MIPL package provides Mobile IPv6 support against Linux systems; the latest version is 2.0.2. The first standard followed is IETF Draft, and the latest version follows RFC 3775 (Mobility Support in IPv6) against Linux kernel 2.6.16. Moreover, MIPL also releases NEPL (NEMO Platform for Linux) to support network mobility function. The latest version is 0.2 against 2.6.15 and is extended from MIPL version 2.0.1 following RFC3963 specification.

3 Design and Implementation of Wireless Access Point

3.1 Overview of Wireless Access Point

Fig. 1 depicts the functions of wireless access point which performs interworking between 3G or more advanced cellular networks and wireless LAN or Wi-Fi. Many portable devices such as laptop, notebook, PDA and smartphone can access wireless Internet via wireless access point simultaneously. Wireless access point should forwards packets between cellular networks and wireless LAN areas in seamless manner without packet loss. In wireless access point, proper types of modems can be equipped to access different cellular networks such as CDMA, GSM, WCDMA(3G), HSDPA and LTE(4G). Also, wireless access point can be extended to perform as a multihoming interworking device that supports many different cellular networks simultaneously. In this case, each portable device can select a proper cellular network before connection establishment with cellular network to provide flexibility of connection. Anyway, in this paper, implemented wireless access point supports only HSDPA network, and HSDPA network is considered to evaluate the performance metrics.

3.2 Design of Wireless Access Point

As shown in Fig. 2, the design of wireless access point has two stages of development. At the first stage, a prototype of wireless access point based on a general-purpose SBC is implemented to verify the correct operation of interworking function of wireless access point, and the second stage implements a dedicated device which is an expansion of a prototype of wireless access point.

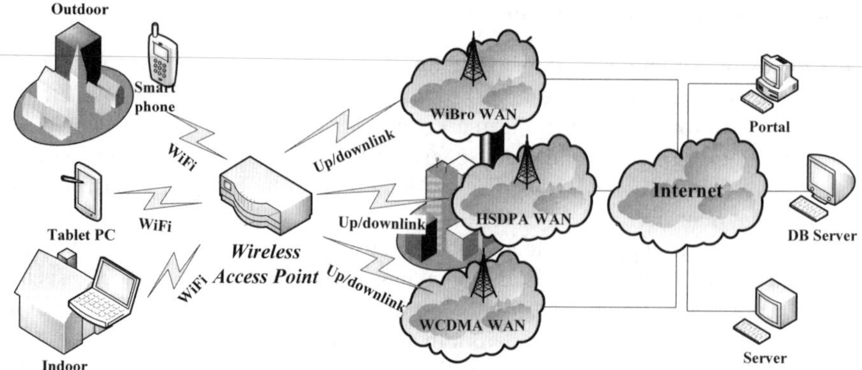

Fig. 1. The functionality of wireless access point

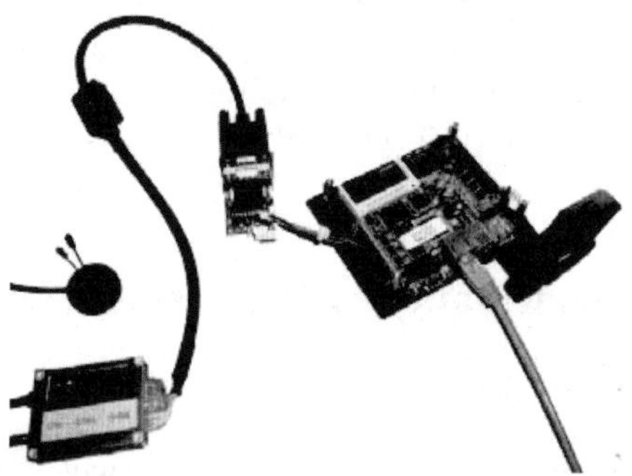

(a) Prototype of wireless access point based on general-purpose embedded board

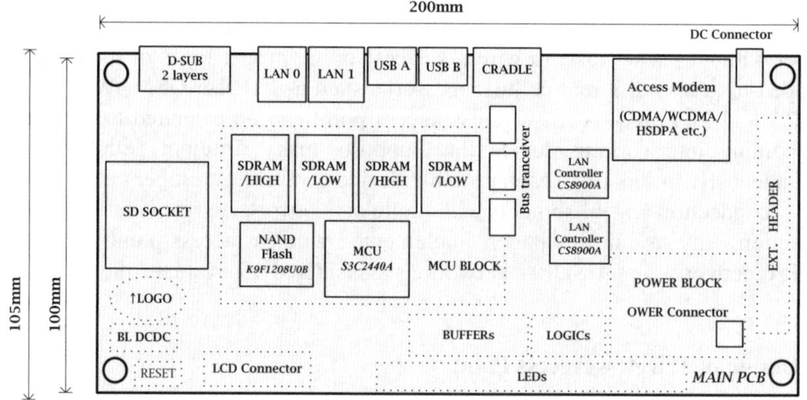

(b) Circuit board layout of mobile access point based on S3C2440-A processor

Fig. 2. Design and implementation of wireless access point

This section explains the design and implementation details of wireless access point and specifications of it. MCU block contains MCU, NAND Flash and SDRAM in the layout of circuit board of wireless access point as shown in Fig. 2(b). Wireless access point can support interworking between wireless WAN and wired or wireless LAN by attaching a variety of wireless WAN access modem such as CDMA, WCDMA, HSDPA etc. Two wired LAN interfaces for connecting mobile devices or another networking devices are provided, and additionally access modems can be attached by plugging into USB interfaces besides of internal access modem. In addition, LCD module can be equipped with LCD connector. Users can identify the operation status of wireless access point by the LEDs that indicates power on/off, normal operation, error occurrence, link status of LAN port etc. Also, user or developer can monitor details of operation through D-Sub interface which can sends current operation status of wireless access point to serial port of computer.

Table 1. Specifications of dedicate device of wireless access point

Item		**Description**
MCU		SAMSUNG ARM920T S3C2440A(400MHz)
Memory	NAND Flash	64MByte, SAMSUNG K9F1208U0B
	SDRAM	64MByte, SAMSUNG K4S511632D
IP Address Allocation	NAT(masquerade) mode and Half-bridge mode	
HSDPA Modem Type	Access Modem (Carrier, WWAN)	CWE624K (Korea Telecom, supports WCDMA/HSDPA dual modes)
Wired LAN Spec.	Two LAN Ports : 100Base-TX, LAN Controller : CS8900A	

3.3 NAT Mode vs. Half- Bridge Mode

Implemented wireless access poiont provides two IP assignment methods, that is, *NAT* and *half-bridge mode* which optionally can be selected at programming stage by programmer. Fig. 3 illustrates the concept of two IP address assignment methods. *Network address translation* (NAT) is the process of modifying network address information in IP packet headers while in transit across a traffic routing device for the purpose of remapping one IP address space into another. Most often today, NAT is used in conjunction with *network masquerading* (or *IP masquerading*) which is a technique that hides an entire IP address space, usually consisting of private network IP addresses (RFC 1918), behind a single IP address in another, often public address space. This mechanism is implemented in wireless access point that uses stateful translation tables to map the "hidden" addresses into a single IP address and then readdresses the outgoing IP packets on exit so that they appear to originate from wireless access point.

In *half-bridge mode*, a public IP address assigned by carrier does not be modified within wireless access point, thus, original IP address is directly assigned to subscriber's device through wireless access point. In this mode, there is no need for modifying network address information in IP packet headers while in transit across wireless access point. However, in this mode, wireless access point can assign only one public IP address per cellular network or wireless WAN interface within wireless access point to a mobile device. So, this mode optionally can be used in specific purposes or services.

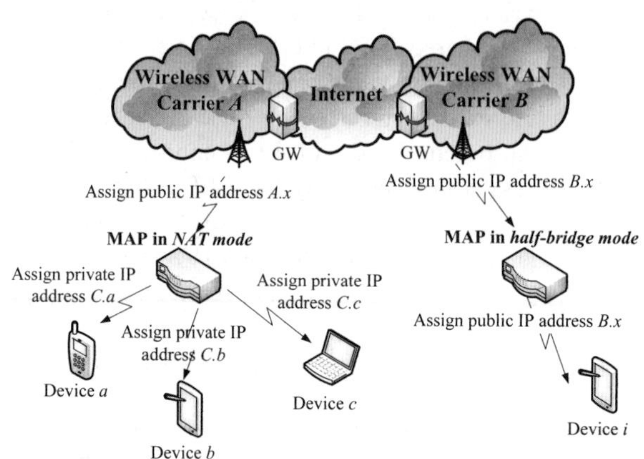

Fig. 3. Two IP Address Allocation Methods

```
PROCEDURE : NAT// Pseudo codes for masq_NAT() procedure

m_call_hsdpa(); // Dial HSDPA Modem to connection establishment.
m_udhcpd_init(); // Initializing DHCP
m_makeNATinit(); // Initializing NAT mode in WAP
// Run deamon for checking data error in background
system("packetcheck&");
for( ; ; ) {   // Check if modem is established successfully
  switch(netdev_main(DEV_PPP,CONN_CHECK)) {
    case DEV_PPP_CONNECT : // In case PPP connection is exist
      if(netdev_main(DEV_PPP, PACK_CHECK)) {
        Chk_Cell_Networks();}// Check if connection is established.
      else if(netdev_main(DEV_PPP, PACK_CHECK) == 0)
        printf("\nDON'T RECEIVED PACKET:warning reboot");
      break;
    case DEV_PPP_DISCONNECT : // In case PPP connection is released
      if(ppp_call_count < 10) {
        m_call_hsdpa();
        ppp_call_count++; }
      else {
        printf("\n NO DEVICE : warning reboot system");
        system("reboot"); }
     break; } } // End of for-loop
```

Fig. 4. Codes for connection establishment and termination in NAT mode

```
PROCEDURE : Half-bridge // Pseudo codes for Half_Bridging() procedure

while(1) {
  switch(led_flag) { // WATCHDOG
    case LED_OFF : printf("\nWATCHDOG_DEV 1st SIGNAL"); break;
    case LED_ON : printf("\nWATCHDOG_DEV 2nd SIGNAL"); break; }
  switch(MODE_FLAG) {
    case BOOT_MODE : h_call_hsdpa(); h_ppp_call_count++;
      if(h_ppp_call_count>6)  //Reset  system  if  retry  count  excess  6
times
        system("reboot");
        if(netdev_main(DEV_PPP,CONN_CHECK)){
           h_Edev_check(DEV_PPP); // Check HSDPA modem interface
           if(h_change_dhcp()==1) { // Check IP information
             system("ppp-off"); printf("\nIP Error");
           if(dhcp_errorCount>3) // Reset system in case failure of modem
             system("reboot");
           dhcp_errorCount++;
        } // End of inner if-statement
      else {
        system("packetcheck&");
         h_half_bridge(); // Set WAP to half-bridge mode
         MODE_FLAG = CONNECT_MODE;  dhcp_errorCount = 1;
         h_udhcpd_init(); } // Update DHCP infomation
       h_ppp_call_count = 0;
     } // End of outer if-statement
     break;
   case CONNECT_MODE : led_buf[0]=0xFF; write(ledDEV_run,led_buf,1);
     if(netdev_main(DEV_PPP,CONN_CHECK)){//Check connection establishment
        if(netdev_main(DEV_PPP,PACK_CHECK) == 0 ) { // Check packet error
           printf("\n DON'T RECEIVED PACKET : Warning reboot system");
           system("reboot"); }
      }
     else { // Transition to re-dial mode
         MODE_FLAG = REDIAL_MODE; system("kill all packet check");
         led_buf[0] = 0x00; write(outDEV_PowON, led_buf, 1); sleep(1);
         led_buf[0] = 0xFF; write(outDEV_PowON, led_buf, 1);
     }
     break;
   case REDIAL_MODE : h_DELhalf_bridge(); h_call_hsdpa();
     h_ppp_call_count++;
     if(h_ppp_call_count > 6) { system("ppp-off"); system("reboot"); }
     if(netdev_main(DEV_PPP, CONN_CHECK)) provide_connectivity();
     else {
       h_kill_udhcpd(); system("packetcheck&"); h_half_bridge();
       MODE_FLAG = CONNECT_MODE; dhcp_errorCount = 1; h_udhcpd_init();
     }
     h_ppp_call_count = 0; break;
  } // End of switch-statement
} // End of while-loop
```

Fig. 5. Codes for connection establishment and termination in half-bridge mode

3.4 Implementation of Wireless Access Point

Wireless access point is implemented according to design details which already were shown in Fig. 2(b). Wireless access point has several interfaces to connect peripherals such as external WWAN access modem and wired or wireless LAN devices.

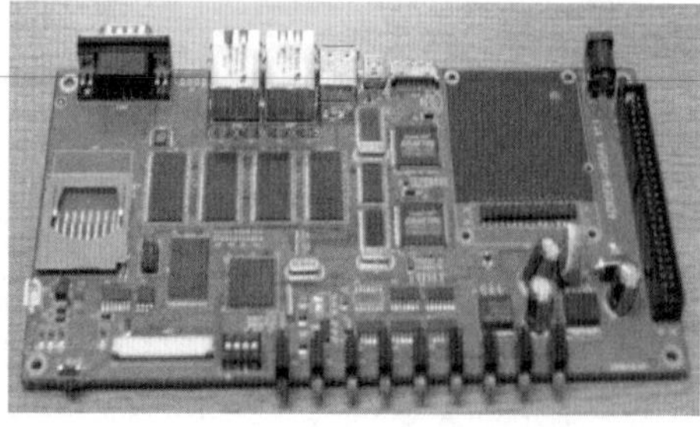

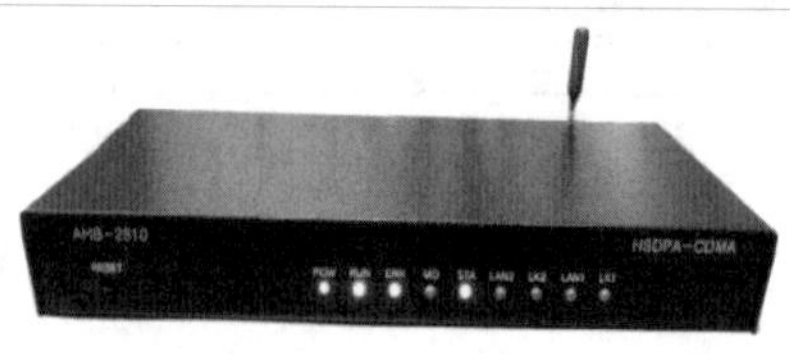

Fig. 6. A dedicate device of wireless access point. The left figure shows internal circuit board, the right figure shows the front of wireless access point respectively.

Table 2. Development environment and tools

Item	Description
Host PC	Linux fedora core6 (kernel-2.6.22)
Target Board	Prototype of WAP is implemented on LN2440SBC, and final dedicated device of WAP is implemented on designed circuit board equipped with Samsung MCU S3C2440A .
Programming Language	C, C++ and Bash Shell Script
Development Tools & Compiler	QplusESC-1.0.2, Jflash-1.1.1 Arm-gp2x-linux-3.4.3, arm-linux-gcc-3, ppp-2.4.4, iptables-1.3.8, dhcpd-0.9.8

4 Test and Evaluation

To investigate the experimental performance of implemented wireless access point, five test scenarios is set. Each scenario is different to each other in connection with wireless access point at physical layer. To get the validity of performance measurement, we use two commercial products for interworking between Ethernet link and Wi-Fi link.

Table 3. Summary of experiment environment

Items	Description
Time of measurement	Five time periods : A.M.08, A.M.11, P.M.06, P.M.09, P.M.11
Location of measurement	Engineering hall(indoor), Catholic Uni. of Daegu, Korea
The number of measurement	Perform 10 experiments per scenario, 50 experiments in total for all of five scenarios in only NAT mode.
Device model	**Dedicate device of WAP**: The designed circuit board based on Samsung S3C2440A-40 processor. **HSDPA modem**: CWE624K, supports WCDMA/HSDPA. **Commercial products**:(i)LGAP:APA-2000, (ii)UCAP:BW-850

Test environments and scenarios are summarized in Table 3 and Table 4 respectively. In table 4, LGAP indicates that APA-2000 of commercial product is used for connecting wireless access point and end device with Ethernet link or Wi-Fi link at physical layer. Also, UCAP means BW-850 model of product.

This chapter also shows the test results of implemented wireless access point over HSDPA and wireless LAN in cases of five different scenarios as mentioned in section 4.1. Table 5 summarizes test results of five scenarios in view of major performance metrics including uplink/downlink throughput, round trip time and standard deviation of RTT. More detailed test result per scenario is shown in Fig. 6.

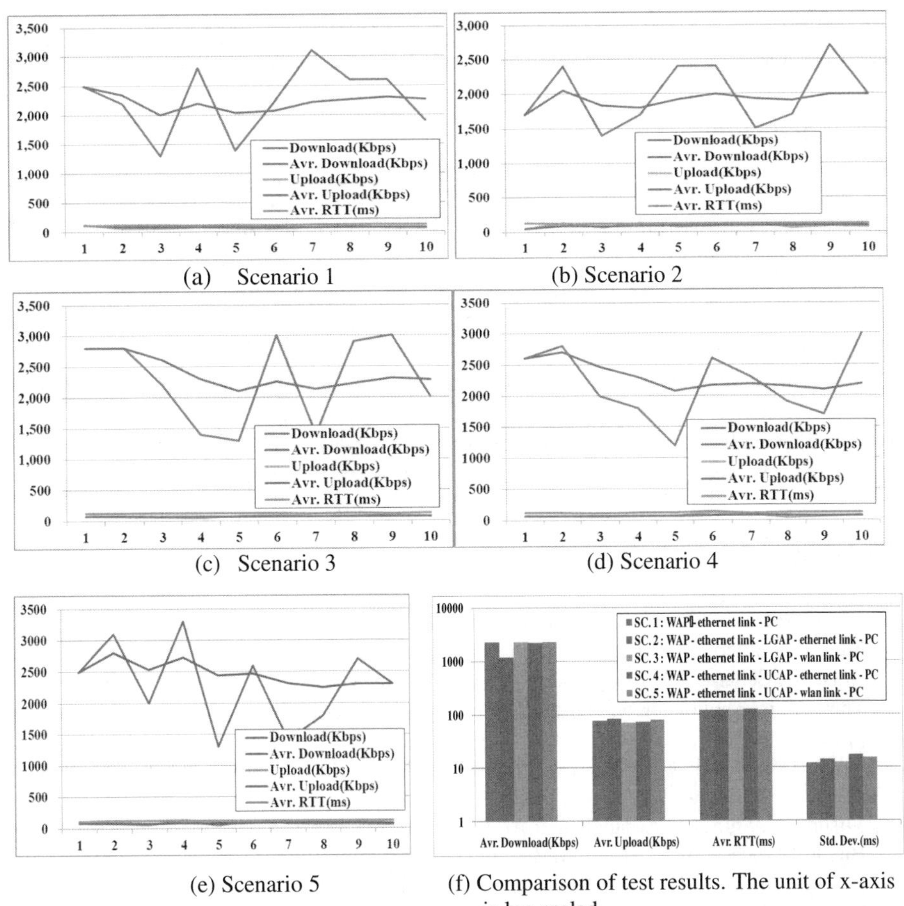

(a) Scenario 1 (b) Scenario 2

(c) Scenario 3 (d) Scenario 4

(e) Scenario 5 (f) Comparison of test results. The unit of x-axis is log scaled.

Fig. 7. Test results in five scenarios

Table 4. Test scenarios for performance measurements

Scenarios	Description
Scen.1	← HSDPA *link* → WAP ← *ethernet link* → PC
Scen. 2	← HSDPA *link* → WAP ← *ethernet link* → LGAP ← *ethernet link* → PC
Scen. 3	← HSDPA *link* → WAP ← *ethernet link* → LGAP ← *WLAN link* → PC
Scen. 4	← HSDPA *link* → WAP ← *ethernet link* → UCAP ← *ethernet link* → PC
Scen. 5	← HSDPA *link* → WAP ← *ethernet link* → UCAP ← *WLAN link* → PC

Table 5. Summary of performance measurements of wireless access point

Scenarios	Performance Metrics			
	Avg. Download Throughput(Kbps)	Avg. Upload Throughput(Kbps)	Avg. RTT (ms)	Std. Dev. (ms)
Scenario 1	***2260***	***74.70***	***118.11***	***12.13***
Scenario 2	***1990***	***84.30***	***120.89***	***14.19***
Scenario 3	***2280***	***69.40***	***118.34***	***12.26***
Scenario 4	***2190***	***71.80***	***121.12***	***17.10***
Scenario 5	***2300***	***77.40***	***118.23***	***15.15***

5 Conclusion

An embedded-based wireless access point is implemented in this paper. Network performance interworking HSDPA network and Wi-Fi is investigated in terms of round-trip time and latency.

As shown in performance measurements, implemented embedded-based wireless access point provides an equivalent performance to commercial access modem in view of throughput and round-trip time. Based on simultaneous support of end devices, it has enough performance using the embedded wireless access point when there are more than two mobile nodes. The future work is focused on combining wireless access point and vehicle-to-vehicle (V2V) communication. Subscribers can exchange safety-related information between moving vehicles using wireless access point.

References

1. Devarapalli, V., Wakikawa, R., Petrescu, A., Thubert, P.: Network Mobility (NEMO) Basic Support Protocol. In: RFC, vol. 3963 (2005)
2. Ernst, T., Uehara, K., Mitsuya, K.: Network Mobility from the InternetCAR Perspective. In: The 17th International Conference on Advanced Information Networking and Applications, pp. 19–25 (2003)
3. MIPL (Mobile IPv6 for Linux) Project, NEPL (NEMO Platform for Linux) Project, `http://mobile-ipv6.org`
4. Mishra, A., Shin, M., Arbaugh, W.: An Empirical Analysis of the IEEE 802.11 MAC Layer Handoff Process. ACM SIGCOMM Computer Communication Review 33(2) (2003)
5. He, J., Yang, J.S., Kim, Y., Kim, A.S.: System-Level Time-Domain Behavioral Modeling for a Mobile WiMax Transceiver. In: The 2006 IEEE International on Behavioral Modeling and Simulation Workshop, pp. 138–143 (2006)
6. Gozalvez, J.: Mobile WiMAX Rollouts Announced (Mobile Radio). IEEE Vehicular Technology Magazine 1(3), 53–59 (2006)
7. Chen, J., Wei, S., Chang, Y., Ma, Y.: Design and Implementation of an Embedded Linux-Based Mobile Router for Telematics Computing. In: ACIT, pp. 8–13 (2008)

VSAM: Virtual Sensor Agent-Oriented Middleware for Distributed and Heterogeneous WSNs

Joon-Min Gil[1], Kwang-Jin Paek[2], and Ui-Sung Song[3]

[1] School of Computer and Information Communications Engineering, Catholic University of Daegu
330 Geumnak, Hayang-eup, Gyeongsan-si, Gyeongbuk 712-701, Korea
jmgil@cu.ac.kr

[2] Software Development Center, ROKAF
com9214@gmail.com

[3] Dept. of Computer Science Education, Busan National University of Education
37 Gyodae-ro, Yeonje-gu, Busan 611-736, Korea
ussong@bnue.ac.kr

Abstract. Since the emergence of WSNs (Wireless Sensor Networks), various middleware architectures have been proposed to achieve a suitable abstraction from the distribution and management tasks of sensor devices. This allows users to focus on application development. In the near future, WSNs will be more pervasive, common, and distributed. Programming on WSNs requires a novel programming paradigm and middleware, especially in distributed and heterogeneous WSNs. We propose Virtual Sensor Agent-Oriented Middleware (VSAM), a middleware system for distributed and heterogeneous WSNs, which provides data dissemination protocol-independent Application Programming Interface (API) and an integrated platform for sensor applications. VSAM makes it possible to integrate WSNs with traditional networks.

Keywords: virtual sensor network, middleware, agent system, lifetime, energy efficiency, QoS.

1 Introduction

The area of Wireless Sensor Networks (WSNs) is an emerging research field, which brings novel problems and challenges to programming. Innovative middleware paradigms are required for the new WSN environment [1,7].

WSNs can contain hundreds or thousands of sensing nodes. Since sensors are equipped with limited battery power and usually have to operate unattended for long periods of time, energy consumption is a critical issue. It is desirable for nodes to be as energy-efficient as possible while the high quality of functions are executed. Sensor nodes contain one or more sensing devices and have limited computing and storage capacity. Their function is to collect, aggregate, and transmit their own data and neighboring data [2]. In general, a WSN has several

T.-h. Kim et al. (Eds.): GDC/CA 2010, CCIS 121, pp. 155–166, 2010.

sensor nodes and one or more sink nodes that act as exit points from the network. Sink nodes have more commutating power than sensor nodes because they have no energy restrictions.

Our research is motivated by the consideration of the heterogeneous deployment of sensors in and around a chemical plant that manufactures hazardous chemicals. In our research, we consider WSNs where:

- The sink node is fixed and located far from the sensor nodes.
- The sensor nodes are heterogeneous, energy-constrained, have a unique ID (Identification) and can move between different WSNs.
- The proposed system can use all routing protocols for WSNs.
- Client programs request a sequence of queries.
- The sensor nodes are hard to be recharged and maintained in unreachable environment.

The level of Quality of Service (QoS) for transmitting data to the sink node requires only selected nodes to transmit (selective transition) on demand to the sink node. This makes it possible to avoid unnecessary data transmission, extending the lifetime of WSNs. In our research, we remove redundant transmissions in the temporal and spatial crossing areas of each rectangle.

There are many routing protocols in WSNs (See Section 2.3). Although these protocols are effective in extending the lifetime of sensor networks, the gap between the protocol and the application is often too large to allow the protocols to be effectively used by application developers [6]. Application developers need novel and flexible middleware for WSNs.

Recently, various middleware architectures have been proposed to achieve a suitable abstraction from distribution and management tasks of sensor devices. Much work has targeted middleware specifically designed to meet the challenges of WSNs, focusing on the longevity and resource-constrained aspects of these systems. AutoSec [16] and DSWare [17] manage resources in a sensor network by providing access control for applications so that QoS requests are maintained. While these middlewares focus on the form of the data presented to the user applications, Impala [18] considers the application itself, exploiting mobile code techniques to change the functionality of middleware executing at a remote sensor. Although each of these middleware architectures are designed for efficient use of the WSN, they have focused on designing new network-level protocols without considering the existing standards or how applications use the protocols.

Sensor network applications may be built on top of the existing protocols, and require a coordination framework to allow for the flexibility that exists in both standardized and non-standardized network protocols. A middleware for WSNs has to support the properties of WSNs and Internet middleware. We especially focused on the application layer of the protocol stack used by the sink and all sensor nodes.

The rest of this paper is organized as follows. In Section 2, we describe our middleware and its components and operation. Section 3 presents system evaluation. Finally, our conclusion and future work are given in Section 4.

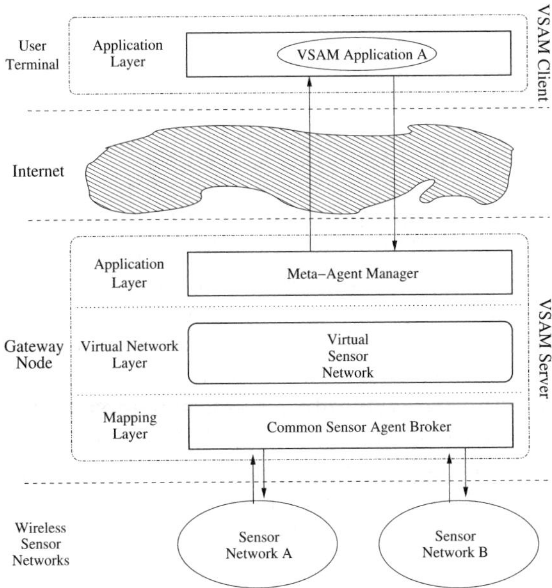

Fig. 1. VSAM Middleware Architecture

2 VSAM System Description

Figure 1 illustrates the deployment and layered architecture of the Virtual Sensor Agent Middleware (VSAM). The VSAM system is a mobile agent system that comprises six components:

- Meta-Agent Manager (MAM)
- Virtual Sensor Network (VSN)
- Common Sensor Agent Broker (CSAB)
- Service Agent (SA)
- Work Agent (WA)
- VSAM Client

The VSAM prototype system was made of Java Development Kit (JDK) 6 and Java Data Objects (JDO) [4]. To transmit the mobile work agents to VSAM client, we also use Java object serialization Application Programming Interface (API). In addition, VSAM provides VSAM API as Java packages for VSAM client developers.

2.1 Virtual Sensor Network

The central concept of our infrastructure is the virtual counterpart, which encapsulates the state and behavior of a sensor node. Figure 2 shows the organization of VSN.

In Figure 2, *GP* indicates a sensor node group, *VN* a virtual sensor node, *sn* a sensor node, and *AR* a partial area of *VSN*. The following equations show the relationship for each set of nodes.

$$VSN \supseteq GP \supseteq VN \supseteq \{sn|sn \in VSN\}$$
$$VSN \supseteq AR \supseteq \{sn|sn \in VSN\}$$

GP is the user-defined node group. Users can construct GPs with arbitrary nodes or nodes with specific attributes. AR is the location-based node group. Nodes from one AR belong to the same specific area. VN is a special node group, which acts as one node and is useful for fault tolerance.

The scope of middleware for WSNs is not restricted to the sensor network alone, but also covers devices and networks connected to WSNs. Classical mechanisms and infrastructures are typically not well suited to interaction with WSNs. One reason for this is the limited resources of WSNs, which may make it necessary to execute resource-intensive functions or store large amounts of data in external components. This may result in the close interaction of processes executing in WSNs and traditional networks. Thus, middlewares for sensor networks should provide a holistic view of both WSNs and traditional networks, which is a challenge for architectural design and implementation [7].

The central concept of our middleware is the VSN. An sn in the VSN replicates the state and behavior of a real sensor node in the WSN. There is one-to-one mapping between the real sensor nodes and their sn. A VN as a single virtual counterpart makes a collection of multiple sns, implementing an n-to-one mapping of sn to VN (a single state and behavior). As a virtual meta-counterpart, VN implements collective state and behavior for a group of sns, virtually maintaining a single state and acting as a single node.

Sensor nodes are influenced by hardware constraints such as limited power and memory. As a result, each sensor node cannot store large amounts of data, and acknowledgements are too costly for sensor networks. VSN is a virtual counterpart of a real sensor network. In VSAM, each sensor node has its own virtual sn as its counterpart. Virtual sensor agents contain and manage all the data, profile, history and meta data of their real sensor node.

The VSN manages the energy content of each sensor node with each sensor node maintaining its energy level. VN, GP, AR, and VSN (node groups) manage the average and total energy level of their sensor nodes. When the data of each sensor node is updated, its energy level, the average and total energy level of its node groups are decreased (see Eqs. (1) and (2) in Section 3.2). The time stamp of the data entry is then updated.

2.2 Query API Types

The VSAM has the minimum acceptable level of QoS for each variable (environmental measurement value). The level of QoS is classified into five categories:

- Area Group node level
- Sensor node level

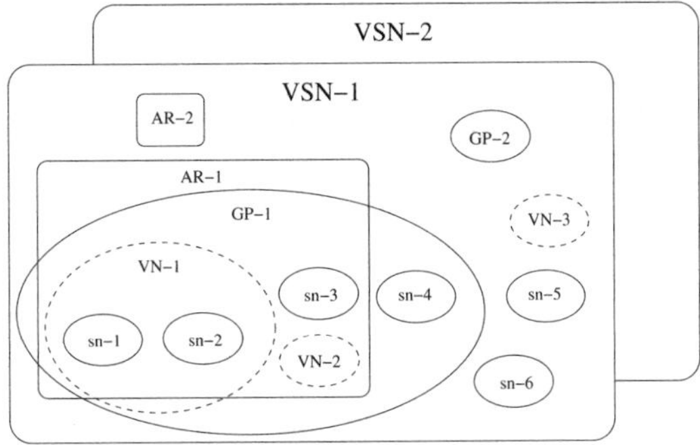

Fig. 2. Virtual Sensor Network Architecture

- Virtual node level
- Group node level
- Virtual sensor network level

VSAM provides three query types, Group Query (GQ), Area Query (AQ) and Node Query (NQ). The following notation describes these two query types, ΔT indicates tolerant time, $N\%$ the percentage of nodes which should be sensed and ND the node ID for a query. The ND can be VN or sn ID. GP is an attribute-based set of NDs and AR is a location-based set of NDs. For example, GP1 is a set of nodes which are at the altitude of 130 meters.

All the elements (sn, VN, GP, and AR) of VSN (See Figure 2) have their own time stamp field. Sensor nodes can maintain various sensor data and each sensor data entity has its time stamped. Each element of VSN updates its time stamp field when the data entity of its subset node is updated. ΔT is the tolerant time between the time stamp of data and the query time.

- $GQ(GP, \Delta T, N\%)$: Attribute-based Group Query
- $AQ(AR, \Delta T, N\%)$: Location-based Area Query
- $NQ(ND, \Delta T, N\%)$: Node Query

Special, temporal, and percentage factors are important parameters for reducing the number of active nodes and the frequency of the query.

WSNs have a high density of nodes, generating high redundancy in the reported data. Such redundancy can be exploited as a mechanism for fault tolerance, or to increase the accuracy of the supplied data. However, if all available nodes are always kept active, network lifetime will decrease. Therefore, data accuracy can be traded off against energy consumption, and the percentage of active nodes can be a parameter for implementing a middleware adaptation policy. VSAM allows application programmers to control energy consumption and accuracy to suit the application.

2.3 CSAB: Common Sensor Agent Broker

The CSAB functions as an adaptation layer between the WSN and VSAM. It provides a uniform sensing interface by abstracting the sensor network protocol. It's two major roles are:

- Query aggregation.
- Sensor data update.

In query aggregation, the CSAB collects queries of VSN sensor nodes. This mechanism optimizes queries by eliminating redundant raw queries. When updates of sensor data are performed, the time stamp of data is also updated. Although CSAB should be implemented at a sink node, other VSAM components don't have to be, as CSAB can communicate with VSAM through TCP/IP.

CSAB can support arbitrary routing protocols for WSNs. The following are types of routing protocols in WSNs:

- Low-level node collaboration (aggregating data locally): LEACH [8].
- Turning nodes off whenever possible: S-MAC [9], ASCENT [10], Span [11], STEM [12], and Lint [13].
- Tailoring the routing protocol: Rumor Routing [14] and TEEN [15].

CSAB selects the optimal protocol according to the query type. For example, when the application is concerned with the continuous data delivery of all nodes, CSAB will choose the LEACH protocol. When the application is concerned with the event-driven data delivery of some nodes, CSAB will choose the TEEN protocol.

2.4 MAM: Meta-Agent Manager

The MAM acts as an execution environment for the two types of agents: Service Agents (SA) and Work Agents (WA). SA is a stationary agent and WA is a mobile agent. The MAM is responsible for agent instantiation, migration, and destruction and monitors VSN events by subscribing to update events of the sensor nodes. VSAM clients can make SA and WA with VSAM API. These agents are migrated to MAM and conduct their operation with their own threads. After the WA completes its operation, it returns to its home VSAM client with the result (e.g., query result). If an application request queries continuously, sending a stationary agent once and remaining at the VSAM server is more efficient than sending a mobile agent each time and returning to the VSAM client. When an application needs to monitor some nodes, the SA is able to do so.

2.5 VSAM Communication Model

From the application perspective, WSNs can be classified in terms of the data delivery required by the application (observer) interest. They may be classified

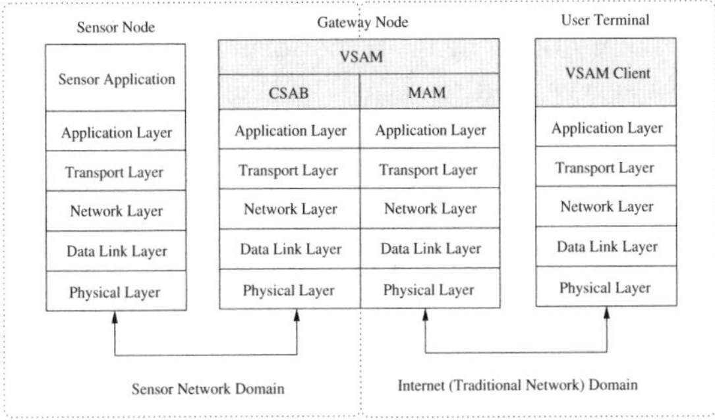

Fig. 3. VSAM Architecture in Network Domains

as: continuous, event-driven, observer-initiated and hybrid. These models govern the generation of application traffic. For any of the above-mentioned models, we can classify the routing approach as: flooding (broadcast-based), unicast, or multicast/other. It is likely that the interaction between the data delivery model from the application and the routing model employed by the network protocol will significantly impact the performance of the network.

VSAM communication models between MAM and VSAM clients support the above-mentioned models. VSAM API is data dissemination protocol-independent. VSAM provides an optimized interaction mechanism by using CSAB. In VSAM, application programmers only have to consider the data delivery model and not the type of dissemination protocol to be adopted. CSAB either selects the best type of data dissemination protocol for the data delivery model or adapts the data delivery model to the type of data dissemination. VSAM supports all data delivery models through CSAB. Figure 3 illustrates the location of the VSAM components in the network protocol stack of each network domain.

3 System Evaluation

3.1 Analysis

In the case of RPC (Remote Procedure Call) communication, there are typically several flows between the client and server in order to perform even a simple transaction. In VSAM, it is expected that these flows could be reduced to a single mobile agent with a corresponding reduction in network traffic, most importantly on the low-bandwidth access network.

Mobile devices such as laptop and notebook computers, as well as emerging classes such personal communicators, are only intermittently connected to a network, hence have only intermittent access to a server. The advantage lies in the mobile VSAM client's ability to develop an agent request – possibly while disconnected – launch the agent during a brief connection session, and then immediately disconnect. The response, if any, is collected during a subsequent connection session. They have limited storage and processing capacity. The advantage lies in the ability of an agent to perform both information retrieval and filtering at a VSAM server, and to return to the VSAM client only the relevant information. Thus, the information transmitted to the device is minimized and the device does not itself need to perform filtering.

The asynchronous nature of mobile agents appears likely to enable higher transaction rates between servers and clients, but a similar result could be achieved by messaging alone. As a method of supporting simple queries and transactions, mobile agents benefit from the scalability inherent in messaging.

CSAB merges all queries, removes redundant parts of merged queries, compares query arrival time and duration time with time stamp of data entry in sn, and filters out useless portions of queries. CSAB achieves query aggregation through these processes.

VSAM provides routing protocol-independent API, and it was made with pure Java, except for CSAB. CSAB used native code for every routing protocol of WSNs. If VSAM applications don't contain native code, they are inherently platform and routing protocol-independent by using pure Java and VSAM API.

We implemented the original version of VSAM as a single monolithic program. The implementation merged VSAM in a rather complex state machine, and it was difficult for programmers to develop applications in a complex environment. We implemented the current version of VSAM and separated the three conceptual parts on the implementation level by using virtual counterpart concept for smart environments. There is a clear separation of the conceptual components of the application at the implementation level, which eases further development of the application and makes it less prone to programming errors than the monolithic approach used in the original version of VSAM.

The technical advantages of VSAM identified in the analysis are:

- Reduction of network traffic
- Support for disconnected operation
- Support for weak clients
- Scalability
- Query aggregation in application layer
- Platform and routing protocol-independent programming
- Support for smart environment by using virtual counterpart

While none of the individual advantages of VSAM given above is overwhelmingly strong, we believe that the aggregate advantage of VSAM is extremely strong, because:

- It can provide a pervasive, open, generalized framework for the development and personalization of WSNs.
- While alternatives to VSAM can be advanced for each of the individual advantages, there is no single alterative to all of the functionality supported by VSAM framework.
- Since Mobile agents can provide an effective means for dealing with the problems of finding services and information, VSAM is expected to be integrated with Internet middleware.

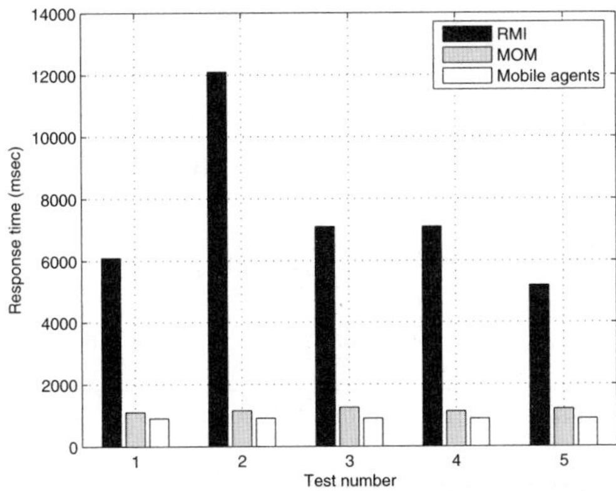

Fig. 4. Results of response time

3.2 Simulation

In sensor network middleware, the response time for requests of clients is a important factor, so we simulate mobile agent of VSAM, RMI (Remote Method Invocation: RPC), and MOM (Message Oriented Middleware) [3]. We implemented these programs with pure Java. The connection was established across the distance between Busan and Seoul, 455 Km. Figure 4 shows measurements of each simulation. Sequentially, packet loss rates are 22%, 29%, 14%, 12%, and 9%. Each test is the average of 10 results. In these results, the mobile agents are less dependent on network bandwidth; it will be more stable than client-server-based (RMI) applications.

Energy efficiency is one of the most important factors in WSNs. To evaluate the energy efficiency of VSAM, we measured the average round when 100 nodes die and average energy after 10,000 rounds for evaluating sensor network lifetime. As we were not interested in simulating any specific communication protocol, we assumed direct transmission without data loss. We assumed a simple model where the radio dissipates $P_{com} = 50\ nJ/bit$ to run the transmitter or receiver circuitry, and $P_{amp} = 100\, pJ/bit/m^2$ for the transmit amplifier (See Table 1). We assumed the overall distance for transmission to be r. The minimum receiving power at a node for a given transmission error rate is $P_{receive}$, and the power at a transmission node is P_{send}. The RF (radio-frequency) attenuation model near the ground is given by

$$P_{receive} \propto \frac{P_{send}}{r^{\alpha}},$$

where α is the RF attenuation exponent. Due to multipath and other interference effects, α is typically in the range of 2 to 5 [5]. We assumed α to be 2. Thus, to transmit a k-bit message with distance r, we used Eq. (1).

$$P_{send}(k, r) = P_{com} * k + P_{amp} * k * r^2 \qquad (1)$$

Table 1. Radio Dissipated Energy

Operation	Energy Dissipated
Transmitter Electronics Receiver Electronics $P_{T-com} = P_{R-com} = P_{com}$	$50\ nJ/bit$
Transmit Amplifier(P_{amp})	$100\ pJ/bit/m^2$

Table 2. Average energy and round using different amounts of initial energy

Energy (J/node)	Simulation Environment	Average Round 100 nodes die	Average energy (nJ) after 10000 rounds
0.25	Exponential	3465	22683210
	Gamma	2980	21742044
	0 tolerant	2699	21201168
0.5	Exponential	6989	88143617
	Gamma	6036	83407250
	0 tolerant	5385	80724393
1	Exponential	13864	339649559
	Gamma	12038	309619661
	0 tolerant	10842	291374934

To receive this message, the radio expends as follows:

$$P_{receive}(k) = P_{com} * k \tag{2}$$

Using Eqs. (1) and (2) and a random 200-node network, we simulated transmission of data from every node to the sink node, which was located within 50 m (at x=50, y=-50). For our experiments, we assumed that the data delivery model is observer-initiated and transmission is direct routing. Each node had a 2000-bit packet to send to the sink node and received a 1000-bit control packet from the sink node. A query area was made of uniformly distributed random numbers.

We used Exponential distribution and Gamma distribution for the requested arrival time of clients.

$$y = f(x|a,b) = \frac{1}{b^a \Gamma(a)}\ x^{a-1} e^{\frac{x}{b}} \tag{3}$$

$$y = f(x|\mu) = \frac{1}{\mu}\ e^{\frac{x}{\mu}} \tag{4}$$

For random request arrival time, we used random numbers from the Gamma distribution (Eq. (3)) with $a = 2$ and $b = 0.5$ and the Exponential distribution

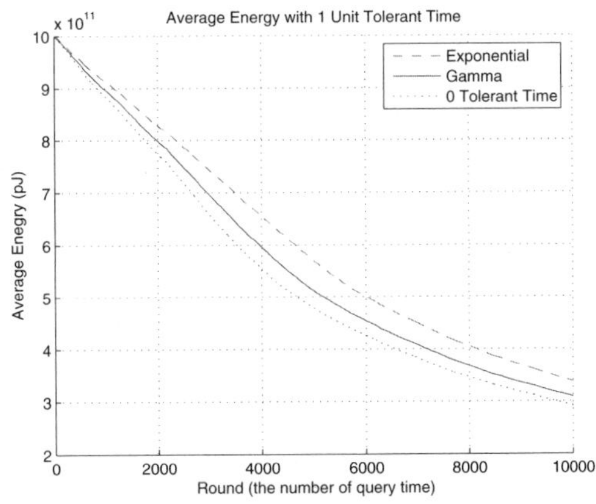

Fig. 5. Average energy of sensor network using 1 unit tolerant time and 1J/node for 200-node random network

(Eq. (4)) with $\mu = 0.5$. We set the tolerant time to 1 unit time and ran the simulation more than 100 times for each case.

We ran similar experiments with 0 and 1 tolerant time (Exponential and Gamma distribution). We found that no matter how energy each node is given and no matter what distribution is used, it takes approximately 10% longer for 100 nodes to die and saves maximally 16% energy with 1 tolerant time. The data from these experiments is shown in Table 2. The advantage of using Query Aggregation can be clearly seen in Figure 5 (An initial energy is 1 J/node).

4 Conclusion and Future Work

In this paper, we described VSAM, a virtual sensor network-based and agent-oriented middleware system. VSAM is a unified middleware system that integrates distributed heterogeneous WSNs into a single virtual sensor network. Because of loosely coupled VSAM components, it can provide a VSAM API that is independent of sensor network protocols. VSN is the conceptual network integrating diverse WSNs. This agent based approach is a very powerful design abstraction. It is scalable so that new agents can be continually added to the system and it is a simple enough to be extended in a variety of ways. It also has the flexibility to be adapted to a variety of network architectures. In addition, we achieved a clear separation of the conceptual components of the application at the implementation level, easing further development of the application.

The current version of VSAM is the first step to flexible, data dissemination protocol-independent and integrated middleware for distributed and heterogeneous WSNs. Our future work will include supporting security API for secure communications and new routing protocols in VSAM.

References

1. Römer, K.: Programming Paradigms and Middleware for Sensor Networks, GI/ITG Fachgespraech Sensornetze, Karlsruhe (Febraury 26-27, 2004)
2. Delicato, F., et al.: Service Oriented Middleware for Wireless Sensor Networks, TR. NCE04/04
3. Message Oriented Middleware Association (MOMA), A Middleware Taxonomy (1998), `http://www.momainc.org/deucation/taxonomy.html`
4. Mahmoud, Q.H.: Getting started With Java Data Objects (JDO): A Standard Mechanism for Persisting Plain Java Technology Objects, Technical Article, Sun Developer Network (August 2005)
5. Zhao, F., Guibas, L.J.: Wireless Sensor Networks: An Information Processing Approach. Elsevier, Oxford (2004)
6. Heinzelman, W.B., Murphy, A.L., Carvalho, H.S., Perillo, M.A.: Middleware to support sensor network applications. IEEE Network Mag. 18(1), 6–14 (2004)
7. Römer, K., Kasten, O., Mattern, F.: Middleware challenges for wireless sensor networks. Mobile. Computing and Communications Review 6(2) (2002)
8. Heinzelman, W., Chandrakasan, A., Balakrishana, H.: Energy-Efficient Communication Protocol for Wireless Microsensor Networks. IEEE Transactions on Wireless Communication 1(4), 660–670 (2002)
9. Wei, Y., Heidemann, J., Estrin, D.: An Energy-Efficient MAC Protocol for Wireless Sensor Networks, In: INFOCOM 2002(June 2002)
10. Cerpa, A., Estrin, D.: ASCENT: Adaptive Self-Configuring Sensor Network Topologies. In: INFOCOM 2002 (June 2002)
11. Chen, B., Jamieson, K., Balakrishana, H., Morris, R.: Span: An Energy-Efficient Coordination Algorithm for Topology Maintenance in Ad Hoc Wireless Networks. ACM Wireless Networks 8(5) (September 2002)
12. Schurgers, C., Tsiatsis, V., Ganeriwal, S., Srivastava, M.: Optimizing Sensor Networks in the Energy-Latency-Density Design Space. IEEE Transactions on Mobile Computing 1(1), 70–80 (2002)
13. Ramanathan, R., Rosales-Hain, R.: Topology Control of Multihop Wireless Networks Using Transmit Power Adjustment. In: INFOCOM 2000, pp. 404–413 (March 2000)
14. Braginsky, D., Estrin, D.: Rumor Routing Algorithm for Sensor Networks. In: 1st ACM Int. Workshop on Wireless Sensor Networks and Applications (2002)
15. Agarwal, D.P., Manjeshwar, A.: TEEN: a routing protocol for enhanced efficiency in wireless sensor networks. In: Proc. of IC3N 2001, pp. 304–309 (2001)
16. Han, Q., Venkatasubramanian, N.: Autosec: An integrated middleware framework for dynamic service brokering. IEEE Distributed Systems Online 2(7) (2001)
17. Li, S., Son, S., Stankovic, J.: Event detection services using data service middleware in distributed sensor network. In: 2nd Int. Workshop on Information Processing in Sensor Networks (April 2003)
18. Liu, T., Martonosi, M.: Impala: A middleware system for manageing autonomic, parallel sensor system. In: PPoPP 2003 (June 2003)

Stream Execution of Object Queries

Piotr Tabor[1] and Krzysztof Stencel[1,2]

[1] Institute of Informatics, University of Warsaw, Poland
[2] Faculty of Mathematics and Computer Science, Nicolaus Copernicus University
{ptab,stencel}@mimuw.edu.pl

Abstract. We show a novel execution method of queries over structural data. We present the idea in detail on SBQL (a.k.a. AOQL)—a powerful language with clean semantics. SBQL stands for the Stack-Based Query Language. The stack used in its name and semantics is a heavy and centralised structure which makes parallel and stream processing unfeasible. We propose to process stack-based queries without a stack. The stack-less execution of stack-based queries is done by a network of components connected by streams. Source streams of the network are populated with necessary fragments of objects retrieved from the database. Output streams produce results of the query. This paper focuses on methods of construction, optimisation and effective execution of such a networks. Although this research was inspired by SBQL/AOQL, eventually we achieved a universal execution method for other object-oriented, object-relational and semi-structured language. Especially promising are the optimisation and parallelisation possibilities offered by the presented execution model.

Keywords: Distributed query processing, databases, structural data, SBQL, AOQL, XML.

1 Introduction

The execution of queries as a stream processing network has a number of significant advantages. First, it allows distributing the workload among many processing units like threads, cores, CPUs, servers and data centres in order to provide the best performance and resource usage. In particular it facilitates processing and aggregating data near nodes where they are stored. This way we can avoid unnecessary network traffic. Second, such execution engine can be used to process data from stream data sources like SAX events [1], sensor data or dynamic results of Event Driven Architecture systems. Third, it is step toward a fully-fledged stream query language [2] and integration of ideas connected to Data Stream Management Systems and Object-Oriented Databases. Fourth, the execution of a number of simple and similar operations allows improving performance on the level of system architecture, since one can avoid excessive data exchange between processor cache and main memory. Moreover, the compiler can optimise the computation using SIMD processor command [3]). Fourth, the execution method and the data flow can be comprehensively (graphically)

T.-h. Kim et al. (Eds.): GDC/CA 2010, CCIS 121, pp. 167–176, 2010.

presented. Fifth, the physical retrieval can be better coordinated, since the components reading the mass memory can be purposely designed.

SBQL (Stack-Based Query Language) [4,5,6] has been adopted by the OMG's Object Database Technology Working Group as the perspective base of the next generation object-database standard [7]. This working group introduced a new name for this language: AOQL (Abstract Object Query Language). The semantics of SBQL is described by operations that are using two stacks: the environment stack and the result stack. Direct implementation of that semantic is quite easy, but since it introduced centralized entities (the stacks), it is hardly possible to employ parallel and distributed execution of SBQL queries. In this paper we propose a stream-oriented execution approach which neither uses any stack nor other type of shared memory. Every query is translated into network composed by components and streams providing one-way communication.

The main contribution of the paper is the algorithm generating a network of components which together execute a query formulated in SBQL/AOQL. The resulting execution method seems to be universal enough to be adapted for query languages other that SBQL/AOQL. The data model used can be object-oriented, object-relational or semi-structured. Execution networks are composed of simple streaming components. This makes many optimisations possible, like adaptive query processing and massive parallelism.

The source database (organized as an AS0 store [5,6]) is available as one or more data streams which emit the data necessary for a particular query. Initially, for the sake of simplicity we will assume that the whole database is dismissed into the input stream. In Section 4.3 we will show how to minimize the data transfer. The result of a query will be collected from a network output stream.

In Section 2 we present streams and components to be used in query execution networks. Next, in Section 3 we discuss the process of static analysis of queries and the algorithm to build query execution networks. We also sketch there some methods to simplify and optimise initially created networks. Section 4 is devoted to practical implementation of the algorithm in the jLoXiM database.

2 Query Processing Networks

Components are processing units which listen to input streams, receive data from them, process the data and send them to output streams. One component can have a number of output streams connected. An exact copy of each output message is put into each output stream.

Components are of different types. Each component type may have a number of instances in a single execution network. Instances of components are parameterised with streams they are connected to and with some data values which drive their execution. This parameterisation occurs at the construction of an execution network and is not altered at the run-time. Components may have state, i.e. a local memory retained between processing of subsequent messages.

While data items flow through the execution network, they can be split into slices in order to be processed independently according to the semantics of the query. Then, the results for slices of one data item are to be combined together. The advantage of this processing model consists in the possibility to limit the amount of data flowing through the network so that only necessary data are passed. As a consequence, however, we have to tag data slices with control data to be used in the result assembly. Those tags will be further called *control records*.

When constructed, execution networks advocated in this paper are compositional and they reflect the structure of the query. Later, as a result of the optimisation process, they can gain uglier shape, since the optimisation does not have to preserve the composition structure.

2.1 Data Model

Components read packets from their input streams and emit packets to their output streams. Each packet consists of a control record and an n-tuple composed of data items.

Control records have been implemented as vectors of non-negative integers. Some entries in a control record can be irrelevant for a given packet. Such entries are filled with zeros and are called *unset*. For clarity we will use $\emptyset$ as their printed representation. For each stream, it is known which control entries are unset, so they can be not transmitted. It will especially profitable if the packets are stored column-oriented.

The data stored method are defined by the data model for a particular query language. In this paper we will use rich model of SBQL Resultset [5,6], which is a superset of XML. For clarity in the examples we will used XML-like notation

There are also some special packets like EOS and FLUSH.

2.2 Components

Components have various roles. They drive the data flow (⟨Stamp⟩ and ⟨Merge⟩), change the data arrangement (⟨MakeBag⟩, ⟨BreakBag⟩, ⟨GetNested⟩), and perform algebraic transformations (arithmetic, logical, set-theoretic, aggregation and ⟨Select⟩). Figure 1 shows an example execution network with sample data flowing through streams.

The component ⟨**Store**⟩ reads persistent object store. It produces a single packet with all significant data. Thus it can be parameterised with a regular expression used to select data paths which influence the result of the query. This allows limiting the number of read data items so only necessary information is pushed into the execution network (see Section 4.3).

The component ⟨**GetNested**⟩ retrieves subobjects with the given name from the objects read from the input stream. The component is parameterised by an external name as used in queries. It produces a single packet for each outgoing packet (if there is more then one matching subobject a bag of such subobjects is a created in the resulting packet).

The component ⟨**Stamp**⟩ is used to mark split streams in such a way that later they can be appropriately joined together. It has one input stream and

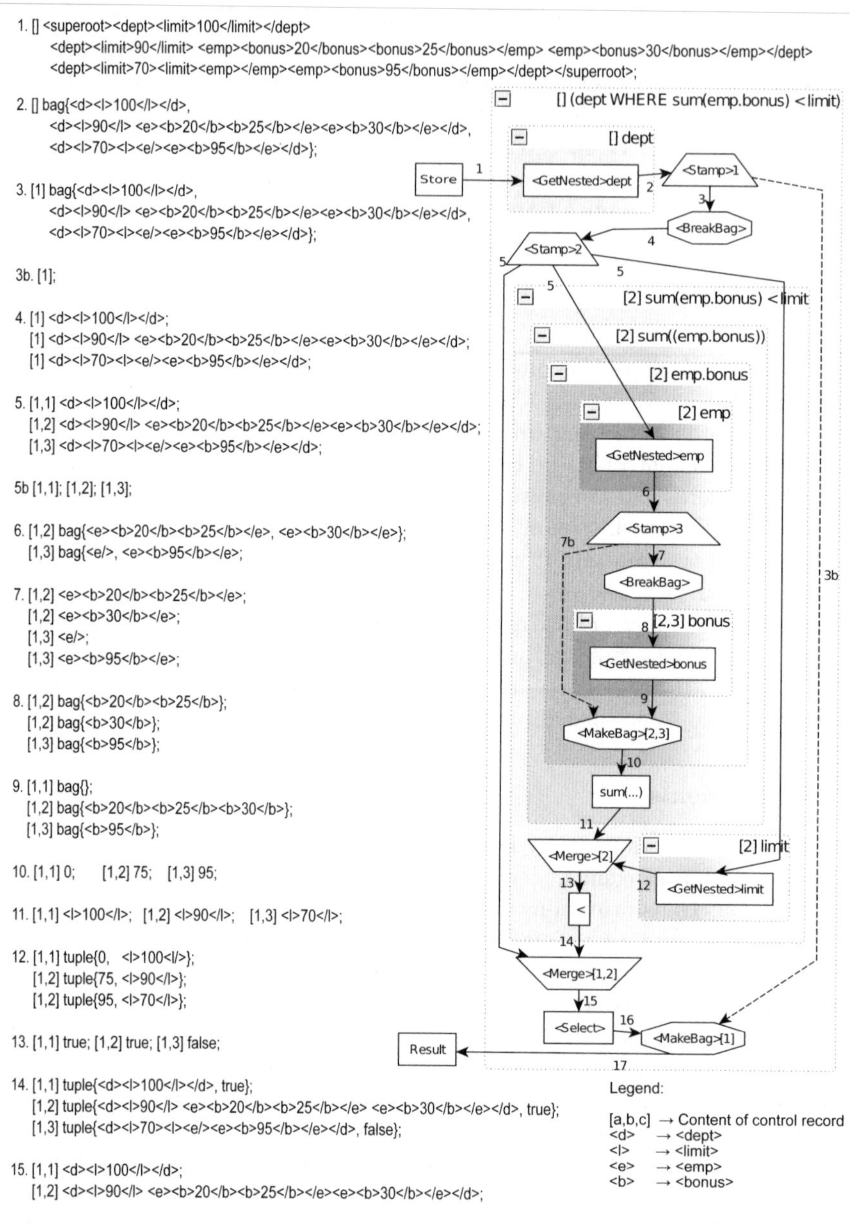

Fig. 1. Network for query: *dept* **where** *sum*(*emp.bonus*) < *limit*

is parameterised by position in the control record vector. Its task is to set the position in the record to the sequential number of the message processed.

In the Fig. 1 the ⟨Stamp⟩1 output is split into two streams (3, 3b). The dashed stream transmits control records only (used to guarantee that at least an empty value will be returned from the network). After the ⟨Stamp⟩2 a stream containing departments (4) is duplicated into 3 streams, responsible for (from left to right): returned value if condition is passed, data needed to evaluate the condition (for "emps" and "limit" subobjects retrieval separately).

The component ⟨**BreakBag**⟩ tokenises received bags and outputs their items one by one (in separate packet) to the output stream. If the input is not a bag, it is passed intact to the output stream. This component preserves control records of the original components. Thus it is possible that many packets with identical control record will be returned.

The component ⟨**MakeBag**⟩ merges many packets with similar control record into a packet containing a bag of all this values. The transformation is parameterised with set of positions in the control record and it works on two input streams (a main and an auxiliary).

For each control record from the auxiliary stream, the component creates a bag of values received from the main stream, which conform together (have the same values on given set of positions). If there is no such messages in the main stream, the empty bag is created and passed to the output stream. All packets returned from this component have control record truncated to given set of positions.

The component ⟨**Merge**⟩ is used to synchronize data arriving at the input streams according to the data sealed in the control records. It has n input streams and is parameterised by E — set of positions in control record.

The component produces k-tuples with k is the number of input streams containing data (not only CRs). Such constructed k-tuples are consumed then by ⟨Select⟩ or other algebraic component (function with k arguments)

From the Cartesian product of data from all input streams we select those tuples $(m_1, m_2, \ldots, m_n)$ which are conformant with respect to positions E (have the same value or are unset on all positions $e \in E$). For each such a tuple, we define a new control record set on each position to the same value as one of source messages $m_{1..n}$ (or unset if the position is not set in any of the messages).

Although this might seem very complex, this component can be efficiently implemented, because all its input streams are ordered. Implementation is similar to merge-sort and in fact it make sense to check conformation condition only on the highest positions of the control record.

Let us emphasise two aspects of the semantics described above. First, result records are emitted to the output stream, only if all inputs transmit matching records. Thus it may happen that data coming from one of input streams never appear at any output, since they have not been matched. Since the data streams are ordered by control records, we are sure that they will not match against anything in the future. Second, some input data can be replicated and transferred through a number of output streams. This may happen, when a control record matches more than one control record from another stream. We can observe it in Example on Fig. 4, where once computed the result of a subquery is many times used in the execution of its superquery. Furthermore, also the constants that are used many times are replicated by component ⟨Merge⟩. This apparent misuse of ⟨Merge⟩ has advantages. It is one of two components which accumulate internal state (the other is ⟨MakeBag⟩). This aids optimisations and reconfigurations during adaptive query processing.

The component ⟨**Select**⟩ transforms a stream of tuples ⟨value, bool⟩ into stream of values having bool = true. It is used to filter out data that does not match the condition.

There are many other components that can be classified as algebraic. For each consumed packet from the input stream, the operators produce a single packet with the same control record, containing transformed data. All standard operations: arithmetic, logical, on strings and other user provided functions are in the category. Moreover aggregation functions (sum, avg, count) matches the category also. They process a bag of values and returns an aggregated result.

3 Construction Rules of Execution Networks

The construction of an execution network is driven by the results of the static analysis of a query, the database schema (or other data structures similar to DataGuides [8]) and the characteristics of the execution environment (the number and properties of processing units and connections among them).

3.1 Static Name Binding with SBQL Operators

The key issue during the construction of an execution network is to identify sources of data for each operator from the query. Such a source is either another operator or the data store.

In the case of SBQL such an analysis consists in binding each identifier from the query with the set of non-algebraic operators which can introduce this name to the binding environment. If the schema is known, each name will be associated with at most one operator. Identifiers which have not been associated are direct references to database roots.

This association of operators is computed using an enhanced version of *static_eval* [5,9]. Procedure *static_eval* simulates the behaviour of all operators in query and their actions performed on the execution stack. It performs the simulation using signatures instead of actual run-time values. A signature is pushed onto the stack together with the identifier of the non-algebraic operator which caused this push. Thus, when we later bind this name using the stack, along with its signature we will also get the operator that recently processed it.

3.2 Construction of a Network

Execution networks are built recursively by traversing abstract syntax trees of queries. The construction rules are presented on Figs. 2 and 3.

Each query (as a whole) is evaluated in the context of a ⟨Store⟩ components and its ⟨Stamp⟩0 component. Non-algebraic components extend the contexts for their right subqueries by the component ⟨Stamp⟩y. This is the key component for name binding. As described in Section 3.1, each name is associated with store or one or more non-algebraic components.

If a name n is associated with store, then the component ⟨GetNested⟩n will be connected to the output stream of ⟨Stamp⟩0. Otherwise a name n is associated with at least a single non-algebraic operator, so ⟨GetNested⟩n will be connected to ⟨Stamp⟩y associated with this non-algebraic operator. If there are many sources, an ⟨HighestDefined⟩ component is added in order to select the non-empty result from the highest index. This way we simulate binding on the stack from its top to the bottom.

3.3 Optimisation of Execution Networks

A network built according to the rules from Section 3.2 can be the subject of optimisation. Since such a network as a graph directly describes all dependencies and the execution flow, it is a good starting point to a number of transformations: trivial graph simplifing rules, state of the art SBQL optimisations [11] and possibly a bigger number of new methods which we expect to present in sequel papers.

4 Implementation

4.1 Realization of Streams

So far we have treated a stream as an abstract channel which is used to pass complex messages. We have assumed that all operations on streams are atomic. However, it is much wiser to implement coarser communication and to allow components to work on much smaller data chunks. Therefore we implemented the channels as streams of events similar to SAX parsers of XML. This way the components may emit events as soon as they gather indispensable information to do so. On the other hand we need to avoid read of items in one by one manner. Instead we read a whole vector of available values in one call. It gives us benefits of vectorised processing especially for arithmetic and Boolean operators.

4.2 Local Streams and Shared Memory

The approach advocated in this paper allows executing each component in a different environment communicating with other environments solely by streams. However, if a number components reside within a single computer, serialization and deserialization of passed messages will be a senseless overhead. Components presented in this paper mostly operate on topmost objects, while the nested objects are usually passed intact to output streams.

Each stream is remote or local. Local streams connect components which have access to a common shared data structure — *clipboard*. The execution framework

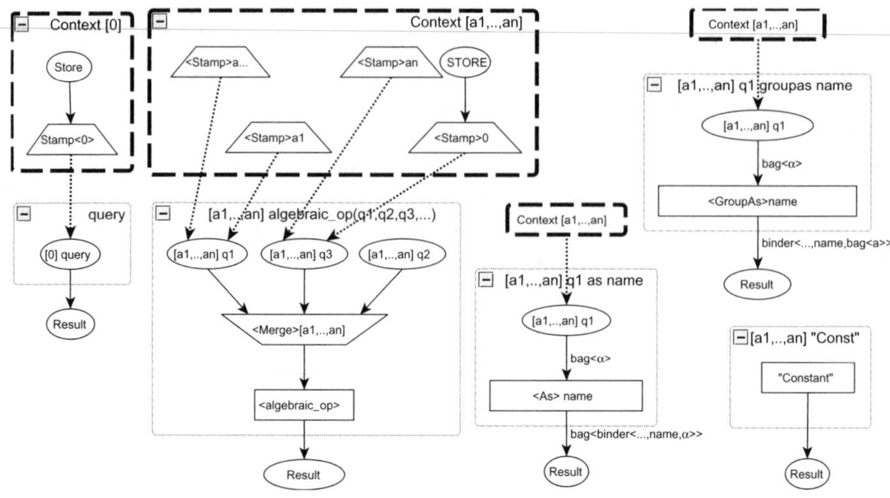

Fig. 2. The construction rules for elementary queries an algebraic operators

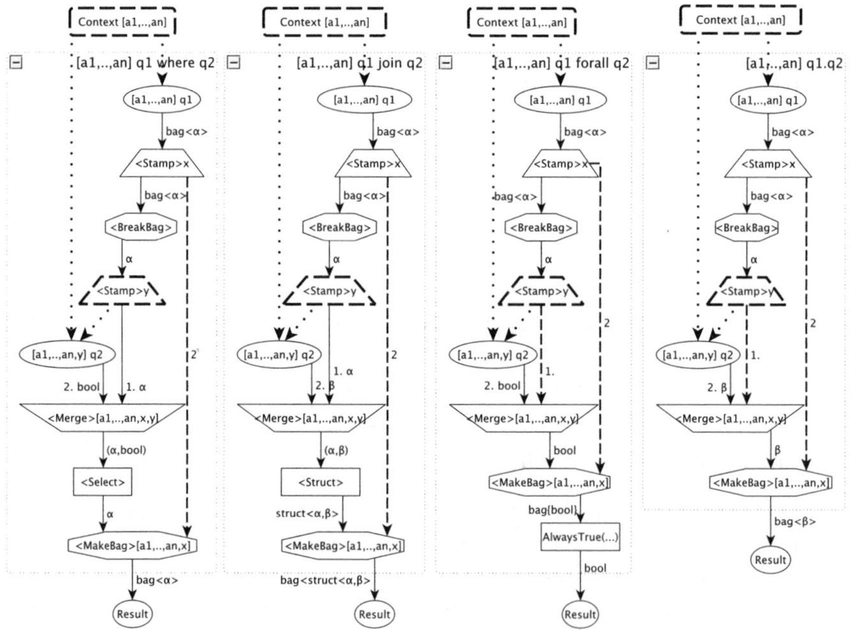

Fig. 3. The construction rules for non-algebraic operators

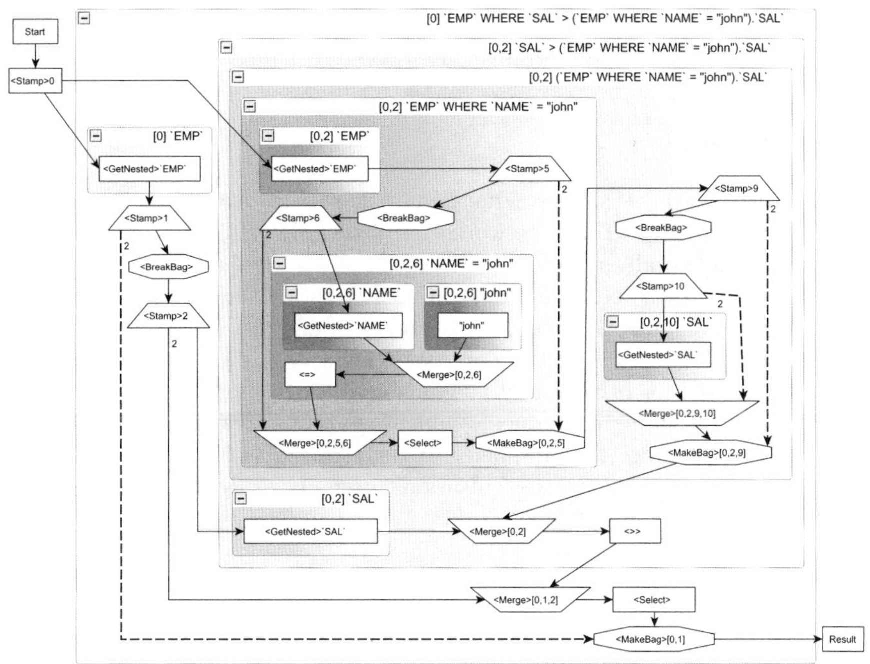

Fig. 4. Network for: Emp where (sal > (Emp where name = 'John').sal) shows that factoring of independent subquery *(Emp where name = 'John').sal* has been spontaneously performed without the application of the method from [10]

can store immutable objects in the clipboard and pass only references throught the local streams.

4.3 Minimizing Store Retrieval

So far we have assumed that the whole database is pushed into the input stream by the component ⟨Store⟩. This assumption is unacceptable in practical implementations, if the data are provided in other than streamed form. The data read have to be limited solely to those which influence the result of the query.

In order to detect this subset of data, we build a subgraph of the execution network which contains only the components ⟨Store⟩, ⟨GetNested⟩ and ⟨RefMaterializer⟩ and directed edges representing paths existing among these components in the original execution network. Analysing this graph as a finite automaton, we compute the regular language which describes the data actually affecting the result of the query.

4.4 JLoXiM - The Experimental Platform

Ideas described in this paper are implemented in a prototype database management system JLoXiM (*http://jloxim.mimuw.edu.pl/*). It is an open-source development project of an object and semi-structured database with transactional support and a number of query processing engines.

5 Conclusion

In this paper we have shown a method to construct execution networks for AOQL/SBQL queries. These networks use streaming interfaces between their components and totally avoid the notion of the environment stack inherent in SBA. The lack of this central execution facility establishes a high potential to execute queries in multi-threaded, multi-processor and distributed environments. As a side effect of this research we obtained a simple and compositional stream execution method for other query languages. The resulting execution networks are composed of simple components which use only streams to communicate. This is promising since the simplicity of the structure of such networks make them an easy subject to many optimisations methods, as well as massive parallel and adaptive execution.

References

1. Brownell, D.: SAX2. O'Reilly, Sebastopol (2002)
2. Golab, L., Ozsu, M.T.: Issues in data stream management. ACM Sigmod Record 32, 5–14 (2003)
3. Boncz, P.A., Zukowski, M., Nes, N.: MonetDB/X100: Hyper-Pipelining Query Execution. In: Proceedings of the Biennial Conference on Innovative Data Systems Research (CIDR), Asilomar, CA, USA, pp. 225–237 (2005)
4. Subieta, K., Kambayashi, Y., Leszczylowski, J.: Procedures in object-oriented query languages. In: Dayal, U., Gray, P.M.D., Nishio, S. (eds.) VLDB, pp. 182–193. Morgan Kaufmann, San Francisco (1995)
5. Subieta, K.: Teoria i konstrukcja obiektowych języków zapytań. Monografie naukowe. Wydawnictwo PJWSTK, Warszawa (2004)
6. Subieta, K.: Stack-based approach and stack-based query language (2008-2010), `http://sbql.pl`
7. Subieta, K.: Omg next-generation object database standarization white paper (2007) (dostęp: 2009-02-29 21:58Z)
8. McHugh, J., Abiteboul, S., Goldman, R., Quass, D., Widom, J.: Lore: A database management system for semistructured data. SIGMOD Record 26, 54–66 (1997)
9. Stencel, K.: Półmocna kontrola typów w językach programowania baz danych. Monografie naukowe, vol. 207. Wydawnictwo PJWSTK, Warszawa (2006)
10. Płodzień, J., Kraken, A.: Object query optimization through detecting independent subqueries. In: Inf. Syst. (2000)
11. Płodzień, J.: Optimization Methods in Object Query Languages. PhD thesis, The Instititue of Computer Science, The Polish Academy of Sciences (2000)

Application of Extended DFT for Fault Detection of Electric Motors

Juggrapong Treetrong

Department of Teacher Training in Mechanical Engineering, Technical Education Faculty King Mongkut's University of Technology North Bangkok, Thailand
juggrapong@yahoo.com

Abstract. This paper proposes a method of fault detection and quantification for induction motors. The method is based on Extended Discrete-Furrier Transform or EDFT. The principle is that any fault either in the stator or the rotor may distort the sinusoidal response of the motor RPM and the main frequency. Because the EDFT relates to both amplitude and frequency of number of harmonics in a signal, hence it is expected to show some harmonics around the mains frequency and some frequencies which have ability to differentiate the faults. The method is tested on 3 different motor conditions: healthy, stator fault, and rotor fault motor at full load condition. The experiments show that it can differentiate conditions clearly by observing the change in specific harmonic amplitudes. The method can also indicate the level of the fault severity by observing the percent change in the harmonic amplitudes.

Keywords: Signal Processing Extended Discrete-Furrier Transform, Extended DFT, Fault Detection, Induction Motors.

1 Introduction

An induction motor is the popular electric drives applied in many groups of industries such as chemical industries, car production industries, and agricultural industries and so on. Thus, the motor is the important mechanism driver in processes of the industries. It can be called the industrial electric motor because of their high level of reliability, efficiency and safety. However, the motor can be suffered with undesirable environments, wrong application and overload uses during operation. Hence it may lead the motor to early-stage failure or increase to server problems until the motor's breakdown which it is an important issue to stop all the mechanism processes of line production.

Some researchers have surveyed the failure that has often occurred in the motor. The research has show that 30-40% of all recorded faults happening in the stator or armature faults caused due to the shorting of stator phase winding and 5-10% fault happening in the rotor (broken bar and/or end ring fault) [1]. Online condition

T.-h. Kim et al. (Eds.): GDC/CA 2010, CCIS 121, pp. 177–185, 2010.

monitoring is an important technique used to check the health of the motor during its operation at the early stage. The information that we obtain from the technique will be used for maintenance planning so that the remedial action can be done in much planned way to reduce the machine downtime and to maintain the overall plant safety.

Signal processing is one of effective tools used to monitor the motor condition. One of them is called Motor Current Signature Analysis (MCSA) which is one of the most spread techniques for condition monitoring of the motor since decades. The main reason is that the other techniques need invasive sensor accessing to the motor and they also need extra equipment/sensors for measuring the required signals.

Popularly, the MCSA is mostly based on frequency analysis. Sometime it is called spectrum method. Some researchers have applied the spectrum for stator fault [2-6] and the rotor fault [7-12] by which the principle was generally based on the observation of the side band, its harmonics around the main frequency, or its other harmonics. However from the previous research [13], the spectrum method cannot show the side band clearly for detecting both rotor and stator by which the stator phase current signals were used as input data. It also has a limitation for identifying the level of fault severity.

Thus from the limitation, this paper proposes a new method of motor condition monitoring. The proposed method is expected to differentiate the motor condition clearly and also be able to identify the level of the faults severity with high accuracy. Extended Discrete Furrier Transform or EDFT is used as a technique for fault quantification in this paper. It is extended from DFT in the purpose of using with limited-signal. Because the EDFT relates to both amplitude and frequency of number of harmonics in a signal, hence it is expected to show some harmonics around the mains frequency and some frequencies which has ability to differentiate the faults. There are the motor faults used to test the proposed method in this research: healthy, stator short turn circuit and broken rotor bar faults of 3 phase induction motors. Following section, this paper introduces the concept of the EDFT. The EDFT results of the experimental cases are presented. Finally, the discussion and conclusion are shown.

2 Extended Discrete-Fourier Transform

Extended Discrete Fourier Transform or EDFT algorithm produces N-point DFT of sequence X (input data) where N is greater than the length of input data. Unlike the Fast Fourier Transform (FFT), where unknown readings outside of X are zero-padded, the EDFT algorithm for calculation of the DFT using only available data and the extended frequency set (therefore, named 'Extended DFT'). The EDFT is one of signal processing techniques which have been mainly adopted from DFT in order to use it with a limitation of a signal input. The EDFT can increase frequency resolution. Because it is well known that zero-padding do not increase frequency resolution by DFT technique, therefore the resolution of the FFT algorithm is limited at N for all frequencies, while EDFT is able to increase the resolution on some frequencies and decrease on others. The EDFT can estimate amplitudes and phases of sinusoidal components in sequence X. the EDFT can be separated for continuous and discrete frequency. The calculation of the EDTFT for continuous frequency can be shown as [13]

$$F_{\propto}(\omega) = |S(\omega)|^2 XR^{-1}E_{\omega}; \quad -\Omega \leq \omega \leq \Omega, \tag{1}$$

$$x_{\alpha}(\omega) = XR^{-1}E_t; \quad -\infty < t < \infty, \tag{2}$$

$$S_{\alpha}(\omega) = \frac{XR^{-1}E_{\omega}}{E_{\omega}^{H}R^{-1}E_{\omega}} \tag{3}$$

where subscript -1 denote the inverse matrix and superscript H denote the Hermitian matrix. $S_{\alpha}(\omega)$ is the signal amplitude spectrum, $F_{\alpha}(\omega)$ is the power spectrum density, $x_{\alpha}(\omega)$ is relative frequency resolution at $\omega_0 = \omega$. X is data input of a signal. R is a unit matrix. E is Fourier Transform basis matrix. For discrete frequency set $-\Omega \leq 2\pi f_n < \Omega$, $n = 0,1,2,\dots,N-1$, The EDFT can be expressed by the following iterative algorithm

$$x = \frac{1}{N} EW^{(i)}E^{H}, \tag{4}$$

$$F^{(i)} = XR^{-1}EW^{(i)} \tag{5}$$

$$S^{(i)} = \frac{XR^{-1}E}{\operatorname{diag}(ER^{-1}E)} \tag{6}$$

where the iteration number $i = 1,2,3,\dots I$. The diagonal weight matrix $W^{(i)}$ (NxN) for the first iteration is a unit matrix, $W^{(i)} = I$, and for the next iterations are derived from the amplitude spectrum $W^{(i+1)} = \operatorname{diag}|S^{(i)}|^2$. The matrix E (KxN) has elements $e^{-j2\pi f_n t_k}$. The $\operatorname{diag}(E^H R^{-1} E)$ (1xN) means extracting the main diagonal elements from quadratic matrix. The EDFT output F(1xN) and S(1xN) are calculated from the results of the last performed iteration I.

3 Experimental Verification

The structure of the test rig is shown in Figure 1. The test rig consists of an induction motor (4kW, 1400RPM) with load cell with a facility to collect the 3-phase current data directly to the PC at the user define sampling frequency. The motors in the test rig used in this experiment can be divided into 3 different conditions – Healthy, Stator Fault (short circuits) and Rotor Faults (broken rotor bars). The load of the motors is set at full load conditions. The data are collected at the sampling frequency of 1280 samples/s. The stator fault motor can be adjusted into 3 server level of the short circuits - 5 turn shot circuit, 10 turn short circuit and 15 turn short circuit while the rotor fault motor is one broken rotor bar.

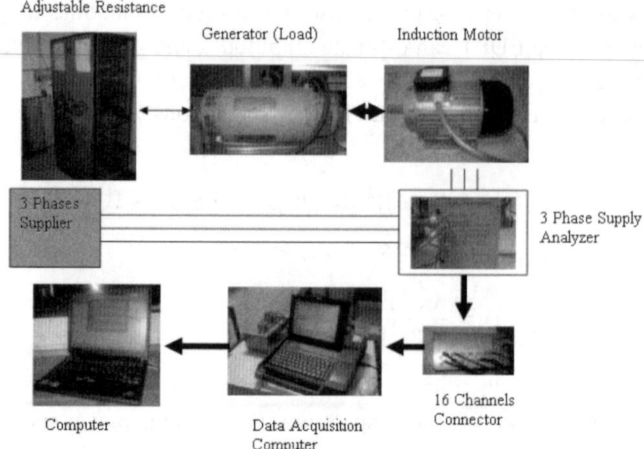

Fig. 1. Schematic of the test rig of an induction motor (4kW, 1400RPM) with load cell

4 Results

A typical stator phase current plot for the healthy motor operating at 100% load is shown in Figure 2. The rated current for the motor is close to 10 Ampere. The frequency analysis and the time-frequency analysis methods have also been estimated for all the experimental data. The frequency resolution was kept 1.25Hz with 90% overlap and number of average 82 for all the signal processing. The computation time using the Pentium-IV PC for both frequency and time-frequency analysis was less than 25 sec which is definitely quick process for the health monitoring purpose.

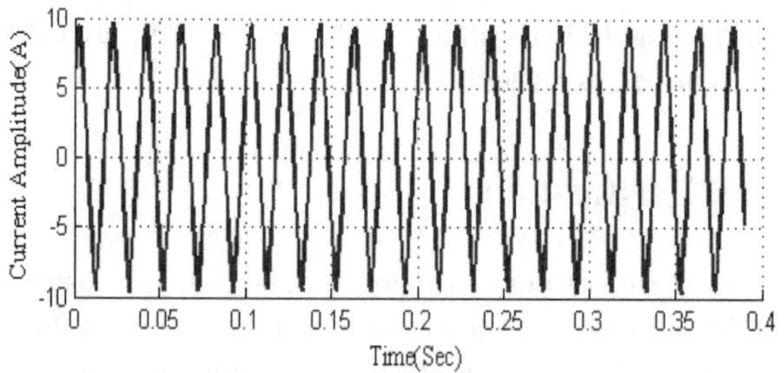

Fig. 2. A typical stator phase current plot for the healthy motor

The proposed method is the Extended Discrete Furrier Transform or EDFT. Power spectrum estimation, power spectrum density and relative frequency resolutions based

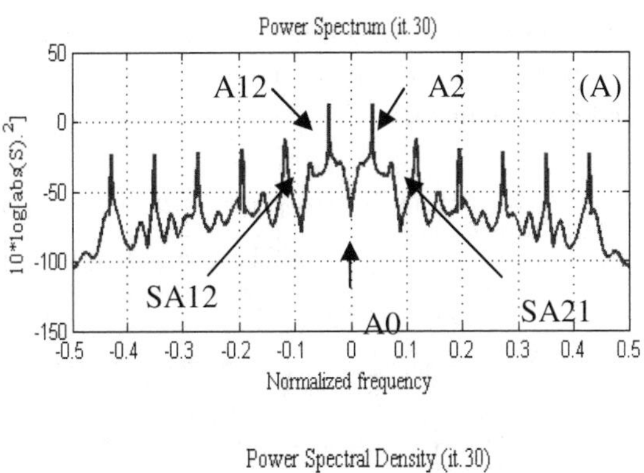

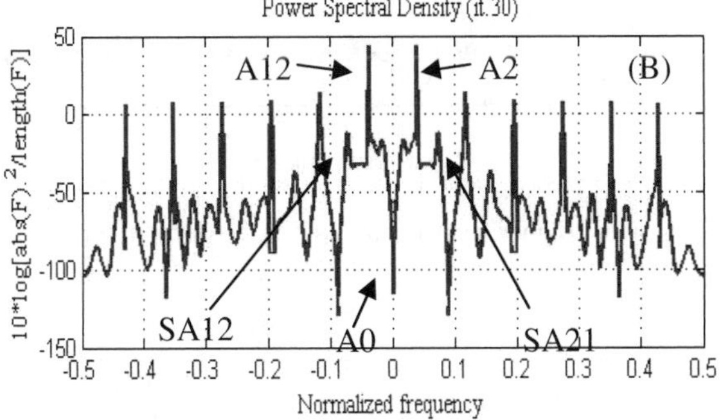

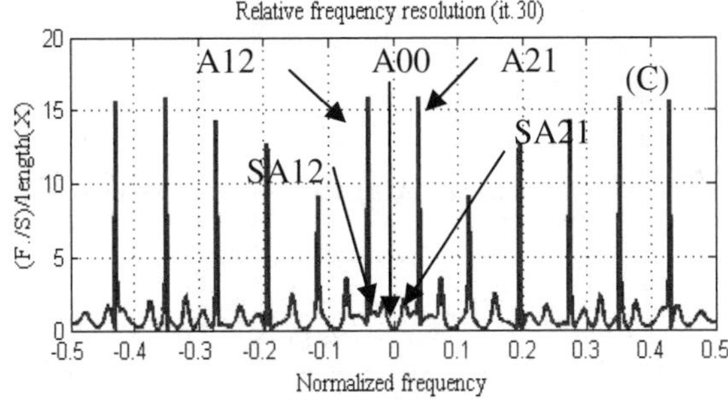

Fig. 3. The EDFT of stator phase current of healthy motor: (A) Power Spectrum, (B) Power Spectrum Density, (C) Relative frequency resolution

on the EDFT are used to classify the motor condition. The power spectrum shows relation between normalize frequency and $10 * log[abs(S)^2]$ which S is amplitude spectrum in Ampere unit. The power spectrum density shows relation between normalize frequency and $10 * log[abs(F)^2/N]$. The relative frequency resolutions shows relation between normalize frequency and $(\frac{F}{S})/K$.

The power spectrum, power spectrum density and relative frequency resolutions of stator currents from healthy motor condition can be seen in Figure 3 (A-C). Assume that A00 is a harmonic appearing at zero frequency or called 'main frequency', A12 (=A21) is a harmonic appearing next to main frequency and SA12 (=SA21) is a side-band appearing around main frequency.

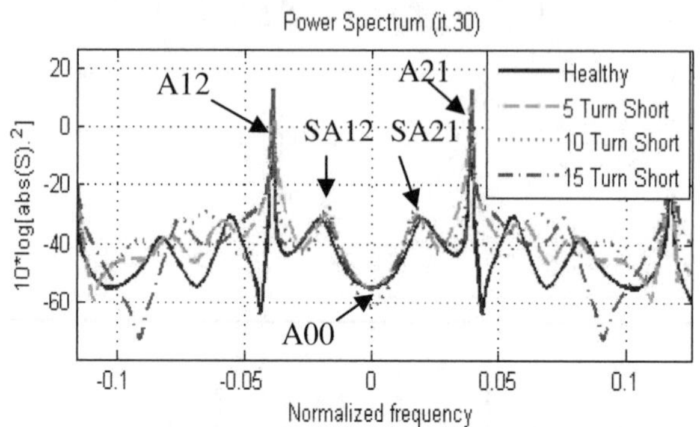

Fig. 4. The spectrum power comparison of healthy, 5 turn short, 10 turn short, and 15 turn short

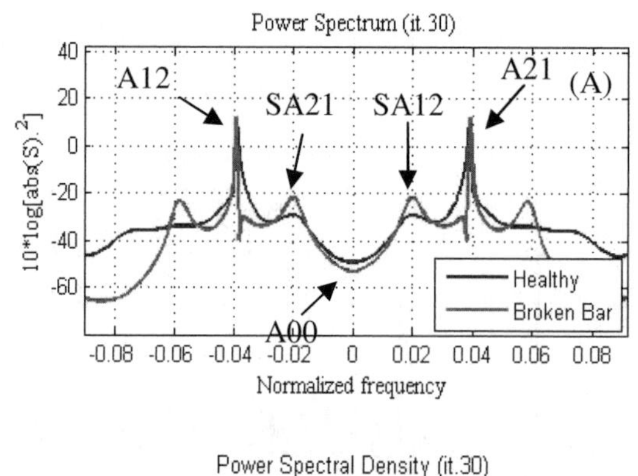

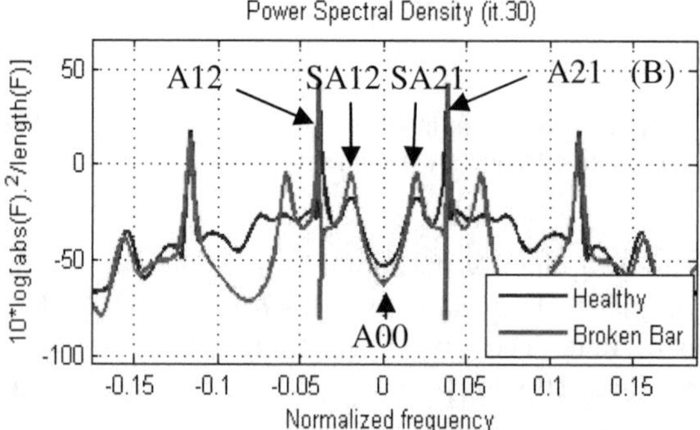

Fig. 5. The comparison between healthy and broken bar motor of: (A) power spectrum, (B) power spectrum Density, (C) relative frequency resolution

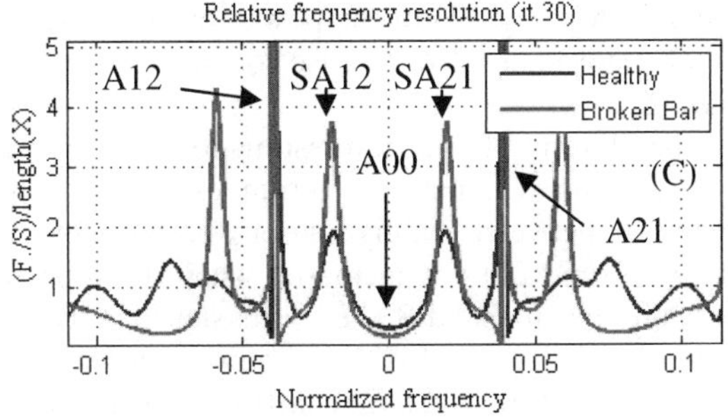

Fig. 5. *(continued)*

Table 1. Harmonic height of power spectrum at specific frequency

Conditions	A00	A12 =A21	SA12=SA21
healthy	-68.13	12.51	-30.65
5 Turn short	-54.22	12.83	-29.52
10 Turn short	-61.58	13.31	-33.85
15 Turn short	-70.34	14.03	-29.99
Broken bar	-59.30	12.43	-10.68

Table 2. Harmonic height of power spectral density at specific frequency

Condition	A00	A12 =A21	SA12=SA21
healthy	-116.01	42.53	-22.31
5 Turn short	-63.04	42.83	-18.55
10 Turn short	-80.53	43.31	-24.48
15 Turn short	-96.73	44.09	-19.36
Broken bar	-72.43	42.41	-1.40

Table 3. Harmonic height of Relative frequency resolution at specific frequency

Condition	A00	A12 =A21	SA12=SA21
healthy	0.002	16.50	1.305
5 Turn short	0.181	17.25	1.767
10 Turn short	0.056	17.92	1.470
15 Turn short	0.023	18.77	1.392
Broken bar	0.110	16.41	4.600

From the tests, the EDFT seem to identify the faults clearly as can be seen in Figures 4 and Figure 5. Figure 4 shows the plotting of power spectrum estimation with healthy condition and 3 different severities of stator faults. The harmonic A12 (=A21) seem to grow when the number of the short circuit turns increases (around 2.55% for 5 turns short, 6.39% for turns short, 12.15% for turns short compared to healthy condition) while the harmonic A12 of the rotor faults seems to remain (as can be seen in

Table 1). The harmonic A12 (=A21) of the power spectrum density and relative frequency resolution for stator faults also increase compared to the healthy condition (As seen in Table 2 and 3).

Figure 5 shows the plotting of spectrum estimation, power spectrum density, and relative frequency resolution. The power spectrum estimation (Figure 5-A) is plotted by comparing the results between healthy and broken bar motor. It can be observed that the sideband SA12 (=SA21) has increased when the broken rotor bar happens (around 65.15 %) while the sideband SA12 of the stator faults seem to remain. The harmonics of the sideband SA12 (=SA21) of power spectrum density and relative frequency resolution (Figure 5-B) and 5-C) can also show the growth in the same way (around 93.72% for the power spectrum density and 253.84% for the relative frequency resolution compared to the healthy condition). The proposed method has been tested with several sets of the motor data in each condition which all the tests are able to provide similar results. But, the measurement noises may slightly affect the accuracy of the results.

6 Conclusion

Because any fault either in the stator or the rotor may distort the sinusoidal response of the motor phase current signal which results in number of harmonics of the motor RPM and the mains frequency, hence the Extended Discrete-Furrier Transform or EDFT is proposed here for the motor fault detection (The EDFT is the modification of the DFT extended in the purpose of using with limited-signal). Because the EDFT is a tool which can show the relation between amplitude and frequency of number of harmonics in a signal, hence the EDFT is expected to show some harmonics around the mains frequency and some frequencies which have ability to differentiate the faults. Based on The experiments, the EDFT can differentiate the motor condition clearly with the harmonic amplitude and the method can also indicate the level of the fault severity by observing the percent change in the measured height of the harmonic amplitudes. Thus, it concludes that the EDFT method is a tool which has ability to use for fault detection and quantification. However base on observation, the accuracy of the method may be affected by measurement noises. Further modification of the method is planned for future work.

References

1. Nandi, S., Toliyat, H.A., Li, X.: Condition Monitoring and Fault Diagnosis of Electrical Motors—A Review. IEEE Transactions on Energy Conversion 20(4), 719–729 (2005)
2. Schoen, R.R., Habetler, T.G.: Effects of time-varying loads on rotor fault detection in induction machines. IEEE Transactions on Industry Applications 31(4), 900–906 (1995)
3. Bellini, A., Filippetti, F., Franceschini, G., Tassoni, C., Kliman, G.B.: Quantitative evaluation of induction motor broken bars by means of electrical signature analysis. IEEE Transactions on Industry Applications 37(5), 1248–1255 (2001)
4. Ayhan, B., Chow, M.Y., Song, M.H.: Multiple Signature Processing-Based Fault Detection Schemes for Broken Rotor Bar in Induction Motors. IEEE Transactions on Energy Conversion 20(2), 336–343 (2005)

5. Henao, H., Razik, H., Capolino, G.-A.: Analytical approach of the stator current frequency harmonics computation for detection of induction machine rotor faults. IEEE Transactions on Industry Applications 41(3), 801–807 (2005)
6. Didier, G., Ternisien, E., Caspary, O., Razik, H.: A new approach to detect broken rotor bars in induction machines by current spectrum analysis. Mechanical Systems and Signal Processing 21, 1127–1142 (2007)
7. Kia, S.H., Henao, H., Capolino, G.-A.: A High-Resolution Frequency Estimation Method for Three-Phase Induction Machine Fault Detection. IEEE Transactions on Industrial Electronics 54(4), 2305–2314 (2007)
8. Marques Cardoso, A.J., Cruz, S.M.A., Fonseca, D.S.B.: Inter-turn stator winding fault diagnosis in three-phase induction motors' by Park's vector approach. IEEE Transaction on Energy Conversion 14(3), 595–598 (1999)
9. Bellini, A., Filippetti, F., Franceschini, G., Tassoni, C.: Closed-loop control impact on the diagnosis of induction motors faults. IEEE Transactions on Industry Applications 36(5), 1318–1329 (2000)
10. Tallam, R.M., Habetler, T.G., Harley, R.G.: Stator winding turn-fault detection for closed-loop induction motor drives. IEEE Transactions on Industry Applications 39(3), 720–724 (2003)
11. Henao, H., Martis, C., Capolino, G.-A.: An equivalent internal circuit of the induction machine for advanced spectral analysis. IEEE Transactions on Industry Applications 40(3), 726–734 (2004)
12. Aroquiadassou, G., Henao, H., Capolino, G.-A.: Experimental Analysis of the dq0 Stator Current Component Spectra of a 42V Fault-Tolerant Six-Phase Induction Machine Drive with Opened Stator Phases. In: IEEE International Symposium on Diagnostics for Electric Machines, Power Electronics and Drives (SDEMPED 2007), September 6-8 , pp. 52–57 (2007)
13. Liepins, V.: Extended Fourier analysis of signals, PhD dissertation, University of Latvia (1998)

On the Complexity of the Classification of Synchronizing Graphs

Eduardo Canale*, Pablo Monzón, and Franco Robledo

IMERL-IIE-Facultad de Ingeniería, Udelar, Montevideo, Uruguay
{canale,monzon,frobledo}@fing.edu.uy
http://www.fing.edu.uy/imerl,
http://iie.fing.edu.uy/

Abstract. This article deals with the general ideas of almost global synchronization of Kuramoto coupled oscillators and synchronizing graphs. It reviews the main existing results and gives some new results about the complexity of the problem. It is proved that any connected graph can be transformed into a synchronized one by making suitable groups of twin vertices. As a corollary it is deduced that any connected graph is the induced subgraph of a synchronizing graph. This implies a big structural complexity of synchronizability. Finally the former is applied to find a two integer parameter family $G(a,b)$ of connected graphs such that if b is the k-th power of 10, the synchronizability of $G(a,b)$ is equivalent to find the k-th digit in the expansion in base 10 of the square root of 2. Thus, the complexity of classify $G(a,b)$ is of the same order than the computation of square root of 2. This is the first result so far about the computational complexity of the synchronizability problem.

Keywords: Network synchronization, coupled oscillators, synchronizing graphs, graph complexity.

1 Introduction

Kuramoto's mathematical model for coupled oscillator represents a wide variety of real systems, from biology to engineering, in which the coordination of several individuals is relevant [1–3]. The i-th oscillator or *agent* is described by its phase $\theta_i : \mathbb{R} \to \mathbb{R}$ and the differential equation

$$\dot{\theta}_i = \sum_{j \in \mathcal{N}_i} \sin(\theta_j - \theta_i) \quad , \quad i = 1, \dots, n \tag{1}$$

models the variation of this phase as a result of the influences of the other oscillators[1]. $\mathcal{N}_i$ denotes the *neighbors* of agent i. These sets can be described by a graph. The natural state space is the n-dimensional torus $\mathbb{T}^n$, since the function sin is 2π-periodic. Thus, we will consider $\theta_i \in [0, 2\pi)$, $i = 1, \dots, n$.

* The authors want to thank the support of PEDECIBA-Informática.

[1] Equation (1) describes the Kuramoto model for weakly coupled identical oscillators; see [1] for more general descriptions.

T.-h. Kim et al. (Eds.): GDC/CA 2010, CCIS 121, pp. 186–195, 2010.

We work with mutual influence between agents, i.e., $i \in \mathcal{N}_j$ if and only if $j \in \mathcal{N}_i$. Synchronization of oscillators is a classical topic in electrical engineering [4]. In the last years, several works in the control community have addressed the problem of analyzing local stability properties of the Kuramoto model [5–8]. Global properties were explored in [9–13]. When a system has the almost global stability, the origin of the system attracts all the initial conditions, with the possible exception of a zero Lebesgue measure set [9]. From an engineering point of view, it is a desirable situation, specially when the system has several equilibrium points. For a Kuramoto model, the origin represents the *consensus* or *synchronization* of all the agents. *Almost global synchronization* (AGS) means that almost every initial condition leads to synchronization [9]. We denote by $\theta \in \mathbb{T}^n$ the vector of phases. Interaction between agents is modeled by using a non-oriented graph G, with nodes representing the agents and links showing the interconnections [14]. If we endow G with an arbitrary orientation, we obtain the respective incidence matrix B and the compact description [5]

$$\dot{\theta} = -B. \sin(B^T \theta) \tag{2}$$

for equation (1). We can write $V(\theta) = m - \mathbf{1}_m. \cos(B^T\theta)$ and $V''(\theta) = -B.diag[\cos(B^T\theta)].B^T$. So, (2) is a *gradient* system (see [5, 7]). Since the *Laplacian* of G is the square matrix $L = B.B^T$ [14], $V''(\theta)$ can be thought as a weighted laplacian. This fact gives a direct link between dynamical properties of system (2) and algebraic properties of graph G. When system (2) has the AGS property, we say that the graph G *synchronizes* or is *synchronizing.* As Kuramoto suggested, each oscillator can be thought as a running particle on the unit circumference, where the respective phase defines its position. So, each oscillator may be represented by a phasor $V_i = e^{j\theta_i}$, $i = 1, \ldots, n$, where $j = \sqrt{-1}$. For each agent i, we introduce the complex numbers

$$\alpha_i(\theta) = \frac{1}{V_i} \sum_{k \in \mathcal{N}_i} V_k = \sum_{k \in \mathcal{N}_i} \frac{V_k}{V_i} = \sum_{k \in \mathcal{N}_i} e^{j(\theta_k - \theta_i)} \tag{3}$$

As we have mentioned,

$$\dot{U}(\theta) = -\|\dot{\theta}\|^2 \tag{4}$$

So, U decreases along the trajectories of system (2). For $U_0 = m$, U is non negative and generalizes in some sense the square of the *order parameter* defined by Kuramoto ([5]). Since, in this case, $U(c\mathbf{1}_n) = 0$ for every $c \in [0, 2\pi)$, we may see U as a local Lyapunov function that proves the local stability of the consensus (see [5, 15]). Moving towards global properties, we wonder what happens when we start far from the consensus curve. Equation (4) says that the potential is non increasing along the trajectories of the system. Since we are working on a compact state space, we may apply LaSalle result and conclude that every trajectory converge to an equilibrium point of (2) (see [15]). Moreover, the only attractors of the system are the equilibria. So, in order to have the AGS property, the consensus must be the only attractor of the state space or, equivalently, every non consensus equilibria must be unstable. Our main tool for classifying the equilibria is Jacobian linearization. At an equilibrium point $\bar{\theta}$, the Jacobian matrix $M_{n\times n}$ of system (2) is symmetric and takes the explicit form

$$m_{ii} = -\sum_{k\in\mathcal{N}_i}\cos(\bar{\theta}_k - \bar{\theta}_i) = -\alpha_i(\bar{\theta}) \quad , \quad m_{hi} = \begin{cases}\cos(\bar{\theta}_h - \bar{\theta}_i) & , h \in \mathcal{N}_i \\ 0 & , h \notin \mathcal{N}_i\end{cases} \tag{5}$$

or, in a compact notation: $M = -B.diag\left[\cos(B^T\bar{\theta})\right].B^T$, which can be thought as a *weighted* laplacian. Observe that always $M.\mathbf{1}_n = 0$ and M has a null eigenvalue. This is related to the fact that the system is invariant under translations parallel to vector $\mathbf{1} \in \mathbb{T}^n$. Due to this invariance, we only care about the rest of the eigenvalues. If M has a positive eigenvalue, then $\bar{\theta}$ is unstable; if M has $n-1$ negative eigenvalues, $\bar{\theta}$ is stable. If the null eigenvalue is not simple, then Jacobian linearization is not enough for proving stability of $\bar{\theta}$. Without looking directly to the eigenvalues, we can work with the quadratic form induced by M. Let $x \in \mathbb{R}^n$ and denote by ik the link between nodes i and k, when it exists. Then,

$$x^T M x = -\sum_{ik\in E}(x_k - x_i)^2\cos(\theta_k - \theta_i) \tag{6}$$

In Section 2, we quickly review the main properties of *synchronizing* graphs. In Section 3, we introduce the idea of twin vertices and later, in Section 4, we analyze the classification of a given family of graphs and we introduce some findings about its complexity. Finally, we present some conclusions.

2 Main Properties

In this Section, we will focus on the general properties of equation (2), its equilibria and its relationships with the underlying interconnection graph. We have the following general results.

Lemma 1. *$\bar{\theta} \in \mathbb{T}^n$ is an equilibrium point if and only if $\alpha_i(\bar{\theta})$ is real, for $i = 1,\ldots,n$.*

Proof: From equation (3), is clear that $\alpha_i(\theta) = \sum_{k\in\mathcal{N}_i}\cos(\theta_k - \theta_i) + j\sum_{k\in\mathcal{N}_i}\sin(\theta_k - \theta_i)$. So, at an equilibrium point, the imaginary part vanishes and the numbers α_i are all real. ■

Lemma 2. *Let $\bar{\theta} \in \mathbb{T}^n$ be an equilibrium point.*

i) If $\cos(\bar{\theta}_i - \bar{\theta}_j) > 0$ for every connected pair of nodes i, j, then $\bar{\theta}$ is stable.
ii) If for some i, the number $\alpha_i(\bar{\theta})$ is negative, then $\bar{\theta}$ is unstable.
iii) If for some i, the number $\alpha_i(\bar{\theta})$ is null, then $\bar{\theta}$ is unstable.
iv) If for a suitable reference, some $\bar{\theta}_i \in (0, \frac{\pi}{2})$ and the rest of the agents' phases are in $(\pi, \frac{3\pi}{2})$, then $\bar{\theta}$ is unstable.

v) If all the agents' phases are located inside a semi circumference, then $\bar{\theta}$ is a consensus equilibria.

vi) If $\bar{\theta}$ is a partial synchronized equilibrium point, then $\bar{\theta}$ is unstable.

vii) Consider an agent i with only two neighbors: $\mathcal{N}_i = \{h, k\}$. Let $\bar{\theta}$ be a stable equilibrium point and define the angles $\varphi_{ik} = |\bar{\theta}_i - \bar{\theta}_k|$ and $\varphi_{ih} = |\bar{\theta}_i - \bar{\theta}_h|$. Then, $\varphi_{ik} = \varphi_{ih}$.

Proof: We only prove item *vii)*; the rest of the proofs can be found in [16]. The equilibrium condition at agent i implies that $\sin(\varphi_{ik}) = \sin(\varphi_{ih})$. Then, it must be true that either $\varphi_{ik} = \varphi_{ih}$ or $\varphi_{ik} + \varphi_{ih} = \pi$. But in the last case, we have $\alpha_i(\bar{\theta}) = 0$ and $\bar{\theta}$ should be unstable. ■

3 Twin Vertices

In this Section we introduce the idea of *twin vertices*, together with its main properties.

Definition 1. *Consider two nodes u and v of a graph G. We say they are twins if the have the same set of neighbors: $\mathcal{N}_u = \mathcal{N}_v$.* ♢

Slightly modifying previous definition, we also say that two vertices are *adjacent twins* if they are adjacent and $\mathcal{N}_u \setminus \{v\} = \mathcal{N}_v \setminus \{u\}$. Concerning synchronization, twins vertices act as a *team* in order to get equilibrium in equation (2). The following result concerns the necessary behavior of twins and will be useful for the complexity analysis we will perform.

Lemma 3. *Consider the system (2) with graph G. Let $\bar{\theta}$ be an equilibrium point of the system and v a vertex of G, with associated phasor V_v. Let T be the set of twins of v and $\mathcal{N}$ the set of common neighbors. If the real number $\alpha_v = \frac{1}{V_v}\sum_{w\in\mathcal{N}} V_w$ is nonzero, the twins of v are partially or fully coordinated with it, that is, the phasors V_h, with $h \in \mathcal{N}_v$ are all parallel to V_v. Moreover, if $\bar{\theta}$ is* ***stable****, the agents in T are fully coordinated.*

Proof: See [12]. ■

We may define an equivalence relationship in the node set of a graph: two nodes are *equivalent* if they are twins. So, we can obtain a *quotient* graph by direct identification of equivalent nodes. The quotient graph can be seen as an induced subgraph of the original one and reciprocally, we can *cover* a given graph by a larger graph, obtained by the addition of twins. These lead us to the following results.

Theorem 1. *Any connected graph G admits an AGS twin cover.*

Proof: Let us suppose that the set of vertices of G is $\{1,\ldots,n\}$ and that we have constructed the cover $\bar{G}$ by splitting each vertex i of G in a number a_i of adjacent twins vertices. Then, if θ is a non linearly stable equilibrium of $\bar{G}$, by Lemma 3, the twins must be synchronized and for a given vertex i, we have: $\sum_{j\in N_i} a_j \sin(\theta_j - \theta_i) = 0$, since all the twins of vertex i have phase θ_i. Then, for any $k \in N_i$:

$$a_k \sin(\theta_k - \theta_i) = -\sum_{j\in N_i, j\neq k} a_j \sin(\theta_j - \theta_i) \quad , \quad |\sin(\theta_k - \theta_i)| \leq \frac{\sum_{j\in N_i, j\neq k} a_j}{a_k}$$

Then, if the second member is small enough to ensure that the sine in the first member is small we are done. Indeed, small sines, say smaller than $\sqrt{2}/D$ where D is the diameter of G, implies phasors in opposite quarter circumference, but by Lemma 2-*iv)* this implies unstability. Then the phasor must be in a quarter circumference, which implies by Lemma 2-*v)* that the equilibrium is a consensus. We can in fact do something weaker, bounding the sines of adjacent vertices in a spanning tree of G by $\epsilon = \sqrt{2}/H$, where H is the height of the tree. In order to do this, we will construct a rooted directed spanning tree T of $G = (V, E)$ and then for each i we will take as k to be the father of i in this tree. Let S_h be the vertices at distance h from vertex 1. Then sort each set S_h with an order $<_h$. We consider the following "lexicographical" order on V: given two vertices $u \in S_i$ and $w \in S_j$ we say that $u < w$ if $i > j$ or if $i = j$ and $u <_i w$. The order defined in this way is total, therefore we can label the vertices following this order so that $1 = v_1 > v_2 > \ldots > v_n$. Next, set $a_i = \lceil (\Delta/\epsilon)^{|V|-i} \rceil$, where Δ is the maximum degree of a vertex in G. Then the arcs of T will be those $v_k v_i$ such that $ki \in E$ and $a_k = \max_{j\in N_i} a_j$. Notice that $v_k > v_i$. We must prove that T is a tree. Indeed, it is acyclic, because for each $i > 1$ any vertex in S_i is adjacent from exactly one vertex in S_{i-1}. Besides v_1 reaches every vertex, thus T is connected as well. Let us now find an upper bound for the sine of the difference between adjacent vertices of T. Let v_i and v_k be adjacent vertices of T with $i > k$, then

$$|\sin(\theta_k - \theta_i)| \leq \frac{1}{a_k} \sum_{j\in N_i, j\neq k} a_j \leq \frac{(\Delta - 1)\left[(\Delta/\epsilon)^{n-k-1} + 1\right]}{(\Delta/\epsilon)^{n-k}} < \epsilon$$

for any $\epsilon < \Delta$. ■

This result tells that the class of synchronizing graphs could be quite large, but not necessarily complex, since its complement could be small. Nevertheless, we will prove that any 2-connected graph is homeomorphic to a non AGS graph telling us that the complement to AGS graphs is also quite big and complex. In order to do it we will prove a stronger result, namely, that doing an enough amount of elementary subdivision in any edge produces a non AGS graph. We conjecture that it is enough to do three subdivisions.

Theorem 2. *If e is a non bridge edge of a graph G then there is an integer n_0 such that the graph obtained from G by making $n > n_0$ elementary subdivisions of e is non AGS.*

Proof: The idea is the following: since the cycle C_n is non AGS for $n \geq 5$, we can replace one of its edges, say uv by $G-e$ identifying the extremes of e with u and v. If n is large enough the "force" induced by C_n will be weak enough to change a consensus of $G-e$ to another still stable equilibrium. Let us denote by $v_1, \ldots, v_m$ be the vertices of G and let $e = v_1 v_2$. Since e is not a bridge, $G' = G - e$ is connected and then the consensus $\theta = (0, 0, \ldots, 0)$ is stable in $G' - e$. Now, connect the vertices v_1 and v_2 of G' through a path $P_n : v_1 = w_1, \ldots, w_n = v_2$ to obtain a graph $\tilde{G}$ with vertices $\tilde{V} = \{w_1, \ldots, w_n, v_3, \ldots, v_m\}$. We want to prove that for n large enough there exist an $\epsilon > 0$ and phases θ_i^ϵ for $3 \leq i \leq m$ such that $\theta^\epsilon : \tilde{V} \to \mathbb{R}$ defined by:

$$\theta_x^\epsilon = \begin{cases} i\epsilon, \text{ if } x = w_i; \\ \theta_i^\epsilon, \text{ if } x = v_i, \end{cases}$$

is a stable equilibrium point of $\tilde{G}$. In order θ^ϵ to be an equilibrium it must satisfies $\sum_{y \in \tilde{N}_x} \sin(\theta_y^\epsilon - \theta_x^\epsilon) = 0$ for all $x \in \tilde{V}$. These equations are trivially fulfilled for $x = w_2, \ldots, w_{n-1}$. Thus, it remains the following equations:

$$\begin{cases} \sum\limits_{y \in N'_{v_1}} \sin(\theta_y^\epsilon - \theta_{v_1}^\epsilon) + \sin(\epsilon) = 0, \\ \sum\limits_{y \in N'_{v_2}} \sin(\theta_y^\epsilon - \theta_{v_2}^\epsilon) - \sin(\epsilon) = 0, \\ \sum\limits_{y \in N_x} \sin(\theta_y^\epsilon - \theta_x^\epsilon) = 0 \qquad x \in V \setminus \{v_1, v_2\}, \end{cases}$$

where N and N' denote neighbors in G and G' respectively. This system can be thought as an ϵ–perturbation of the system that defines the equilibrium of G'. Moreover, if we add an adequate equation, e.g. $\theta_{v_1} = 0$, the system verifies the hypothesis of the implicit function theorem for $\theta = \mathbf{0}_m$ and $\epsilon = 0$. Thus it implicitly defines the angles θ_x^ϵ as a function of ϵ, for each node of G, in a neighborhood $(-\epsilon_0, \epsilon_0)$ of 0. Moreover, we will have that θ^ϵ is a C^∞–curve in $\mathbb{R}^m$ passing through $\mathbf{0}_m$ for $\epsilon = 0$. Finally, in order to prove the stability, we notice that the cosines $\cos(i\epsilon - (i-1)\epsilon) > 0$ for ϵ small enough. Besides, when $\epsilon = 0$ all the cosines $\cos(\theta_i^\epsilon - \theta_j^\epsilon)$ are positive and since ϵ is small enough, by the continuity of θ_i^ϵ as a function of ϵ, the cosines $\cos(\theta_i^\epsilon - \theta_j^\epsilon)$ will remain positive, thus, by Lemma 2-*i)*, the equilibrium is stable. Therefore, it suffices to take $n_0 > 2\pi/\epsilon_0$. ∎

4 Complexity Analysis for a Graph Family

In this Section we use the previous ideas in order to analyze some complexity issues of the classification of AGS graphs. It is clear that the classification of a given graph requires some knowledge of the structure of the set of equilibrium points of (2). In some cases, this set is quite simple or has a well understood behavior[2]. But in general, this set is very complicated and its study can be

[2] For example, when G is a tree, a cycle or a complete graph. See [9, 17].

hard. In order to illustrate the complexity of the problem, we present a result concerning a class of graphs whose classification is as hard as the computation of $\sqrt{2}$. Let n, a and b be natural numbers and consider the cycle C_{n+2}. We build a new graph $G_n(a,b)$, adding a twins to agent 1 and b twins to the rest of the agents. We will explore the existence of other equilibrium points besides consensus. We will also impose conditions on n, a and b in order to have or not the AGS property.

Theorem 3. *Given positive integers a, b and n, the graph $G_n(a,b)$ is AGS if*

$$n > 3,\ a < \sin(\frac{\pi}{n})b \quad , \quad n = 3,\ \frac{\sqrt{3}}{2}b < a < \sqrt{2}b \tag{7}$$

Proof: from Lemma 2-*vii)* and Lemma 3, a stable non-consensus equilibrium candidate configuration can be easily derived, as is shown in Fig. 1. We retain the reference nodes 1 to $n+2$ from the original graph. We denote by α and β the two involved angles. Equilibrium conditions for node 1 and nodes i, $i = 3,\ldots,n+1$ are trivially satisfied. Equilibrium conditions for nodes 2 and $n+2$ results in the following equations for α and β: $a\sin(\alpha) = b\sin(\beta)$ and $2\alpha + n\beta = 2\pi$. So, since $\alpha = \pi - n\frac{\beta}{2}$ and $\sin\left(\pi - n\frac{\beta}{2}\right) = \sin\left(n\frac{\beta}{2}\right)$, we have this implicit equation for β:

$$\frac{a}{b}\sin\left(n\frac{\beta}{2}\right) = \sin(\beta)$$

We define the auxiliary function $f_n(\beta) = \frac{a}{b}\sin\left(n\frac{\beta}{2}\right)$. Notice we have the trivial solution $\beta = 0$, and the respective $\alpha = \pi$, which correspond to a partial consensus equilibrium configuration, which is unstable. So, we rule out this solution. In Figure 2, we show many distinct possibilities of the relative position of the curves $\sin(\beta)$ and $f_n(\beta)$, for the case $n = 3$. We will only look for solutions $\beta \in [0,\pi]$ and $n \geq 1$. A β greater than π is only possible for $n = 1$ but the respective number $\alpha = \pi - \frac{\beta}{2}$ will be greater than $\frac{\pi}{2}$ and will have a negative cosine, given an unstable equilibrium point. Note that the number n affects the frequency of function $f_n(\beta)$. An immediate condition for the existence of a non-consensus equilibrium is $f'(0) > 1$:

$$f'(0) = \frac{na}{2b} > 1 \Leftrightarrow a > \frac{2}{n}b \tag{8}$$

If it does not happens, $G_n(a,b)$ is synchronizing. Now, we assume that condition (8) is fulfilled and we have at least one solution $\beta^* \in [0,\pi]$ (and its corresponding α^*). We perform a stability analysis of the corresponding equilibrium point. According Lemma 2, a sufficient condition for stability is that $\cos(\beta^*) > 0$ and $\cos(\alpha^*) > 0$, while a sufficient condition for unstability is that either $\cos(\beta^*) < 0$ or $\cos(\alpha^*) < 0$, since this numbers directly defines the sign of all the involved numbers $\alpha_i(\bar{\theta})$. Consider first $\cos(\beta^*)$. Then, $\cos(\beta^*) > 0$ if and only if $n > 3$ or

$n = 3$ and $f(\pi/2) < 1$. This implies that $n > 3$ or $n = 3$ and $\frac{a}{b}\sin(n\pi/4) < 1$. So, we have the following condition for synchronizability: $n > 3$ or $n = 3$ and $a < \sqrt{2}b$. Consider now $\cos(\alpha^*)$. Then, $\cos(\alpha^*) > 0$ if and only if $\pi - n\frac{\beta}{2} < \frac{\pi}{2}$, which is equivalent to $\beta > \pi/n$. This implies the inequality $f(\pi/n) > \sin(\pi/n)$, since f attains its maximum at π/n (see Fig. 2 for the case $n = 3$). So, we obtain the following condition for synchronizability: $a < b\sin(\pi/n)$. Therefore, putting all things together, and considering that $\sin(\pi/n) > \frac{2}{n}$ and $\sin(\frac{\pi}{3}) = \frac{\sqrt{3}}{2}$, we have that the candidate equilibrium is stable if

$$\begin{aligned} &n > 3\ ,\ a < b\sin(\pi/n), \\ &n = 3\ ,\ \tfrac{\sqrt{3}}{2}b < a < \sqrt{2}b \end{aligned} \tag{9}$$

Conditions (9) are summarized in Figs. 3 and 4. ■

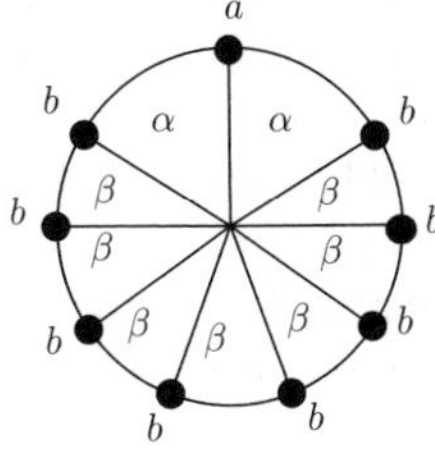

Fig. 1. A candidate equilibrium point for C_{n+2}. At each position, there are a or b twins.

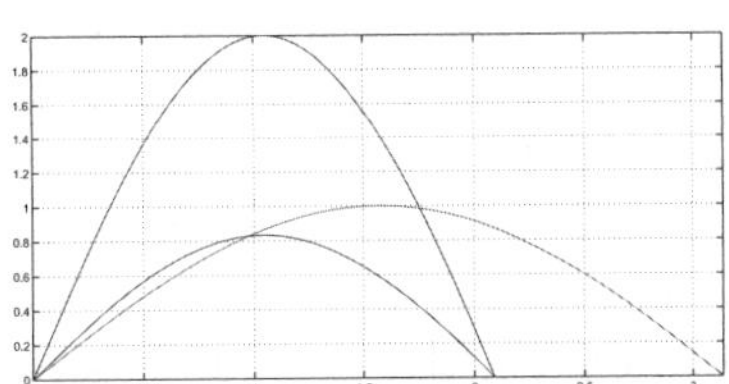

Fig. 2. Situation for $n = 3$

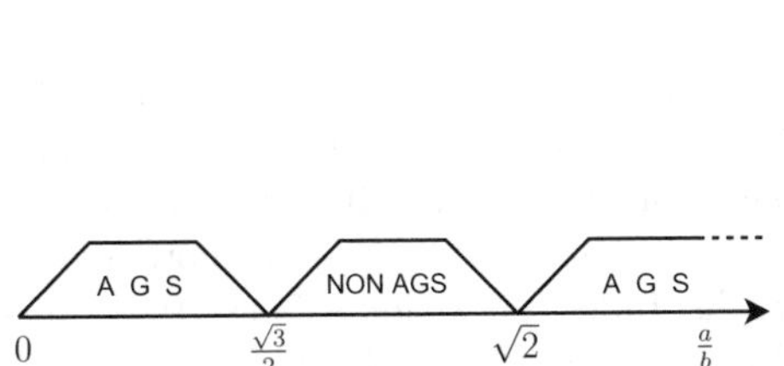

Fig. 3. Synchronizability condition on $\frac{\mathbf{a}}{\mathbf{b}}$

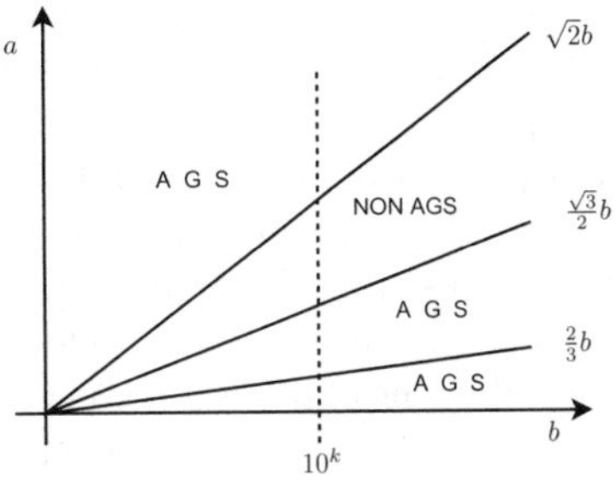

Fig. 4. $(\mathbf{a}, \mathbf{b})$ diagram for synchronizability ($n = 3$)

As an immediate consequence, we have the following result on the complexity of the classification of AGS graphs.

Theorem 4. *The classification of the family of graphs*

$$\mathcal{G} = \{G_3(a, 10^k)\ ,\ a > 0\ , k \geq 0\}$$

has the same order of complexity than the computation of $\sqrt{2}$.

Proof: from Theorem 3, we know that $G_3(a, 10^k)$ is AGS if $\frac{\sqrt{3}}{2}.10^k < a < \sqrt{2}.10^k$. Suppose we know c_k and d_k, the k-th elements of the decimal expansion of $\sqrt{3}$ and $\sqrt{2}$ respectively. Then, a sufficient condition for synchronizability is $\frac{c_k}{2} < a < d_k$. ∎

5 Conclusions

In this work we present evidence about the hardness of the classification of graph as synchronizing or not. On one hand, the class $\mathbb{SG}$ of synchronizing graphs is a combinatorial one, but on the other hand, its definition is made in terms of the differential equations associated with them throughout the Kuramoto model of coupled oscillators. This does not make easy to answer questions like those about the computational complexity of the decision problem of classification. In other contexts, where similar non combinatorial definitions have been made, like for planar graphs, an structural theorem arises that enable the study of the computational complexity. However, in our case, Theorem 1 and 2 (1=every connected graph can be made synchronizing; 2= every graph with a non bridge edge can be made not synchronizing) tell that the class of synchronizing graph is quite complex from an structural point of view, and not such theorems like the Kuratowski one, can be given.

Nevertheless, in this work we present an infinite family whose classification is computational equivalent to find the n-th digit of square root of two. This result seems to tell that there is no a combinatorial definition of synchronizing graphs. However, there are many combinatorial problems where square of root appears, but they are of a enumerations nature. Therefore, if a combinatorial classification theorem exists, it seems to be in terms of amount of structures in the graphs.

As further works, we should find new families whose classification give new light over the computational complexity of the general classification problem. However, this could be a difficult task, since our present result rest over the well known equilibrium points of cycles, while we do not have a complete knowledge of the equilibriums of other 2-connected graphs. Indeed, if we identify the twins vertices of $G(n, m)$, we obtain a cycle, and that is why the equilibriums of $G(n, m)$ are quite similar to those of cycles. However, for other known 2-connected synchronizing graphs, named, complete graphs and wheels, the former are invariant over twins operations, while for the latter we have no idea of its equilibria.

References

1. Kuramoto, Y.: International Symposium on Mathematical Problems in Theoretical Physics. Lecture Notes in Physics, vol. 39, p. 420 (1975)
2. Winfree, A.: The geometry of biological time. Springer, Heidelberg (1980)
3. Strogatz, S.H.: From Kuramoto to Crawford: exploring the onset of synchronization in populations of coupled nonlinear oscillators. Physica D (143), 1–20 (2000)

4. van der Pol, B.: The nonlinear theory of electrical oscillations. Proc. of the Institute of Radio Engineers 22(9), 1051–1086 (1934)
5. Jadbabaie, A., Barahona, M., Motee, N.: On the stability of the Kuramoto model of coupled nonlinear oscillators. In: Proc. of the American Control Conference (2004)
6. Monzón, P., Paganini, F.: Global considerations on the kuramoto model of sinusoidally coupled oscillators. In: Proc. of the 44th IEEE CDC and ECC, Sevilla, Spain, pp. 3923–3928 (2005)
7. Lin, Lin: The mathematical research for the Kuramoto model of the describing neuronal synchrony in the brain. Commun. Nonlinear Sci. Numer. Simulat. 14, 3258–3260 (2009)
8. Chopra, Spong: On exponential synchronization of Kuramoto coupled oscillators. IEEE Transactions on Automatic Control 54(2), 353–357 (2009)
9. Monzón, P.: Almost global stabilityt of dynamical systems. Ph.D. dissertation, Udelar, Uruguay (2006)
10. Canale, E., Monzón, P.: Gluing Kuramoto coupled oscillators networks. In: Proc. of the 46th IEEE Conference on Decision and Control, New Orleans, USA, pp. 4596–4601 (2007)
11. Canale, E., Monzón, P.: Synchronizing graphs, In: Workshop on Spectral Graph Theory with applications on computer science, combinatorial optimization and chemistry (2008)
12. Canale, E., Monzón, P., Robledo, F.: Global Synchronization Properties for Different Classes of Underlying Interconnection Graphs for Kuramoto Coupled Oscillators. In: Lee, Y.-h., Kim, T.-h., Fang, W.-c., Ślęzak, D. (eds.) FGIT 2009. LNCS, vol. 5899, pp. 104–111. Springer, Heidelberg (2009)
13. Mallada, Tang: Synchronization of Phase-coupled oscillators with arbitrary topology. In: American Control Conference (2010)
14. Biggs, N.: Algebraic Graph theory. Cambridge University Press, Cambridge (1993)
15. Khalil, H.: Nonlinear Systems. Prentice-Hall, Ed. Prentice-Hall, Englewood Cliffs (1996)
16. Canale, E., Monzón, P.: On the characterization of Families of Synchronizing Graphs of Kuramoto Coupled Oscillators. In: IFAC Workshop on Estimation and Control of Networked Systems (NecSys 2009), Venice, Italy (2009)
17. Canale, E., Monzón, P.: Global properties of Kuramoto bidirectionally coupled oscillators in a ring structure. In: IEEE International Conference on Control Applications (CCA) & International Symposium on Intelligent Control (ISIC), Saint Petersburg, Russia, pp. 183–188 (2009)

Low Frequency Compensator of Multi-variable Tele-control System

Faramarz Asharif, Shiro Tamaki, Tsutomu Nagado, and Mohammad Reza Asharif

Faculty of engineering, University of the Ryukyus
1 Senbaru, Nishihara, Okinawa 903-0213
faramarz@neo.ie.u-ryukyu.ac.jp

Abstract. The aim of this research is to compensate the multivariable Tele-control system's performance and preserve the stability of closed loop system. Generally in Tele-control systems, it contains with 2 time-delay elements. One is input delay and the other is feedback delay. Therefore the closed loop system's performances become poor and lose the stability due to time-delay elements. Here by using low frequency compensator, it preserves the stability and realizes a good performance of Tele-control system.

Keywords: Tele-Control System, Multivariable system, Low frequency compensator, Time-delay system, Robust Control.

1 Introduction

The purpose of this paper is to stabilize the closed loop of multi variable system and realize a good performance. Generally, time-delay occurs when plant has input delay, output delay or internal delay. But, in Tele-control systems, there are two time-delay elements due to utilization of communication systems. Therefore, closed loop system contains with one input delay and the other delay is feedback delay [1], [2], [3]. Stabilization of time-delay system was considered in many schemes and methods such as PID (Proportional Integrator Derivative) controller for classical method [4], [5], [6], LQI (Linear Quadratic Integration) for Modern method. However improvement of system's performance is quite hard due to existence of time-delay element. Therefore, in this research by using low frequency compensator, tracking performance of system is improved. It is well known that time-delay element has a large phase lag which drops suddenly. This may cause instability in the closed loop system even though the plant itself is stable. Therefore, it is required to internally stabilize the closed loop system. To this end, the parameters of the low frequency compensator are tuned in order to assure the performance improvement. Low frequency compensator, internally stabilize the closed loop system and by tuning the parameters of compensator and as a result the performance can be improved. Therefore, in this paper, the closed loop system internally stabilized and performance of system is improved by low frequency compensator and then evaluation of proposed method is simulated to confirm the stability of closed loop system and performance. In following we have discussed about time-delay element, low frequency compensator, numerical analysis, results and finally conclude the paper.

T.-h. Kim et al. (Eds.): GDC/CA 2010, CCIS 121, pp. 196–205, 2010.

2 Time-Delay System

In this research, we consider a round trip time-delay system input signal has one time-delay element to reach plant and the output signal of the plant or as a feedback signal of the system, has the other time-delay element in order to compare with reference signal. Fig. 1 shows the illustration of the Tele-control system. Also the equivalent system of Fig. 1 has been shown in Fig.2 with the block diagram of a round trip time-delay system with controller.

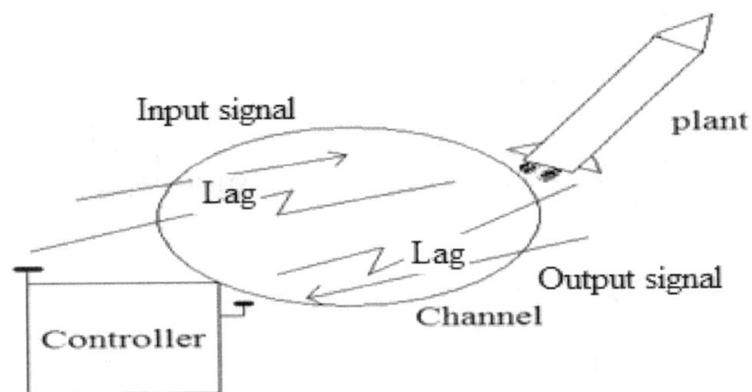

Fig. 1. Illustration of Tele-Control system

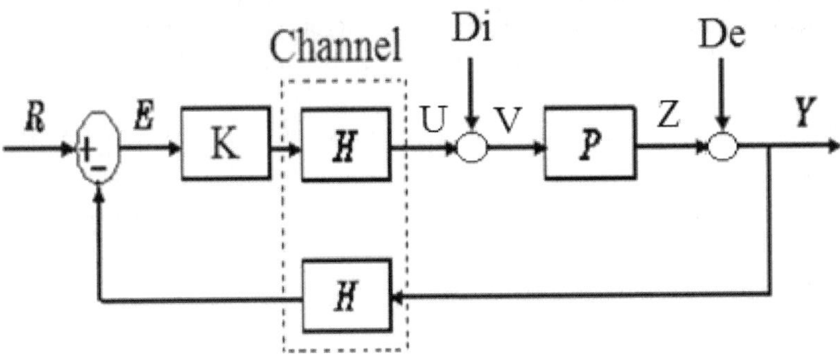

Fig. 2. Tele-control system with compensator

There are various transfer function in Fig. 2. These are for inputs vector of[R Di De]^T which transfer to outputs vector of[Y Z V U E]^T.where "K" is controller, "P" is plant, "H" is time-delay element and "Di" and "De" are internal and external disturbances, respectively. Here, controller has the role of stabilization the closed loop system and tracking for a better performance. By minimizing the error that is the transfer functions from "R" to "E", it can improve the performance of closed loop. Because when system has less error then we have better performance. However, necessary condition of improving the performance is to internally stabilize the closed loop system. The equation (1) is internally stable if and only if guarantee the stability of the gang of four transfer function which contains the complementary sensitivity signal from R to Y, load sensitivity signal from Di to Z, disturbance sensitivity signal from U to R and sensitivity signal from R to E. [7], [8], [9], [10]. The gang of four functions is shown in table 1.

Transfer Function of Fig. 2 is shown in equation (1).

Table 1. Gang of four

Complementary Sensitivity: $(I+PKH^2)^{-1}PKH$	Load Sensitivity: $(I+PKH^2)^{-1}P$
Disturbance Sensitivity: $(I+PKH^2)^{-1}KH$	Sensitivity: $(I+PKH^2)^{-1}$

$$\begin{bmatrix} Y \\ Z \\ V \\ U \\ E \end{bmatrix} = \begin{bmatrix} \Delta PKH & \Delta P & \Delta \\ \Delta PHK & \Delta P & -\Delta KHPH \\ \Delta KH & \Delta & -\Delta KH \\ \Delta KH & -\Delta PHKH & -\Delta HKH \\ \Delta & -\Delta PH & -\Delta H \end{bmatrix} \begin{bmatrix} R \\ Di \\ Do \end{bmatrix} \quad (1)$$

where, $\Delta = (I+PKH^2)^{-1}$ is Sensitivity function.

Here, bode diagram of time-delay element $H(s) = e^{-sL}$ is shown in Fig. 3. It is clear that it contains 0 dB gain and for phase suddenly drops by increasing frequency. If we express phase of time-delay mathematically then we have $\text{phase}(H) = -L\omega$ which is proportionally decreasing with L. That is if L is large then phase decrease rapidly with respect to frequency. Therefore, this may cause the instability of closed loop system. Because if cross gain frequency is larger than cross phase frequency then gain margin will be less than 1, hence closed loop become unstable.

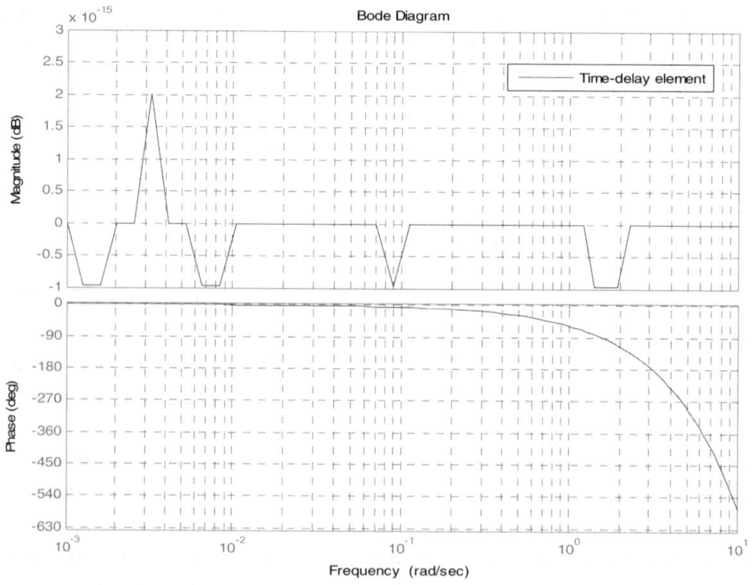

Fig. 3. Bode diagram of Time-delay element e^{-sL} $(L = 1)$

Here we consider an open loop transfer function for stable case. Cross gain frequency is the frequency at which gain of open loop becomes 1(0 [dB]) and also cross phase frequency is the frequency at which phase of open loop becomes -180°. The condition of stability of closed loop system is the case that phase margin larger than 0°and gain margin larger than 1 (0[dB]). Let us approach in mathematical expression. Supposed that the open loop transfer function is $G(j\omega) = |G(j\omega)|e^{j\gamma(\omega)}$ where $\gamma(\omega)$is phase of $G(j\omega)$ When $\omega = \omega_{cg}$ where ω_{cg} is cross gain frequency, then for stability condition we have $\varphi_{margin} = 180 - \gamma(\omega_{cg}) > 0$. For gain margin we have $\omega = \omega_{cp}$ where ω_{cp} is cross phase frequency, then we have gain margin $G_{margin} = G(\omega_{cp})^{-1}$ and stability condition is $G_{margin} > 1$.

For example, we take two open loop transfer functions in which G_1 is stable and G_2 is unstable which has been shown in Nyquist diagram in Fig. 4.

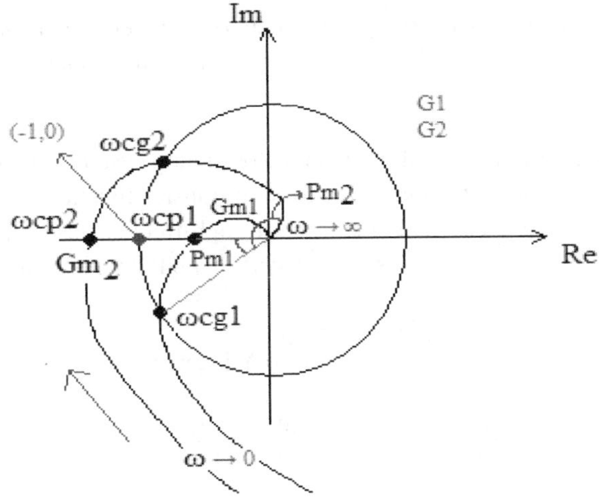

Fig. 4. Nyquist diagram of G1 and G2 Gm : Gain margin Pm: Phase margin

As it is clear that Fig. 4, in the case of G_1 we have $\omega_{cg1} < \omega_{cp1}$ therefore, the closed loop of G_1 is stable. However, in the case of G_2 we have $\omega_{cp2} < \omega_{cg2}$ that means gain margin is less than 1 and closed loop system is unstable. Therefore, the existence of time-delay element may occurs the instability of the closed loop system as the same as G_2's conditions.

Here, the stability condition of controller is well-posed that has been shown in the following equation:

$$I + P(j\omega)K(j\omega)H^2(j\omega) \neq 0 \text{ for } \forall\omega \tag{2}$$

The equation (2) means that singular values of open loop system in high frequency must have small values. However, for good performance of system with time-delay, singular values of open loop in low frequencies should have large values. Therefore, by using the low frequency compensator, we can increase the singular values in low frequencies. This is because of low frequency compensator has the roll of increasing the singular values in low frequencies. Also the performance of system is adjustable by tuning the controller's parameters in order to avoid the overshoots in output signals.

3 Low Frequency Compensator

As we discussed previously, the system including time-delay element, has large phase lag especially in high frequency. Therefore, controller is required to reduce the gain in high frequency. In other words, if and only if open loop has large gain in low frequencies and small gain in high frequencies, the time-delay has no influence in the closed loop system. To confirm this fact, we give the next theorem to prove by a scalar transfer function from R to Y in Fig. 2.

In this case, polar expression of "P","K" and "H" is given as below.

$P = r_P e^{j\theta_P}$, $K = r_K e^{j\theta_K}$ and $H = e^{-j\omega L}$ where "L" is time-delay.

[Theorem 1]

The necessary and sufficient conditions for a closed loop system to be internally stable is that it possess the characteristics of open loop transfer function, HPKH, which has large gain in low frequencies and small one in high frequencies. This condition will improve the performance of the closed loop system, and robust disturbances.

The necessity conditions are explained below:

From Fig. 2, the transfer function from R to Y is given by

$$Y = \frac{PKH}{1+PKH^2}R \rightarrow \frac{Y}{R} = \frac{PKH}{1+PKH^2} = \frac{r_P e^{j\theta_P} r_K e^{j\theta_K} e^{-j\omega L}}{1+r_P e^{j\theta_P} r_K e^{j\theta_K} e^{-j2\omega L}}.$$

$$= \frac{r_P r_K e^{j(\theta_P+\theta_K-\omega L)}}{1+r_P r_K e^{j(\theta_P+\theta_K-2\omega L)}} = \frac{R_{ol} e^{j\varphi}}{1+R_{ol} e^{j\theta}}.$$

Here, we take $R_{ol} = r_P r_K$, $\theta = \theta_P + \theta_K - 2\omega L$ and $\varphi = \theta_P + \theta_K - \omega L$

Then, we have closed-loop function for complementary sensitivity function which given by

$$\frac{R_{ol} e^{j\varphi}}{1+R_{ol} e^{j\theta}} = \frac{R_{ol}}{\sqrt{R_{ol}{}^2+2R_{ol}\cos\theta+1}} e^{j(\varphi-\tan^{-1}\frac{R_{ol}\sin\theta}{1+R_{ol}\cos\theta})} = R_{cl} e^{j\theta_{cl}}.$$

In this case, we assume that the open-loop system has monotony decreasing transfer function in frequency domain. Then, we consider two cases, one is for low frequencies and the other is for high frequencies. This means that for $\omega \ll 1$, then we have $R_{ol} \gg 1$ and for $\omega \gg 1$, then we have $R_{ol} \ll 1$.

From the above assumption, the summation of the phase of plant and controller is given by $\theta_P + \theta_K \approx -90°$ for $\forall\omega$.

Then we have 2 cases,

- For $\omega \ll 1$ we have $R_{cl} \approx 1$ and $\theta_{cl} \approx 0$, therefore, here we have $R_{cl} = 1$.

Such that Y=R, hence, the error is reduced, then the performance is improved.

- For $\omega \gg 1$ we have $R_{cl} \approx 0$ and $\theta_{cl} = -90° - \omega L \approx -\infty$ that means there is not any influence of time-delay element in high frequencies and it is robust to disturbances.

The Sufficient condition is indicates as following:

The sufficient condition of stabilization of closed loop is axiomatic in small gain theorem given by following.

$$\|PKH^2\|_\infty < 1 \tag{3}$$

■

This theorem is expanded to multivariable case, by evaluation of singular values as shown in below.

$$\overline{\sigma}(KHPH) < 1 \tag{4}$$

Where, $\overline{\sigma}(.)$ indicate the maximum singular values.

From these conditions the controller for MIMO system can be chosen as following for the stability:

$$K(s) = \text{diag}\{\frac{1+\alpha Ts}{Ts}, \ldots, \frac{1+\alpha Ts}{Ts}\} \tag{5}$$

Here, α and T are tuning parameters of the controller.

4 Numerical Analysis of MIMO System

Previously, we had discussed the necessity of SISO system for stability and performance. Here we expand for MIMO systems in order to evaluate the LFC (Low frequency Compensator), we have simulated a multivariable system including time-delay. Bode diagram of open loop is shown in Fig. 5. Also step response of the system with and without controller has been shown in Fig. 6 and singular values of gang of four and the open loop system is shown in Fig. 7and Fig. 8, respectively. The specifications of simulation are shown as follows.

$$\text{Plant: } P(s) = \begin{bmatrix} \frac{s+4}{s^2+6s+5} & \frac{1}{s+5} \\ \frac{s+1}{s^2+10s+100} & \frac{2}{2s+1} \end{bmatrix}, \text{ Time-Delay: } H(s) = \text{diag}\{e^{-Ls}, e^{-Ls}\}$$

(L=1[second]), Controller: $K(s) = \text{diag}\{\frac{1+\alpha Ts}{Ts}, \frac{1+\alpha Ts}{Ts}\}$ tuning parameters: ($\alpha = 0.4, T = 5$) Also we assume that the system contains the internal and external step disturbances.

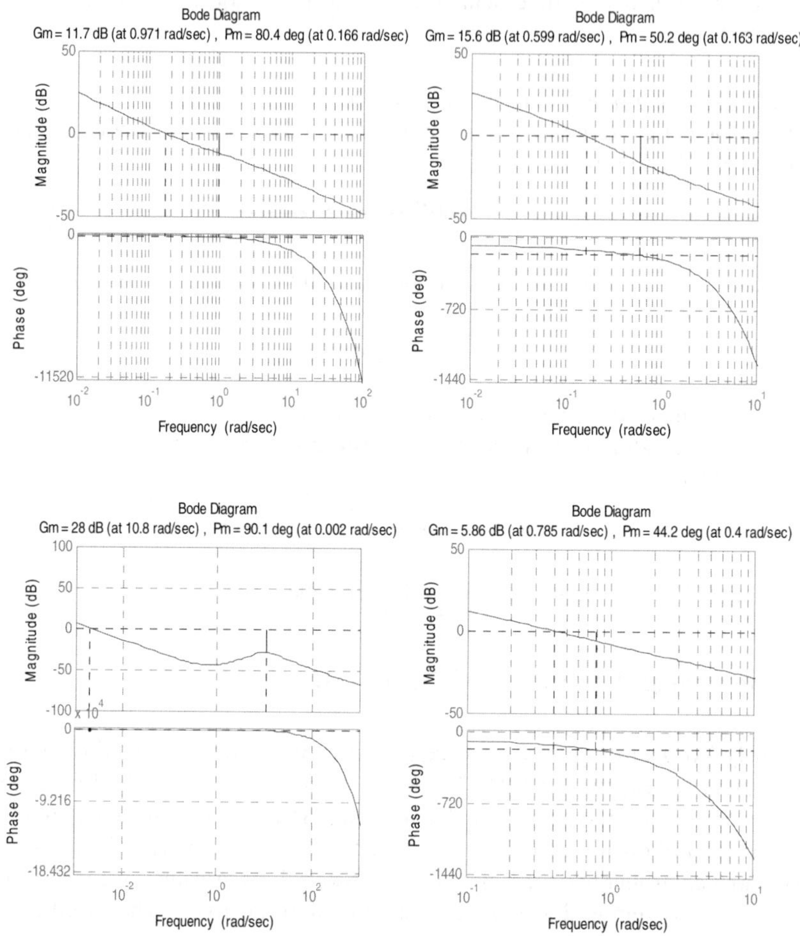

Fig. 5. Bode diagram of open loop with controller Gm (cross phase frequency) and Pm (cross gain frequency) Gm: gain margin Pm: Phase margin

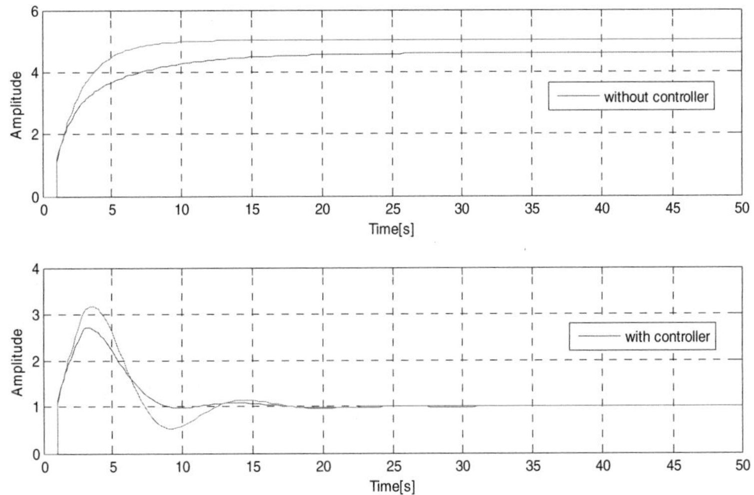

Fig. 6. Step response of system with internal and external disturbances

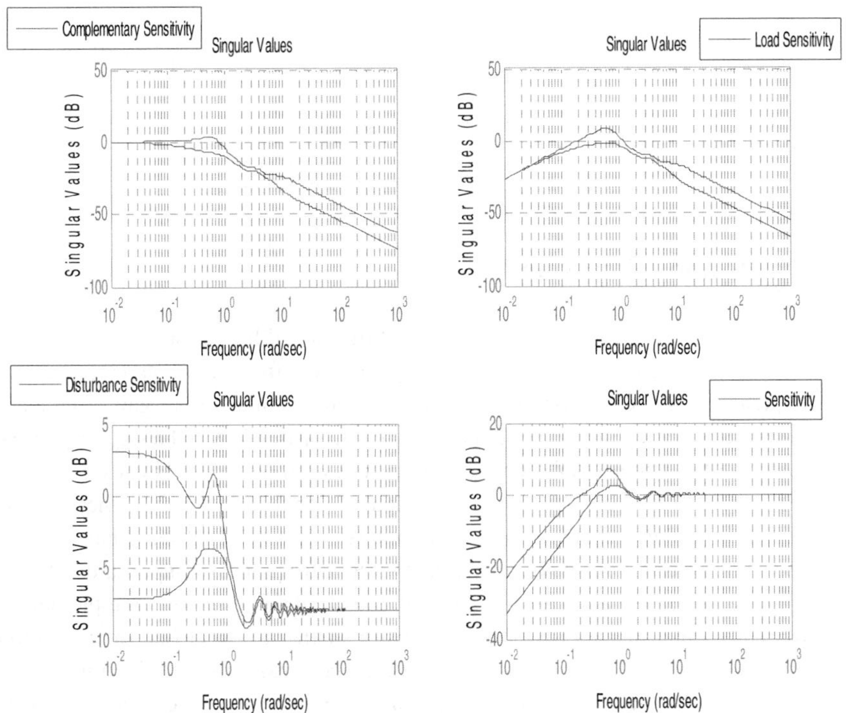

Fig. 7. Singular values of the gang of four functions

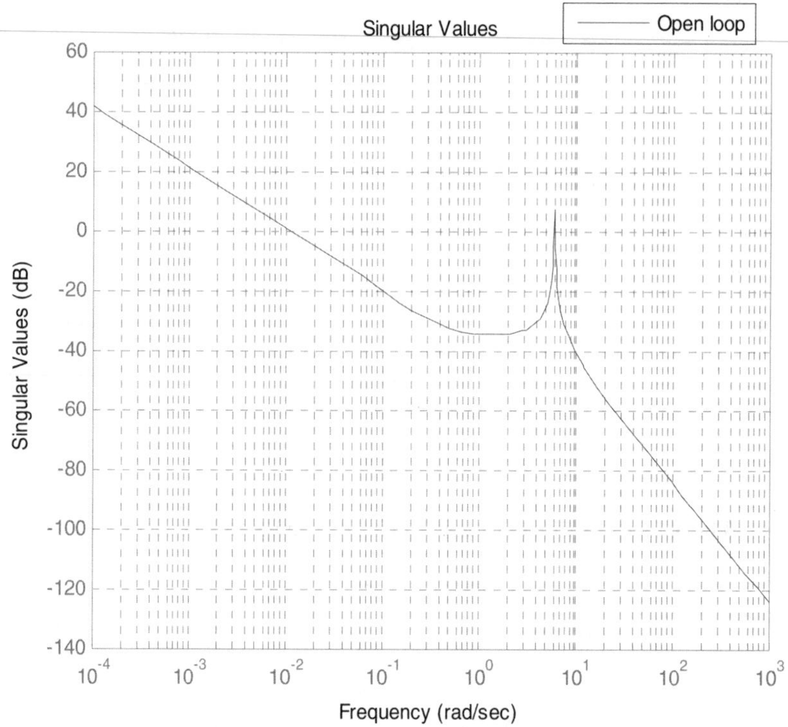

Fig. 8. Singular values of open loop functions

5 Results and Discussion

From simulation results it can be confirmed that the closed loop system is stable. As it clear in Fig. 5, the open loop system has large gain in low frequencies and small gain in high frequencies and cross phase frequency is larger than cross gain frequency. Therefore the time-delay influences almost canceled. Also in Fig. 6 the step response of disturbances without controller is converting to undesired behavior. However by using controller output signal convergence to reference signal and preserve the stability. Therefore, in time-delay systems even if the internal and external disturbances exist, the closed loop system, preserve the stability by low frequency compensator. Also in Fig. 7 the two singular values of the gang of four transfer function, complementary sensitivity shows that in high frequency it contain small gain so closed loop system is robust to disturbance and time-delay. Furthermore, the sensitivity transfer function it is clear that has small gain in low frequencies and 0 dB in high frequencies so the error signal is reduced, hence performance is improved. Fig. 8 shows that the open loop system has high values in low frequencies and small values in high frequencies region, hence, we can confirm the validation of given theorem.

6 Conclusion

In this research, we achieved the internally stabilization of the closed loop system including time-delay elements and disturbances by using LFC and also the performance of system is improved. As it can be confirmed the outputs of system without controller converges to unreferenced signal. However by using LPC output signal though it contains overshoot but converges to desirable signal. Also the stability of closed loop system is clear that the open loop of system's cross phase frequency is larger than cross gain frequency. Therefore, in order to stabilize the closed loop system, the controller's parameters are depending on the length of time-delay to avoid instability and overshoot. Our future works is to design a controller for time-delay system which includes uncertainty in the plant.

Acknowledgment

This work was supported by Grant-in-Aid for Scientific Research(C). We wish to express our gratitude of this grant.

References

[1] Dorf, R.C., Bishop, R.H.: Modern Control System. Prentice-Hall, Englewood Cliffs (2002)
[2] Pedrycz, W.: Robust Control Design an Optimal Control Approach. Wiley, Chichester (2007)
[3] Franklin, G.F., Powell, J.D., Workman, M.: Digital Control of Dynamic System. Addison -Wesley, Reading (1997)
[4] Oboe, R., Natori, K., Ohnishi, K.: A Novel Structure of Time Delay Control System with Communication Disturbance Observe. IEEE, Los Alamitos (2008)
[5] Normey-Rico, J.E., Camach, E.F.: Control of dead-time processes. Springer, Heidelberg (2007)
[6] Silva, G.J., Datta, A., Bhattacharyya, S.R.: PID Controller for Time-Delay System. Birkhauser, Basel (2004)
[7] Dugard, L., Verriest, E.I.: Stability and Control of Time-delay Systmes. Springer, Heidelberg (1998)
[8] Balas, G.J., Doyle, J.C., Glover, K., Packard, A., Smith, R.: Robust ControlToolbox TM 3 User'S Guide. The Math Works
[9] Skogestad, S., Postlethwaite, I.: Multi Variabla Feedback Control Analysis and Design. John Wiley & Sons, Chichester (1996)
[10] Asharif, F., Tamaki, S., Nagado, T., Nagata, T., Rashid, M., Asharif, M.: Feedback Control of Linear Quadratic Integration Including Time-Delay System. In: ITC-CSCC 2009 (2009)

A Differential Evolution Based Approach to Estimate the Shape and Size of Complex Shaped Anomalies Using EIT Measurements

Ahmar Rashid[1], Anil Kumar Khambampati[2], Bong Seok Kim[3], Dong Liu[1], Sin Kim[4], and Kyung Youn Kim[1]

[1] Department of Electronic Engineering, Jeju National University, Jeju, South Korea
[2] BK21 Clean Energy Training & Education Center, Jeju National University, Jeju, South Korea
[3] Applied Radiological Science Research Institute, Jeju National University, Jeju, South Korea
[4] Department of Nuclear and Energy Engineering, Jeju National University, Jeju, South Korea

{ahmar,anil,bongsk3,liudong,kyungyk,sinkim}@jejunu.ac.kr

Abstract. EIT image reconstruction is an ill-posed problem, the spatial resolution of the estimated conductivity distribution is usually poor and the external voltage measurements are subject to variable noise. Therefore, EIT conductivity estimation cannot be used in the raw form to correctly estimate the shape and size of complex shaped regional anomalies. An efficient algorithm employing a shape based estimation scheme is needed. The performance of traditional inverse algorithms, such as the Newton Raphson method, used for this purpose is below par and depends upon the initial guess and the gradient of the cost functional. This paper presents the application of differential evolution (DE) algorithm to estimate complex shaped region boundaries, expressed as coefficients of truncated Fourier series, using EIT. DE is a simple yet powerful population-based, heuristic algorithm with the desired features to solve global optimization problems under realistic conditions. The performance of the algorithm has been tested through numerical simulations, comparing its results with that of the traditional modified Newton Raphson (mNR) method.

Keywords: EIT boundary estimation, truncated Fourier series, differential evolution (DE) algorithm.

1 Introduction

Electrical impedance tomography (EIT) is a non-invasive measurement technique in which the conductivity distribution inside an object is reconstructed through the measurement of boundary potentials across the electrodes attached to the surface of the object [1]. EIT has several applications. For example, in medical imaging, EIT has been proposed for breast cancer detection [2] and to monitor several physiological

T.-h. Kim et al. (Eds.): GDC/CA 2010, CCIS 121, pp. 206–215, 2010.

phenomena, such as cardiac, pulmonary and respiratory functions [3], [4]. In the process industry, it can be employed to monitor the multi-phase flow pipelines, the mixing phenomenon [5], the sedimentation phenomenon [6] and etc. In medical imaging the unknown information is the boundaries of the organs instead of their conductivity values. Similarly, in industrial processes, one is often interested in the estiamtion of location, size and shape of the bubbles inside a liquid medium. EIT image reconstruction is a non-linear ill-posed problem and suffers from a poor spatial resolution. Due to the poor spatial resolution of EIT it is very difficult to estimate the region boundaries with reasonable accuracy. If the number of distinctive regions and the respective conductivity values inside a domain are assumed to be known then the inverse problem to be solved, using EIT, is the estimation of shape, size and location of these regions. Such an estimation scheme significantly reduces the size of the problem, at the same time, increasing the resoltuon of the image.The ill-posedness of the problem is often eliminated this way, bypassing the need for any regularization technique used otherwise. The EIT boundary estimation is not a new problem. Different boundary estimation techniques have been proposed before [7], [8]. In this paper, the region boundaries are expressed as coefficients of truncated Fourier series [8]. The same approach has been employed in a previous study for the dynamic estimation of heart ventricle boundary [9]. The unknown boundary was assumed to be elliptic thus requiring only six Fourier Coefficients to be estimated by the inverse algorithm. Kolehmainen et al. [8], on the other hand, reconstructed non-elliptic boundaries resembling the organs such as the lungs and the heart, which in turn required the estimation of 12 Fourier coefficients. Extended Kalman filter (EKF) was used as an inverse algorithm in both these studies (i.e., [8] and [9]). Kolehmainen et al also tried to reconstruct the non-elliptic boundaries using the traditional Gauss-Newton method. However, the Gauss Newton method has been reported to encounter serious convergence problems with a tendency to produce self-intersecting boundaries for this problem. Even the results obtained using the EKF suggested room for improvement in the estimation of complex shaped anomalies (i.e., anomalies which are not elliptic in nature and thus require higher modes of Fourier coefficients to be estimated). The traditional inverse algorithms (such as Gauss Newton method and EKF) are very sensitive to initial guess and require the calculation of a gradient matrix. Given the poor spatial resolution of EIT and considering the inevitable discretization of the problem domain, the gradient of the higher order Fourier coefficients in the case of the non-elliptic targets is subject to large calculation errors, thus severely undermining the performance of the said algorithms. The presence of usually high measurement noise magnifies this problem to several orders of magnitude.

A derivative-free algorithm (which does not require the gradient matrix calculation) less sensitive to the initial guess is largely expected to improve the capability of EIT boundary estimation. One class of such algorithms is the set of evolutionary algorithms (EAs). EAs are population-based global optimization algorithms with the desired features to solve global optimization problems under realistic conditions [10]. This paper presents a Differential Evolution (DE) based optimization algorithm [11] to estimate the shape, size and location of region boundaries inside a circular domain. DE is a simple but powerful population-based, heuristic algorithm which uses the distance and direction information from the current population to guide the further search. The primary advantages of DE are its simple structure, ease of use, robustness, the ability to run in a parallel mode and the straightforward incorporation of *a priori* information into the problem solution. Numerical simulations have been carried out to verify the performance of the algorithm. The boundaries are expressed as coefficients of truncated Fourier series and the conductivity of each region is assumed to be known a priori. With this approach, it is possible to reconstruct simple circular shaped anomalies (such as air bubbles and etc) as well as complex shaped boundaries (such as non-elliptic organ boundaries inside a human being).

2 EIT Boundary Estimation

Electrical impedance tomography is an imaging modality in which the internal electrical conductivity distribution is reconstructed based on the imposed currents and the measured voltages across the electrodes placed on the surface of an object. The physical relationship between the internal conductivity $\sigma(x,y)$ and the electrical potential $u(x,y)$ on the object $\Omega \subset \Re^2$ is governed by a partial differential equation with appropriate boundary conditions. EIT consists of forward and inverse problem. The forward problem calculates the boundary voltages by using the assumed conductivity distribution. The forward problem is usually solved using the finite element method (FEM). The detailed FEM formulation of EIT can be found in [1]. The inverse problem reconstructs the conductivity distribution minimizing the difference between the measured and the calculated boundary voltages.

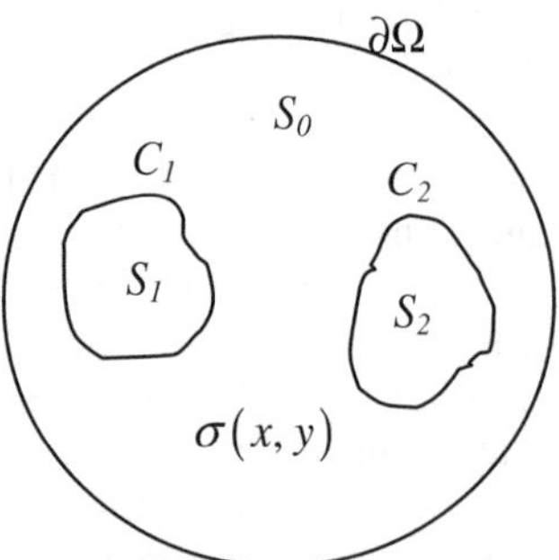

Fig. 1. A schematic diagram describing a circular domain $\Omega \subset \Re^2$ with conductivity distribution $\sigma(x,y)$, enclosed by the boundary $\partial\Omega$. C_1 and C_2 denote the boundaries of the two anomalies S_1 and S_2, respectively, inside the domain.

$$\Phi(\gamma_k) = \frac{1}{2}\left[V(\gamma_k) - U\right]^T \left[V(\gamma_k) - U\right] \tag{1}$$

where $\gamma_k \in \Re^{2MN_\theta}$ are the coefficients of truncated Fourier series of order N_θ representing M boundaries [8]. $V(\gamma_k) \in \Re^{L^*K\times 1}$ is the forward solution based on FEM that gives the calculated voltages based on given Fourier coefficients γ_k, $U \in \Re^{L^*K\times 1}$ is the measured voltage, k represent the iteration number, and LK is the number of measurements at each iteration. $\Phi(\gamma_k)$ is the EIT cost functional. This paper considers the problem of estimating the boundaries of two noncircular regions. A schematic diagram describing a circular domain $\Omega \subset \Re^2$ with conductivity distribution $\sigma(x,y)$, enclosed by the a known boundary $\partial\Omega$ is shown in Fig. 1. In the figure, C_1 and C_2 denote the boundaries of the two anomalies S_1 and S_2, respectively, inside the domain.

2.1 The Fourier Series Boundary Representation

Let us consider an objet domain schematically shown in Fig. 1. The outer boundary $\partial\Omega$ of the object is assumed to be known. The boundary $C_l(s)$ of any enclosed region is assumed to be sufficiently smooth to be expressed as coefficients of truncated Fourier series of order N_θ [8]

$$C_l(s) = \begin{pmatrix} x_l(s) \\ y_l(s) \end{pmatrix} = \sum_{n=1}^{N_\theta} \begin{pmatrix} \gamma_n^{x_l} \theta_n^x(s) \\ \gamma_n^{y_l} \theta_n^y(s) \end{pmatrix}, l = 1,2,\ldots,M \tag{2}$$

where $\theta_n(s)$ is the periodic and smooth basis function of the form

$$\begin{aligned} \theta_n^\alpha &= 1, & n &= 1 \\ \theta_n^\alpha &= \sin(2\pi \frac{n}{2} s), & n &= 2,4,6,\ldots \\ \theta_n^\alpha &= \cos(2\pi \frac{n-1}{2} s), & n &= 3,5,7,\ldots \end{aligned} \tag{3}$$

Here, $s \in [0,1]$, α denotes x or y and M is the number of boundaries. Expanding (2) and (3), the boundaries C_l can be represented as γ of the shape coefficients, i.e.,

$$\gamma = (\gamma_1^{x_1},\ldots,\gamma_{N_\theta}^{x_1},\gamma_1^{y_1},\ldots,\gamma_{N_\theta}^{y_1},\ldots,\ldots\gamma_1^{x_M},\ldots,\gamma_{N_\theta}^{x_M},\gamma_1^{y_M},\ldots,\gamma_{N_\theta}^{y_M})^{\mathrm{T}} \tag{4}$$

where $\gamma \in \Re^{2MN_\theta}$.

3 Differential Evolution Algorithm

Evolutionary algorithms (EAs) [10] are well known population-based global optimization algorithms in which a set of candidate solutions compete amongst themselves to reach the final solution. EAs work on the principal of mutation and recombination, the latter often referred to as the crossover. The crossover creates new candidate solutions by combining two or more existing solutions, while the mutation corresponds to the erroneous duplication of the previous solutions. The cross over step tends to increase the correlation among the current set of candidate solutions, whereas the mutation keeps the search space open to new solutions, thus increasing the population diversity. Both the approaches have their own advantages and disadvantages and the right balance between them has been studied before [12].

The DE algorithm is an evolutionary algorithm which uses the distance and direction information derived from the current population to explore the search space [11]. DE employs three control parameters for its operation: $N_{P,}$ the size of the population, F, the mutation scaling factor and CR, the probability of crossover. Although DE is a simple, yet powerful evolutionary algorithm, its optimum performance is dependent upon the fine tuning of its control parameters. This issue, however, can be resolved by using self adaptive variants of DE [13], [14]. A major advantage of the DE algorithm is its ability to incorporate *a priori* information into the problem solution. This is particularly beneficial in the case of EIT boundary estimation, which usually suffers from large measurement and round-off errors and under realistic conditions it is often impossible to be solved without any prior information. The *a priori* information can be incorporated in several ways. One way to do it is simply rejecting all the infeasible solutions (e.g., in the case of multi-region boundary estimation, the boundaries cannot cross each other). However, this can be computationally expensive. Another way to do it is the use of such mutation and cross over schemes which make sure that only feasible solutions are generated. In DE, a new solution replaces the previous solution only if the former is more suitable than the latter. Although it follows a greedy selection schemes, DE is an extremely efficient algorithm to establish the global minimum and often performs better than other evolutionary algorithms. A further advantage of the DE algorithm is its inherent ability to be adapted for its parallel execution. Given the availability of parallel-mode modern computer architectures, DE proves to be a fast and efficient optimization easily outperforming the traditional gradient-based algorithms such as Newton Raphson method.

The general mechanism of DE resembles that of the genetic algorithms (GAs) [15],[16] which constitute another popular class of evolutionary algorithms, nonetheless, it has certain distinctive features of its own. For example, the GA replaces a small subset of all candidate solution whereas DE attempts to replace all the previous solutions in each generation. Another key difference lies in the implementation of the mutation scheme. In GA the mutation steps consists of a small modification in each of the selected individual while the DE mutation comprises of a more complex arithmetic combination of individual. A comparison of the DE with other evolutionary algorithms including GA can be found in the reference [17]. The pseudo-code of the DE algorithm applied to ETI boundary estimation is given below.

```
Generate the initial population P
Evaluate the fitness for each individual in P
while Exit condition is not satisfied do
for i = 1 to N_P (for all population) do
    Select uniformly distributed random numbers
     r1 ≠ r2 ≠ r3 ≠ i
    Randomly select the Fourier coefficient C_rand
     to be modified
     for c = 1 to N_C do
       if Rand[0, 1] < CR or c = C_rand then
         Y_i(c) = X_r1(c) + F × (X_r2(c) − X_r3(c))
       else
         Y_i(c) = X_i(c)
       end if
     end for
   end for
   for i = 1 to N_P do
      Evaluate the offspring Y_i
      if Y_i is better than the parent P_i then
        P_i = Y_i
      end if
   end for
end while
```

Here, $N_c = 2MN_\theta$ is the total number of Fourier coefficients to express the M boundaries, $X_i(c)$ is the c-th variable of the solution X_i, Y_i is the offspring and Rand[0, 1] is a uniformly distributed random real number between 0 and 1.

It should be noted that DE algorithm is very good at exhausting the global search space in order to establish the location of the global minimum. However, it fails to properly exploit the solution, which can result in convergence to a local minimum around the global minimum. This issue can be addressed with the use of a Hybrid algorithm, combining DE with another algorithm such as BBO which is good exploitation of the solution space [18].

4 Results and Discussions

A circular shape phantom of 15 cm radius is considered to carry out the numerical simulations to verify the performance of the proposed method. FEM mesh structures with 8928 and 2232 triangular elements have been used to solve the forward and inverse problems, respectively. The so-called trigonometric current injection patterns are injected into 32 electrodes attached to the boundary of the circular phantom. The complete electrode model with effective electrode contact impedance of 0.005 Ωcm^2 has been used to enforce the boundary conditions for the EIT problem. In EIT, the voltage measurements are often noisy in nature. Therefore, zero-mean Gaussian noise

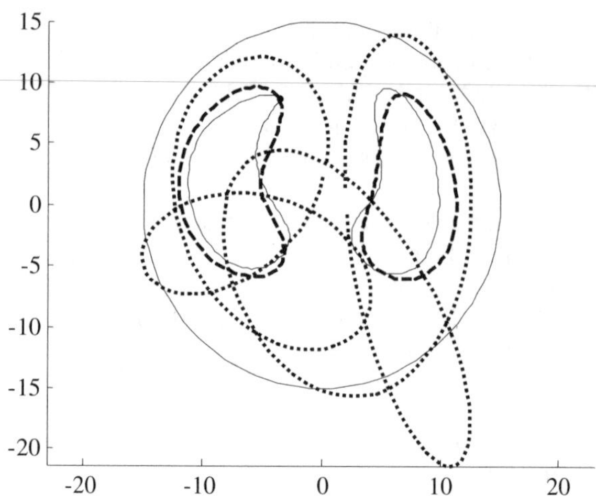

Fig. 2. Estimated region boundaries using DE and mNR. The solid black lines are used to draw the true region boundaries, the broken line is used to show the estimated boundaries using the DE while the dotted line shows the mNR estimated boundaries.

with a standard deviation of 1.0 relative to the corresponding measured voltages has been added to the observed voltage data to simulate realistic measurements.

This paper considers the problem of estimating the boundaries of two noncircular regions. The number of Fourier Coefficient required to reconstruct a boundary is not exactly known. Therefore, a different number of the Fourier coefficients are used in the inverse problem than the number used while generating the true data. The number of Fourier coefficients to represent each of the true boundaries is 14 ($N_\theta = 7$). In the inverse problem, the number of Fourier coefficients used to reconstruct each boundary is 10 ($N_\theta = 5$).

The selection of the size N_P of the initial population and the number of iterations required to reach the desired solution are key considerations affecting the performance of the population-based direct search algorithms. The selection of these parameters is problem dependent. Given a state vector of size N_c, for DE, a value between $4N_c$ and $10N_c$ has been recommended [12], [16]. The authors have analyzed the performance of the algorithm for uniformly distributed populations with different sizes and iteration counts. Of course, the estimation performance of the algorithm is improved as the size of the population and the number of iterations for the algorithm are increased. However, the cost functional calculation in EIT boundary estimation is computationally expensive and accounts for the major portion of the running time of the algorithm It is, therefore, recommended to use $N_P \sim 5N_c$, with a maximum iteration count of 10. The performance of the algorithm is reasonable with this selection of the populations and the iteration count, even though there is still room for improvement. The dispersion of the initial population is also a major player in the performance of the algorithm. A densely populated set of candidate solutions around the true solution is bound to show fast convergence as compared to a loosely coupled population chosen away from the respective true values. This selection is also problem dependent. In the medical applications, for example, the shape and location of the organs inside a human body are roughly known. On the other hand, in industrial applications the shape and location of the anomalies cannot be known in advance. A closely distributed population can be chosen for the former application whereas a more scattered initial population is generally required to estimate the latter. In one set of simulations a uniformly distributed initial population comprising of 60 candidate solutions has been generated, such that the Fourier coefficients representing the location (x- and y-coordinates) of the region boundaries are distributed with a maximum deviation of 5 cm form their respective true values, whereas the rest of the Fourier coefficients are distributed with a maximum deviation of 1 cm form their respective true values. This kind of initial population selection depicts the scenario in which the number, shape and size of the targets is roughly known, however, very poor information regarding the locations of the targets is available. The values of crossover operator CR and the mutation parameter F are set as 0.7 and 0.5 respectively.

The performance of the algorithm has been verified by running it 10 times, each time with a different noise seed, and a different set of initial population, chosen from the same range as discussed before. The authors have also reconstructed the noncircular region boundaries using one step modified Newton Raphson (mNR) algorithm. The execution of one-step mNR has also been repeated for 10 runs, each time with a different initial guess, randomly chosen from a uniform distribution with a standard deviation of 0.5 cm centred at its respective true values. The initial guess chosen for the mNR is much closer to the true value, as compared to that chosen for DE. Even with a very close initial guess the estimated results for the mNR are very poor. The results for the two algorithms have also been compared using the root means square error (RMSE) which is a measure of the estimation error with respect to the true values. The RMSE values using the mNR are significantly higher as compared to that for the DE algorithm. The RMSE can be calculated as follows

$$\mathrm{RMSE}_{\gamma} = \sqrt{\frac{(\hat{\gamma}-\gamma_{true})^{\mathrm{T}}(\hat{\gamma}-\gamma_{true})}{\gamma_{true}^{\mathrm{T}}\gamma_{true}}} \tag{5}$$

$$\overline{\mathrm{RMSE}_{\gamma}} = \frac{1}{n}\sum_{i=1}^{n}\left(\mathrm{RMSE}_{\gamma_i}\right) \tag{6}$$

where $\hat{\gamma}$ is the estimated value while γ_{true} is the true value of the respective Fourier coefficient. n is used to denote the number of repeated executions of the algorithm, and $\overline{\mathrm{RMSE}_{\gamma}}$ denotes the mean RMSE of the estimated Fourier coefficients (calculated over $n = 10$ runs). The comparison of the $\overline{\mathrm{RMSE}_{\gamma}}$ values for the two algorithms has been reported in Table 1. Note that the RMSE values have been calculated for the aggregated Fourier coefficients for each of the left and right region boundaries, respectively. Clearly, the RMSE values using mNR are significantly higher as compared to those with DE.

Table 1. RMSE values

	RMSE values of the aggregated Fourier Coefficients	
	DE	**mNR**
$RMSE_{Left}$	0.1759	1.3477
$RMSE_{Right}$	0.2053	2.1134
$RMSE_{Overall}$	0.1914	1.8152

5 Conclusions

A differential evolution based 2D EIT measurement technique has been used to recover the region boundaries in a circular domain, expressed as truncated Fourier series coefficients. Zero-mean Gaussian-distributed measurement noise has been added to simulate voltage measurement errors. The performance of the DE algorithm has been compared with the traditional mNR method. Results obtained through numerical simulations using a circular mesh structure demonstrate the superiority of the DE algorithm as compared to the mNR method. DE is an effective global optimization algorithm in terms of exploring the search space. However, it lacks the ability to properly exploit the solution space. Future work includes the extension of the method to 3D EIT for experimental measurements, the simultaneous reconstruction of region boundaries and their conductivities and the application of hybrid population based algorithms to EIT boundary estimation.

Acknowledgments

This work was supported by the National Research Foundation of Korea (NRF) grant funded by the Korean Government (MEST) [No. 2010-0014962].

References

1. Vauhkonen, M.: Electrical impedance tomography and prior information. PhD Thesis University of Kuopio, Finland (1997), `http://venda.uku.fi/~mvauhkon`
2. Kim, B.S., Isaacson, D., Xia, H., Kao, T., Newell, J., Saulnier, G.: A method for analyzing electrical impedance spectroscopy data from breast cancer patients. Physiol. Meas. 28, S237–S246 (2007)
3. Brown, B.H., Barber, D.C., Morica, A.H., Leathard, A.D.: Cardiac and respiratory related electric impedance changes in the human thorax. IEEE Trans. Biomed. Eng. 41, 729–733 (1994)
4. Deibele, J.M., Luepschen, H., Leonhardt, S.: Dynamic separation of pulmonary and cardiac changes in electrical impedance tomography. Physiol. Meas. 29, S1–S14 (2008)
5. Mann, R., Dickin, F.J., Wang, M., Dyakowski, T., Williams, R.A., Edwards, R.B., et al.: Application of electrical resistance tomography to interrogate mixing processes at plant scale. Chem. Eng. Sci. 52, 2087–2097 (1997)

6. Khambampati, A.K., Rashid, A., Kim, S., Soleimani, M., Kim, K.Y.: Unscented Kalman filter approach to track moving interfacial boundary in sedimentation process using three-dimensional electrical impedance tomography. Phil. Trans. R. Soc. A. 367, 3095–3120 (2009)
7. Han, D.K., Prosperetti, A.: A shape decomposition technique in electrical impedance tomography. J. Comput. Phys. 155, 75–95 (1999)
8. Kolehmainen, V., Voutilainen, A., Kaipio, J.P.: Estimation of non-stationary region boundaries in EIT—state estimation approach. Inverse Problems 17, 1937–1956 (2001)
9. Rashid, A., Kim, B.S., Khambampati, A.K., Liu, D., Kim, S., Kim, K.Y.: Dynamic boundary estimation of human heart within a complete cardiac cycle using electrical impedance tomography. J.Phys.: Conf. Ser. 224, 012042 (2010)
10. Back, T., Schwefel, H.-P.: An overview of evolutionary algorithms for parameter optimization. Evolut. Comput. 1, 1–23 (1993)
11. Storn, R., Price, K.: Differential evolution - A simple and efficient heuristic for global optimization over continuous spaces. J. of Global Optim. 11, 341–359 (1997)
12. Spears, W.: Crossover or Mutation? In: Foundations of Genetic Algorithms Workshop, vol. 2, pp. 221–237 (1992)
13. Brest, J., Boškovic, B., Greiner, S., Žumer, V., Sepesy Maucec, M.: Performance comparison of self-adaptive and adaptive differential evolution algorithms. Soft. Comput. 11, 617–629 (2007)
14. Brest, J., Greiner, S., Boškovic, B., Mernik, M., Žumer, V.: Selfadapting control parameters in differential evolution: a comparative study on numerical benchmark problems. IEEE Trans. Evol. Comput. 10, 646–657 (2006)
15. Goldberg, D.: Genetic algorithms in search, optimization and machine learning. Addison-Wesley Publishing Company, Reading (1989)
16. Rolnik, V.P., Seleghim Jr. P.: A specialized genetic algorithm for the electrical impedance tomography of two-phase flows. J. Braz. Soc. Mech. Sci. & Eng. 28, 378–389 (2006)
17. Ali, M.M., Törn, A.: Population set-based global optimization algorithms: some modifications and numerical studies. Comput. Oper. Res. 31, 1703–1725 (2004)
18. Gong, W., Cai, Z., Ling, C.X.: DE/BBO: a hybrid differential evolution with biogeography-based optimization for global numerical optimization. Soft Comput, 1–21 (2010)

Tracking Extrema in Dynamic Environments Using a Learning Automata-Based Immune Algorithm

Alireza Rezvanian[1] and Mohammad Reza Meybodi[2]

[1] Department of Computer Engineering, Islamic Azad University, Hamedan branch, Iran
[2] Department of Computer & IT Engineering, Amirkabir University of Technology, Tehran, Iran
rezvan@iauh.ac.ir, mmeybodi@aut.ac.ir

Abstract. In recent years, bio-inspired algorithms have increasingly been used by researchers for solving various optimization problems increasingly. Many real world problems are mostly time varying optimization problems, which require special mechanisms for detecting changes in environment and then responding to them. The present paper has been proposed to combination the learning automata and artificial immune algorithm in order to improve the performance of immune system algorithm in dynamic environments. In the proposed algorithm, the immune cells are equipped with a learning automaton. So they can increase diversity in response the dynamic environments. Learning automata based immune algorithm for dynamic environment has been tested in the moving parabola as a popular standard dynamic environment and compared by several famous algorithms in dynamic environments.

Keywords: Artificial Immune Algorithm, Learning Automata, Dynamic Environments, Time Varying Problems.

1 Introduction

Most real world problems are known as optimization problems. In these problems, the extrema change along the landscape during time [1]. Due to lack of traditional optimization algorithms to trace the optima they failed in the non-stationary environments. Therefore, bio-inspired algorithms are more frequently used for solving different optimization problems such as dynamic optimization problems [2]. In dynamic optimizations, not only do the algorithms have to detect the changes but also must respond to the changes in the landscape. Several suggestions which have been proposed for dealing with time varying optimization based on population based algorithms in [3-5].

Artificial Immune Systems (AIS) are bio-inspired algorithms that take their inspiration from the complex defensive mechanism of human immune system for protecting against pathogens [6, 26]. The immune algorithms have been used for many different applications such as optimization problems [7-13]. More recently, also in [4] and [14], AIS has been implemented for optimization in dynamic environments. Moreover, the development of these algorithms has not been widespread and they are not much developed in comparison with other population-based methods such as

T.-h. Kim et al. (Eds.): GDC/CA 2010, CCIS 121, pp. 216–225, 2010.

Particle Swarm Optimization (PSO) [1, 15]. Learning Automaton (LA) is a general purpose stochastic optimization tool with finite states. It has been developed as a model for learning systems. LA tries to determine, iteratively, the optimal action to apply to the environment from a finite number of actions that are available to it. The environment returns a reinforcement signal that shows the relative quality of an action of the LA, and then LA adjusts itself by means of a learning algorithm [7, 16]. Previously, LAs were successfully used in many applications such as evolutionary algorithms, in order to enhance the learning and adaptation abilities of different parameters in genetic algorithm (GA) [17], PSO [8], Ant Colony Optimization (ACO), and recently in AIS [19]. So this paper presents a new method to improve the AIS increasing diversity which occurs when changes in dynamic environment happen. This is done by the use of LA as a solution for improving AIS in dynamic environments. The rest of the paper is organized as follows: the next section briefly introduces Immune Algorithms (IA). LA will be presented in the third section. The forth section considers the proposed algorithms and finally in the last section the results of simulation for the dynamic environments of moving parabola are presented.

2 Immune Algorithms

Immune algorithms are bio-inspired algorithms which have been inspired by human immune system [6, 26]. Human immune system is divided into innate immune and adaptive immune. The algorithms have been modeled based on the latter. In addition, according to different theories for natural immune system, the inspired algorithms are categorized into several groups: negative selection, clonal selection, bone marrow, immune network, and danger theory, which are utilized with a wide variety of application such as optimization in static environments [7]. Theoretically, the mechanism of the human immune system can handle well the changes in the environment and can react to these changes; however, the AIS algorithms are unable to trace the changes in dynamic environments. As a result, some mechanisms are needed in AIS algorithm to detect and respond to the changes [14]. In [20] the immune network algorithm has undergone some changes to be used in dynamic environments. In [4], after the comparison of different mutations of immune network and clonal selection, the performance of these algorithms has been compared with each other.

3 Learning Automata

Learning Automaton (LA) has finite set of actions and at each stage chooses one of them. The choice of an action depends on the state of LA represented by an action probability vector. For the action chosen by the LA the environment gives a reinforcement signal with unknown probability distribution. Then, based on this signal, the LA updates its action probability vector using a learning algorithm. A class of LA called *variable structure learning automata* are represented by a triple $\langle\beta, \alpha, T\rangle$ where $\beta = \{0, 1\}$ is a set of inputs, $\alpha = \{\alpha_1, \ldots, \alpha_r\}$ is a set of actions, and T is the learning algorithm [27]. In *linear reward-inaction learning algorithm* (L_{R-I}), the action probability vector is updated using equation (1):

$$p_j(k+1) = \begin{cases} p_j(k) + b \times [1 - p_j(n)] & i = j \\ p_j(k) - b \times p_j(k) & i \neq j \end{cases} \quad (1)$$

When the environment rewards and the action probability vector remains unchanged, the environment penalizes the action. Parameters $b \in (0, 1)$ and r represent learning parameter and the number of actions for LA, respectively and α_i is the action chosen at stage k as a sample realization from probability distribution $p(k)$ [28]. LA have been successfully used in many applications such as control of broadcast networks, intrusion detection in sensor networks, database systems, and solving shortest path problem in stochastic networks, to mention a few [16]. The interaction between LA and environment is shown in figure 1.

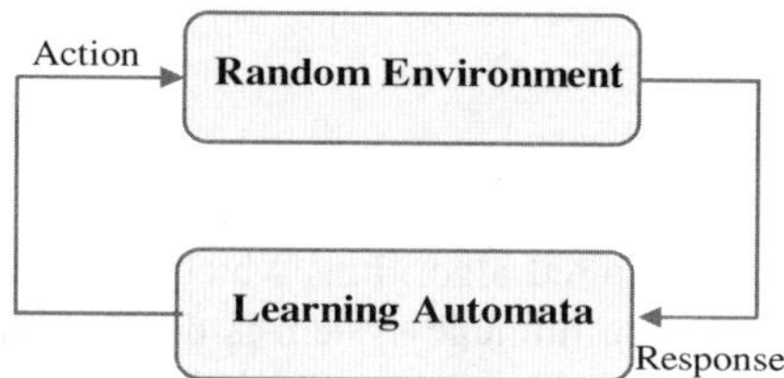

Fig. 1. The interaction between the learning automata and its environment

4 The Proposed Algorithm: Learning Automata Based Immune Algorithm

In IA, mutation, as the only and most important operator, should act effectively, and it is also termed *hypermutation*. The immune cells in immune algorithm suffer the mutation according the probability of mutation rate, which is calculated by a Gaussian distribution following equation (2):

$$\begin{aligned} c' &= c + \alpha \times N(0,1), \\ \alpha &= \frac{1}{\beta} \times exp(-f^*) \end{aligned} \quad (2)$$

Where in equation (1), c' represents mutated cells, and $N(0,1)$ is a Gaussian distribution with a mean of 0 and standard deviation of 1. Here β is taken as the decay parameter to control the inverse exponential function and f^* is the fitness of an individual normalized [20].

Hypermutation in this algorithm is considered as probabilistic and with an affinity between antibody and antigen. Therefore, cells with highest affinity suffer the lowest mutation rate, whereas the lowest affinity cells has high mutation rate. The probability of mutation rate is obtained from equation (3) [21].

$$P_m = \begin{cases} \alpha\left(0.5 - f_d^2\right), & 0 \le f_d \le 0.5, \quad 0 < \alpha \le 1.0 \\ \alpha\left(1 - f_d^2\right)^2, & 0.5 \le f_d \le 1.0, \quad 0 < \alpha \le 1.0 \end{cases} \tag{3}$$

Where p_m is hypermutation rate with a value less than 0.5, α is the scale coefficient with a value less than 0.1 and f_d is the value of normalized fitness. Scale coefficient cannot be assigned a precise value; therefore the LA is used for adaptive setting of the parameter of α scale coefficient. Three actions, namely "*increasing α*", "*decreasing α*" and "*fixing α*" are considered for LA. In each step, LA selects one action according to the probabilistic vector and thus the value of the parameter of scale coefficient becomes modified. Consequently, hypermutation rate mutates antibodies by means of the new value of the scale coefficient. Afterwards, based on evaluating the performance, the probabilistic vector of action becomes up to date. At the beginning, the probability of selecting each action for probabilistic vector is initialized equal. Then, according the selected action and the feedback from the actions it will be update in each step. The general structure of LA has been illustrated in figure 2.

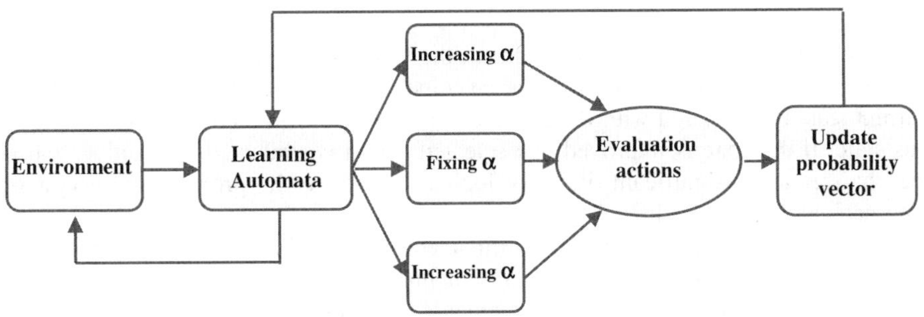

Fig. 2. The structure of the proposed learning automata

At the end of each step, based on the density between individuals, some parts of population are eliminated. The population density of immune cells is relative to the distance between cells. In every step the distance between the two antibodies is calculated by Euclidian distance as follows in equation (4) [19].

$$D = \left[\sum_{i=1}^{n} \left| A(x_i) - B(x_i) \right|^2 \right]^{1/2} \tag{4}$$

Supposing a threshold T, if $D < T$, two immune cells are considered very close to each other, so the one with lower fitness is removed.

In dynamic environments, after detecting environmental changes by memory cells, it is considered that the reaction of the algorithm against these changes is to reset the parameters. Certainly, the initial value of the parameters is not appropriate and the LA can find a proper value of parameters in a stochastic environment.

Now, regarding the above-mentioned points, the steps of the proposed algorithm for dynamic environments can be formed as following pseudo-code in figure 3:

```
1. Initialize immune cells and the probabilistic vector for LA.
2. Repeat the following steps for every immune cell until reaching
stopping criteria.
  2.1. Evaluate the fitness function of immune cells.
  2.2. If the change is detected in the environment:
    2.2.1. Re-initialize the immune cells and the probabilistic vector
     of LA.
    2.2.2. Re-evaluate the fitness function of immune cells.
  2.3. Select the best immune cell.
  2.4. Select one action according to the probabilistic vector of LA.
  2.5. Clone and Mutate immune cells according to the probability
   mutation rate obtained from the selected action of the LA
  2.6. Evaluate the performance of the selected action and update the
   probabilistic vector of the LA.
  2.7. Retain the best antibodies as memory.
  2.8. Calculate the distance between cells.
  2.9. Remove a part of weak immune cells.
  2.10 Replace weak immune cells with new immune cells.
3. Repeat the steps.
```

Fig. 3. The pseudo-code of proposed algorithm

If there is no change in the environment, the method for evaluating the selected action for the automata is as follows: the average performance of immune cells in the current state is compared with the average performance of immune cells in the previous state. If the state is improved, the selected action is evaluated as positive, and if the changes are insignificant, it is not logical to change the probabilistic vector of automata, and otherwise it is evaluated as negative.

Among the important advantages of this method is the adaptation of the scale coefficient parameter according to the environmental changes in order to increase its diversity and high ability in stable environments to escape from local optima or proper convergence. In fact, increase in α leads to expansion of mutation radius and a global search, but decrease in α leads to reduction of mutation radius and a local search in the search space.

5 Experimental Results

In order to evaluate the efficiency of the results of the algorithm, Offline Error (oe) was used which is the famous criterion in different papers for evaluating the average deviation of the best value since the last change from the optimum. It is computed by equation (5) [4]:

$$\mathit{Offline\ Error} = \frac{1}{N_c}\sum_{j=1}^{N_c}\left(\frac{1}{N_e(j)}\sum_{i=1}^{N_e(j)}\left(f_j^* - f_{ji}^*\right)\right) \tag{5}$$

Where N_c is the total number of fitness landscape changes within a single experiment, $N_e(j)$ is the number of solutions evaluations performed for the jth state of the environment, f^*_j, is the value of optimal solution for the jth landscape, and f^{*ji} is the current best fitness value found for the jth landscape [4].

Since most real world problems are dynamic spontaneously, so the environments change within the time. For evaluating the proposed algorithm in uncertainty environments termed *Angeline* method [22] was used. It is also known as the *moving parabolas* mentioned in [23] and [24]. In moving parabolas three types of movement, namely linear, circular and Gaussian, are present, and changes are controlled by two parameters of step size (τ) and change frequency (f). The movement in Angeline method is calculated for linear, circular and Gaussian respectively by the following equations:

$$\Delta k' = \Delta k + \tau \tag{6}$$

$$\Delta k' = \begin{cases} \Delta k + \tau sin\left(\dfrac{2\pi t}{25}\right) & \text{k is even} \\ \Delta k + \tau cos\left(\dfrac{2\pi t}{25}\right) & \text{k is odd} \end{cases} \tag{7}$$

$$\Delta k' = \Delta k + N(0,1) \tag{8}$$

Δk is added to each variable as an update parameter. In order to evaluate the proposed method, the four benchmark functions *Rastrigin*, *Griewank*, *Rosenbrock*, and *Sphere* was used according to the conditions mentioned in table 1 [7]. Initial values and parameters of moving parabolas, according to [20], were set as τ=0.1, f=1.0, and d=30, with a total of 1000 iterations and an average of 10 independent experiments.

Table 1. The benchmark functions and the initialization range

Name	Range	Dimension (N)	Function
Rastrigin	$[-5.12, 5.12]^n$	30	$f_2(x) = \sum_{i=1}^{n} \left(x_i^2 - 10\cos(2\pi x_i) + 10\right)$
Griewank	$[-600, 600]^n$	30	$f_3(x) = \frac{1}{4000}\sum_{i=1}^{n} x_i^2 - \prod_{i=1}^{n} \cos\left(\frac{x_i}{\sqrt{i}}\right) + 1$
Rosenbrock	$[-100, 100]^n$	30	$f_4(x) = \sum_{i=1}^{n-1} \left(100(x_{i+1} - x_i)^2 + (x_i - 1)^2\right)$
Sphere	$[-1.28, 1.28]^n$	30	$f_1(x) = \sum_{i=1}^{n} x_i^2$

Among these functions, Sphere and Rosenbrock are well known as single-modal, Rastrigin and Griewank are known as multi-modal [8].

In order to make a comparison based on *OE* and standard deviation of OE, in addition to the proposed method which is termed *Lopt-aiNet*, use was also made of an immune network algorithm method named *Opt-aiNet* [25], dynamic immune network algorithm called *Dopt-aiNet* [20] and the multi-population immune network algorithm named *Mopt-aiNet* [14].

The results of these experiments, according to the mentioned conditions, are presented in table 2 to 5 respectively for Sphere, Rastrigin, Griewank, and Rosenbrock.

Table 2. The Comparison of the OE of the proposed algorithm with that of different algorithms in dynamic environment for *Sphere* function

Algorithm	**OE±STD**		
	Linear	**Circular**	**Gaussian**
Opt-aiNet	1.21±1.13	1.35±1.79	1.26±1.37
Dopt-aiNet	0.02±0.22	0.32±0.18	0.02±0.02
Mopt-aiNet	0.03±0.08	0.14±0.09	0.03±0.03
Lopt-aiNet	0.02±0.05	0.15±0.07	0.01±0.02

Table 3. Comparison of the OE of the proposed algorithm with that of different algorithms in dynamic environment for *Rastrigin* function

Algorithm	**OE±STD**		
	Linear	**Circular**	**Gaussian**
Opt-aiNet	3.13±2.24	5.12±2.28	3.91±1.74
Dopt-aiNet	0.50±0.17	0.57±0.24	0.22±0.17
Mopt-aiNet	0.11±0.08	0.14±0.39	0.17±0.13
Lopt-aiNet	0.12±0.07	0.15±0.33	0.19±0.09

Table 4. Comparison of the OE of the proposed algorithm with that of different algorithms in dynamic environment for *Griewank* function

Algorithm	**OE±STD**		
	Linear	**Circular**	**Gaussian**
Opt-aiNet	1.93±2.01	1.77±1.93	0.96±1.78
Dopt-aiNet	0.13±1.76	0.33±0.17	7.57±5.79
Mopt-aiNet	0.03±0.12	0.29±0.12	0.02±0.13
Lopt-aiNet	0.03±0.02	0.31±0.07	0.02±0.02

Table 5. Comparison of the OE of the proposed algorithm with that of different algorithms in dynamic environment for *Rosenbrock* function

Algorithm	**OE±STD**		
	Linear	**Circular**	**Gaussian**
Opt-aiNet	1.53±1.91	4.81±1.25	1.38±1.26
Dopt-aiNet	0.03±0.16	0.38±0.58	0.03±0.16
Mopt-aiNet	0.10±0.82	0.27±0.12	0.41±2.13
Lopt-aiNet	0.03±0.12	0.32±0.12	0.01±0.02

In figure 4, the behavior of the proposed algorithm for different functions is shown in a logarithmic form as shown; the algorithm can very well follow the optima and some oscillations are observed, but Rosenbrock function has more oscillations than do other functions due to its many plateaus.

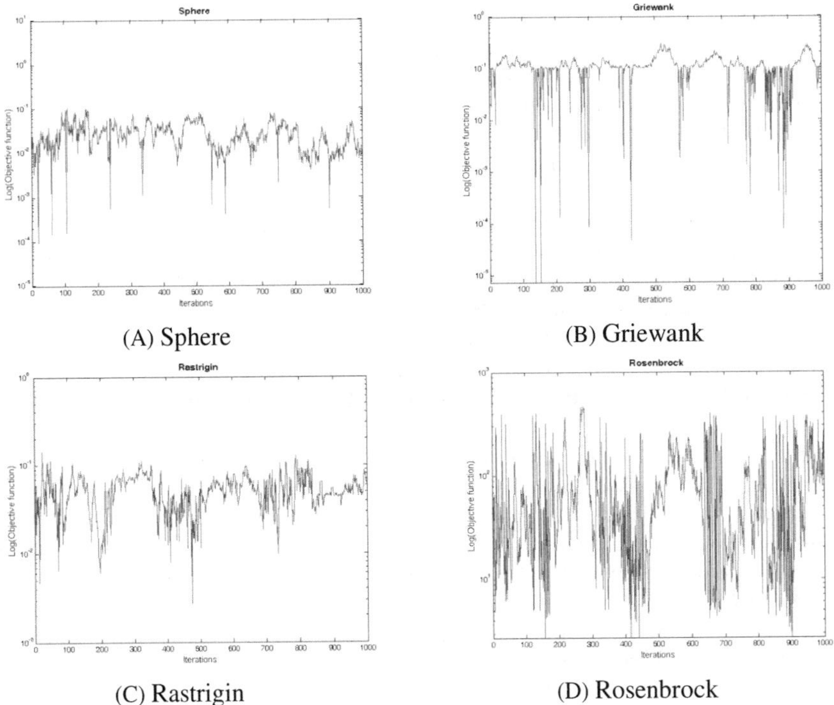

(A) Sphere (B) Griewank

(C) Rastrigin (D) Rosenbrock

Fig. 4. Logarithmic behavior of the proposed algorithm on dynamic environments (τ= 0.1, f= 1.0 and circular displacement)

6 Conclusion

This paper proposes a combination of the LA and AIS in order to improve the standard immune algorithm in dynamic environments. Since after detecting an environmental change there is no guarantee for the parameter values of execution of the standard algorithms, the parameter values of the probabilistic of hypermutation rate are set and thus the LA approaches the proper values by feedback from the environment. The main advantage of the proposed method is that it does not require parameter tuning. The simulation results of the proposed algorithm on the moving parabolas as linear, circular and Gaussian displacement show that this algorithm is relatively more improved than other methods based on immune algorithm. Among the future works of the authors, assessing other methods of hypermutation in the proposed algorithm is to be mentioned.

Acknowledgments. The authors thank Mr. Arash Moradi and Mr. Masoud Safaee for some improvements.

References

1. Lung, R.I., Dumitrescu, D.: Evolutionary Swarm Cooperative Optimization in Dynamic Environments. Natural Computing 9, 83–94 (2010)
2. Pelta, D., Cruz, C., Gonzalez, J.R.: A Study on Diversity and Cooperation in a Multiagent Strategy for Dynamic Optimization Problems. International Journal of Intelligent Systems 24, 844–861 (2009)
3. Wang, H., Wang, D., Yang, S.: A Memetic Algorithm with Adaptive Hill Climbing Strategy for Dynamic Optimization Problems. Soft Computing-A Fusion of Foundations, Methodologies and Applications 13, 763–780 (2009)
4. Trojanowski, K., Wierzchon, S.T.: Immune-based Algorithms for Dynamic Optimization. Information Sciences 179, 1495–1515 (2009)
5. Yang, S., Yao, X.: Population-based Incremental Learning with Associative Memory for Dynamic Environments. IEEE Transactions on Evolutionary Computation 12, 542–561 (2008)
6. De Castro, L.N., Von Zuben, F.J.: Learning and Optimization using the Clonal Selection Principle. IEEE Transactions on Evolutionary Computation 6, 239–251 (2002)
7. Rezvanian, A., Meybodi, M.R.: LACAIS: Learning Automata based Cooperative Artificial Immune System for Function Optimization. In: Ranka, S., et al. (eds.) 3rd International Conference on Contemporary Computing (IC3 2010), Noida, India. Contemporary Computing, CCIS, vol. 94, pp. 64–75. Springer, Heidelberg (2010)
8. Rezvanian, A., Meybodi, M.R.: Improving Artificial Immune System using Fuzzy Logic. In: 10th Iranian Conference on Fuzzy Systems (IFS 2010), Tehran, Iran, pp. 173–177. IFSS, Tehran (2010)
9. Khaled, A., Abdul-Kader, H.M., Ismail, N.A.: Artificial Immune Clonal Selection Algorithms: A Comparative Study of CLONALG, opt-IA, and BCA with Numerical Optimization Problems. International Journal of Computer Science and Network Security 10, 24–30 (2010)
10. Aragon, V.S., Esquivel, S.C., Coello, C.A.: Artificial Immune System for Solving Global Optimization Problems. Inteligencia Artificial 46, 3–16 (2010)
11. Xu, Q., Wang, L., Si, J.: Predication based Immune Network for Multimodal Function Optimization. Engineering Applications of Artificial Intelligence 23, 495–504 (2010)
12. Gao, J., Wang, J.: WBMOAIS: A Novel Artificial Immune System for Multiobjective Optimization. Computers & Operations Research 37, 50–61 (2010)
13. Verbeeck, K., Nowe, A.: Colonies of Learning Automata. IEEE Transactions on Systems, Man, and Cybernetics, Part B: Cybernetics 32, 772–780 (2002)
14. Xuhua, S., Feng, Q.: An Optimization Algorithm Based on Multi-population Artificial Immune Network. In: 5th International Conference on Natural Computation (ICNC 2009), vol. 5, pp. 379–383. IEEE Press, New York (2009)
15. Hu, C., Wang, B., Wang, Y.: Multi-swarm Particle Swarm Optimiser with Cauchy Mutation for Dynamic Optimisation Problems. International Journal of Innovative Computing and Applications 2, 123–132 (2009)
16. Beigy, H., Meybodi, M.R.: Cellular Learning Automata with Multiple Learning Automata in each Cell and its Applications. IEEE Transactions on Systems, Man, and Cybernetics, Part B: Cybernetics 40, 54–65 (2010)
17. Abtahi, F., Meybodi, M.R., Ebadzadeh, M.M., Maani, R.: Learning Automata-based Coevolutionary Genetic Algorithms for Function Optimization. In: 6th International Symposium on Intelligent Systems and Informatics (SISY 2008), Subotica, Serbia, pp. 1–5. IEEE Press, New York (2008)

18. Hashemi, A.B., Meybodi, M.R.: Adaptive Parameter Selection Scheme for PSO: A Learning Automata Approach. In: 14th International CSI Computer Conference (CSICC 2009), Tehran, Iran, pp. 403–411. IEEE Press, New York (2009)
19. Rezvanian, A., Meybodi, M.R.: A New Method for Function Optimization using Artificial Immune System and Learning Automata. In: 3rd Joint Congress on Fuzzy and Intelligent Systems (IFS 2009), Yazd, Iran, pp. 1–7. IFSS, Tehran (2009)
20. De Franca, F.O., Von Zuben, F.J., De Castro, L.N.: An Artificial Immune Network for Multimodal Function Optimization on Dynamic Environments. In: Conference on Genetic and Evolutionary Computation (GECCO 2005), Washington, DC, USA, pp. 289–296. ACM, New York (2005)
21. Yongshou, D., Yuanyuan, L., Lei, W., Junling, W., Deling, Z.: Adaptive Immune-genetic Algorithm for Global Optimization to Multivariable Function. Journal of Systems Engineering and Electronics 18, 655–660 (2007)
22. Angeline, P.: Tracking Extrema in Dynamic Environments. In: Angeline, P.J., McDonnell, J.R., Reynolds, R.G., Eberhart, R. (eds.) EP 1997. LNCS, vol. 1213, pp. 335–345. Springer, Heidelberg (1997)
23. Woldesenbet, Y.G., Yen, G.G.: Dynamic Evolutionary Algorithm with Variable Relocation. IEEE Transactions on Evolutionary Computation 13, 500–513 (2009)
24. Dempsey, I., O'Neill, M., Brabazon, A.: Foundations in Grammatical Evolution for Dynamic Environments. Springer, Heidelberg (2009)
25. Walker, J.H., Garrett, S.M.: Dynamic Function Optimisation: Comparing the Performance of Clonal Selection and Evolution Strategies. In: Timmis, J., Bentley, P.J., Hart, E. (eds.) ICARIS 2003. LNCS, vol. 2787, pp. 273–284. Springer, Heidelberg (2003)
26. Timmis, J., Hone, A., Stibor, T., Clark, E.: Theoretical Advances in Artificial Immune Systems. Theoretical Computer Science 403, 11–32 (2008)
27. Narendra, K.S., Thathachar, M.A.L.: Learning Automata: An Introduction. Prentice-Hall, New York (1989)
28. Beigy, H., Meybodi, M.R.: Asynchronous Cellular Learning Automata. Automatica 44, 1350–1357 (2008)

TDOA/FDOA Geolocation with Adaptive Extended Kalman Filter

Hongshuo Shao, Dongkyun Kim, and Kwanho You

Sungkyunkwan University, Suwon, 440-746, Korea
hong2009@skku.edu, kidkyun@skku.edu, khyou@ece.skku.ac.kr

Abstract. In this paper, we propose a moving target tracking algorithm using the measurement signals of time difference of arrival (TDOA) and the frequency difference of arrival (FDOA). As the conventional target tracking using TDOA measurement is not accurate enough to estimate the target location, we use the TDOA and FDOA measurement signals together to estimate the location and the velocity of a target at discrete times. Although, the Kalman filter shows remarkable performance in calculation and location estimation, the estimation error can be large when the priori noise covariances are assumed with improper values. We suggest an adaptive extended Kalman filter (AEKF) to update the noise covariance at each measurement and estimation process. The simulation results show that the algorithm efficiently reduces the position error and it also greatly improves the accuracy of target tracking.

Keywords: Adaptive extended Kalman filter, time difference of arrival, frequency difference of arrival, target tracking, geolocation.

1 Introduction

Target tracking is an important technique in wide range of areas, such as wireless communications, search and rescue using satellites, locating and identifying a target in electronic warfare, *etc*. As main techniques for target tracking, there are several generally used methods: difference of arrival, time difference of arrival, frequency difference of arrival, *etc*. Many researches have been performed for position calculation. The Taylor-series expansion [1] method uses an iterative scheme to find an optimal solution of the position equation, and it needs an approximate initial position guess. Therefore, when the initial position is proper, it can get a high precision and the convergence is also good and fast. However, the problem is that it is hard to get the initial value in the real environment which has much disturbance. Chan [2] proposed a two-stage weighted least square algorithm to linearize the TDOA and FDOA measurement. When the TDOA measurement is obtained by signal processing, the feature of TDOA measurement error can be indentified and the nonlinear equations of TDOA measurement can be transformed into linear equations by some mathematical operation. The analytic solution to the measurement with some constrains is introduced in [3]: DOA, TDOA, FDOA, the combination of TDOA and FDOA, *etc*.

T.-h. Kim et al. (Eds.): GDC/CA 2010, CCIS 121, pp. 226–235, 2010.

The DOA is one of the passive conventional techniques with low location accuracy. The TDOA uses the hyperbola curves. The accuracy is higher than the DOA and it does not require any time reference [4]. The location of a target can be tracked by the signal intercepted at several sensors; one of the most effective methods is to use the measurement signals of time difference of arrival and/or frequency difference of arrival between pairs of signals received from the sensors. This method involves two problems concerning the estimation of position: one is the signal processing to collect a set of TDOA and FDOA estimates, and the other is to process the results from the TDOA/FDOA data to estimate the target location. As a conventional way, target tracking uses only TDOA measurements which are not accurate to estimate the target location when the number of receivers is not enough [5]. To solve this problem, we use the TDOA and FDOA measurement signals together to estimate the location and the velocity of the target.

The Kalman filter is well-known for solving the problem of the target location. To overcome the nonlinear problems, the extended Kalman filter (EKF) estimates the state through a linearization process. The EKF uses priori guess to estimate the process and measurement noise covariance. As the circumstances change at different times, it's difficult to track the position precisely when the priori values are estimated with too much error from the real values. In this paper, we propose an adaptive extended Kalman filter for precise position tracking. Using the adaptive factor, the process and measurement error covariance can be modified to approach the real values. In section 2, we introduce the system modeling for target localization. Section 3 designs the adaptive extended Kalman filter algorithm for geolocation. The simulation results show the improved tracking accuracy in section 4. Conclusions are drawn in section 5.

2 System Modeling for Target Localization

The localization method is based on using the time difference of arrival (TDOA) and the frequency difference of arrival (FDOA) signals collected from receiver sensors or UGVs receiver equipped with sensors under the interference noise. To follow the fast moving target's location, it is required to reduce the computational process in real time system. In the real situations, the TDOA and FDOA signals are mostly affected by the external noises.

$$s = s_e + \Delta s \tag{1}$$

where s_e is the ideal measurement value without noises and Δs is an added noise value. As a robust estimation solution, Kalman filter algorithm is a classic and efficient method to estimate the position using TDOA and FDOA as measurement output.

To apply Kalman filter algorithm in the localization problem, the state-space equation needs to be formulated. Therefore the target tracking problem can be modeled as a discrete equation in two dimensions as following.

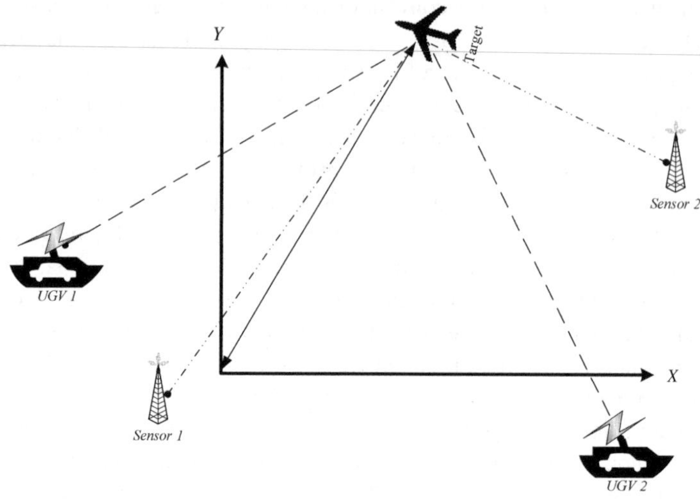

Fig. 1. Concept of target location using TDOA and FDOA measurements

$$s(k+1) = As(k) + Bu(k) + w(k),$$
$$A = \begin{bmatrix} 1 & 0 & 1 & 0 \\ 0 & 1 & 0 & 1 \\ 0 & 0 & 0 & 0 \\ 0 & 0 & 0 & 0 \end{bmatrix}, \quad B = \begin{bmatrix} 0 & 0 \\ 0 & 0 \\ T_S & 0 \\ 0 & T_S \end{bmatrix} \tag{2}$$

where$s(k) = [x \quad y \quad \Delta x \quad \Delta y]^T$, $(x,\ y)$ is the target position, $(\Delta x,\ \Delta y)$ is the positional variation at each sampling time T_S, $u(k) = \left[v_x \ v_y\right]^T$ is the velocity of the moving target, and $w(k)$ is the process noise modeled as a zero-mean white Gaussian noise. The output equation can be formulated using the measurements of TDOA and FDOA signals.

$$z(k) = h\big(s(k), n(k)\big) \tag{3}$$

where $n(k)$ is the measurement noise also modeled as a white Gaussian noise. The output $z(k)$ is the TDOA and FDOA measurements obtained from the definition in the following analytical methods. In this model, because of the nonlinear terms in the measurement output equation, we use the partial derivative approximate as measurement transition matrix.

$$H(k) \approx \frac{\partial \mathrm{h(s, n\,)}}{\partial \mathrm{s}} \tag{4}$$

The transmitted signal has a time difference and a frequency difference when it is sent to each receiver with known position and velocity by a moving target emitter with unknown position and velocity. To simplify the location process, we choose two pairs of receivers as shown in Fig. 1; one pair is just composed of receiver sensors, the other pair includes two UGVs equipped with sensors. The analytic method to find the target position can be summarized as follows.

Let the position and velocity of two receivers be denoted by $r_1, r_2 \in R^2$ and $v_1, v_2 \in R^2$, respectively. The unit position vectors from the unknown target position r with velocity of v to the receivers are given by:

$$u_i = \frac{r_i - r}{\|r_i - r\|}, \quad i = 1, 2 \tag{5}$$

Although more receiver sensors can be used to identify for more accuracy, we just use two receivers for a simple model in this paper. Here, TDOA and FDOA measurements obtain signals from the two receiver sensors as following.

$$TDOA = \frac{1}{C}(\|r_2 - r\| - \|r_1 - r\|)$$

$$FDOA = -\frac{f_0}{c}[(v_2 - v)^T u_2 - (v_1 - v)^T u_1] \tag{6}$$

where c is the signal propagation velocity and f_0 is the signal frequency. The TDOA and FDOA measurements are the nonlinear processes. To apply the EKF algorithm, we need to linearize the output measurement through the partial differentiation. The gradients are:

$$\Delta TDOA = -\frac{1}{c}(u_2 - u_1)$$

$$\Delta FDOA = \frac{f_0}{c}\left[\frac{[I - u_2 u_2^T](v_2 - v)}{\|r_2 - r\|} - \frac{[I - u_1 u_1^T](v_1 - v)}{\|r_1 - r\|}\right] \tag{7}$$

The above equation of (7) can be set as the measurement output matrix.

$$H(k) \approx \begin{bmatrix} \Delta TDOA \\ \Delta FDOA \end{bmatrix} = \frac{f_0}{c}\begin{bmatrix} -\frac{1}{f_0}(u_2 - u_1) \\ \frac{[I - u_2 u_2^T](v_2 - v)}{\|r_2 - r\|} - \frac{[I - u_1 u_1^T](v_1 - v)}{\|r_1 - r\|} \end{bmatrix} \tag{8}$$

3 Localization Using Adaptive Extended Kalman Filter

The extended Kalman filter (EKF) for target tracking is widely used in the position estimation of nonlinear system. However, the divergence of estimated results caused by a modeling error is considered to be a crucial weakness. Generally, the dynamic properties and errors are considered together in Kalman filter. The EKF algorithm uses a fixed priori estimates for the process and measurement noise covariances during the whole estimation process. However, the divergence of the nonlinear system model based on the TDOA and FDOA measurement values can happen in real environment if the real position values do not match with the values of estimated model system. It becomes difficult to apply the EKF method to track the accurate position with the past static priori values during the target's fast movement [6]. As a solution to prevent the divergence of extended Kalman filter, the adaptive extended Kalman filter (AEKF) is proposed to update the covariance of process noise and measurement noise in current states. As the AEKF algorithm uses the recent covariance values in the process and measurement state, it is effective to overcome the disturbance problem.

The summary for EKF algorithm consists of two parts and is given as [7]:

1) Time update (prediction part)
(a) The state projection:

$$\hat{s}^{-}(k) = f\big(\hat{s}(k-1), u(k), w(k)\big), \tag{9}$$

(b) The error covariance projection:

$$P^{-}(k) = A(k)P(k-1)A(k)^{T} + W(k)Q(k)W(k)^{T}, \tag{10}$$

2) Measurement update (correcting part)
(a) Kalman gain update:

$$K(k) = P^{-}(k)H(k)^{T}[H(k)P^{-}(k)H(k)^{T} + V(k)R(k)V(k)^{T}]^{-1}, \tag{11}$$

(b) The error covariance update:

$$P(k) = [I - K(k)H(k)]P^{-}(k), \tag{12}$$

(c) The estimate update with measurement $z(k)$:

$$\hat{s}(k) = \hat{s}^{-}(k) + K(k)[z(k) - \hat{z}(k)]. \tag{13}$$

Here $\hat{s}(k)$ is the predicted estimate of state at *k-th* step, $\hat{s}^{-}(k)$ is a posteriori estimate of state at *k-th* step, $u(k)$ is the control input with a velocity of a moving target, $P^{-}(k)$ is the error covariance of $\hat{s}^{-}(k)$, $A(k)$ is the state transition matrix, $K(k)$ is the gain matrix, and $Q(k)$ and $R(k)$ represent the process and measurement noise covariance, respectively.

The initial condition s_0 is designed to be a zero-mean Gaussian random variable with a covariance p_0 ($p_0 > 0$), and $w(k)$ and $v(k)$ are independent zero-mean white Gaussian noises. We assume the process and measurement noise as,

$$E[w(i)w(k)^{T}] = \begin{cases} Q(k), & i = k, \\ 0, & i \neq k, \end{cases}$$

$$E[v(i)v(k)^{T}] = \begin{cases} R(k), & i = k, \\ 0, & i \neq k, \end{cases}$$

$$E[w(i)v(k)^{T}] = 0\,, \quad \text{for all } k \text{ and } i. \tag{14}$$

In Fig. 2, with initial values of s_0, p_0 in time update process, we evaluate the estimate of system state by time flow and we calibrate the state estimation by comparing the differences between a real measurement and an estimate through a system modeling in measurement update process.

The implementation of Kalman filter requires a priori statistical knowledge of the process noise and measurement noise. Poor knowledge of the noise values may seriously degrade the function of Kalman filter and the divergence problem in the filtering process may happen. To fulfill the accuracy requirement, the adaptive Kalman filter can be utilized as the noise-adaptive filter to estimate the process and measurement noise covariance matrices $Q(k), R(k)$.

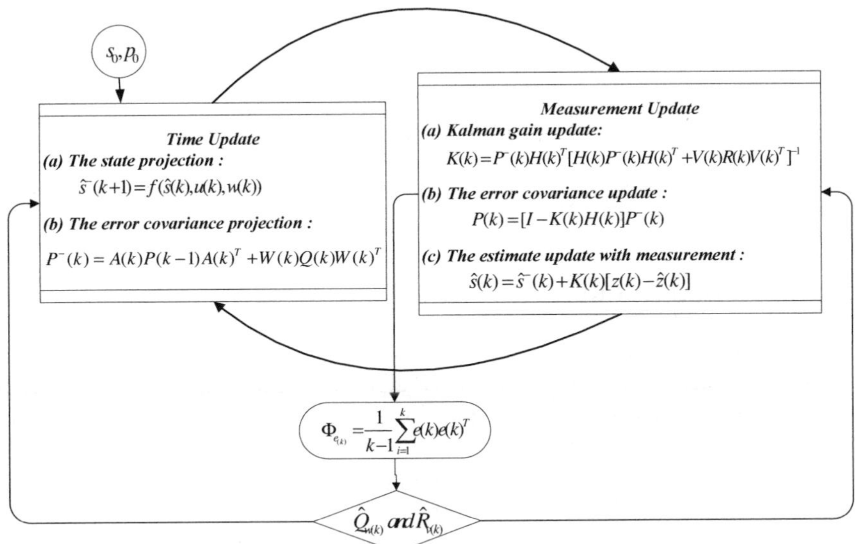

Fig. 2. Operation of adaptive extended Kalman filter

An innovation sequence utilizes the correlation and covariance matching techniques to estimate the noise covariance. Here, the maximum-likelihood estimation for the multivariate normal distribution approach is to make the actual value of the covariance consistent with its theoretical value. From the incoming measurement $z(k)$ and the optimal prediction $h(\hat{s}^-(k), u(k), v(k))$ obtained in the previous step, the innovation sequence is defined as $e(k) = z(k) - \hat{z}(k)$.

The innovation sequence can be written as:

$$e(k) \approx H(k)\big(s(k) - \hat{s}^-(k)\big) + v(k). \tag{15}$$

The covariance can be obtained by taking the variance on both sides of the Eq. (15).

$$\Phi_{e(k)} = H(k)P^-(k)H(k)^T + R_{v(k).} \tag{16}$$

The covariance of $e(k)$ is written as

$$\Phi_{e(k)} = E[e(k)e(k)^T]. \tag{17}$$

According the maximum-likelihood estimation for the multivariate normal distribution approach, the statistical sample variance of $\Phi_{e(k)}$:

$$\hat{\Phi}_{e(k)} = \frac{1}{k}\sum_{i=1}^{k} e(k)\, e(k)^T. \tag{18}$$

From Eq. (16), the estimate of the measurement noise covariance is as

$$\hat{R}_{v(k)} = \hat{\Phi}_{e(k)} - H(k)P^-(k)H(k)^T. \tag{19}$$

The estimate of the process noise covariance is

$$\hat{Q}_{w(k)} = \frac{1}{k}\sum_{i=1}^{k}\left(s(k) - \hat{s}^{-}(k)\right)\left(s(k) - \hat{s}^{-}(k)\right)^T + P(k) - A(k)P(k-1)A(k)^T$$
$$\approx K(k)\hat{\Phi}_{e(k)}K(k)^T. \tag{20}$$

Two important values for the process and measurement noise covariance are modified adaptively by using the Eqs. (19) and (20)

4 Simulation Results

In this section, through some simulation results, we demonstrate the effectiveness of the proposed tracking method using AEKF algorithm. The simulation conditions are as follows: the first receiver's sensor position is set as (8, 30) km, the initial velocity is set as (1, 0.9) km/s; the second receiver sensor is set as (70, 4) km, the velocity is set as (1, 0.5) km/s. The UGVs are also equipped with sensors as receivers. The positions of UGVs are set separately as (5, 6) km and (5, 15) km with a constant altitude and the UGV is moving following a circular orbit with a radius of 1 km.

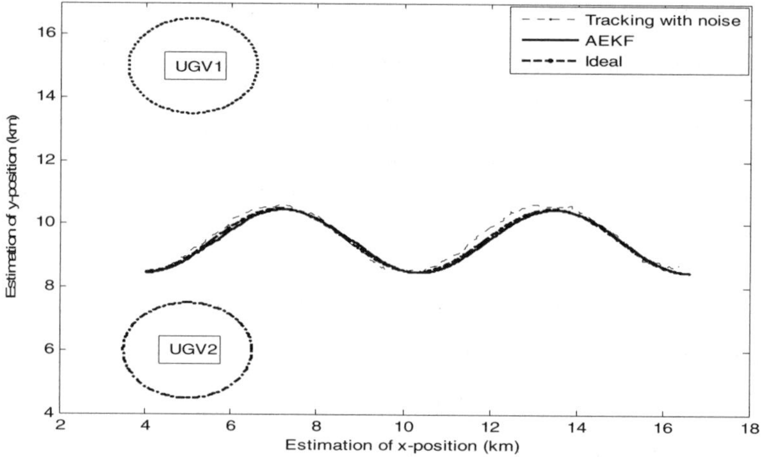

Fig. 3. Position estimation of a sinusoidal movement

Figure. 3 shows the position estimate of AEKF compared with the ideal position and the position tracking with noise. The ideal position without noise in Fig. 3 is indicated by the long-dashed line as a reference, the estimate of position tracking with noise is indicated by the short-dashed line. The solid line is the position estimate using the AEKF algorithm. It also confirms that the adaptive estimate algorithm updates the process and measurement noise covariance for each sampling time. The simulation proves that the AEKF method can track the target more accurately compared with the tracking result with noise. It also illustrates that the updated

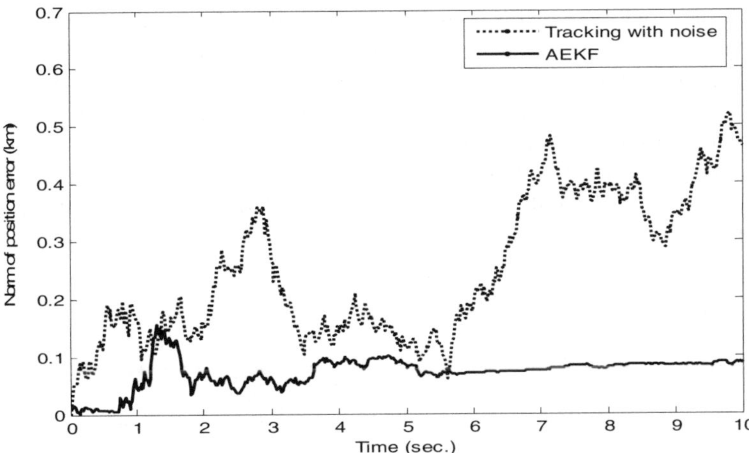

Fig. 4. Norm of position error for sinusoidal movement

information on process and measurement noises plays an important role in locating the real position in localization problem.

Figure. 4 represents the norm of position error. The dotted line represents the norm of position error between the ideal position and the position tracking with error, the solid line means the norm of position error between the ideal value and the position estimate using the AEKF algorithm in Fig. 3. Fig. 4 shows that the position error of target is reduced when we use the AEKF algorithm and the proposed algorithm can estimate more closely to the real position with two moving UGVs' receivers.

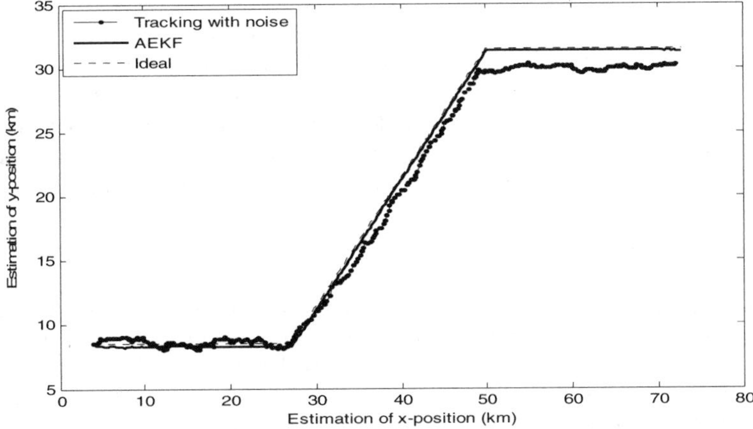

Fig. 5. Position estimation of a transitional movement

Figure. 5 shows the simulation results with a different trajectory. The ideal position without noise is indicated by the dotted line as reference for comparison and the position tracking with noise is indicated by the dash-dotted line. The solid line is the AEKF algorithm estimate which updates the process and measurement noise covariance in the process. In the simulation, we use two sensors as receivers with different location and constant velocity. Using the TDOA and FDOA measurement signals together to estimate the location and velocity of the target at different times, the simulation results prove that the AEKF method is effective to reduce the error and that the accuracy of the target tracking is increased.

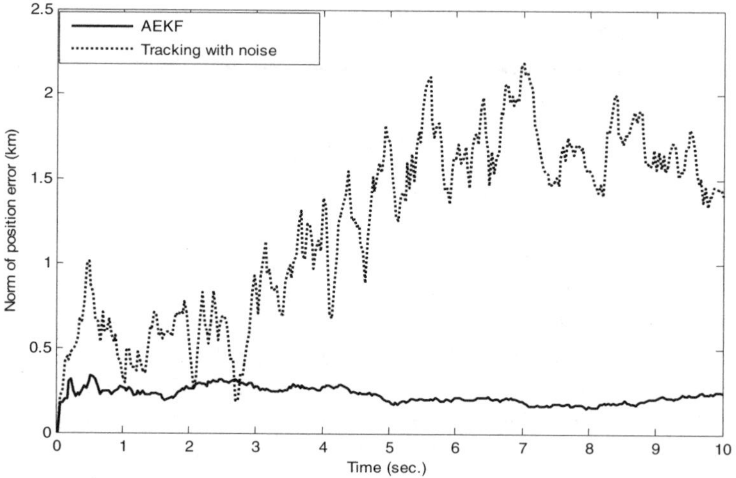

Fig. 6. Norm of position error for a transitional movement

Figure. 6 represents the norm of position error. The norm of position error between the ideal position and position tracking with error is compared with that between the ideal position and position estimate using the AEKF algorithm. Fig. 6 shows that the position error with noise fluctuates widely more than that of AEKF. Through the AEKF algorithm, the position error is limited within the boundary of 0.25 km. The simulation result proves the effectiveness of the AEKF algorithm in target tracking.

5 Conclusions

This paper proposes an AEKF algorithm for tacking the target position using the TDOA and FDOA measurement signals together from the two UGVs' receivers and two general receivers in the modeling. The method that uses only TDOA measurement signals is not sufficient for estimating the velocity of the target. Therefore we use the TDOA and FDOA signals together to estimate the location and the velocity of the target at discrete times. Generally, EKF algorithm is easily and widely applied to the target tracking through linearization of the nonlinear process. However, the EKF algorithm uses a past static priori values as the process and measurement noise covariance during the update process. When the priori values are incorrectly estimated and when it deviates from the true values under the irregular environmental condition, it's difficult to track the accurate position of the target. We proposed the AEKF algorithm which updates the current process and the measurement noise covariance according to the changing environment at discrete times. Through the simulation results, the proposed estimate algorithm achieved more accurate target position and reduced the position error.

Acknowledgement

This paper was supported by Faculty Research Fund, Sungkyunkwan University, 2009.

References

1. Foy, W.H.: Position Location Solutions by Taylor Series Estimation. IEEE Trans. Aerospace Electronic Systems 12(2), 187–194 (1976)
2. Chan, Y.T.: A Simple and Efficient Estimator for Hyperbolic Location. IEEE Trans. Signal Processing 42(8), 1905–1915 (1994)
3. Ho, K.C., Chan, Y.T.: Geolocation of a Known Altitude Object from TDOA and FDOA Measurements. IEEE Trans. Aerospace Electronic Systems 33(3) (1997)
4. Li, W.C., Xiao, X.C.: Robust TDOA-based Location Method and Its Performance Analysis. Sci. China. Ser. F-Inf. Sci. 52(5), 876–882 (2009)
5. Takabayashi, Y., Matsuzaki, T., Kameda, H., Ito, M.: Target Tracking using TDOA/FDOA Measurements in the Distributed Sensor Network. The University Electro-Communications, Japan (2008)
6. Han, J.H., Kim, D.C., Sunwoo, M.H.: State-of-charge Estimation of Lead-acid Batteries Using an Adaptive Extended Kalman Filter. Journal of Power Sources 188, 606–612 (2009)
7. Kluge, S., Reif, K., Brokate, M.: Stochastic Stability of the Extended Kalman Filter With Intermittent Observations. IEEE Trans. Automatic Control 55(2), 514–518 (2010)

A Very Low Cost BCH Decoder for High Immunity of On-Chip Memories

Haejun Seo[1], Sehwan Han[2], Yoonseok Heo[1], and Taewon Cho[2]

[1] School of Electrical & Electronics Engineering, Chungcheong University
[2] Department of Electronics Engineering, College of Electrical & Computer Engineering, Chungbuk National University
hjseo@ok.ac.kr, shhan@dsd.cbnu.ac.kr

Abstract. BCH(Bose-Chaudhuri-Hoquenbhem) code, a type of block codes-cyclic codes, has very strong error-correcting ability which is vital for performing the error protection on the memory system. BCH code has many kinds of dual algorithms, PGZ(Pererson-Gorenstein-Zierler) algorithm out of them is advantageous in view of correcting the errors through the simple calculation in t value. However, this is problematic when this becomes 0 (divided by zero) in case $v \neq t$. In this paper, the circuit would be simplified by suggesting the multi-mode hardware architecture in preparation that v were 0~3. First, production cost would be less thanks to the smaller number of gates. Second, lessening power consumption could lengthen the recharging period. The very low cost and simple datapath make our design a good choice in small-footprint SoC(System on Chip) as ECC(Error Correction Code/Circuit) in memory system.

1 Introduction

As portable devices introduced in daily life, convenient and long-term rechargeable devices are being attractive to consumers. Also, devices support high performance and high resolution so that the capacity of memory has been increased to satisfy the performance. Cutting edge technology is applied to narrow area for a number of functions and the various operating conditions are required for huge memory devices. The ripple of supply voltage is no longer ignorable since the method reduce power consumption by lowering operating voltage is common. Hence, highly error-correcting BCH (Bose-Chaudhuri-Hoquembhem)code has been rised as error incidencerate of conventional circuits were increased [1]. Current highly error-correcting circuits are not suitable for multi error correcting code due to large size. To solve these disadvantages[2-3] Chein, Berlekamp, syndrome symmetric matrix and PGZ (Peterson, Gorenstein, Zierler)decoder were suggested. Among them, PGZ decode algorithm is commonly used because the circuit is remarkably simple. This paper suggests a method to reduce power consumption and area for PGZ decoder which is used in conventional BCH code. and verifies through design of structure and area calculation. Organization is as follow: Section 2 describes decoding method of BCH encode. Section 3 analyzes conventional PGZ algorithm technique and section 4 describes proposing multi-mode decoder. Section 5 concludes with brief evaluation.

T.-h. Kim et al. (Eds.): GDC/CA 2010, CCIS 121, pp. 236–244, 2010.

2 Decoding of BCH Encode

Decoding method solves syndrome equations and searches error position number $\alpha^{j\lambda}$, λ =1, 2, … , v from syndrome factors. Each syndrome factor, s_k , is same as the value of calculated error form, *e(x)*, from $x = \alpha^k$. So it is expressed with the factor of GF(2m). Suppose errors of v(1≤v≤t) come from unknown position $j_1, j_2, \ldots, j_v$. Error form can be expressed as (1).

$$e(x) = \sum_{\lambda=1}^{v} x^{j\lambda}, 0 \le j_\lambda \le n-1 \tag{1}$$

From (1), syndrome factor is expressed by (2).

$$s_k = \sum_{\lambda=1}^{v} (\alpha^k)^{j\lambda} = \sum_{\lambda=1}^{v} (\alpha^{j\lambda})^k = \sum_{\lambda=1}^{v} (\beta_\lambda)^k \tag{2}$$

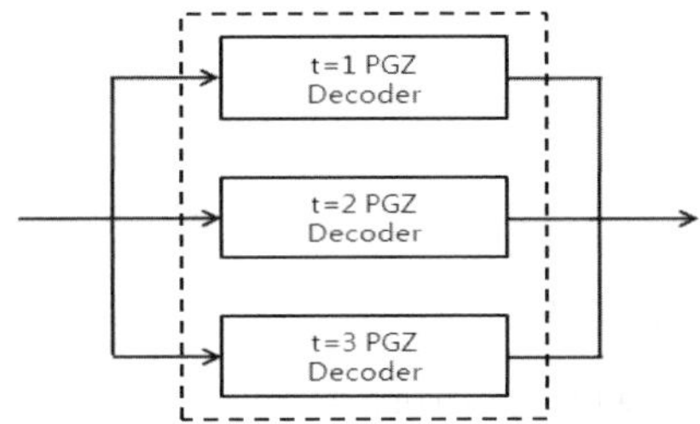

Fig. 1. Architecture of conventional PGZ decoder

This equation forms equation set between syndrome factor, $s_k, 1 \le k \le 2t$ and error position number, $\beta_\lambda = \alpha^{j\lambda}, 1 \le \lambda \le v$. (3) describes equation set.

$$s_1 = \sum_{\lambda=1}^{v} \beta_\lambda,\ s_2 = \sum_{\lambda=1}^{v} (\beta_\lambda)^2 \ldots\ s_3 = \sum_{\lambda=1}^{v} (\beta_\lambda)^{2t} \tag{3}$$

These $2t$ equations are called syndrome equation or prime power symmetric function. Decoder of BCH encode analyzes these syndrome equations and searches error position from syndrome factors.

3 Peterson, Gorenstein, Zierler Algorithm

BCH encode which is highly error correcting encode can correct multi errors. PGZ algorithm for dual BCH encode is generalized. Typical PGZ algorithm needs a correcting circuit to correct one error. As depicted in Figure 1, individual encoder is necessary for triple error correction in t=1, 2, 3. It makes hardware size to be proportioned by t. For error t=3, decoder of t=2 cannot obtain correct value. While, for error decoder of produces 0 in all cases, then it cannot obtain correct value [3]. PGZ algorithm is composed of two main processes. First one is to find Newton's identities.

$$\begin{bmatrix} s_1 & s_2 & \cdots & s_\nu \\ s_2 & s_3 & \cdots & s_{\nu+1} \\ \vdots & & & \vdots \\ s_\nu & s_{\nu+1} & \cdots & s_{2\nu-1} \end{bmatrix} \bullet \begin{bmatrix} \sigma_\nu \\ \sigma_{\nu-1} \\ \vdots \\ \sigma_1 \end{bmatrix} = \begin{bmatrix} -s_{\nu+1} \\ -s_{\nu+2} \\ \vdots \\ -s_{2\nu} \end{bmatrix} \tag{4}$$

In here, syndrome value is used to evaluate root of σ. Chien demonstrated that require time for the procedure to evaluate root of σ(x) is about 3tn clock. Hence, triple error correction (31,16) BCH encode has 3tn= (3)(3)(31)=279 clock. Generally, an error position polynomial to correct t times errors is expressed as (5), where $\sigma_0 = 1$. Error position number, α^{n-j}, $0 \leq j \leq n-1$ is inverse of $\alpha^{j\lambda}$ which is a root of σ(x). So it is important to solve σ(x).

$$\sigma(x) = \sigma_0 + \sigma_1 x + \cdots + \sigma_{t-1} x^{t-1} + \sigma_t x^t$$
$$= \sum_{j=0}^{t} \sigma_j x^j \tag{5}$$

3.1 One-Error PGZ Algorithm

For (4), determinant is same with (6) when t=1,

$$[s_1] \bullet [\sigma_1] = [-s_2], \text{ and } \sigma_1 = \frac{s_2}{s_1} \tag{6}$$

Error position polynomial is expressed as (7) [3-5].

$$\sigma(x) = 1 + \sigma_1 x \tag{7}$$

3.2 Double-Error PGZ Algorithm

For (4), determinant is same with (8) when t=2,

$$\begin{bmatrix} s_1 & s_2 \\ s_2 & s_3 \end{bmatrix} \bullet \begin{bmatrix} \sigma_2 \\ \sigma_1 \end{bmatrix} = \begin{bmatrix} s_3 \\ s_4 \end{bmatrix} \tag{8}$$

For 2x2 matrix, M, if detM≠0 inverse matrix of M is $M^{-1} = (1/\det M)(adjM)$. That is expressed as (9).

$$\begin{bmatrix} \sigma_2 \\ \sigma_1 \end{bmatrix} = \frac{1}{s_1 s_3 - s_2^2} \begin{bmatrix} s_3 & s_2 \\ s_2 & s_1 \end{bmatrix} \bullet \begin{bmatrix} s_3 \\ s_4 \end{bmatrix} \tag{9}$$

For next, root of $\sigma(x)$ to decide error position number is expressed as (10).

$$\sigma_1 = \frac{s_2 s_3 + s_1 s_4}{s_1 s_3 - s_2^2}$$

$$\sigma_2 = \frac{s_3^2 + s_2 s_4}{s_1 s_3 - s_2^2} \tag{10}$$

Therefore, error position polynomial $\sigma(x)$ can be expressed as (11).

$$\sigma(x) = 1 + \sigma_1 x + \sigma_2 x^2 \tag{11}$$

3.3 Triple-Error PGZ Algorithm

For (4), determinant is same with (12) when t=2,

$$\begin{bmatrix} s_1 & s_2 & s_3 \\ s_2 & s_3 & s_4 \\ s_3 & s_4 & s_5 \end{bmatrix} \bullet \begin{bmatrix} \sigma_3 \\ \sigma_2 \\ \sigma_1 \end{bmatrix} = \begin{bmatrix} s_4 \\ s_5 \\ s_6 \end{bmatrix} \tag{12}$$

By applying inverse matrix M^{-1} Newton's identities for t=3 can be expressed as (13). Root of $\sigma(x)$ to decide error position number is (14).

$$\begin{bmatrix} \sigma_3 \\ \sigma_2 \\ \sigma_1 \end{bmatrix} = \frac{1}{s_1 s_3 s_5 + s_2 s_3 s_4 + s_2 s_3 s_4 - s_3 s_3 s_3 - s_1 s_4 s_4 - s_2 s_2 s_5} \bullet \begin{bmatrix} s_3 s_5 - s_4^2 & s_2 s_5 - s_3 s_4 & s_2 s_4 - s_3^2 \\ s_2 s_5 - s_3 s_4 & s_1 s_5 - s_3^2 & s_1 s_4 - s_2 s_3 \\ s_2 s_4 - s_3^2 & s_1 s_4 - s_2 s_3 & s_1 s_3 - s_2^2 \end{bmatrix} \begin{bmatrix} s_4 \\ s_5 \\ s_6 \end{bmatrix} \tag{13}$$

$$\sigma_1 = \frac{s_2 s_4 s_4 + s_3 s_3 s_4 + s_1 s_4 s_5 + s_2 s_3 s_5 + s_1 s_3 s_6 + s_2 s_2 s_6}{s_1 s_3 s_5 + s_2 s_3 s_4 + s_2 s_3 s_4 + s_3 s_3 s_3 + s_1 s_4 s_4 + s_2 s_2 s_5}$$

$$\sigma_2 = \frac{s_2 s_4 s_5 + s_3 s_4 s_4 + s_1 s_5 s_5 + s_3 s_3 s_5 + s_1 s_4 s_6 + s_2 s_3 s_6}{s_1 s_3 s_5 + s_2 s_3 s_4 + s_2 s_3 s_4 + s_3 s_3 s_3 + s_1 s_4 s_4 + s_2 s_2 s_5} \tag{14}$$

$$\sigma_3 = \frac{s_3 s_4 s_5 + s_4 s_4 s_4 + s_2 s_5 s_5 + s_3 s_4 s_5 + s_2 s_4 s_6 + s_3 s_3 s_6}{s_1 s_3 s_5 + s_2 s_3 s_4 + s_2 s_3 s_4 + s_3 s_3 s_3 + s_1 s_4 s_4 + s_2 s_2 s_5}$$

Error position polynomial, $\sigma(x)$ is as follow [3-5].

$$\sigma(x) = 1 + \sigma_1 x + \sigma_2 x^2 + \sigma_3 x^3 \tag{15}$$

$$\begin{bmatrix} s_1 \\ s_2 \\ s_3 \end{bmatrix} = \alpha \begin{bmatrix} s_2 \\ s_3 \\ s_4 \end{bmatrix} = \beta \begin{bmatrix} s_3 \\ s_4 \\ s_5 \end{bmatrix} \tag{16}$$

4 Proposed Multi-mode Decoder

4.1 Problem for Conventional Structure

Figure 2 shows block diagram correcting when error occurs to 3-bits of received code. If error occurs for the bits less than 3-bits, all of result values are 0. In this case, *t*=3 PGZ decoder circuit is not used. When the result value is 0, it is called divided-by-zero.

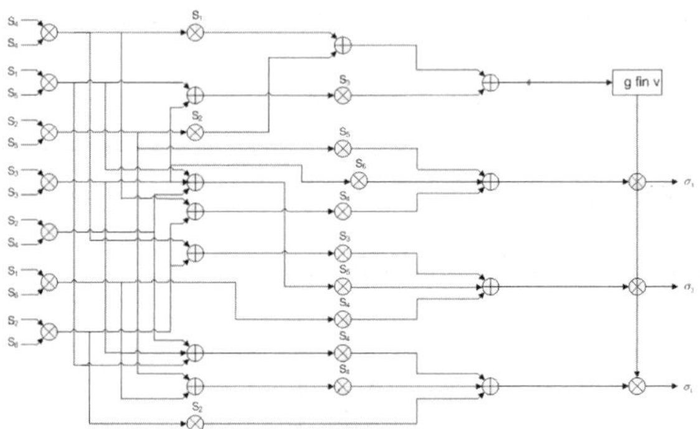

Fig. 2. Architecture of conventional PGZ decoder

Consider the determinant to correct triple errors, (12). If the number of error bits is less than 3-bits, every column has linear characteristics and determinant of M results 0.

For denominators of (14), $s_2s_3s_4$+$s_2s_3s_4$ is eliminated by Boolean expression, *A*+*A*=0. For a numerator of σ_3, $s_3s_4s_5$+$s_3s_4s_5$ is eliminated so that results the value expressed as (17). It is also applicable when bit error less than 2-bits occurs for *t*=2 PGZ decoder and results the value expressed as (18). In Figure 1, each *t*=1,2,3 decoder is existing. However, only one decoder operates and the others operate unnecessary. Multi-mode structure is proposed to solve those problems and it is depicted in Figure 3. Figure 4 shows the process to track the number of errors. For decision the number of errors, syndrome matrix is expressed as (19).

$$\begin{aligned}
&s_1s_3s_5+s_3s_3s_3+s_1s_4s_4+s_2s_2s_5=0\\
&s_4s_4s_4+s_2s_5s_5+s_2s_4s_6+s_3s_3s_6=0\\
&s_2s_4s_4+s_3s_3s_4+s_1s_4s_5+s_2s_3s_5+s_1s_3s_6+s_2s_2s_6=0\\
&s_2s_4s_5+s_3s_4s_4+s_1s_5s_5+s_3s_3s_5+s_1s_4s_6+s_2s_3s_6=0
\end{aligned} \tag{17}$$

$$\begin{aligned}
&s_1s_3+s_2^2=0\\
&s_2s_3+s_1s_4=0\\
&s_3^2+s_2s_4=0
\end{aligned} \tag{18}$$

$$s_1s_3s_5+s_3s_3s_3+s_1s_4s_4+s_2s_2s_5\neq 0 \tag{19}$$

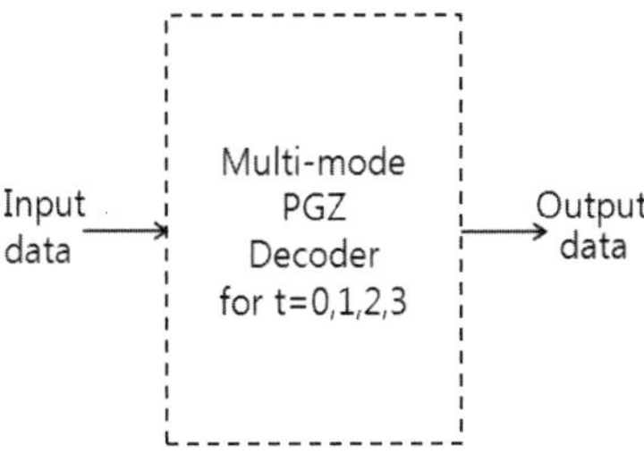

Fig. 3. Block diagram of the proposed multi-mode PGZ decoder

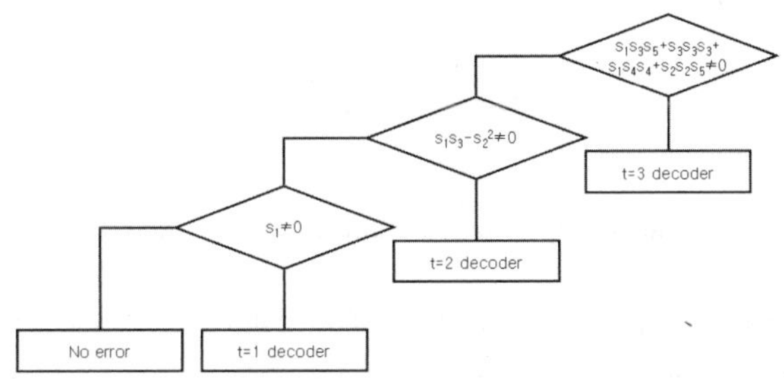

Fig. 4. Error trace algorithm of the proposed BCH decoder

If $t \neq 3$, polynomial matrix is 0 then checks t=2 due to t=v-1. When t=2, syndrome matrix M has same property of (20). When $t \neq 2$, M is 0 as expressed (18) and check t=1 due to t=v-1. If t=1, syndrome matrix M is $s_1 \neq 0$ and for $t \neq 1$, there is no errors.

$$s_1 s_3 + s_2^2 \neq 0 \tag{20}$$

4.2 Proposed Multi-mode PGZ Decoder

Substantial advantage with multi-mode structure is that reduction of power consumption and manu-facturing cost. It is important to set element of multi-mode for optimization. Because the number of gates is decided by a set of element.

s_1s_3, s_2s_2, s_2s_3, and s_1s_4, s_3s_3, s_2s_4 are chosen for t=2 in (18). These elements are essential to generate the path of t=2. There are a number of elements for t=3 in (17), but one of high frequent elements, s_4s_4, s_2s_5 and s_1s_5, s_2s_6, s_3s_4 s_3s_5, s_3s_6 is chosen. In Figure 5, the circuit has been implemented with applying s_1s_5. It tracks the number of errors with denominator polynomial and choose the mode, simultaneously.

4.3 Performance Evaluation

The criterion of evaluation in this paper is defined with the area and operation speed. The number of gates is a simple characteristic to show reduction of circuit size. The more gates used, the more power is consumed. Moreover, it makes circuit bigger and results high manufacturing cost. Table 1 presents the comparison of the number of gates. FFM(Finite-Field Mutipliers) and FFA(Finite-Field Adders) reduced 25.0 %

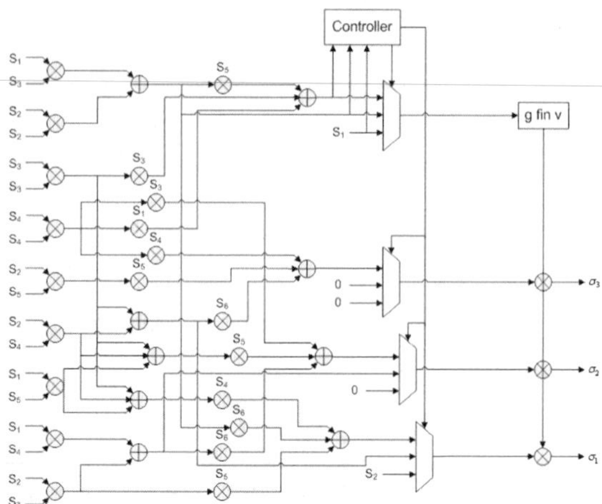

Fig. 5. Architecture of the proposed multi-mode PGZ decoder with t=1,2,3

Table 1. Comparisons of circuit sizes for the design of PGZ algorithm

	Existing t=1,2,3 PGZ	Proposed t=1,2,3 PGZ	Area ratio [%]
FFM[EA]	32	24	-25.0
FFA[EA]	14	9	-35.7
FFD[EA]	3	1	-66.7

and 66.7 %, respectively. In general, proposed one reduced 31.7 % comparing to conventional PGZ decoder. For approvement of processing speed, the time from the input to the output was computed. In the case of a single path, glitch is prevented in advance by choosing the longest path. Because this paper excepts the evaluation with full-custom method, delay time by wiring is not considered. The output load capacitance C_L of 0.1 pF is supposed as 0 since the unit of average delay time is nano second [3]. Figure 6 shows the longest path of conventional PGZ decoder. In this case, it consists of three FFM, two FFA and a FFD. FFM and FFD are expressed by AND gate, FFA is expressd by XOR gates. AND gate is represented as $A \cdot B = \overline{\overline{A \cdot B}}$ and XOR gate is represented as:

$$A \oplus B = \overline{A}B + A\overline{B} = \overline{\overline{\overline{A}B + A\overline{B}}} = \overline{(\overline{\overline{A}B}) \cdot (\overline{A\overline{B}})}\,.$$

NOT, NOR and NAND gate can be added. By referring to [3] delay time for the longest path of conventional PGZ decoder, DConv. can be found.

Assume the delay of NOT and NAND2 as . DConv. is expressed as (21).

$$D_{Conv.} = 2(\alpha + 2\beta) + 4(\alpha + \beta) \\ = 6\alpha + 8\beta \quad (21)$$

Delay time of the longest path of conventional PGZ decoder is 3.62ns.

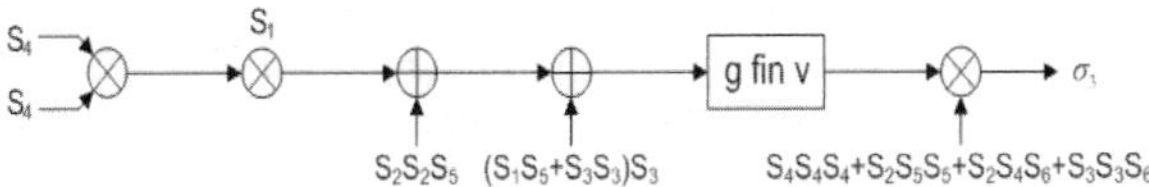

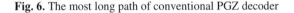

Fig. 6. The most long path of conventional PGZ decoder

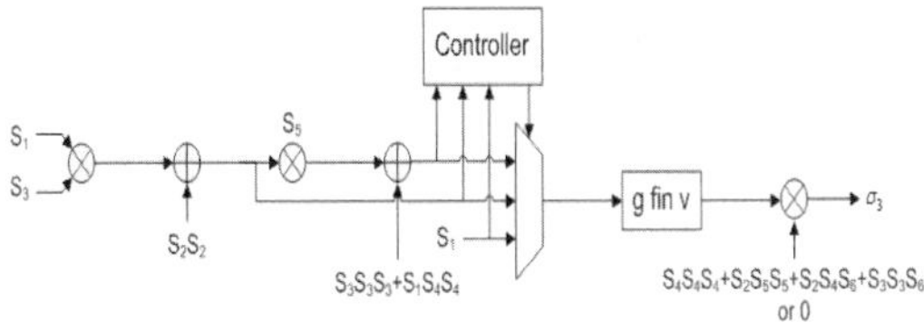

Fig. 7. The most long path of the proposed multi-mode PGZ decoder

Figure 7 presents the longest path of proposed multi-mode PGZ decoder. It consists of three FFM, two FFA and a FFA. For multi-mode choice delay time for the longest path of proposed multi-mode PGZ decoder can be found with table 2. Assume the delay of NOT, NAND2 and NAND3 as α, β and β'. DProp. is expressed as (22).

$$D_{Prop.} = 2(\alpha + 2\beta) + 4(\alpha + \beta) + \alpha + \beta' \\ = 7\alpha + 8\beta + \beta' \quad (22)$$

Delay time of the longest path of proposed PGZ decoder is 4.19 ns. For performance evaluation the size reduced by 30.1 % and processing speed increased by 15.7 %. Table 2 is based on the area of [3] and almost twice of area reduction has been accomplished comparing with the increase of processing speed.

Table 2. Size computation of the designed PGZ algorithm decoder

	Existing decoder	Proposed decoder	Area ratio [%]
FFM[EA] /Area	77/231	(52+3) /(156+12)	-28.3
FFA[EA] /Area	63/126	41 /82	-35.0
Total area	357	238+12	-30.1

5 Conclusion

PGZ decoder with multi-mode applied to ECC is proposed in this paper. A proposed PGZ decoder with multi-mode reduced the number of unnecessary gates by merging PGZ decoders to one and power consumption with selective using of gates. Besides, it has an advantage of lower manufacturing cost with minimizing the area.

For evaluation, FFM is reduced by 25.0 % and FFA, FFD are advanced by 35.7 %, 66.7 %, respectively, comparing to PGZ decoder. Delay time for direct path is increased to 15.2 %, however reduction of the area has been achieved over twice.

Considering area reduction has been significant as capacity of memory increases, proposed PGZ decoder with multi-mode has advantages of power con-sumption and area so that is applied to ECC for wireless communication memory field. For further research course, the possibility of realization will be evaluated by implementing the hardware of PGZ decoder.

References

[1] Maiz, J., Hareland, S., Zhang, K., Armstrong, P.: Characterization of multi-bit soft error events in advanced SRAMs. In: International Electron Devices Meeting, IEDM 2003, 8-10, pp. 21.4.1 -21.4.4 (December 2003)

[2] Andrea, B., Danilo, R., Michele, T., Cosimo, T.: Memory device with reduced power dissipation. U.S. Patent 6,061, 286, May 9 (2000)

[3] hee, R., Young, M.: Error-correcting coding theory. McGraw-Hill, New York (1989)

[4] Stevens, P.: Extension of the BCH decoding algorithm to decode binary cyclic codes up to their maximum error correction capacities. IEEE Transactions on Information Theory 34(5), 1332–1340 (1988)

Improved Non Linear Time Series Forecasting Using Non Linear Analysis Techniques and RBF Neural Networks for MRS Signals and Chaotic Diode Resonator Circuits

D.A. Karras and M.P. Hanias

Chalkis Institute of Technology, Greece, Automation Dept., Psachna, Evoia, Hellas (Greece) P.C. 34400
dakarras@teihal.gr, dakarras@ieee.org

Abstract. A novel non linear signal prediction method is presented using non linear signal analysis and deterministic chaos techniques in combination with Radial Basis Functions (RBF) Neural Networks for diode resonator chaotic circuits, used in industrial processes, as well as for Magnetic Resonance Spectroscopy (MRS) processes. The Time series analysis is performed by the method proposed by Grasberger and Procaccia, involving estimation of the correlation and minimum embedding dimension as well as of the corresponding Kolmogorov entropy. These parameters are used to construct the first stage of a one step / multistep predictor while an RBF Artificial Neural Network (ANN) is involved in the second stage to enhance prediction results. The novelty of the proposed two stage predictor lies on that the RBF ANN is employed as a second order predictor, that is, as an error predictor of the non-linear signal analysis stage application. This novel two stage predictor is evaluated through an extensive experimental study for both resonator circuits for industrial processes as well as for MRS signals in a preliminary stage of analysis. Different types of Neural Networks are compared as well.

Keywords: time series forecasting, non- linear signal analysis, diode resonator circuits, chaos, correlation dimension, RBF neural networks, MRS.

1 Introduction

A novel two-stage time series forecasting method is presented in this paper and is applied to the prediction of a chaotic signal produced by a diode resonator chaotic circuit used in industrial processes as well as to artificial MRS signals. Regarding diode resonator circuit, being quite simple, it illustrates how chaos can be generated. We have selected Multisim [1] to simulate circuits since it provides an interface as close as possible to the real implementation environment for industrial processes. In addition, complete circuits implementation and oscilloscope graphical plots are all presented. While non-linear signal analysis methods have been quite extensively studied and applied in several systems presenting chaos, chaotic time series prediction for electronic circuits is a field not too deeply investigated so far but of paramount importance in industrial processes. Chaos has already been recognized to be present in

T.-h. Kim et al. (Eds.): GDC/CA 2010, CCIS 121, pp. 245–256, 2010.

electronic circuits [2]-[5]. Some preliminary investigations on such time series prediction have been performed by the authors in [6]. The present paper aims at developing efficient predictors for such chaotic time series that are involved in industrial processes. To this end, the classical nonlinear signal analysis (i.e [7]-[8]) has been involved as a first stage of the proposed predictor, while RBF neural networks have been employed in the second stage to enhance first stage results, being a second order predictor for the first time in the relevant literature. An extensive experimental study shows that the proposed predictor is very favorably evaluated in terms of accuracy compared with the classical nonlinear signal analysis methodology as well as with other neural based predictors.

As a second step, after defining and evaluating our methodology in well recognized chaotic signals, we attempt, at a preliminary stage, to apply it in MRS processes where the produced signals are too complex but chaotic and nonlinear analysis tools have not actually been evaluated so far. The herein presented results are quite promising although further evaluation is needed.

2 The RL Diode Circuit Used in Industrial Processes

A non autonomous chaotic circuit referred to as the driven RL-diode circuit (RLD) [2-4] shown in Fig 1.

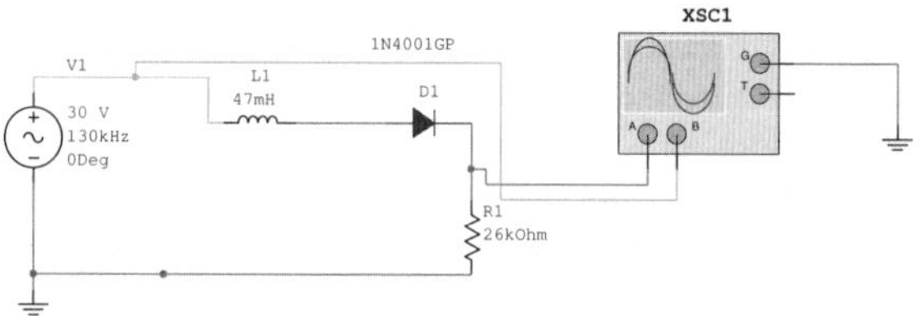

Fig. 1. RL-Diode chaotic circuit

It consists of a series connection of an ac-voltage source, a linear resistor R1, a linear inductor L1 and a diode D1 type 1N4001GP, that is the only nonlinear circuit element. An important feature of this circuit is that the current i (or the voltage across the resistor R) can be chaotic although the input voltage V1 is non-chaotic. The usual procedure is to choose a parameter that strongly affects the system. We found that for V1=32V RMS and input frequency f=135 KHz, inductance L1=47mH, the response is a chaotic one. The results of the Multisim simulation are shown in Fig. 2. The RL-diode was implemented and the voltage oscillations across the resistor VR1 and its phase portrait V1 vs VR1 are shown in Fig. 2.

3 The Proposed Novel Forecasting Methodology

First Stage: The Non Linear Signal Analysis Process

Time series prediction takes an existing series of data $x_{t-n}, \dots, x_{t-2}, x_{t-1}, x_t$ (1) and forecasts the future

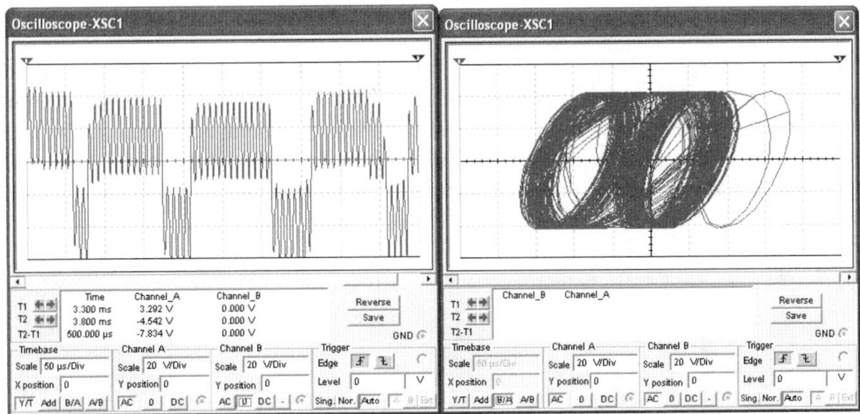

Fig. 2. Time series V_{R1} (t) (left) Phase portrait of V_1versus VR1 (right)

$x_{t+1}, x_{t+2}, \ldots$ (2) data values. Taking into account this point of view we could interpret the data produced by the RLD circuit as a non-linear chaotic time series. The same could be considered for complex signals lime the ones produced in MRS Spectroscopy processes. The goal is to observe or model the existing data series to enable future unknown data values to be forecasted accurately. If such a goal is achieved the conclusion is that the predictor involved could be considered a successful model of the physical phenomenon underlying the industrial process or the biomedical process as in the case of MRS.

To evaluate the resulted time series, the method proposed by Grasberger and Procaccia [7,8] and successfully applied in similar cases [9-11] has been applied in order to define the first stage of the proposed predictor. According to Takens theory [12] the measured time series were used to reconstruct the original phase space. For this purpose we calculated the correlation integral, for the simulated signal, defined by the following relation [13].

$$C_m(r) = \lim \frac{2}{(N)(N+1)} \sum_{i=1}^{N} \sum_{j=1+1}^{N} H\{r - (\sum_{k=1}^{m} [x_{i+k} - x_{j+k}]^2)^{\frac{1}{2}}\} \quad (3)$$

for lim r→ ∞ , where

N......................is the number of points,

H.......................is the Heaviside function,

m is the embedding dimension

In the above equation N is the number of the experimental points, here N=16337, Xi is a point in the m dimensional phase space with Xi given by the following relation [12], $X_i = \{VR1_{(ti)}, VR1_{(ti+\tau)}, VR1_{(ti+2\tau)} \ldots . VR1_{(ti+(m-1)\tau)}\}$ (4)

The vector

$X_t=\{VR1_{(ti)}, VR1_{(ti+\tau)}, VR1_{(ti+2\tau)}.....VR1_{(ti+(m-1)\tau)}\}$, represents a point to the m dimensional phase space in which the attractor is embedded each time, where τ is the time delay τ=iΔt determined by the first minimum of the time delayed mutual information ,I(τ) [13-16]. In our case, regarding RLD circuits, because of sample rate Δt=4.8x10-7 s, the mutual information function exhibits a local minimum at τ=6 time steps as shown at Fig -3.

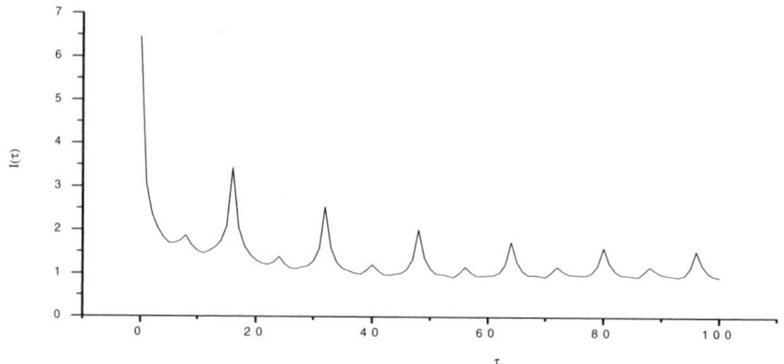

Fig. 3. Average Mutulal Information vs time delay τ

We used this value for the reconstruction of phase space. With (3) dividing this space into hypercubes with a linear dimension r we count all points with mutual distance less than r. It has been proven [7-8] that if our attractor is a strange one, the correlation integral is proportional to rv where v is a measure of the dimension of the attractor, called the correlation dimension. The correlation integral C(r) has been numerically calculated as a function of r from formula (3), for embedding dimensions m=1..10. In Fig 4 (upper insert) the slopes v of the lower linear parts of these double logarithmic curves give information characterizing the attractor.

In fig 4 (lower insert) the corresponding average slopes v are given as a function of the embedding dimension m It is obvious from these curves that v tends to saturate, for higher m's , at non integer value v=2.23 with this value of v the minimum embedding dimension could be min=3 [13]. So the minimum embedding dimension of the attractor for one to one embedding is 3.

In order to get more precise measurements of the strength of the chaos present in the oscillations we have introduced the Kolmogorov entropy. According to [13] the method described above also gives an estimate of the Kolmogorov entropy, i.e. the correlation integral C (r) scales with the embedding dimension m according to the following relation.

$C(r) \sim e^{-m\tau K_2}$ (5) where, K2 is a lower bound to the Kolomogorov entropy. From the plateau of fig 5 we estimate K2=0.11 bit/s

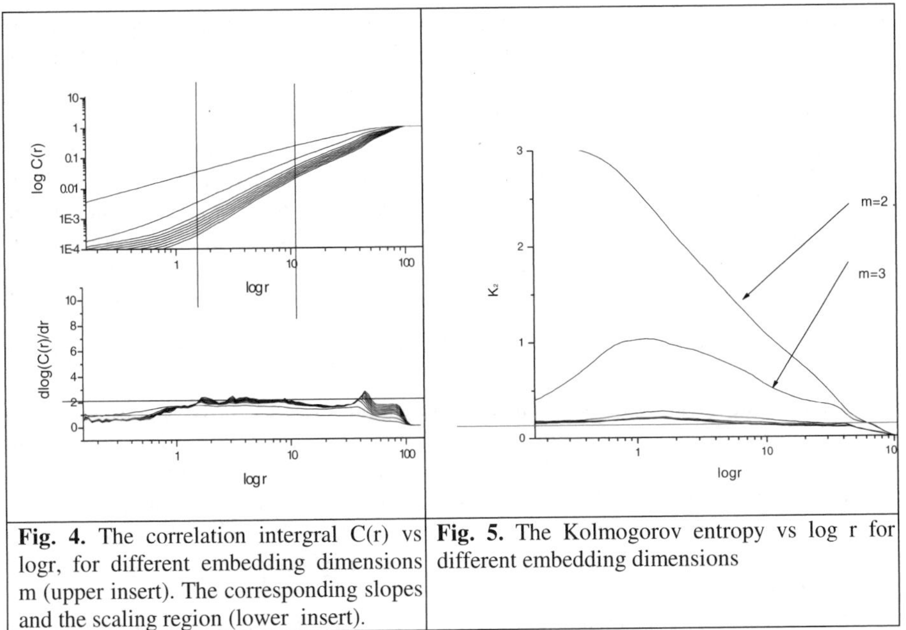

Fig. 4. The correlation intergral C(r) vs logr, for different embedding dimensions m (upper insert). The corresponding slopes and the scaling region (lower insert).

Fig. 5. The Kolmogorov entropy vs log r for different embedding dimensions

Second Stage: The RBF ANN as a Second Order Multistep Predictor Involving an Optimized Nearest Neighbor Methodology

The proposed novel algorithm to enhance non-linear signal analysis prediction is as follows:

1. To predict points V_{i+1}, V_{i+2}, V_{i+3}, ….. V_{i+q} we determine the last known state of the system as represented by vector $X = [V_i, V_{i-\tau}, V_{i-2\tau}, V_{i-(m-1)\tau}]$, where m is the embedding dimension and τ is the time delay.
2. With optimum values of delay time and embedding dimension m we then search the time series to find k similar states that have occurred in the past, where "similarity" is determined by evaluating the distance between vector X and its neighbour vector X' in the m-dimensional state space. So k close states (usually nearest neighbours of X) of the system that have occurred in the past are found, by computing their distances from X.
3. We used a fixed size of nearest neighbours K (calculated for optimizing prediction performance in the training phase) <u>as an initial value for k</u>. if a state $X'= [V'_i, V'_{i-\tau}, V'_{i-2\tau}, \ldots V'_{i-(m-1)\tau}]$ in the neighbourhood of X resulted in the observation V'_{i+1} in the past, then the point V_{i+1} which we want to predict must be somewhere near V'_{i+1}. In the sequel, concerning points V_{i+2}, V_{i+3}, ….. V_{i+q} , using sliding windows of the same length m, we apply recursively the same technique described above. For instance, state $X''= [V'_{i+1}, V'_{i+1-\tau}, V'_{i+1-2\tau}, \ldots V'_{i+1-(m-1)\tau}]$ results in the prediction of V'_{i+2}, which must be somewhere near to the real point V_{i+2} to be predicted, and so on. This is the main concept of nonlinear signal analysis of first order approximation. In order to enhance results we herein propose a novel optimized scheme for selecting parameter k in the nearest neighbour methodology.

4. More specifically, let's consider the above proposed first order approximation strategy resulted in a series of predictions V_{i+1}, V_{i+2}, V_{i+3}, ... V_{i+q} based on signal values $X = [V_i, V_{i-\tau}, V_{i-2\tau}, \ldots V_{i-(m-1)\tau}]$ and so on. At this point we start in reverse order, that is we consider state $Y= [V_{i+q-(m-1)\tau}, \ldots V_{i+q-3\tau}, V_{i+q-2\tau}, V_{i+q-\tau}, \ldots V_{i+q}]$ and by applying an equivalent predictor as above, we attempt to approximate $V_{i+q-(m)\tau}$, that is the previous point defined by Y (which belongs in the known dataset) in the time series. This reverse prediction process is performed for all points $V_{i+q-(m)\tau}$, which belong to the known data set produced considering all forward multistep prediction points V_{i+1}, V_{i+2}, V_{i+3}, ... V_{i+q} with the reverse estimation scheme outlined above. Let's the reverse prediction error for all such $V_{i+q-(m)\tau}$ points be Error_reverse(k) = $\sum_q (V_{i+q-(m)\hat{o}} - V'_{i+q-(m)\hat{o}})^2$ for the specific value of k, i.e the number of nearest neighbours in the above specified nearest neighbour methodology. Starting from initial value K for the nearest neighbour methodology, as explained above, we apply the algorithm of steps 3 and 4 above for values of k=K, K-1, K-2, ..., K-λ, (for λ=4 in our experiments), until we find the minimum Error_reverse(k). Then, we keep this value for k as the optimum value and thus, the optimized nearest neighbour methodology has been completely defined.
5. It is reasonable to calculate $V_{i+1} = (\Sigma q_k V'_k)/ \Sigma q_k$ where q_k the distance between current state X and neighboring state X_k, whereas V'_k the corresponding prediction from X'_k vector (from the training set). The above sum is considered for all k X neighbors, where k has been found from steps 3 and 4 above
6. Our proposition to enhance prediction results is to write down $V_{i+1} = (\Sigma q_k V'_k)/ \Sigma q_k$ + error_V_{i+1}, where $(\Sigma q_k V'_k)/ \Sigma q_k$ is the first order prediction and error_V_{i+1}, is the prediction error to be minimized provided it is calculated properly. Therefore, it is a second order approximation proposal to predict such an error. This error_V_{i+1}, could be calculated through a suitable neural network as an error predictor. This is exactly the main concept of the proposed novel methodology. Different Neural Models could be involved but we herein compare RBFs and Backpropagation error models [18].
7. Suppose err_k the corresponding prediction error measured through the above procedure for each neighboring state X'_k of given current state X above (out of the K optimal neighbours of X defined in steps 3, 4 above). This err_k is known through the training set, since for each X'_k in the training set we can calculate its corresponding K neighbours from the training set, and then, estimate, using step 6 above, the associated err_k. Therefore, for k we construct all K such err_k. Then, we feed these K values as inputs to an RBF neural network of K-L-1 architecture, with L the number of hidden nodes considered to be Gaussian type radial basis functions. This network, trained with the normal RBF algorithm [18], should be able to predict state's X error error_V_{i+1}.
8. The training set needed for step 7 is constructed for each state X of the training set by estimating all corresponding err_k of its K neighbours and its associated error_V_{i+1} , which of course serves as the desired output of the corresponding input pattern.

4 Experimental Study with RLD Circuits in Industrial Processes and with MRS Processes Using Simulated Data

We have conducted an experimental study to evaluate the proposed methodology when applied to forecasting and modeling of signals produced by RLD circuits in industrial processes as well as to complex MRS signals produced in MRS spectroscopy.

Regarding the first series of experiments, we have used a simulated time series from RLD circuit with V1=32V RMS and input frequency f=135 KHz and we predict the voltage V across the resistor. We use locally linear models to predict the one step and the multistep procedures. That is, instead of fitting one complex model with many coefficients to the entire data set, we fit many simple models (low order polynomials) to small portion of the data set depending on the geometry of the local neighborhood of the dynamical system. [17].The general procedure is the following: To predict point Vi+1, we determine the last known state of the system as represented by vector X = [Vi, Vi-τ, Vi-2τ, Vi-(m-1)τ], where m is the embedding dimension and τ is the time delay. So we use as a delay time the value of τ=6 as before.. From previous analysis the correlation dimension for RLD circuit is found v=2.23. With optimum values of delay time and embedding dimension m=3 we then search the time series to find k similar states that have occurred in the past, where "similarity" is determined by evaluating the distance between vector X and its neighbor vector X' in the m-dimensional state space. So k close states (usually nearest neighbors of X) of the system that have occurred in the past are found, by computing their distances from X as explained above.

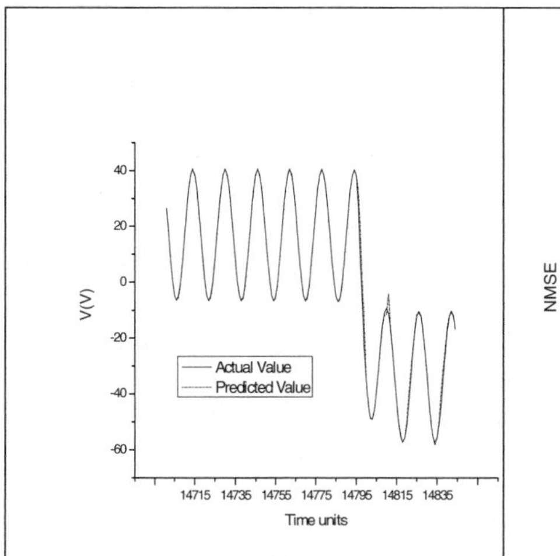

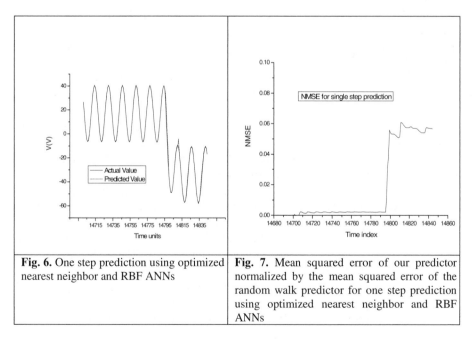

Fig. 6. One step prediction using optimized nearest neighbor and RBF ANNs

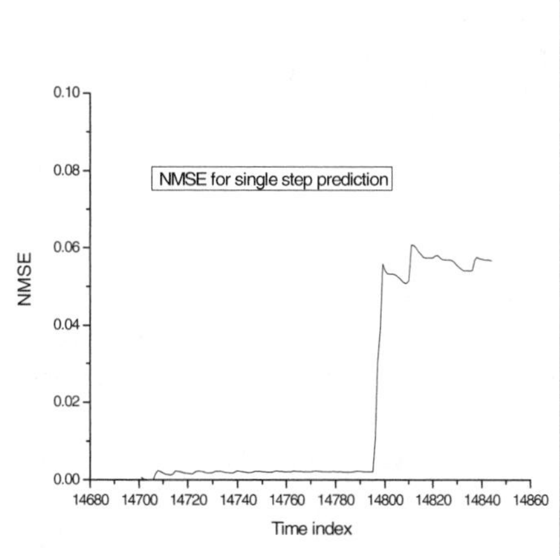

Fig. 7. Mean squared error of our predictor normalized by the mean squared error of the random walk predictor for one step prediction using optimized nearest neighbor and RBF ANNs

The idea is to fit a map which extrapolates X and its k nearest neighbors to determine the next value. If the observable signal was generated by some deterministic map M(Vi,Vi-τ, Vi-2τ, V(i-(m-1)τ) = Vi+τ, that map can be recovered (reconstructed) from the data by looking at its behavior in the neighborhood of X. Using this map, an approximate value of Vi+1 can be obtained. By involving the optimized nearest neighbor methodology outlined above we have found that k= 32 nearest neighbors. Now we can use this map to predict Vi+1 In other words, we make an assumption that M is fairly smooth around X, and so if a state X'= [V'i, V'i-τ, V'i-2τ, V'i-(m-1)τ] in the neighborhood of X resulted in the observation V'i+1 in the past, then the point Vi+1 which we want to predict must be somewhere near V'i+1. [17]. We have employed both the one step and multistep ahead prediction methods. In the one step ahead prediction, after each step in the future is predicted, the actual value is utilized for the next one –step prediction. In contrast, the multistep prediction is based only on the initial k states.

The calculated performance is otherwise known as the Normalized Mean Squared Error (NMSE) is calculated by (5-1),

$$NMSE = MAX\left(\frac{\sum_{i=1}^{NP} (\tilde{V}_i - V_i)^2}{\sum_{i=1}^{NP} (\overline{V}_i - V_i)^2}, \frac{\sum_{i=1}^{NP} (\tilde{V}_i - V_i)^2}{\sum_{i=1}^{NP} (V_{i-1} - V_i)^2} \right) \quad (5\text{-}1),$$

where $\tilde{V}_i$ is the predicted value, Vi, the actual value, $\overline{V}$ is the average actual value, and NP is the range of values in the prediction interval.

From (5-1), it can be seen that NMSE is the mean squared error of our predictor normalized by the mean squared error a random walk predictor. By definition, the minimum value of NMSE is 0. At that value, there is the exact match between the actual and predicted values. The higher NMSE, the worse is our prediction as compared to the trivial predictors. If NMSE is equal to 1, our prediction is as good as the prediction by the trivial predictor. If NMSE is greater than 1, our prediction worsens. With values of τ=6, m=3 we achieved the minimum NMSE.

The second stage RBF ANN is of 32-60-1 architecture. We have, also, employed a back-propagation ANN of 32-60-60-1 architecture for comparison reasons.

We used 14700 data points and predicted the evolution for 889 succeeding dimensionless time steps. The results for the proposed methodology are shown at fig 6 where the one step ahead predicted values are coming from prediction out-of-sample set, where we pretend that we know the data only up to a given point, and we try to predict from there on. The NMSE is shown at fig 7 for the one step prediction.

We use the same procedure as before but with multi-step ahead predictions. The results are shown at Fig - 8 for the proposed methodology. The NMSE is shown at Fig - 9 for the multi step prediction

In comparison, when a first stage only predictor is used without the proposed RBF neural network of stage 2, on average, for the 889 unknown data points we have achieved 9.3% worse performance in the one-step prediction for the NMSE and 8.3% worse performance in the multistep prediction experiments. If, instead of RBF, we use backpropagation ANNs in the second stage of the proposed method, we have achieved 0.8% worse performance in the one-step prediction for the NMSE and 0.5% worse performance in the multistep prediction experiments, with regards to RBF performance. Therefore, the proposed methodology is worth evaluating it further in larger scale experiments for such RLD circuits involved in industrial processes with real data and not only simulated ones as herein presented.

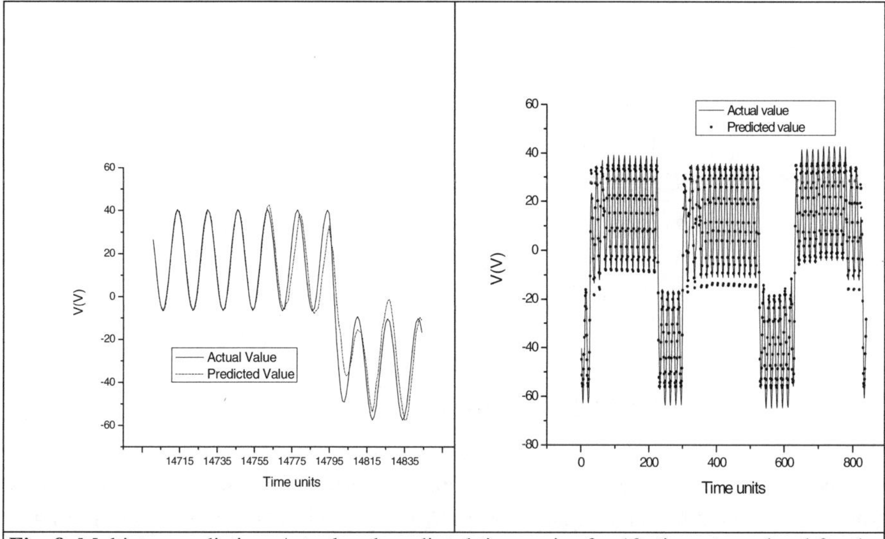

Fig. 8. Multistep prediction, Actual and predicted time series for 10 time steps ahead for the total set of points and the unknown time series (right insert, in detail) using optimized nearest neighbor and RBF ANNs

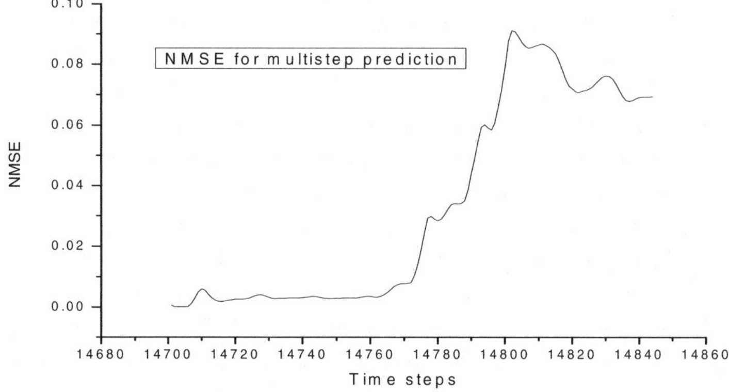

Fig. 9. Mean squared error of our predictor normalized by the mean squared error of the random walk predictor for multistep prediction using optimized nearest neighbor and RBF ANNs

Regarding the series of experiments associated with the application of the proposed methodology to MRS signals we could report the following. We have considered the simulated MRS signal of figure 10 and we applied the same optimized methodology for RLD circuit based chaotic signals forecasting and modeling. This MRS signal is created as a simulation signal, with 11 peaks, derived from a typical in-vivo 31P spectrum measured in the human brain. The signal consists of 11 exponentials.

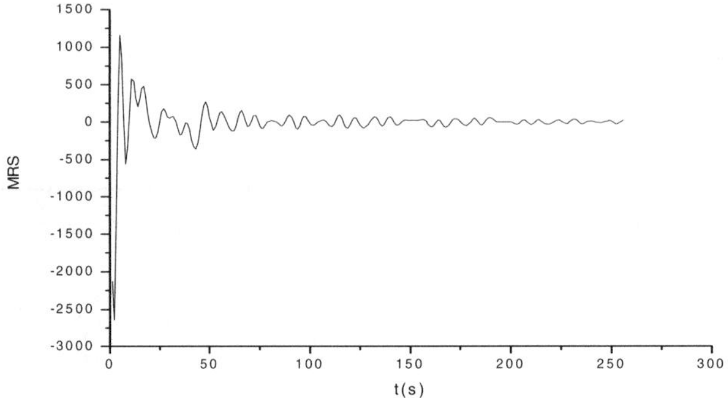

Fig. 10. Time series of MRS with N=256 points

The 31P peaks from brain tissue, phosphomonoesters, inorganic phosphate, phosphodiesters, phosphocreatine, Gamma-ATP, Alpha-ATP and Beta-ATP are present in this simulation signal. The time sampling interval is 0.333 msec. The number of samples in the simulation signal can easily be modified. The question to be resolved through the herein conducted experiments has been to examine whether given these samples of MRS "time series" we could investigate best features for analyzing and facilitating multistep prediction and thus acquiring modeling of the signal as well as whether we could successfully involve the proposed methodology for feature extraction by identification of its nonlinear "deterministic chaos" characteristics and for forecasting via RBF ANNs as defined and optimized above for RLD circuits. Following the steps outlined above, we first show in figure 11, how delay τ is defined by the first minimum of the mutual information to be in this case τ =2 time steps. We also, show that m=4, as derived from the same figure 11 below.

Given the above data and following steps 1-7 above, with m=4 and τ = 2, we have achieved an NMSE of 0.26 which is rather promising, despite the very few time series points. In our simulations we have used the 200 points out of 256 as known and the rest 56 as unknown. The above result for NMSE is considered for a 56 points multi-step prediction, as outlined previously. The average result for NMSE, when one step-ahead prediction is considered, has been found equal to 0.11 in our simulations. Of course further experimentation is needed but these results are rather promising in modelling MRS signals even though only as preliminary could be considered.

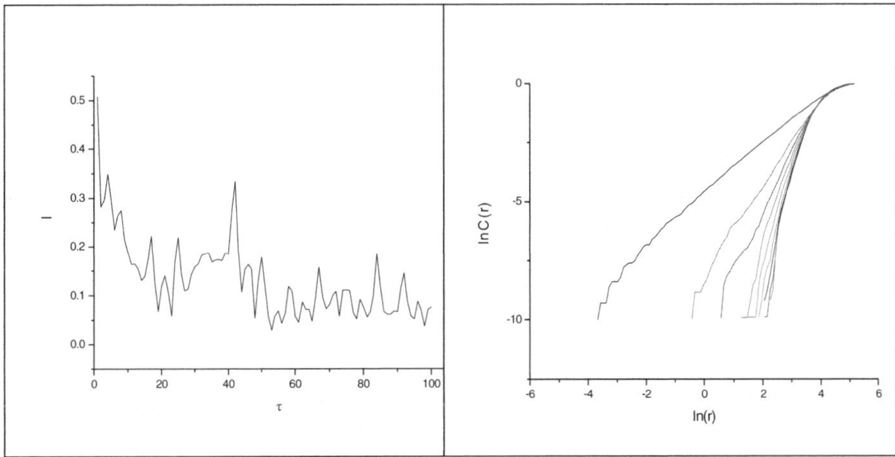

Fig. 11. Mutual Information I vs time delay τ for N=256 points (left), and the correlation integral, lnC(r) vs lnr, for different embedding dimensions m, for MRS with N=256 points (right)

5 Conclusions and Future Trends

We have proposed a novel two-stage time series prediction scheme based on established nonlinear signal analysis methods and a novel error prediction RBF ANN as well as a novel optimized nearest neighbor methodology. This scheme has been shown to be suitable for modeling signals produced in industrial processes and in MRS spectroscopy processes. Applying the proposed methodology in the analysis of time series data produced by a simple chaotic RLD circuit involved in industrial processes, we found that the strange attractor that governs the phenomenon is a Lorenz type attractor with a correlation dimension v=2.23 stretching and folding in a 3 dimension phase space. We have, also, found that a similar attractor of a 4 dimension phase space exists for the simulated MRS signal presented above. This is also evident from the one step ahead and multistep successful predictions with the use of the corresponding strange attractor invariants as input parameters, the efficient RBF ANN model introduced in the second stage of the proposed predictor as well as with the use of the optimized nearest neighbor above described approach.

We believe that for a detailed understanding of chaos in the RLD circuits as well as in the MRS processes these results must be combined with the reverse-recovery effect and all of its nonlinearities. The proposed prediction methodology might be applied successfully in other chaotic time series too involved in many other industrial or biomedical processes, since it is quite general. This is, also, a future goal for the authors. However, the major future goal of the authors is to investigate how such results could be exploited in improving quantification of complex signals as it is the case in MRS spectroscopy, a task of paramount importance for clinical analysis of MRS signals.

References

[1] Lonngren, K.E.: Notes to accompany a student laboratory experiment on chaos. IEEE Transactions on Education 34(1) (February 1991)
[2] Matsumato, T., Chua, L., Tanaka, S.: Simplest Chaotic Nonautonomous Circuit. Phys. Rev. A 30, 1155–1157 (1984)
[3] Azzouz, A., Hasler, M.: Orbits of the R-L-Diode Circuit. IEEE Transaction on Circuits and Systems 37, 1330–1339 (1990)
[4] Aissi, C.: Introducing chaotic circuits in an undergraduate electronic course. In: Proceedings of the 2002 ASEE Gulf-Southwest Annual Conference, The University of Louisiana at La-fayette, March 20-22, American Society for Engineering Education (2002); Copyright © 2002
[5] de Moraes, R.M., Anlage, S.M.: Phys. Rev. E. 68, 26201 (2003)
[6] Hanias, M.P., Giannaris, G., Spyridakis, A., Rigas, A.: Time series Analysis in chaotic diode resonator circuit. Chaos Solitons & fractals 27(#2), 569–573 (2006)
[7] Grassberger, P., Procaccia, I.: Phys. Rev Lett. 50, 346–349 (1983)
[8] Grassberger, P., Procaccia, I.: Physica D 9, 189 (1983)
[9] Hanias, M.P., Karras, D.A.: On efficient multistep non-linear time series prediction in chaotic diode resonator circuits by optimizing the combination of non-linear time series analysis and neural networks. Engineering Applications of Artificial Intelligence 22(1), 32–39 (2009)
[10] Mozdy, E., Newell, T.C., Alsing, P.M., Kovanis, V., Gavrielides, A.: Synchroniza-tion and control in a unidirectionally coupled array of chaotic diode resonators. Physical Review E 51(6), 5371–5376 (1995)
[11] Abarbanel, H.D.I.: Analysis of Observed Chaotic Data. Springer, New York (1996)
[12] Takens, F.: Lecture Notes in Mathematics, vol. 898 (1981)
[13] Kantz, H., Schreiber, T.: Nonlinear Time Series Analysis. Cambridge University Press, Cambridge (1997)
[14] Aasen, T., Kugiumtzis, D., Nordahl, S.H.G.: Computers and Biomedical Research 30, 95-116 (1997)
[15] Fraser, A.M., Swinney, H.L.: Phys. Rev. A 33, 1134 (1986)
[16] Fraser, A.M.: IEEE Transaction of Information Theory 35, 245 (1989)
[17] Kononov, E.: Virtual Recurrence Analysis, Version 4.9 (2006), Email: eugenek@ix.net.com.com
[18] Haykin, S.: Neural Networks, a comprehensive foundation, 2nd edn. Prentice Hall, Englewood Cliffs (1999)

A Constrained Genetic Algorithm with Adaptively Defined Fitness Function in MRS Quantification

G.A. Papakostas[1], D.A. Karras[2], B.G. Mertzios[1], D. Graveron-Demilly[3], and D.van Ormondt[4]

[1] Department of Electrical and Computer Engineering Democritus University of Thrace (DUTH) Xanthi, Greece
gpapakos@ee.duth.gr
[2] Chalkis Institute of Technology, Automation Dept, Psachna, Evoia, 34400, Greece
dakarras@ieee.org, dakarras@teihal.gr, dakarras@usa.net
[3] Laboratoire Creatis-LRMN , CNRS UMR 5220, INSERM U630, Université Claude Bernard Lyon1, Villeurbanne, France
[4] Applied Physics, Lorentzweg 1, 2628CJ, TUDelft
D.vanOrmondt@tudelft.nl

Abstract. MRS Signal quantification is a rather involved procedure and has attracted the interest of the medical engineering community, regarding the development of computationally efficient methodologies. Significant contributions based on Computational Intelligence tools, such as Neural Networks (NNs), demonstrated a good performance but not without drawbacks already discussed by the authors. On the other hand preliminary application of Genetic Algorithms (GA) has already been reported in the literature by the authors regarding the peak detection problem encountered in MRS quantification using the Voigt line shape model. This paper investigates a novel constrained genetic algorithm involving a generic and adaptively defined fitness function which extends the simple genetic algorithm methodology in case of noisy signals. The applicability of this new algorithm is scrutinized through experimentation in artificial MRS signals interleaved with noise, regarding its signal fitting capabilities. Although extensive experiments with real world MRS signals are necessary, the herein shown performance illustrates the method's potential to be established as a generic MRS metabolites quantification procedure.

Keywords: MRSI, metabolites quantification, genetic algorithms.

1 Introduction

There has been passed a long time since the introduction of the Magnetic Resonance Imaging (MRSI) in medical diagnostics. The main advantage of this diagnostic method is that it is non-invasive and gives anatomic and morphology information about a human's body part.

Recently, an opportunity to measure the chemical information of the human tissues is given by a novel methodology called Magnetic Resonance Spectroscopy Imaging (MRSI). This technique extracts a specific spectrum having a number of peaks each

T.-h. Kim et al. (Eds.): GDC/CA 2010, CCIS 121, pp. 257–268, 2010.

one corresponding to a specific metabolite. The area under a peak corresponds to the concentration of this metabolite, which can be measured by applying a procedure called quantification.

The MRSI metabolites quantification procedure has attracted the scientific interest of the engineering community, regarding the development of noninvasive and computational efficient methodologies. Significant contributions based on Artificial Intelligence (AI) tools, such as Neural Networks (NNs), with accurate results have been presented lately [1-6]. However, the usage of NNs to approximate the metabolites of a retrieved spectrum has the drawback of constructing many different neural models to address the possible characteristics of the spectrum in process.

The paper is organized by presenting the proposed quantification methodology in section 2. Section 3 draws a detailed experimental study on artificial data and section IV summarizes the main conclusions and future research directions are stated.

2 Proposed Methodology

The long time training procedures, the need for constructing many neural models to address possible characteristics of the peaks in process are some drawbacks, which make the usage of Neural Networks as metabolites quantifiers inefficient.

In addition, a main issue needed to be encountered is the case of overlapping peaks existing in the spectrum, which only partially and with difficulty might be addressed by the NNs approximators.

Taking into account that each peak can be approximated by the Voigt line shape [6], consisting of a Lorentzian and a Gaussian part, the process of peak detection in such spectrums, constitutes a typical optimization problem. This is exactly our view compared to that of the state of the art.

More specifically, the metabolites peaks can be approximated by the Voigt line shape approach based on the following definition.

$$F(u) = \mu L(u) + (1-\mu) G(u) \tag{1}$$

where

$$L(u) = \frac{b}{1 + \left(\frac{u - u_0}{h} \right)^2} \tag{2}$$

is the *Lorentzian peak* and

$$G(u) = b e^{-\ln(2)\left(\frac{u-u_0}{h}\right)^2} \tag{3}$$

the *Gaussian peak*.

In the above (1)-(3) formulas, b is the amplitude, h the linewidth, μ the proportion of Lorentzian and u_0 the central frequency.

Once the parameters b, h, μ and u_0 are found the concentration of the metabolites, which is proportional to the area of the peak, can be calculated using the following equations.

$$A(l) = bh\pi \tag{4}$$

$$A(g) = bh\sqrt{\frac{\pi}{\ln(2)}} \tag{5}$$

$$Area\ of\ peak = \mu A(l) + (1-\mu) A(g) \tag{6}$$

where A(l), A(g) are the areas of Lorentzian and Gaussian peak respectively.

Based on the previous assumptions the quantification problem can be more naturally considered as a typical global optimization problem. For this purpose, a simple Genetic Algorithm (GA) is proposed to be used, in order to find the appropriate set of Voigt models that best approximate the metabolites spectrum under quantification.

This optimization problem is defined as: "*find the parameters amplitude (b), line width (h), proportion of Lorentzian (μ), central frequency (u₀) and the number of peaks that best approximate the spectrum in process in terms of an error objective function (7)*".

In contrast to linear model methods traditionally used SVD etc. – as well as in contrast to ANN problem solving a function approximation approach, the above optimization problem is resolved by using the simple genetic algorithm (GA) only as a starting point, while many more options are available with evolutionary strategies.

In the herein proposed model, preliminarily proposed in [7], the chromosome structure is defined as

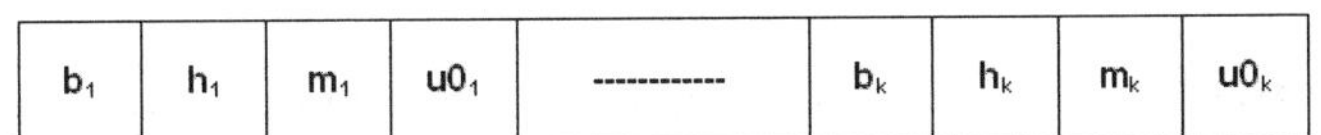

Fig. 1. Chromosome structure

where, b_i is the amplitude , h_i the linewidth , k the maximum number of curves , m_i the proportion of Lorentzian and u_{0i} the central frequency, of the ith chromosome.

This is actually the simple genetic algorithm approach which shows good results in case of overlapping peaks but not in noisy signals as it will be discussed in the experimental study.

In order to address the issue of metabolite quantification, especially in noisy and artificial MRS signals case a more sophisticated genetic algorithm approach will be herein investigated.

First, the MRS signal is most commonly defined as a model function using a sum of exponentially damped sinusoids,

$$MRS\_Signal = \sum_{k=1}^{K} a_k e^{j\phi_k} e^{(-d_k + j2\pi f_k)t}$$

where,

a_k : the amplitude , **φ_k :** the phase
d_k : the damping factor and **f_k** : the frequency of the kth exponential sinusoid " metabolite"

Based on the previous assumptions the quantification problem can be more naturally considered as a typical global optimization problem, defined as:

"Find the parameters amplitudes , damping factors of the metabolites based on the prior knowledge that frequencies and phases are within certain ranges, that best approximate the spectrum in process in terms of an error objective function (Squared Error)".

In order to solve it we herein propose a constrained genetic algorithm approach as follows.

The chromosome structure is modified, concerning the previously defined simple genetic algorithm approach in figure 1, by the following structure

a_1	d_1	φ_1	f_1	-----------	a_k	d_k	φ_k	f_k	A	B

where

a_k : the amplitude , **φ_k :** the phase
d_k : the damping factor , **f_k** : the frequency of the kth exponential sinusoid " metabolite" while **k :** the number. of "metabolites" in the MRS signal

A and B are parameters of the adaptively defined generic fitness function, to be optimally defined in order to incorporate prior knowledge in the MRS signal fitting process.

The Objective Function (the Fitness function) for the simple genetic algorithm problem previously presented corresponds to the fitting error for a specific number of samples and is defined as

$$Error = \sum_{i=1}^{n} \left(desired\left(i\right) - estimated\left(i\right)\right)^2 \tag{7}$$

In the case now of the constrained genetic algorithm approach herein adopted, the fitness function is modified as follows

$$Error = \sum_{i=0}^{N} (desired - actual)^2 + (\frac{1}{A}) \sum_{j=1}^{K} (f_k - f_{0k})^2 + (\frac{1}{B}) \sum_{j=1}^{K} (\Phi_k - \Phi_{0k})^2$$

where,

f_{0k} and φ_{0k} are reference frequency and phase for the k_{th} metabolite, since for each real metabolite in MRS they are known in principle. On the other hand, amplitudes and damping factors of metabolites are considered unknown. Unknown are the parameters A and B and should be defined by the GA optimization process. The starting values for A, B are near zero in order for the GA process to firstly satisfy the constraints coming from our prior knowledge for the MRS metabolites.

$$\textit{Constraints are}$$

$$minimize\{\sum_{i=0}^{N}\sum_{j=1}^{K}(f_k - f_{0k})^2\}\ and\ minimize\ \{\sum_{j=1}^{K}(\Phi_k - \Phi_{0k})^2\}$$

The main benefits of the introduced methodology are focused on the accurate quantification of the metabolites concentration through the peaks identification in the artificial MRS signals involved in the experimental study of this paper. We also, compare this new methodology with another preliminary one that considers A and B as user defined parameters and not unknown ones to be estimated by the GA global optimization process.

3 Experimental Results

The proposed method has been tested in artificial data and the simulation results are presented in this section. An example of these experiments is illustrated in the next figures based on synthetic MRS data.

For the sake of the experiments a simple genetic algorithm is used with the following settings of Table 1.

Table 1. Genetic Algorithm's Settings

Parameter	Value
Population Size	100
Maximum Generations	200
Crossover Probability	0.8
Mutation Probability	0.01
Selection Method	Stochastic Universal Approximation (SUS)
Elitism	YES, 1 chromosomes
Crossover Points	2 points

Figure 2, shows a spectrum derived by the superposition of two separate peaks models of Voigt type (1)-(3). The generation parameters of each peak is ($b=1$, $h=7$, $\mu=0.3$, $u_0=30$) and ($b=0.7$, $h=10$, $\mu=0.5$, $u_0=60$) respectively.

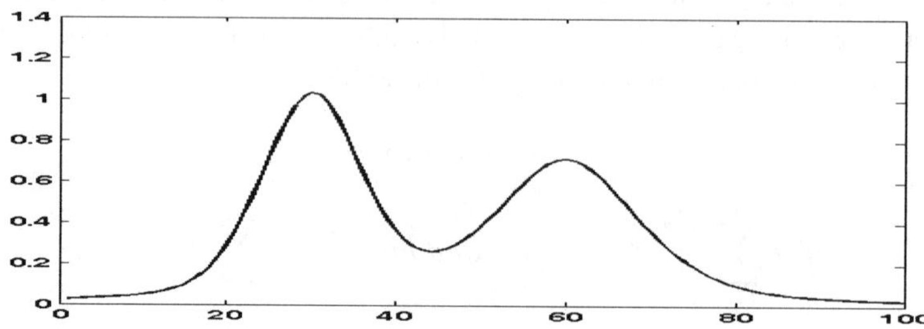

Fig. 2. Portion of a synthetic MRS spectrum with 2 peaks (metabolites). Axes x, y are in Hz and magnitude for the synthetic signal respectively.

The optimization problem of finding the parameters of the peaks that constitute the spectrum depicted in Fig.2, is an easy task for the simple genetic algorithm. In conjunction to the parameters of the possible Voigt models belong to the spectrum, the proposed technique also finds the total number of the spectrum's peaks components.

The performance of the introduced fitting technique for the case of the spectrum of Fig.1 is presented in the following Fig.3 and Fig.4, approximated with 1 and 2 Voigt models respectively.

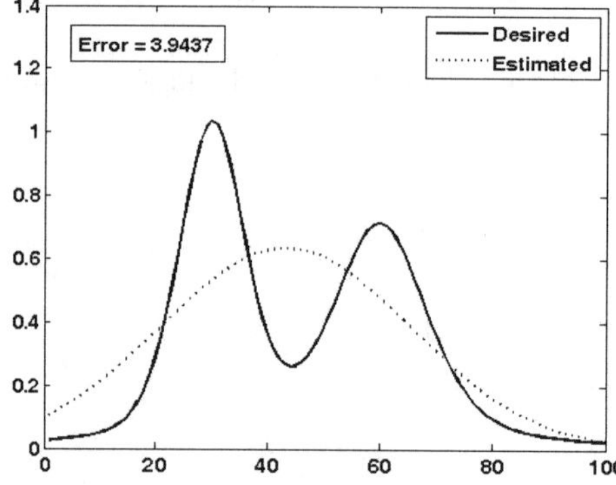

Fig. 3. Approximation with 1 Voigt model. Axes x, y are in Hz and magnitude for a synthetic signal respectively.

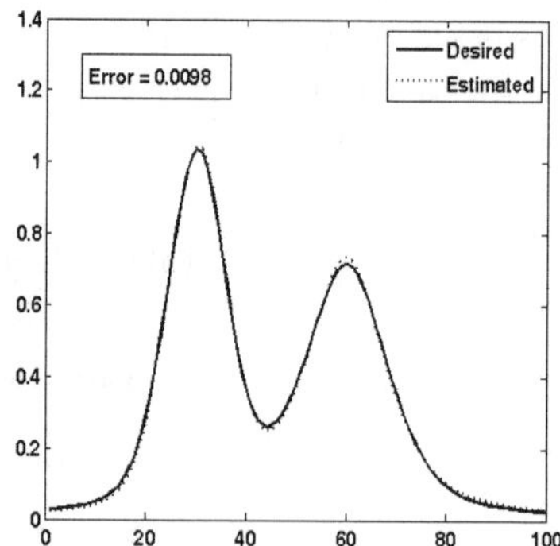

Fig. 4. Approximation with 2 Voigt model. Axes x, y are in Hz and magnitude for the synthetic signal respectively.

The corresponding fitting error of approximating the spectrum with several number of Voigt models is plotted in Fig.5.

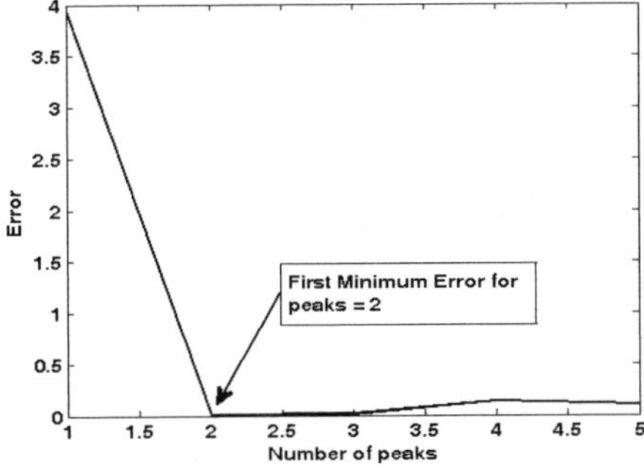

Fig. 5. Error performance for different number of Voigt models

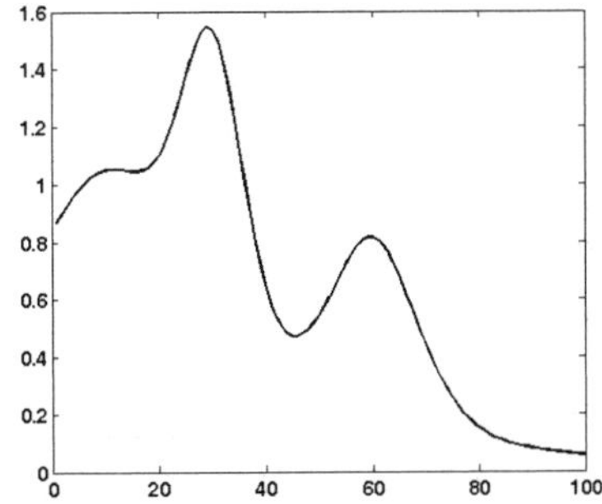

Fig. 6. Portion of a synthetic MRS spectrum with 3 peaks (metabolites). Axes x, y are in Hz and magnitude for the synthetic signal respectively.

By adding another peak with parameters (b=1, h=20, μ=0.7, u_0=10) in the spectrum of Fig.2, a more complicated spectrum with highly overlapped peaks is constructed. The resulted spectrum and the corresponding approximations are presented in the following figures.

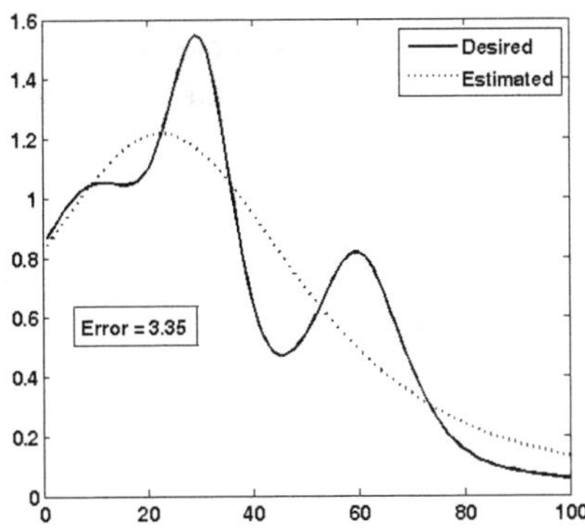

Fig. 7. Approximation with 1 Voigt model. Axes x, y are in Hz and magnitude for the synthetic signal respectively.

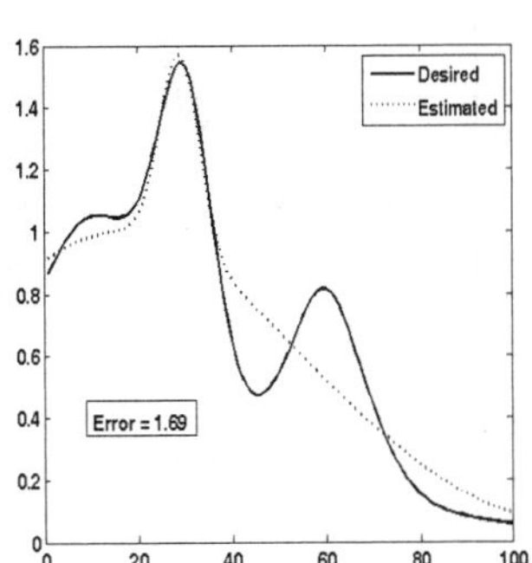

Fig. 8. Approximation with 1 Voigt model. Axes x, y are in Hz and magnitude for the synthetic signal respectively.

From the above figures it is obvious that when the number of Voigt model tends to the real number of including peaks the fitting error is decreased. The corresponding fitting error for the case of the spectrum with 3 peaks varies as follows.

It will be of significant importance to study the performance of the proposed technique under difficult noisy conditions. For this reason a uniform noise with parameters (mean,std) equal to (0,0.01) is added on the spectrum of Fig.6 and the methodology is repeated. The resulted noisy spectrum has the following form.

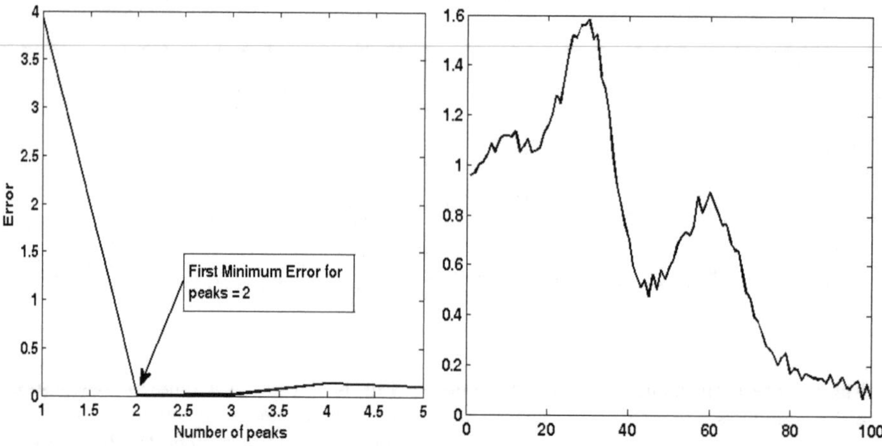

Fig. 9. Error performance for different number of Voigt models

Fig. 10. Portion of a noisy synthetic MRS spectrum with 3 peaks (metabolites). Axes x, y are in Hz and magnitude for the synthetic signal.

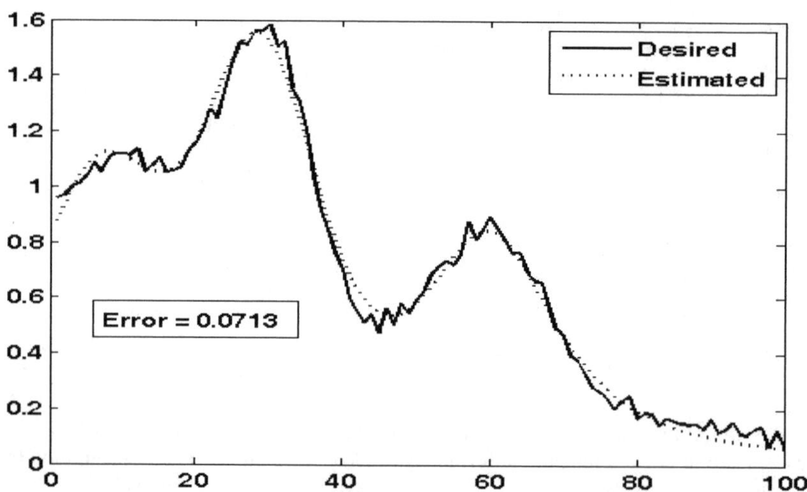

Fig. 11. Approximation with 3 peaks. Axes x, y are in Hz and magnitude for the synthetic signal respectively.

The number of identified peaks is 3 and their parameters (*b*, *h*, μ, *u0*), are presented in Table 2. In this table, the original peak's parameters are illustrated in bold face in order to distinguish them from the estimated ones.

Table 2. Identification Results

Peak Number	b	h	μ	u0
1st Peak	0.63	8.85	0.41	60.38
	0.7	**10**	**0.5**	**60**
2nd Peak	0.8396	6.2609	0.05	29.99
	1	**7**	**0.3**	**30**
3rd Peak	1.10	25.76	0.99	11.20
	1	**20**	**0.7**	**10**

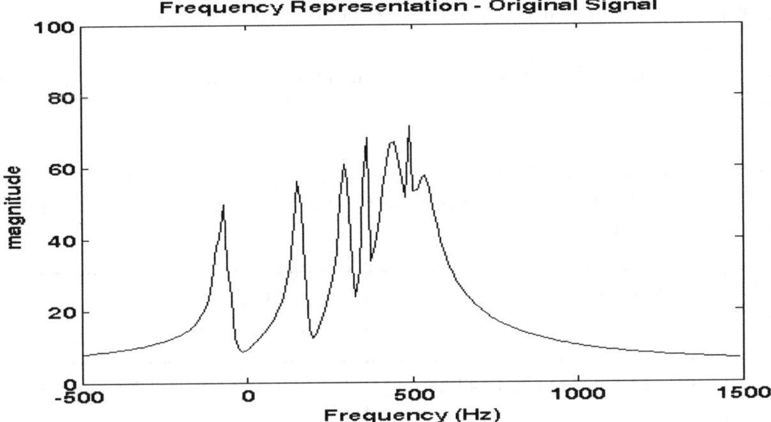

Fig. 12. Original Artificial MRS Test signal for investigating the constrained genetic algorithm

Table 3. Constrained Genetic Algorithm's Settings

Population Size	**100**
Variables Range	**[0,2000]**
Maximum Generations	**1000**
Elitism	**YES, 2 chromosomes**
Crossover Points	**2 points**
Crossover Probability	**0.8**
Mutation Probability	**0.001**
Selection Method	**Stochastic Universal Approximation (SUS)**
Parameters A,B in the fitness function	***METHOD 1) User defined (A=1..10, B=1..10)) constants*** ***METHOD 2 - THE PROPOSED) Adaptively defined by the GA process***

While the performance of the methodology in noisy spectrums seems to be marginal, this study can lead to an improvement of the way the fitting error is measured. However, the previous analysis brings on a new issue in metabolites spectrum fitting which deals with the existence of different parameters set (*b, h, μ, u0*) giving near the same Voigt model.

The previous results show that the simple genetic algorithm approach provides promising results in artificial signals. However, it presents difficulties even in artificial MRS signals and has several limitations. To this end the constrained genetic algorithm has been proposed in this paper and the results of its application in the synthetic MRS data are as follows.

The original test signal used in our experiments, which has also been induced with different noisy levels, is

The application of the constrained genetic algorithm has involved the following parameters.

Table 4. Some Results Using the Constrained Genetic Algorithm (Original Value /Method 1 for A,B Definition (0%-Noise) (10%-Noise)//Method 2-The Proposed one for Adaptively Defining Parameters A,B(0%-Noise) (10%-Noise)

Peak No	d_k (Hz)	a_k (a.u.)
1	50 /(52.6)(39.1)// (52.1)(43.2)	75 /(82.5)(65.9)// //(77.5)(69.8)
2	50 /(46.3)(49)//(51.2)(49.2)	150/(135.7)(143.8)// (145.6)(144.5)
3	50/ (53.9)(65.6)//(51.7)(61.8)	75 /(84.3)(91.2)//(80.3)(83.2)
4	50 /(51.0)(50.6) //(51.0)(50.8)	150/(153.6)(149.6) //(151.8)(149.7)
5	50 /(49.5)(51.4)// (49.5)(50.6)	150/(147.6)(151.3)//(148.5)(151.5)
6	50 /(50.8)(55.7) //(50.5)(53.9)	150/(152.1)(163.1) //(152.1)(158.7)
7	50 /(50)(47.3) //(50)(48.7)	150/(149.6)(143.9)//(149.7)(144.3)
8	25 /(25.3)(26.4)//(25.2)(25.9)	150/(151.3)(156.2) //(149.8)(153.7)
9	285.7 (283.8)(273)//(284.2)(280)	1400/(1392.4)(1339.1)//(1395.1) (1364.4)
10	25/(26.1)(22.8)//(25.7)(23.6)	60/(62.4)(57.4)//(61.9)(58.3)
11	200/(198.7)(212.3)//(199.1)(207.6)	500/(498.4)(539.5) //(498.6)(515.5)

Applying the proposed constrained genetic algorithm we have obtained as a sample the following initial results.

These results are quite promising and show the potential of the method. Especially, they show that the proposed scheme for adaptively defining the parameters A and B, in the proposed fitness function model, provides superior performance with respect to a simple scheme considering them as user defined constants.

4 Conclusion

A novel methodology for the MRS signals quantification and modeling has been presented in this paper based on a novel constrained genetic algorithm using an adaptive scheme for defining a suitable fitness function. This work extends the results of peak identification got by the simple genetic algorithm [7]. By formulating the quantification procedure to a typical optimization problem, which can be dealt with using evolutionary algorithms such as constrained genetic algorithms, an accurate solution can be obtained, especially if the proposed adaptive scheme for defining the selected fitness function is adopted.

Extensive experiments on artificial MRS data distorted, also, by different noise levels show the advantages of the introduced scheme, especially in difficult cases with overlapped peaks. Additional experiments with real data need to be arranged, in order to investigate the method's behavior under real conditions and finally to establish it as a generic quantification procedure.

However, the most important prospect might emerge by defining how to combine the two genetic algorithms herein involved in a sophisticated scheme since this will lead to an accurate estimation of metabolite concentration and not only to peak detection and modeling/quantification of MRS signals.

Acknowledgment

This work has been partially supported by the European Project FAST--Advanced Signal Processing for Ultra Fast Magnetic Resonance Spectroscopic Imaging, and Training, Marie Curie Research Training Network, MRTN-CT-2006-035801.

References

[1] Eason, G., Mierisova, S., Ala-Korpela, M.: MR spectroscopy quantification: a review of frequency domain methods. NMR in Biomedicine 14(4), 247–259 (2001)

[2] Axelson, D., Bakken, I.J., Gribbestad, I.S., Ehrnholm, B., Nilsen, G., Aasly, J.: Applications of neural network analyses to in vivo 1H magnetic resonance spectroscopy of Parkinson disease patients. J. Magn. Reson. Imaging 16(1), 13–20 (2002)

[3] Bakken, I.J., Axelson, D., Kvistad, K.A., Brodtkorb, E., Muller, B., Aasly, J., Gribbestad, I.S.: Applications of neural network analyses to in vivo 1H magnetic resonance spectroscopy of epilepsy patients. Epilepsy Research 35(3), 245–252 (1999)

[4] Kaartinen, J., Mierisova, S., Oja, J.M., Usenius, J.P., Kauppinen, R.A., Hiltunen, Y.: Automated quantification of human brain metabolites by artificial neural network analysis from in vivo single-voxel 1H NMR spectra, vol. 134(1), pp. 176–179 (1998)

[5] Hiltunen, Y., Kaartinen, J., Pulkkinen, J., Hakkinen, A.M., Lundbom, N., Kauppinen, R.A.: Quantification of human brain metabolites from in vivo 1H NMR magnitude spectra using automated artificial neural network analysis. J. Magn. Reson. 154(1), 1–5 (2002)
[6] Bhat, H., Sajja, B.R., Narayana, P.A.: Fast quantification of proton magnetic resonance spectroscopic imaging with artificial neural networks. J. Magn. Reson. 183(1), 110–122 (2006)
[7] Papakostas, G.A., Karras, D.A., Mertzios, B.G.: Dealing with peaks overlapping issue in quantifying metabolites in MRSI. In: International Workshop on Imaging Systems and Techniques, IST 2009, pp. 58–62. IEEE, Los Alamitos (2009), doi: 10.1109/IST.2009.5071602

A Neural-Network Clustering-Based Algorithm for Privacy Preserving Data Mining

S. Tsiafoulis[1], V.C. Zorkadis[1], and D.A. Karras[2]

[1] Data Protection Authority, 1-3 Kifisias Av. 11523 Athens, Greece
zorkadis@dpa.gr
[2] Chalkis Institute of Technology, Automation Dept., Psachna, Evoia, Hellas (Greece) P.C. 34400
dakarras@ieee.org, dakarras@teihal.gr

Abstract. The increasing use of fast and efficient data mining algorithms in huge collections of personal data, facilitated through the exponential growth of technology, in particular in the field of electronic data storage media and processing power, has raised serious ethical, philosophical and legal issues related to privacy protection. To cope with these concerns, several privacy preserving methodologies have been proposed, classified in two categories, methodologies that aim at protecting the sensitive data and those that aim at protecting the mining results. In our work, we focus on sensitive data protection and compare existing techniques according to their anonymity degree achieved, the information loss suffered and their performance characteristics. The ℓ-diversity principle is combined with k-anonymity concepts, so that background information can not be exploited to successfully attack the privacy of data subjects data refer to. Based on Kohonen Self Organizing Feature Maps (SOMs), we firstly organize data sets in subspaces according to their information theoretical distance to each other, then create the most relevant classes paying special attention to rare sensitive attribute values, and finally generalize attribute values to the minimum extend required so that both the data disclosure probability and the information loss are possibly kept negligible. Furthermore, we propose information theoretical measures for assessing the anonymity degree achieved and empirical tests to demonstrate it.

Keywords: Privacy Enhancing Technologies, SOM, k-anonymity, l-diversity.

1 Introduction

Data contained in databases may be personal data, i.e. information that directly or indirectly identifies an individual, as for instance an address and date of birth that can be linked with public available datasets and background knowledge and reveal the identity of an individual. Such a set of attributes is called *Quasi-identifier* (QI) set. Data-mining a database can lead to the disclosure of personal data and the identification of data subjects, i.e. persons the data refer to. But on the other hand exploiting such databases may offer many benefits to the community and support the policy and

T.-h. Kim et al. (Eds.): GDC/CA 2010, CCIS 121, pp. 269–276, 2010.

action plan development process, as for instance in case of pandemic. To address these at first sight contradicting requirements, privacy preserving data mining techniques have been proposed [1, 2, 3, 4, 5, 6, 10].

Existing privacy-preserving data mining algorithms can be classified into two categories: algorithms that protect the sensitive data itself in the mining process, and those that protect the sensitive data mining results [1]. The most popular algorithms in the data mining research community address *k-anonymity* and *ℓ-diversity*. They belong to the first category and apply generalization and suppression methods to the original datasets in order to preserve the anonymity of individuals or entities data refer to.

K-anonymity requires each tuple in the published table to be indistinguishable from at least k-1 other tuples [2]. Tuples with the same or close *QI* values form an *equivalence class*. However, k-anonymity cannot protect against homogeneity and background knowledge attacks [3]. To address these shortcomings, the l-diversity principle was proposed [3], which requires that different values of the sensitive attributes are *well represented* in each *equivalence class*, thus preventing an attacker from guessing the sensitive attribute value for a QI set with probability greater than $1/\ell$ *Distinct ℓ-diversity* requires that for each equivalence class e_i, there are at least ℓ distinct values in $e_i[S]$, where $e_i[S]$ is the multi-set of e_i 's *sensitive attribute* values [2, 3].

In table 1, clustering-, partition- and hierarchy–based algorithms for the implementation of k-anonymity and l-diversity are categorized with respect to their characteristics, attribute type, searching method and analysis approach used. Due to structural similarities of k-anonymity and *ℓ-diversity algorithms*, most of the k-anonymity algorithms can be transformed easily to algorithms for ℓ-diversity [3].

In our work, we use the Adult data set provided by Irvine machine learning repository [4], so that our research results can be compared with those presented in the literature (see section 2), since this database has been used widely in classification experiments. It consists of 30162 complete records, with 6 numerical and 8 categorical attributes.

This paper is organized as follows. Next section is devoted to existing k-anonymity- and l-diversity algorithms. In section 3, we propose a new algorithm to the k-anonymity and l-diversity problem, and in section 4, we introduce measures and tests to evaluate the performance of the proposed algorithm and compare it with the performance of existing algorithms. Finally, we conclude the paper.

2 k-Anonymity and l-Diversity Algorithms

In [5] two greedy algorithms are proposed. The first is clustering-based and conducts a bottom-up search, while the second one is partition-based and works top-down. The selection criterion for an attribute to be merged in an equivalence class is the *weight certainty penalty* (*NCP*). By using this criterion, information loss and record importance are taken into account. In bottom-up search, at the beginning of the anonymization process, each tuple is being treated as an individual group. Each group whose population is less than *k* is being merged with another group such that the combined group has the smallest *NCP*. It iterates until every group has at least *k* tuples. In the end of the process, each group that has more than 2k tuples is being split into such that each group has at least k tuples. In the top-down approach, in the beginning, the two tuples that cause the highest *NCP* in case they are merged in the same group, are being selected and form the two initial groups *Gu*, *Gv*. Then, the other tuples are being assigned to these groups randomly. The assignment of a tuple *w* depends on the *NCP(Gu,w)* and *NCP*(*Gv*,*w*), where *Gu*, *Gv* are the groups formed so far. Tuple *w* is assigned to the group that leads to a lower NCP. The procedure of the partitioning is being conducted recursively while the group has *k* or more tuples. If one group *G* has less than *k* tuples then a group with population greater than *2k-*/*G'*/is being searched. Then from the group that has been formed, *G'*= (*k*-|*G*|) tuples are being selected such that *NCP* (*G*U*G'*) is minimized.

In [6], the algorithm starts with a fully generalized dataset, one in which every tuple is identical to every other, and systematically specializes the dataset into one that is minimally k-anonymous. This algorithm uses a tree search strategy to find the optimal solution. An optimal solution is an optimal generalization with the least information loss and the highest privacy preserving. Considering that this technique can involve scanning and sorting the entire dataset, it may produce an enormous solution space. So it uses *pruning strategies* to reduce the solution space and a dynamic search rearrangement tree search algorithm named OPUS [7]. Opus extends a systematic set-enumeration-search strategy [8] with dynamic tree rearrangement and cost – based pruning for solving optimization problems. A node can be pruned only when the algorithm can determine that none of the descendants or the node itself could be optimal solution. For this determination a lower bound cost must be computed for any node within the subtree rooted beneath it. If this lower bound exceeds the current best cost, the node is pruned. To compute the lower bound cost it uses the *discernibility metric and classification metric [6]*.

[9] proposes a genetic algorithm to find the optimal anonymization. Every possible anonymization is being coded and represented with a chromosome. Then, based on the Genitor algorithm [11], is trying to find the optimal solution, that is the chromosome with the best evaluation value. For the evaluation it uses the criterion of the *weighted certainty penalty* [5]. Also, the generalizations must be consistent with the restrictions set out in *valid generalization* notion that was mentioned in section 3.2.a.

BSGi is an algorithm for the implementation of *ℓ-diversity* anonymization. This algorithm was influenced from *Anatomy* [12], so firstly "bucketize" the tuples according to their SA values. Then recursively "select" ℓ tuples from the ℓ biggest buckets and group them into an equivalence class. Finally "incorporate" the residual tuples into a proper equivalence class. This technique also preserves the *unique distinct ℓ-diversity* model in which each equivalence class has to contain exactly ℓ distinct *SA* values. To ensure that the equivalence classes that BSGI creates are as many as possible a method called *Max-ℓ* is performed. According to this method the tuples are selected from the ℓ biggest buckets. Also, in begin of the selecting step iteration the buckets are sorted according to their sizes. So, in summary, the selection of records and creation of equivalence classes is as follows:

step 1: The tuples of the dataset are bucketized according to their *SA* values to B_i buckets.

step 2: The B_i buckets are sorted according their sizes.

step 3: Randomly one tuple from the first bucket B_1 is selected and creates an equivalence class e.

step 4: From each of the next ℓ-1 B_i groups one tuple is selected that minimize the information loss according to *NCP* metric and incorporated to e.

step 5: While there is a bucket with more than ℓ tuples, steps 1 to 4 are being repeated.

step 6: Incorporating all residual tuples.

3 A Neural Network – Based k-Anonymity and l-Diversity Algorithm

BSGI which was inspired from "*Anatomy*" [12] implements *ℓ-diversity* by firstly "bucketizing" the tuples according to their SA values and then "greedy" group them into equivalence classes depending on the similarity to their *QI* attributes. As it was mentioned on section 4, it randomly selects a tuple from the largest bucket and tries to find *ℓ-1* other tuples from the next largest *ℓ-1* buckets. Assuming that some "better" tuples belong to other */D/- ℓ* buckets then this technique introduces a limitation with possible information loss.

In our algorithm, tuples regrouped according to their *QI* similarity. by clustering the data set using *Kohonen networks* and more precisely *Kohonen Self Organising Feature Maps* (SOMs) Then, the algorithm bucketizes the tuples according their *SA* value in each group. In the next step, in each group it selects a tuple from the smallest bucket and searches for a similar tuple in the *ℓ-1* largest buckets from the same group to create an equivalence class. So, by firstly groupping the tuples according to their similarity the probability to create more uniform classes is significantly increased. This leads to better generalization with less information loss. In addition, by taking care of the rare tuples the probability to suppress rare and valuable tuples is minimized. By doing so, the proposed algorithm satisfies the "utility based anonymization" principle stated in [5], so that crucial information is protected from being suppressed. Also, weights given to tuples improve clustering and give the ability to control the generalization's depth. This algorithm uses the benefits of neural networks for the clustering of the tuples. It starts by clustering the data set using *Kohonen networks* and more precisely *Kohonen Self Organising Feature Maps* (SOMs). After that, in each group that has been created from the Kohonen network the tuples are bucketized according their *SA* value. This algorithm uses three labels for each tuple: one named *QIG* represents the group that a tuple belongs to, another named *SAL* represents the bucket that it belongs, and the third represents the ranking of the buck a tuple belongs, named *SALR*. These labels help to the third step of the algorithm in which the equivalence classes are being created. First, it selects from the smallest buckets a tuple. Then, the algorithm is searching to the biggest ℓ-1 buckets for the *nearest neighborhood* in each of them and creates an equivalence class. This searching is taking place to the group that the selected tuple belongs. At the end of the third step, if a proper tuple could not been found in the same group, the algorithm is searching to the next group which is the most common.

Finally, the *total weight certainty penalty NCP(T)* that mentioned in section 1 and the *discernibility metric* C_{DM} mentioned in section 2 are computed for the evaluation of the algorithm.

4 Coding

Domain Hierarchy

The generalization process of the categorical attributes adopts the model that represented in [9]. It is based on *domain generalization hierarchy* [10] and extends by setting the restriction of the *valid generalization.*

The domain ordering must be supplied by the user. This ordering should correspond to the order in which the leaves are output by the preorder traversal of the hierarchy. According to [9] "a generalization *A* is represented by a set of nodes S_A in the taxonomy tree and it is valid if it satisfies the property that the path from every leaf node *Y* to the root entounters exactly one node *P* in S_A . The value represented by the leaf node *Y* is generalized in *A* to the value represented by the node *P*."

Each value domain is denoted with the least value belonging to the interval of the generalization interval. Even more, values inside a value domain must be ordered. Then, this technique imposes a total ordering over the set of all attribute domains such that the values in the ith attribute domain (Σ_i) all precede the values in any subsequent domain (Σ_j) for $j>i$). The least value from each value domain is being omitted. So, the empty set { } represents the most general anonymization in which the induced equivalence classes consist of only a single equivalence class of identical tuples. Adding a new value to an existing anonymization specializes the data while removing a value generalizes it.

Chromosomes

Each chromosome is formed by concatenating the bit strings corresponding to each potentially identifying column. If the attribute takes numeric values then the length of the string that refers to this attribute is proportional to the granularity at which the generalization intervals are defined. A string representing a numeric attribute formed according to the intervals of the generalization. The bit string for a numeric attribute is made up of one bit for each potential end point in value order. A value of 1 for a bit implies that the corresponding value is used as an interval end point in the generalization [9]. For example if the potential generalization intervals for an attribute are

[0-20](20-40](40-60] (60-80] (80-100]

Then the chromosome 100111 provides that values 0,60,80,100 are end points, so the generalized intervals are [0,60](60,100].

For a categorical attribute with *D* distinct values which are generalized according to the taxonomy tree *T*, the number of bits needed for this attribute is *D-1*. The leaf nodes which are representing the distinct values are arranged in the order resulting from an in-order traversal of *T*. Values of 1 are assigned to the bits of the chromosomes that are between to leaf nodes and represents that those to leaf nodes are separated in the generalization. Because some of the newly chromosomes may not be valid, an additional step to the *Genitor* algorithm modifies them into valid ones.

5 Performance Evaluation of the Proposed Algorithm and Its Comparison with Existing Algorithms

]. Discernibility metric assign a penalty to each tuple based on how many tuples in the transformed dataset are indistinguishable from it. This can be mathematically stated as follows:

$$C_{DM}(g,k) = \sum_{\forall E s.t. |E| \geq k} |E|^2 + \sum_{\forall E s.t. |E| < k} |D||E| \tag{3.1}$$

where |D| the size of the input dataset, E refer to the equivalence classes of tuples in *D* induced by the anonymization *g*.

Classification metric assigns no penalty to an unsuppressed tuple if it belongs to the majority class within its induced equivalence class, while all the other tuples are penalized a value of 1. More precisely:

$$C_{CM}(g,k) = \sum_{\forall E\ s.t. |E| \geq k} \left(|\text{minority}(E)|\right) + \sum_{\forall E\ s.t. |E| < k} |E| \tag{3.2}$$

where E is the equivalence class and minority function accepts a class of equivalence argument and returns all those records which are in the minority class with respect to the sign class. The first sum gives a penalty to those records which have not been suppressed, while the second one penalizes suppressed tuples.

6 Conclusions

Table 2 summarizes the above algorithms according to their effectiveness. To be effective an algorithm for anonymization it has to be fast enough so that could be practical. Also, must be aware of the information loss that causes, so the anonymised table could be useful. The anonymization and the management of medical data must be taken care of with a great concern. The information that those data sets includes is very sensitive so they have to be protected and very crucial for the humanity health. So, algorithms cannot indifferent for the rare attributes values and have to distinguish the more important values from the less important. Our Algorithm is practical while it is taking care of those aspects.

Table 1. Categorization of the Algorithms According to their Characteristics

		Nume-ric	**categorical**			
Utility-Based Anonymization	k-anonymity	Age, education	work class, marital-status, occupation, race, gender, native-country	Greedy	bottom-up	Clustering
					top-down	Partitioning
Data Privacy Through Optimal k-Anonymization	k-anonymity	Age, education	work class, marital-status, occupation, race, gender, native-country	Exhaustive search	Heuristic depth-first tree search	
Transforming Data to Satisfy Privacy Cons-trains	k-anonymity	Age, education	work class, marital-status, occupation, race, gender, native-country	Genetic		
BSGI	ℓ-diversity	Age, final-weight, education, Hours per week	marital-status, race, gender	Greedy	clustering	

Table 2. General Characteristics According the Effectiveness of the Algorithms

	complexity		**average time** (sec)	**technical characteristics**	**Discernability metric**		**Certainty metric**	
					k=25	k=100	k=25	k=100
Utility-Based Anonymization	bottom-up	$O(\log_2 k\lvert T\rvert^2)$	200	512MB RAM 2.0 GHz Pentium iv Microsoft Windows XP				
	top-down	$O(\lvert T\rvert^2)$	60		$2x10^4$	$4x10^4$	$17x10^5$	$15x10^6$
Data Privacy Though Optimal k-Anonymization			5400	2.8 GHz Intel Xeon (only one processor was used) Linux OS (kernel2.4.20)	$15x15^6$	$18x15^6$	k=25 Classification metric =5320	k=100 Classification metric =5460

Table 2. *(Continued)*

Transforming Data to Satisfy Privacy Constrains		18hours (15060 records)	1GB RAM 1GHz Pentium III IBM 6868 Intellistat ion				
BSGI	O(|T|^2)	10-20	1GB RAM 2.8 GHz Pentium D Microsoft Windows Server 2003	ℓ =4 $10x10^4$	ℓ =7 $12x10^4$	ℓ =4 $2x10^3$	ℓ =7 $3x10^3$

References

[1] Gkoulalas-Divanis, A., Verykios, V.S.: An Overview of Privacy Preserving Data Mining. Crossroads archive 15(4), Article No. 6 (June 2009)

[2] Liu, Y., Lv, D., Wang, C., Feng, J., Deng, Q., Ye, Y.: BSGI An Effective Algorithm towards Stronger l-Diversity. In: Yu Liu, D.L. (ed.) Applications table of contents Turin, Italy, pp. 19–32 (2008) (Data Privacy table of contents)

[3] Machanavajjhala, A., Kifer, D., Gehrke, J., Venkitasubramaniam, M.: L-Diversity: Privacy Beyond k-Anonymity. ACM Transactions on Knowledge Discovery from Data 1(1), Article 3, 1:52 (2007)

[4] UCI, Irvin Machine Learning Repository

[5] Xu, J., Wang, W., Pei, J., Wang, X., Shi, B., Fu, A.W.-C.: Utility-Based Anonymization Using Local Recoding (2006)

[6] Bayardo, R., Agrawal, R.: Data privacy through optimal k-anonymization. In: Proceedings on 21st International Conference (2005)

[7] Webb, G.I.: Opus:An Effcient Admissible Algorithm for Unordered Search (1995)

[8] Rymon, R.: Search Through Systematic Set Enumeration (1992)

[9] Iyengar, V.S.: Transforming Data to Satisfy Privacy Constrains (2002)

[10] Sweeney, L.: Achieving k-anonymity privacy protection using generalization and suppression (2002)

[11] Whitley, D.: The Genitor Algorithm and Selective Pressure: Why rank-based allocation of reproductive trials is best. In: Proceedings of Third International Conference on Genetic Algorithms, pp. 116–121 (1989)

[12] Xiao, X., Tao, Y.: Anatomy: Simple and effective privacy preservation. In: VLDB, pp. 139–150 (2006)

On a Novel Simulation Framework and Scheduling Model Integrating Coverage Mechanisms for Sensor Networks and Handling Concurrency

A. Filippou[1], D.A. Karras[2], P.M. Papazoglou[3,*], and R.C. Papademetriou[1]

[1] University of Portsmouth, UK, ECE Department, Anglesea Road, Portsmouth, United Kingdom, PO1 3DJ
alexfilippoy@yahoo.gr

[2] Chalkis Institute of Technology, Greece, Automation Dept., Psachna, Evoia, Hellas (Greece) P.C. 34400
Tel.: +30 6979688870; Fax: +30 210 9945 231, +30 22280 99625
dakarras@ieee.org, dakarras@teihal.gr

[3] Lamia Institute of Technology, Greece

Abstract. Coverage is one of the fundamental metrics used to quantify the quality of service (QoS) of sensor networks. In general, we use this term to measure the ability of the network to observe and react to the phenomena taking place in the area of interest of the network. In addition, coverage is associated with connectivity and energy consumption, both important aspects in the design process of a Wireless Sensor Network (WSN). On the other hand, simulating a WSN involves taking into account different software and hardware aspects. In this paper we attempt to present a simulation framework suitable for integrating coverage mechanisms in WSN emulation using a layered architecture and a fitting scheduling model. The suggested model is derived after a critical overview and presentation of the coverage strategies as well as the simulation approaches for WSN developed so far. The main advantage of the proposed framework is its capability to handle concurrent events occurring at WSN deployment and operation through the suitable layered scheduler integrated.

Keywords: WSN, Simulation WSN, Scheduling, Coverage in WSN, Distributed Sensor Networks.

1 Introduction

Sensor networks are networks consisted of tiny devices (motes or nodes) equipped with a set of sensors, a transceiver, a μC and memory. We use large numbers of such devices to form a network, usually deployed over a large area. Motes collaborate to perform a larger sensing task, in order to provide the user a global view of the area of interest, in which they are deployed.

* Correponding author.

T.-h. Kim et al. (Eds.): GDC/CA 2010, CCIS 121, pp. 277–286, 2010.

Motes in most cases are running on batteries, thus energy efficiency is a major issue during design process.

Deploying redundant motes is a technique to prolong network lifetime. Deriving energy efficient ways of using redundancy is a task equivalent of finding solutions to problems that are usually classified as NP-hard or NP-complete. Since motes have limited CPU power and memory, it is critical that optimal solutions to such problems are not computationally expensive. In this paper we explore the multi dimensional nature of coverage concept aiming at presenting a novel simulation framework for WSNs efficiently integrating coverage mechanisms and a proper scheduling scheme. Before proceeding with the description of the proposed approach let us define main events occurring within WSN deployment and operation.

Environment and events
Motes collaborate to perform a global sensing task, and to be able to propagate information as response to user query. Monitored events may be classified according time and space in two main aspects:

Spatial Distribution (Localized/Distributed): The events of interest may be spatially localized. Wildlife tracking, vehicle tracking, perimeter breach, are considered as such. They are usually detected by a small number of sensors [1] in whose sensing range the events are taking place. The only concern is to locate the current position of the target and plot the movement path. In case of a forest fire, a chemical or biological contamination, the spatial distribution of the phenomenon is required.

Temporal Distribution (Discrete/Continuous): Measuring temperature over a large area, is a procedure that can be scheduled at regular intervals (e.g. every 2 hours) during a day. On the other hand, monitoring industrial machinery, patients in the ER, or seismic data, requires the network performing such tasks to be actively sensing at all times [2].

2 The Coverage Concept in WSN Design

Sensing Models:
A. Boolean or 0/1 Model: We may use a circle as an abstraction of the mote. The mote's location is the centre of the circle and the area of the circle is its sensing radius. The mote provides full coverage within its sensing radius and none outside it.

B. Continuous Model: [3] Taking in consideration that sensing ability diminishes as distance increases and that sensing devices have different hardware features, a more realistic way is to express sensing model S at any point p in the field at a distance d(s,p) from the mote s is the following:

$$S(s,p) = \frac{\lambda}{[d(s,p)]^K}$$

where λ and K are hardware dependent parameters.

Node Deployment Strategies:

A. Deterministic / Manual Placement: We deploy motes over a field uniformly, according to a predefined shape. An example of a uniform deterministic coverage is a grid based sensor deployment where motes are located on the intersection points of a grid (cellular). This requires manual placement, which is realistic for small number of nodes, and an accessible environment. This placement ensures complete coverage of the field with the minimum number of motes. The number of motes needed to cover a, area A is given by[4]:

$$n = \frac{2A}{\sqrt{27}\, r^2}$$

Where r is the sensing radius, n the required number of nodes, an A the area covered.

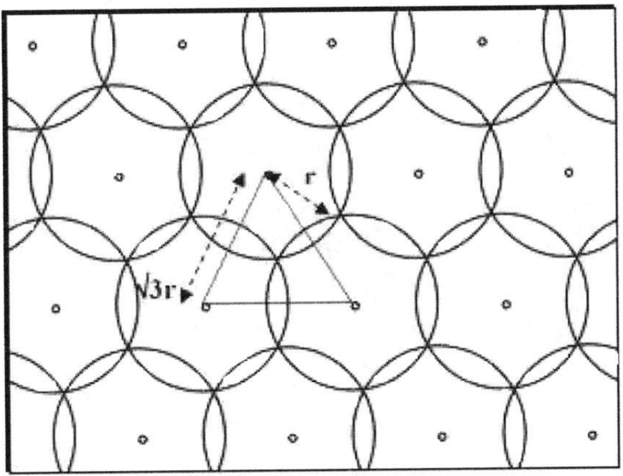

Fig. 1. Optimal Placement of Motes

B. Stochastic Placement: In hostile or inhospitable environments, it's a necessity to deploy motes from a plane, in order to gather data of interest. In this case, motes are deployed randomly, and since they are of low cost, we deploy redundant motes to increase connectivity, coverage and to prolong network lifetime. In this way, some regions may be densely populated or may exhibit blind holes, areas out of any mote's sensing range. In densely populated regions, keeping all motes active causes many packet collisions thus wasting energy. In the next section we discuss coverage schemes that take advantage of the redundancy of motes in energy efficient way.

3 Coverage Protocols

In a dense network, a target is covered by more than one mote. The grade of this depends on the sensing range and density of the network. It is also possible that one mote covers more than one target. The goal is to keep active only the necessary motes to cover an area. Taking it a step further, we could schedule sets of motes, all covering the same area, to be active in turns, saving energy while keeping coverage of the area.

Area Coverage

Slijepcevic and Potkonjak [6] allocate nodes into covers, mutually exclusive sets of motes. The first step is to identify the parts of the area covered by different sensor nodes.

DEFINITION: A field is a set of points. Two points belong to the same field iff they are covered by the same set of sensors.

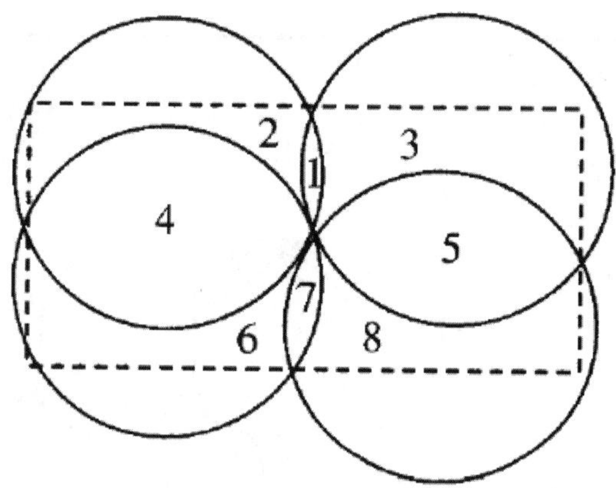

Fig. 2. Four sensors covering the area (dotted rectangle) creating eight fields

The area is modelled as a collection of fields defined above. Any field has the property that any point inside the field is covered by the same set of sensors.

"The most constrained least constraining algorithm computes the disjoint covers successively, selecting sensors that cover the critical element (field covered by a minimal number of sensors), giving priority to sensors that: cover a high number of uncovered fields, cover sparsely covered fields and do not cover fields redundantly"[5].

"The downside to the scheme is that it estimates at most m covers where m is the number of sensors covering the most constrained field in the whole area. This implies that many nodes in the denser regions are not included in any cover and are left idle."[2]

Point Coverage

The maximum disjoint set covers and the maximum lifetime are two different problems [7]. In this MSc, Li Yin proposes an algorithm that finds the schedule that produces the maximum lifetime, instead of trying to find the maximum number of mutually exclusive sets.

Problem Definition: Given a set S of N motes, and a set T of M targets, find a schedule to activate motes that guarantees that at any time, all targets can be covered by active motes, and that maximizes the network lifetime.

The optimal solution is derived using a two phase algorithm. In phase one, the complete set of non redundant covers is computed. Each cover set is a subset of motes belonging to S and completely covers all targets in set T without redundant motes. In phase two, optimal solution is derived by solving the linear program – assigning the time slice for selected set covers, a schedule for sensors to be active or idle in order to achieve maximum lifetime.

Metrics for QoS of Sensor Coverage

Two metrics are proposed [9] p. 69 concerning coverage.

A. "% of uncovered area in the region. This metric is defined as the percentage of area over the entire region not covered by any sensor at a given time. When plotted against time, it gives an assessment of how long the network is able to achieve acceptable levels of coverage."

B. "Time at which the first breach occurs. An obvious quality measure is how long the integrity of the perimeter being sensed is maintained. When enough nodes have died so as to enable an entity to cross the perimeter without detection, a breach occurs and the sensor network effectively fails."

4 Mobile Motes Models

Potential Fields

Potential field techniques were first described by [8] and used for robotic applications such as local navigation and obstacle avoidance.

Mobile motes and objects in the environment exert virtual repulsive force. The vector of that force is calculated and given as direction to the mote's mobility system. In this way motes seem to push away one another and being pushed by obstacles of the environment.

The motes will keep moving till the static equilibrium state is reached. It's the state where every mote's control vector value is 0. Then, parameter could be chosen accordingly, so every mote maintains a desired overlap of its own and neighboring motes sensing range.

This approach does not require models of the environment or communication between motes. Motes cover the area uniformly using a distance sensor which allows every mote to calculate the control vector and move to new position till it reaches static equilibrium [10].

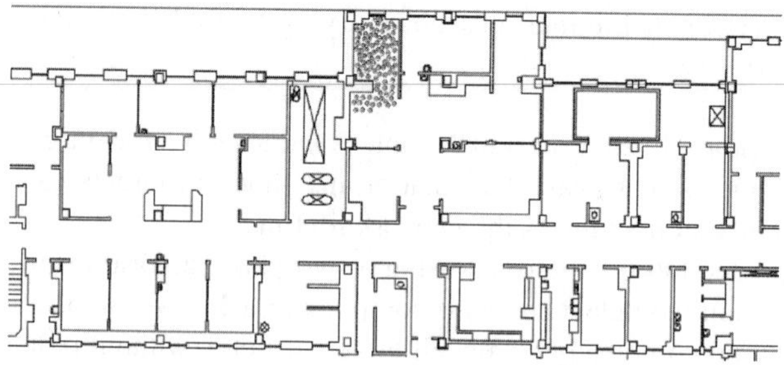

Fig. 3. Initial network configuration

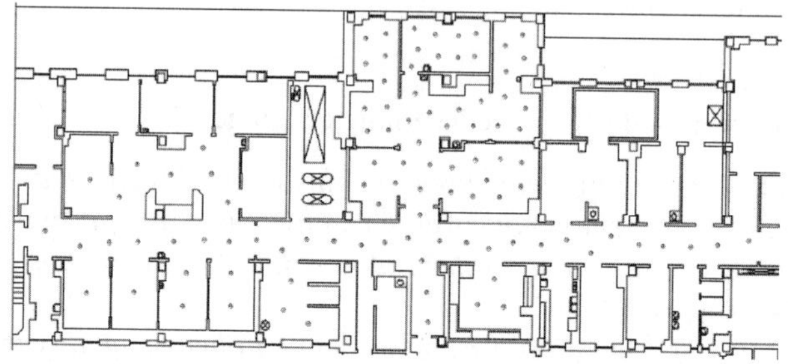

Fig. 4. Final Configuration

5 A Concise Overview of Simulation Models for WSN

WSN containing deployed motes, as previously described, should involve a micro-controller (μC or MCU) per mote, which defines mote's states. It is important, in order to define a simulation model for WSNs to consider emulation of these MCUs.

MCU manufacturers for WSN frequently introduce improvements in two main topics: energy consumption of μCs and CPU power – memory / cost ratio. These features have a major impact in the WSN field, and absorbing them in the design process of a WSN is needed.

The design process is divided into two main fields: Hardware configuration and of course code running on the μC. A WSN may be homogenous concerning hardware or software, meaning the same hardware platform running the same code throughout the network, and heterogeneous, meaning motes with different hardware specs collaborating forming a network, or identical motes running different programs.

The basic tool that completes the design process is simulation. Software simulation tools carrying out the task must be flexible, taking into account hardware features, and providing a detailed simulation of the environment the WSN will operate in.

A WSN simulation is consisted of two model fields: The first contains the environmental event and RF channel models, and the other the mote's component models. Some simulators for example SensorSim, SWAN, SENS, use models of the motes. Such models represent code behavior, and are completely unaware of additive hardware features. They provide metrics concerning network delays, throughputs, packet collisions, and power usage.[11][12][13].

Tossim, Atemu and Avrora, [14][15][16], emulate AVR/Mica2 motes, Tossim emulating hardware except some low level features, Atemu and Avrora run the binary file to be uploaded in real motes, while both can be used for emulation of different platforms. Atemu provides precise timing and Avrora synchronizes when necessary. Tossim's radio model is very simple, the network is a directed graph, in which each vortex is a node, and each edge has a bit error probability. Atemu emulates the CC100 as a receiver / transmitter pair, due to this module's flexibility to use a range of frequencies controlled by software. In SENS environment is defined as a grid of interchangeable tiles, and assigns BER according to traffic conditions [13].

MAC Protocols, Localization protocols need accurate synchronization, because much of the μC program's execution depends on the timing and behavior of devices. Received signal strength, (RSSI) , time of arrival (TOA), are quantities used by protocols to perform topology construction, hence RF channel simulation and code running on μC's should be synchronized.

6 The Proposed Novel Simulation Framework and Scheduling Model Integrating Coverage Mechanisms for WSN

The proposed simulation framework consists first of the main scheduler which is hierarchical and is based on the coverage scheme aspect, in order to seamlessly integrate coverage into the suggested simulation solution. Second, it integrates a proper model for the MCU emulation as depicted in figure 5. The major goal of the proposed methodology is to define a simulation model suitable for handling concurrency of events in an operational WSN. Actually concurrency of events should be an important aspect in our simulation considerations since WSN performance should be finally analyzed with respect to environment events and alarms occurring concurrently.

The coverage mechanism implements a two phase algorithm as discussed in section 2 and these phases should be integrated in the coverage scheduler as shown in figure 6.

Each coverage set, in which the coverage algorithm leads to, has its own scheduler as shown in figure 6. Such a scheduler deals with the motes as events, the active motes included in the specific coverage set.

The layered scheduling set up shown in figure 6 illustrates that a mote event is nothing but a set of MCU component events. With this respect Virtual Memory management, RF channel management, etc. are such components.

We propose an algorithm in which every aspect of the simulation is treated as a component with its own time step. Devices, phenomena, possible targets are treated as functions of time. The emulation of the μC is implemented using an array as its memory, registers, and ports, and a chip specific engine, that alters the contents of this memory according to the instruction executed. The time step of this engine is one machine cycle. The instruction level simulation provides the highest behavioral and timing accuracy for software and is both language and operating system independent, and by default cross layer. In addition, energy consumption of one instruction execution is specified in the specs of the device, allowing the creation of an accurate energy consumption model.

A variable is used as the basic time step. Every component in the simulation has a time step that is multiple of the basic time step. The main simulation loop that synchronizes the components is:

```
For (I=0;;I++)
  {
     If  (I mod a=0) then
        Component (a)
     If (I mod b=0) then
        Component (b)

     ......
  }
```

where, I is the basic time step, a,b etc are time steps and function Component(x) hands over execution to all components within a MCU of a specific mote with time step x multiple of basic step I.

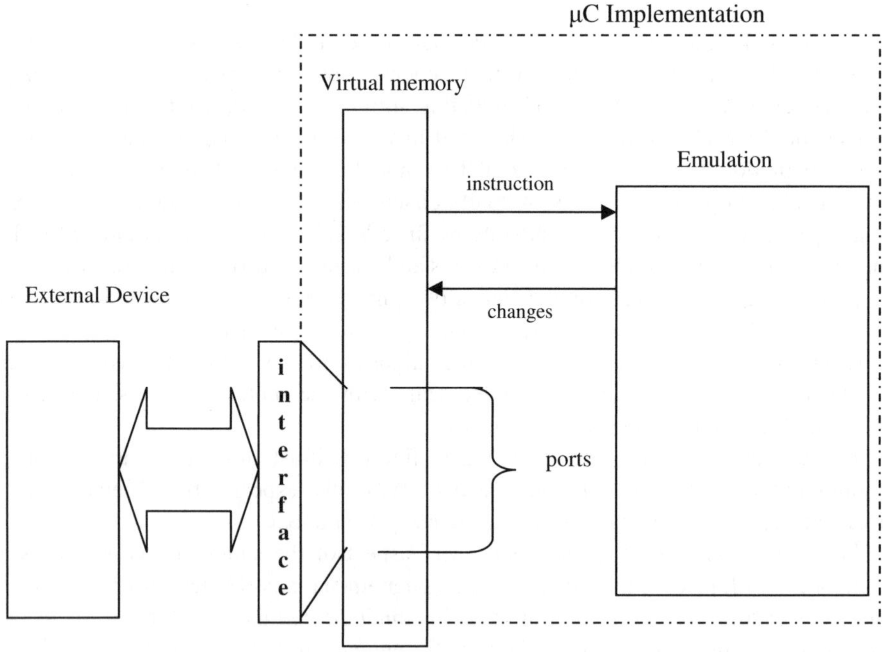

Fig. 5. The μC model in the proposed simulation framework for WSN

Concerning the emulation of a μC, the variable implementing the program counter, fetches the next bytes from μC virtual memory consisting an instruction, and the emulation engine changes virtual memory's contents according to that instruction. Virtual memory's locations that implement ports, are used as an interface for external devices e.g. RF modules.

The above time definitions should be considered within each mote at the lowest layer of the proposed scheduler, layer 1. Therefore, if at layer 2, which schedules events at cover set level, we consider simulation time step equal to T2, then simulation time at layer 1 of mote and MCU level should be estimated as T1 based on the concepts and the algorithm presented above. This is precisely the model for the proposed scheduler of the suggested simulation framework for WSN.

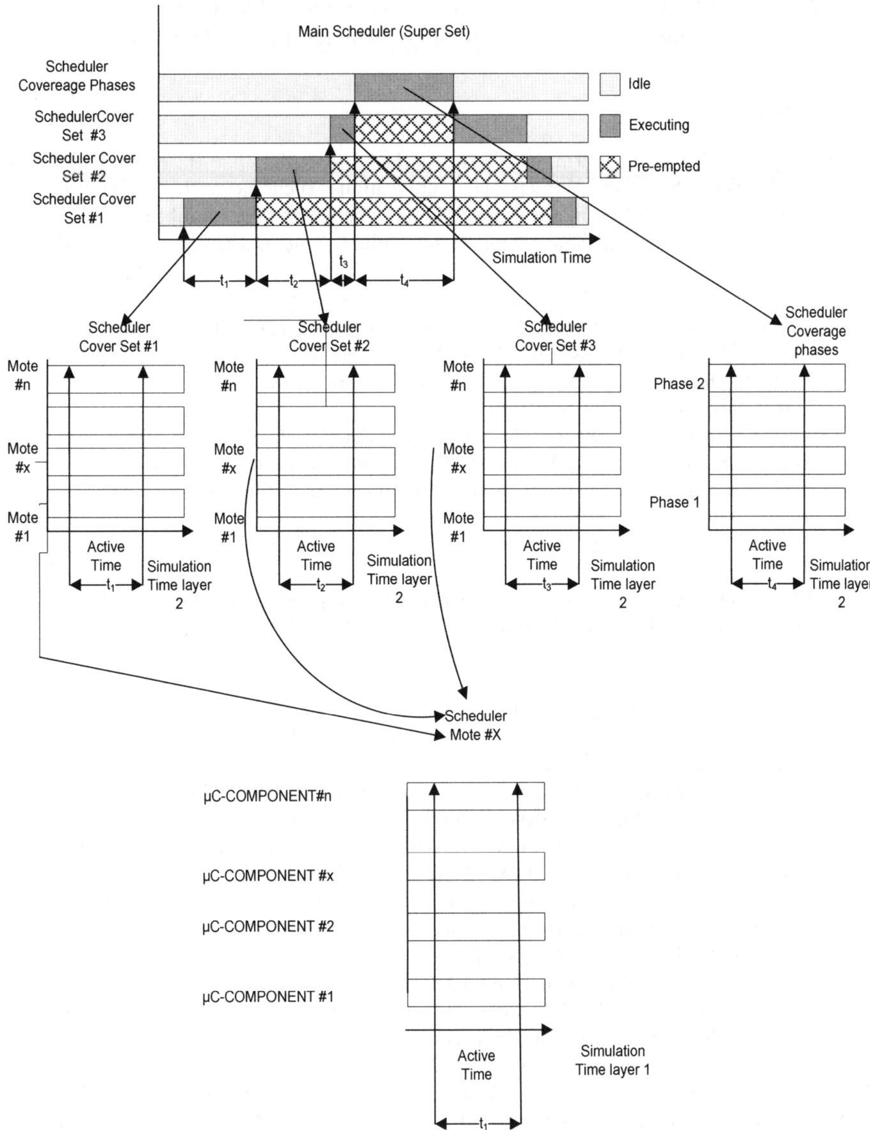

Fig. 6. The Scheduling model in the proposed simulation framework for WSN

7 Conclusion and Prospects

A Simulation framework and a suitable scheduling scheme have been presented in this paper after an analysis and overview of existing simulation solutions and coverage problem solution strategies in WSNs. The proposed methodology seamlessly integrates in a layered architectural model all needed components for an efficient simulation strategy that can deal with the concurrent events occurring during the operation of a WSN. Implementation of this framework and comparison with different approaches using Java multithread technology is under the way by the authors.

References

[1] Cerpa, A., Elson, J., Estrin, D., Girod, L., Hamilton, M., Zhao, J.: Habitat Monitoring: Application Driver for Wireless Communications Technology. In: ACM SIGCOMM Workshop on Data Communications in Latin America and the Caribbean (April 2001)

[2] Seetharaman, Sumathi. Self-organized scheduling of node activity in large-scale sensor networks, http://etd.ohiolink.edu/view.cgi?acc_num=ucin1092939502

[3] Meguerdichian, S., Potkonjak, M.: Low power 0/1 coverage and scheduling techniques in sensor networks, Tech. Report 030001, UCLA (January 2003)

[4] Williams, R.: The geometrical foundation of natural structure: A source book of design. Dover Pub. Inc., New York (1979)

[5] http://www.cse.fau.edu/~mihaela/HTML/PAPERS/coverage_comcom.pdf

[6] Slijepcevic, S., Potkonjak, M.: Power efficient organization of wireless sensor networks. In: Proceedings of IEEE International Conference on Communications, vol. 2, pp. 472–447 (2001)

[7] http://scholarsmine.mst.edu/thesis/Sensor_network_cover_09007dcc80497653.html

[8] Khatib, O.: Real-time obstacle avoidance for manipulators and mobile robots. International Journal of Robotics Research 5(1), 90–98 (1986)

[9] http://scholar.lib.vt.edu/theses/available/etd-07122001-190827/

[10] Howard, A., Poduri, S.: Potential Field Methods for Mobile-Sensor-Network Deployment. In: Bulusu, N., Jha, S. (eds.) Wireless Sensor Networks A System Perspective. Artech House, London (2005)

[11] Park, S., Savvides, A., Srivastava, M.: Sensorsim: a simulation framework for sensor networks. In: Proceedings of MSWiM 2000, 3rd ACM International Workshop on Modeling, Analysis and Simulation of Wireless and Mobile Systems, pp. 104–111 (2000)

[12] Liu, J., Perrone, L.F., Nicol, D.M., Liljenstam, M., Elliott, C., Pearson, D.: Simulation modeling of large-scale ad-hoc sensor networks. In: Proceedings of Euro-SIW 2001, European Simulation Interoperability Workshop (2001)

[13] Sundresh, S., Kim, W., Agha, G.: SENS: A sensor, environment and network simulator. In: Proceedings of 37th Annual Simulation Symposium, pp. 221–230 (2004)

[14] Levis, P., Lee, N., Welsh, M., Culler, D.: TOSSIM: Accurate and scalable simulation of entire TinyOS applications. In: Proceedings of SenSys 2003, First ACM Conference on Embedded Networked Sensor Systems (2003)

[15] Polley, J., Blazakis, D., McGee, J., Rusk, D., Baras, J.S., Karir, M.: ATEMU: A fine-grained sensor network simulator. In: Proceedings of SECON 2004, First IEEE Communications Society Conference on Sensor and Ad Hoc Communications and Networks (2004)

[16] Titzer, B.L.: Avrora: The AVR Simulation and Analysis Framework. Master's thesis, UCLA (June 2004)

Author Index

Author Index

Printing: Mercedes-Druck, Berlin
Binding: Stein + Lehmann, Berlin